KARSH of Ottawa.

The Critical Reputation of

TENNESSEE WILLIAMS

a reference guide

A
Reference
Guide
to
Literature

Jackson Bryer
Editor

The Critical Reputation of

TENNESSEE WILLIAMS

a reference guide

JOHN S. McCANN

G. K. HALL & CO. ● BOSTON, MASSACHUSETTS

Library of Congress Cataloging in Publication Data
McCann, John S.
    The critical reputation of Tennessee Williams.
    (A Reference guide to literature)
    Includes index.
    1. Williams, Tennessee, 1911–   —Bibliography.
I. Title.   II. Series.
Z8976.424.M37   1983   016.812'54   82-15706
[PS3545.15365]
ISBN 0-8161-8635-9

This publication is printed on permanent/durable acid-free paper
MANUFACTURED IN THE UNITED STATES OF AMERICA

To
NJT
SPONSAE, ET ITERVM DICO SPONSAE
SED ET MAGISTRAE MVSAEQVE FIDELI
QVAE LINEA RECTA EST
QVAM DVCERE CONOR

Contents

The Author

John S. McCann studied at and received degrees from St. Edward's University, New York University, and the University of Maryland. He has written previously about Tennessee Williams for the *Washington Post* and the Los Angeles *Times*. Presently he is Professor of English and director of the Honors Program at Prince George's Community College in Largo, Maryland.

Preface

This compilation represents an attempt to reckon with the vast storehouse of material on Tennessee Williams and his work, up to and including 1981. My parameters are basic ones: all popular and scholarly press criticism, with an emphasis on that which has appeared in the United States; production notices limited to Broadway premieres and important revivals, as well as notices from other domestic cities when significant premieres occurred somewhere other than New York; British notices for plays given important productions in London; interviews with Tennessee Williams, biographical material, and book reviews of his nondramatic works wherever they could be found; foreign language material limited to book-length studies; and doctoral dissertations.

Three criteria shared equal weight in my compiling this bibliography: accuracy, completeness, neutrality. And the order there is only alphabetical; there was no hierarchy. Clearly if my entries are in any way inaccurate, they are self-defeating, and I therefore attempted rigidly to force accuracy upon all the stages of these several years' work. Additionally, completeness seems to be so basic a necessity that it is almost a given; at the same time it is necessarily a relative term, subject to the limits of my sources. (More on that later.) And finally, neutrality, as it applies to the annotations, was a consistent watchword; at no point did it seem my prerogative to impose my bias on a critical work nor to characterize it (other than quantitatively) for the reader.

Of all the advice given to me over the years I worked, the most influential was the succinct advice of my mentor, Professor Jackson R. Bryer. His one-sentence admonition contained all that needed to be said: "Never presume the use the reader will make of your bibliography." Hence my three criteria: less than full accuracy would presume no serious reader at all; to omit references would presumptuously define the reader's interests, the reader's research intent; and anything less than neutrality would implicitly predict the ends of any research undertaken.

ix

It is my hope that the only limitations this study sustains are the limitations of my sources. And fortunately I have had access to (and have made thorough use of) the Washington, D.C., area Consortium and non-Consortium university and college libraries, plus the Library of Congress; additionally I made extensive use of the Theatre Collection of New York Public Library's Lincoln Center branch; and further still I gained access to the Tennessee Williams files at Williams' publisher, New Directions, in New York, and the files of Bill Barnes and then Mitch Douglas (two of Williams' former agents) at International Creative Management. With such access, the limitations of sources have been slight. (Items I was not able to obtain for examination are designated by an asterisk preceding the entry number.)

While I rigidly maintained the determination to be neutral in my annotations, they do sometimes, simply by their relative length, signal my judgment of the relative worth of a given work (length of annotation is by no means *always* an indication of that bias, however); further, I cannot and will not deny that the subtleties of vocabulary and syntax in the annotations might betray an attitude toward a work under scrutiny. Finally, I make no secret of my strong personal regard for Tennessee Williams and most of his work; to some extent, that favor has influenced me also. However, for emphasis, let me restate that my aim has been to remain as detached as possible, to produce annotations that allow users to make their own judgments, unprejudiced by me.

The year 1981 is bound to appear somewhat deficient by the time this volume is published since, even as it goes to press, I am still discovering items that need to be included. I apologize in advance for what might seem its paucity.

Arrangement and Form

All works are arranged chronologically by years of publication to illustrate the history and development of Williams' reputation. Arrangement within each year is alphabetical by the last name of the author or, when the work is anonymous, by the first word (exclusive of articles) of the title.

Enumeration is sequential within each year; every new year begins again with no. 1.

For the sake of concision within annotations, Tennessee Williams is consistently referred to as TW, and all Williams' works are referred to by abbreviated codes, as the list to follow will illustrate.

Preface

For convenience and clarity, abbreviations, even the more common and acceptable ones, are never used for serials or newspapers. Full titles, excluding articles, are always provided.

All doctoral dissertations that have been abstracted are so noted; *DA* and *DAI* are used to represent *Dissertation Abstracts* and *Dissertation Abstracts International*, respectively.

Acknowledgments

I am in the debt of so many whose assistance and encouragement have made this book a reality. Merely listing their names cannot begin to do justice to them, since often what they have given me has been so much more subtle than what a traditional statement of gratitude can acknowledge.

To start at the beginning: I am profoundly indebted to Sister Patricia Lee, O.P., and Brother Dunstan Bowles, C.S.C., my teachers, two generous, good, shatteringly intuitive people who, at very different times in my life, taught me more about how to think, feel, and act than I have yet been able to catch up with, two people who—in their root humility—will be surprised even to be mentioned here.

Without question, my gratitude goes to Tennessee Williams, whose personal courtesy to me encouraged, indirectly, the completion of this venture.

Also: my mentor, my former professor, my editor, Jackson R. Bryer of the University of Maryland; Donald Fowle and Roderick Bladel of the Theatre Collection at the Lincoln Center branch of the New York Public Library; Griselda Ohannessian of New Directions; Bill Barnes, Mr. Williams' former agent; Mitch Douglas of International Creative Management, also a former agent of Mr. Williams; John Oliva and Ronald Powell of Prince George's Community College Library; Patricia Tatspaugh and Lloyd Shaw of Prince George's Community College; Pamela Kraus and George J. Siefert, Jr., of The Catholic University of America; Richard A. Steinbach of Georgetown University; Karen Wood, Jean Sansobrino, Lynn Pedigo Robison, and Sarah Pritchard of the Library of Congress; Jeffrey von der Schmalz of the *New York Times*; Christian Williams of the *Washington Post*; Judith Bremmerman, my typist; Dennis Vaughan, my courier; Roger Green; my research assistant, James L. Williamson; my research assistant and indexer, William Triplett.

J. S. McC.
Takoma Park, Maryland

Introduction

In one of the last interviews with Tennesse Williams which this volume includes (1980.46), he plaintively tells us, "I just want to live to complete my life's work." His theater-going public, his readers, his casual students, his popular press critics, as well as the scholars dedicated to his work were probably unanimous in hoping he would have been able to realize that wish.

Williams' sudden death on 24 February 1983 obviously put the final period to his "life's work," although those who respected and admired him are no doubt as sad as he was that the completion he sought never really materialized.

It is a general critical axiom that *The Night of the Iguana* (1961) was Williams' last first-rate play. It is further generally agreed that the last twenty years show a struggling, debilitated Williams trying to fulfill what the quote above indicates he expected of himself and what he continued to believe his public wanted of him: the one final good play that would guarantee the security of his critical reputation.

The difficulty of weighing that critical reputation is certainly the problem of Williams' last twenty rather fallow years (fallow in quality, not quantity of works). It is also a problem of understanding what the critical premises were in the formation of his reputation originally: it is frequently not clear, when reading the criticism of Williams' work, whether the basis of the criticism is the work itself, the work plus the flamboyance of its author's image, or the flamboyance of the author's image accompanied by a tangential curiosity about the work.

Certainly this is particularly a dilemma for any student of Tennessee Williams' work who attempts to contend with the popular press criticism. The sheer mass of the criticism, starting with the first minor notices of 1939 and continuing unabated in its bulk to the present day, could easily disarm the reader who wants a command of the history of

Introduction

Williams' work and its reputation in the tradition of American drama. And since the popular press often seems implicitly to claim Williams as a creature of its own making, it is frequently more than the mass of the criticism that is the difficulty for a serious reader; it is the contentiousness, the opinionation, the gossipy smallness and cynicism that characterize so much of the response to Williams that would daunt and alienate any but the most determined reader.

Bearing this in mind and examining the critical response chronologically, the search becomes a search for premises, for controlling biases, for elements of continuity that might inform the criticism. It is a search for order.

Tennessee Williams' first work to receive any recognition got such resounding denunciation, it was almost his professional undoing. *Battle of Angels* was not only rejected by the popular press critics (the *Boston Evening Transcript* (1940.1) called it "a stumbling, pointless affair"; the *Boston Globe* (1940.9) said "the play gives the audience the sensation of having been dunked in mire"), it was, literally, banned in Boston, and it created a public furor that Williams seemed never to have either forgotten or entirely forgiven. (His *Memoirs'* account of it in 1975 made it seem like recent personal experience.)

After a silence of four years, both in the press and from Williams, he and Audrey Wood (who would remain his devoted agent and adviser for thirty years) chose pre-Christmas Chicago for their renewed attempt to get him an audience, get him a positive press response, and get him on his way to New York with a critical bias already fixed. They got all three. *The Glass Menagerie* opened at Chicago's Civic Theatre on 26 December 1944 and established Tennessee Williams, truly overnight, as the figure we now know to be an indelible presence in the imagination of this half of the twentieth-century. The Chicago critics wrote reviews of the sort that publicists dream of ("... gripping, you are caught in its spell" [*Chicago Daily Tribune*, 1944.1]; "... has the courage of pure poetry couched in colloquial prose" [*Chicago Herald American*, 1944.5]). Their praise was as unanimous as it was quotable; *The Glass Menagerie* and Tennessee Williams were ready for Broadway.

The 31 March 1945 opening of *The Glass Menagerie* at Broadway's Playhouse Theatre received a critical response in the New York dailies that amplified the praise of Chicago, elaborated on its terms and themes, and spilled over into the popular weeklies, biweeklies, and monthlies. Brown praised "its high shimmering virtues" (1945.3); Cotter said it was "a tragedy that is haunting and beautiful" (1945.7); Gibbs referred to it as "a very touching play" (1945.16); Krutch called it "powerful and arresting" (1945.29). The encomium was almost without detracting voices (Freedley said Williams had given Broadway "its highest moment this year" [1945.12]; Morehouse called it "a vivid, eerie and curiously enchanting play" [1945.36]; Waldorf insisted it was the best play to have opened that season [1945.56]); and what little negative response there might have been was simply drowned out in the volume of positive critical acclaim.

What was set in motion by the New York dailies' reviews on 2 April 1945 was a phenomenon whose dimensions critics (and Tennessee Williams) were, until February of 1983, still catching up with. At once, the force of the words of John Chapman, George Freedley, Robert Garland, Otis Guernsey, followed quickly by John Mason Brown, Lewis Nichols, Wolcott Gibbs, Joseph Wood Krutch, and Kappo Phelan, "created" a playwright of significance, one whose work would go on to be given countless future productions on every continent but Antarctica, would become the stock of classroom lectures and doctoral theses, scholarly books and academic colloquia. But just as surely, since his reputation had its inception in the popular press, Tennessee Williams and his work would continue to be the assumed critical possession of those who believed they "made him." As such, his "critical reputation," as this bibliography amply demonstrates, is just as much a reputation spelled out in gossip columns and brief, trivial news items, as in chatty profiles and commentaries on the author's preferences in pots and pans and style of hat. "Critical reputation," as we understand the term, would never be an easily definable term when the subject was Tennessee Williams or his work.

By the time *A Streetcar Named Desire* opened on 3 December 1947, Tennessee Williams' reputation had been set in the popular press; it had been undisturbed by the tepid response to *You Touched Me!* of late 1945, largely, it seems, because the work was produced while *The Glass Menagerie* was still running successfully on Broadway, and because it was coauthored (with Donald Windham). *A Streetcar Named Desire* succeeded in fortifying the reputation that *The Glass Menagerie* had established. It is significant that it received almost twice as much popular press response as *The Glass Menagerie* had, and that the actual vocabulary of the *Streetcar* notices shows critics reaching for deeper criteria than they had two years earlier. (For example, Atkinson's *New York Times* review [1947.1] referred to *Streetcar*'s being "a quietly woven study of intangibles"; Barnes, in the *New York Herald Tribune* [1947.5], mentioned its "disregard for so-called social problems"; Freedley, in the New York *Morning Telegraph* [1947.15], cited its "compelling honesty"; Gibbs, in the *New Yorker* [1947.17], called *Streetcar* an "implacable play about the disintegration of a woman, or, if you like, of a society"; Krutch, in his *Nation* review [1947.23], discussed the play's frankness and pathology.)

  A Streetcar Named Desire was ensconced at the Barrymore Theatre from 3 December 1947 until 17 December 1949, a two-year run of 855 performances, overlapping significant offshoot productions during the same period in Mexico City, Rome, Manchester, London, and Paris. As might be expected, *Life* magazine leapt into the void of biographical data on Williams, engaging Lincoln Barnett to write an elaborate profile. Barnett's "Tennessee Williams: A Dreamy Young Man with an Unconquerable Compulsion to Write Finds Himself at 33 the Most Important Playwright in the U.S. Theatre" (1948.6) was the first profile of any significant length and flourish to appear nationally; it gave the expected biographical details, and it assisted in the creation of a mystique: the popularized image of the slightly bohemian writer, earning astounding amounts of money on Broadway, who calls himself "Tennessee" and who defines things such as security by phrases such as "a kind of death." The month after Barnett insinuated the mystique into the general culture through his profile, Carson McCullers pronounced judgment from the realm of those on the inside; her letter to the editor, in *Life*'s 8 March issue (1948.42), complimented Barnett on his portrait of Tennessee Williams, citing particularly his sensitivity to Williams' "nobility of character and spirit." Seven months later, *Summer and Smoke* was on Broadway; Tennessee Williams was being interviewed and commented on unceasingly in the press; *A Streetcar Named Desire* was winning the Pulitzer Prize, the Drama Critics' Circle Award, and the Donaldson Award; Hollywood was making a film of *The Glass Menagerie*; and Tennessee Williams' critical reputation was ripe for inquiry that would go deeper than newspaper reviews or articles in serials of the ilk of *Life*'s were prepared to go.

  John Gassner attempted (in October 1948 [1948.33]) to trace the idiom and the tradition Tennessee Williams was associating himself with; he invoked Chekhov, Gorki, O'Neill, and Lorca, trying to fit Williams into the schema; with his *College English* article, both Tennessee Williams and Williams criticism, in a manner of speaking, came of age. Gassner's essay clearly delivered Tennessee Williams to the academy, and although the essay was not necessarily more profound than pieces Brooks Atkinson, Harold Clurman, John Mason Brown, Wolcott Gibbs, Joseph Wood Krutch, or Elliot Norton had already written as reviewers, Tennessee Williams' name had taken on currency in a new form. In the summer of 1949, Ray C.B. Brown's "Tennessee Williams: The Poetry of Stagecraft" (1949.4) went briefly, compactly, but certainly a step beyond Gassner, into the concerns of critics of letters as opposed to critics of performances. Brown (who does not seem to have written about Tennessee Williams again) injected considerations of the "conventions of structure" and Tennessee Williams' place among the "experimentalists" into the vocabulary.

By the end of the forties, with one full decade behind him, Tennessee Williams' critical reputation might best be summed up as exalted. He had had four Broadway productions, one published volume of short stories (*One Arm*, 1948), and, within the year 1950, would publish *The Roman Spring of Mrs. Stone*, have *The Glass Menagerie* released as a film, and mount *The Rose Tattoo* on Broadway; he had his one Donaldson Award, his two Drama Critics' Circle Awards, his Pulitzer Prize.

The fifties were Tennessee Williams' most fertile years, and the criticism trailing him from the earliest years of that decade seemed more prepared to reckon with him in an idiom appropriate to his new stature. As early as 1951, when *The Rose Tattoo* opened on Broadway, Howard Barnes sounds a note in the popular press that not only goes beyond what had been expected of reviews published in New York dailies, but directly anticipates the academic criticism to follow. Barnes, in his *Herald Tribune* Sunday-after-premiere review (1951.7), is lavish in his praise of Williams' product, and at first his praise sounds like the sort of reviewer's cant that is so predictable we can almost anticipate its vocabulary and syntax: "Tennessee Williams has written 'The Rose Tattoo' with such imagination, depth of feeling and strange humor that his play now takes definite precedence over any new American play shown here this season." Curiously, after this formulaic beginning, he changes course and calls *The Rose Tattoo* "a terrible [meant as 'strong'] 'Pilgrims Progress'"; he refers to the "great deal of liturgical lore in the lines and situations"; and finally he suggests that *The Rose Tattoo* was inspired by T.S. Eliot's translation of "Anabasis."

Barnes comments, as undeveloped as he left them, indicate a significant new direction in popular press criticism of Williams' plays. The literary references suggest a connection with dramatic tradition that goes beyond the scope of plays on the popular stage. The turn is toward the more serious, and the intent seems as much to treat Williams' new play appropriately as to invite Williams to be equal to the august criticism.

George Freedley, Tennessee Williams' consistently loyal critic whose work appeared in the unlikely forum of the daily racing bulletin, the New York *Morning Telegraph*, stood guard over Williams' popular critical reputation in reviews such as his 1953 notice of *Camino Real* (1953.19): "Certainly the finest play by the most outstanding American dramatist.... It gives encouragement to an adult theatre in America." The totally positive, while generally unpenetrating praise that Freedley would systematically record may not have had the influence of his contemporaries' reviews in the other, more auspicious New York dailies whose notices could make or break a play. But Freedley, as an unwavering Williams ally from the start, had another occupation in addition to his *Morning Telegraph* reviewing—he was curator and director of New York Public Library's Theatre Collection, the collection now housed at the library's Lincoln Center branch. The clippings files on Tennessee Williams that Freedley is responsible for beginning are perhaps the most ample repository of uncatalogued, unindexed Williams criticism collected in any one place. Its resources outdistance the massive collection in his publisher's (New Directions) files, and it is generally agreed that they outdistance what Audrey Wood amassed over the years.

However insignificant the forum of his criticism, Freedley's consistent plaudits did not go unnoticed by his fellow New York critics; and at times, in the *Morning Telegraph*, the lively antagonism of his reviews clashing with Whitney Bolton's gave a vitality to the criticism. Frequently, as soon as Freedley would praise a Tennessee Williams production, Bolton, in the same newspaper within a few days, would blast it; contrariwise, when Freedley would, on rare occasion, find grounds for censuring a Williams play, Bolton would find cause for praising Williams more lavishly than he'd ever before seen fit. (Of note: regarding *27 Wagons Full of Cotton*, Bolton claims [1955.16] that "Mr. Williams has fallen into the low habit of writing dirty words on paper, instead of fences." Freedley several days later [1955.41] claims it is "a MUST show for Broadway playgoers.")

However intriguing such in-house squabbles may be in the history of Williams criticism, it is the works themselves, in staged play, film, and fiction formats, that dominated the news of this decade and fostered evolving critical reputation. There were the indismissible events that had not so much to do with the fact that Williams had written a given work as that it appeared at a particular time, in a particular place, with a particular cast that gave Williams an image of increased stature, and thereby, as a natural consequence, produced a need for still newer critical terminology and critical interest.

One such event was the reappearance of *Summer and Smoke* in 1952. It had run for only three months when it opened on Broadway in 1948, and none of the reviews was so glowing as to give it much of a chance; it closed quickly, to no one's great surprise or regret. It reappeared—to relatively indifferent notice—at the Actors Company in La Jolla, California, as well as in London, in 1950 and 1951, respectively. But when Jose Quintero gave Geraldine Page the role of Alma and took the modest course of staging *Summer and Smoke* at Greenwich Village's Circle-in-the-Square in April of 1952, a success was delivered back to Tennessee Williams that only partially had to do with the intensely positive reviews of Atkinson, Sheaffer, and Wyatt (1952.2, 1952.16, 1952.22). As Stuart Little points out in his *The Prophetic Theater* (1972.28), off-Broadway, as a theatrical reality, a theatrical phenomenon, quite simply *began* on 24 April 1952 when *Summer and Smoke* was revived on Sheridan Square. The production was the first major success below 42nd Street in thirty years. And it is of no minor significance that an event that gave rise to a whole New York theatrical structure, a legitimizing, as it were, of a theatrical arena, was a Tennessee Williams play.

Just as certainly, by whatever means one measures Williams' critical reputation, such an event as this has got to be taken into account: by 1952, Tennessee Williams had in fact become a force who could alter the conventionally understood stature of theater territory. Seven years earlier, only a handful of theater enthusiasts even knew who he was. Now, a play only four years old was having a revival, films were being made of his works, his fiction was being published and he was shaping theatrical history.

By mid-decade there was manifest critical interest—beyond the range of review criticism—abroad. Frederick Lumley, in his 1956 *Trends in 20th Century Drama* (1956.68), addressed himself to Tennessee Williams' themes; he spoke of Williams' pessimism, calling it "typically American"; he went on to speak of language, of symbolism, of "non-naturalistic style," and of folk tragedy in Williams' still small canon. And at the end of the decade, J.G. Weightman would use similar critical perspectives. In his *Twentieth Century* review of *Garden District* (1958.108), he would berate Williams for the "moist smell of rotting Southerners" that he found in *Suddenly Last Summer* particularly, and he would be utterly straightforward in claiming that since Americans were Britishers' "heirs," he found Tennessee Williams' dramatic world-view distressing. Weightman preferred to think of Americans as "big strong men thinking in global terms." Williams' "rotting Southerners" contravened that preference, Weightman took exception, and his critical judgment descended.

This sort of criticism saw itself as clean and right in its vision, and it would not die out, as perhaps it should have, merely because it was generally argued with so little evidence and so narrow (though insistent) a value structure at its base. Indeed, Continental criticism, as limited in volume as it appears to be, persisted with a compelling interest in Tennessee Williams' South, its decaying "smell," its fetid characters (particularly its wilted, semigrotesque women), and what it found to be Tennessee Williams' rhapsodic lyricizing of these very items. German and French criticism particularly (1961.28, 1967.13, 1975.38) pored over this theme, frequently using it as the keystone of critical theories about his work.

More to the point of domestic criticism though, the fifties—the decade that would have Tennessee Williams give us *The Rose Tattoo, Camino Real, Cat on a Hot Tin Roof, Sweet Bird of Youth, Garden District* (containing *Something Unspoken* and *Suddenly Last Summer*), plus the films *The Glass Menagerie, A Streetcar Named Desire, Fugitive Kind*, and *Baby Doll*—would be a decade that more than any other forged his popular reputation for good. The films, particularly *Streetcar* and the hysterically received *Baby Doll*, popularized Tennessee Williams as his plays never could—and that alone dictated the need for critical reassessment. Plays such as *Cat on a Hot Tin Roof* and *Sweet Bird of Youth* took the theater back to Tennessee Williams' South of *Streetcar* and *Summer and Smoke* and pushed deeper at the themes that alarmed as well as excited, the themes that individuated the Williams voice coming across the footlights.

Even apart from the popular havoc of *Baby Doll*, there was a rising critical voice, as the decade drew to a close, that was trying to unscramble the canon and its worth, trying to isolate the staples in Williams' schema. Donald Hall, reviewing *In the Winter of Cities* in the *Yale Review* (1957.41), goes beyond the poems he is apparently criticizing and reaches out for the canon as a whole; he discusses "the faults which undermine the plays" as though it is a given that there *are* pervasive faults and that they *are* undermining. He cites such elements as awkwardness and technical primitivism, Williams' "inability to use the line as a unit of rhythm"—all problems in the poems specifically, but problems endemic as well to the plays. Whether Hall today would continue to subscribe to the then quite young Hall's critical denunciation of an equally young Williams corpus is less important than that in the winter of 1957, while the newspapers coast to coast were steaming and pouting about *Baby Doll*, Hall was talking of rhythm and control of line, of technical primitivism and compositional fraudulency. The vocabulary of the criticism was adding girth.

The same year, Walter Kerr, in his *Pieces at Eight* (1957.52), would attempt to summarize almost a decade of his own criticism of Tennessee Williams. While focusing particularly on *Rose Tattoo* and *Camino Real*, Kerr would generalize his critical inquiry: "The failures of Tennessee Williams are worth talking about." His customarily skilled critical voice would cite the implausibility of so many of Tennessee Williams' "escape-hatch endings," his inability to deliver on what he incites, the paucity of Williams' "own imaginative equipment."

Kerr's concern is echoed the following year in Richard B. Vowles' important *Tulane Drama Review* essay (1958.98). Vowles notes Tennessee Williams' relative success in the popular press, as well as his professional success generally, but he attempts to be precise in assessing the cause of Williams' "slight critical approbation in the literary press." An important question. And, to be sure, Vowles poses it at a crucial time in the development of Williams' reputation. Vowles's own conclusions probably give us more of a clarifying of the territory than any real answers: he claims that an inverse proportion of approbation operates as a matter of course—if one is "too successful" on Broadway (and with its popular press champions), one suffers ipso facto in the literary press. According to Vowles, Williams poses substantial problems for serious critics: his "moral world" is too constricting—and oversimplified—for the more thinking critics; the South itself, as a literary convention, invites critical antagonism. Vowles's argument remains that—an argument. Its value as an argument is its early appearance. No one before seems to have acknowledged this problem as being worth investigating in print.

It's worthy of note that at about the same time, one of the first Tennessee Williams Ph.D. dissertations would appear—Nancy Marie Patterson would complete her "Patterns of Imagery in the Major Plays of Tennessee Williams" (1957.71). Her focus would be on elements at the crux of dramatic-poetic experience, and however unprepossessing a statement it might have been, it would be the first words of a critical voice that would go on to be linked with Williams criticism categorically—Nancy Marie Patterson quickly became Nancy M. Tischler, and the concerns of her last words as a student in the academy just as quickly became what we now know to be the substantial and serious collection of her critical studies of Williams and his work.

Tennessee Williams' critical reputation for the year late-1956 to mid-1957 is inextricable from the reputation of *Baby Doll*. Judging by newspaper and magazine accounts, the furor that *Baby Doll* caused in the social sphere outdistances the notice anything of Williams' ever achieved—before or since. A blitz of words—speeches, sermons, panel discussions, commentaries, editorials, reviews, analyses, charges, counter-charges, letters to editors and letters by the thousands from the public to movie theater managers, legal briefs, governmental position papers—all addressed to what seems to have been a fairly innocuous film whose hyped reputation preceded it. Naturally it redirected critical attention back to its author, and just as naturally, while disclaiming any lurid or unseemly intent, its author gave every appearance of relishing the enfant terrible image the hysteria furthered.

Without belaboring the point, it might be worthwhile to pause and sample the critical torrent. Headlines sometimes give us a full picture, and in this case, the evidence is patent: "Blunt and Banned" (1956.11), " 'Baby Doll' Cancelled" (1956.7), " 'Baby Doll' Risks Legion's Wrath" (1956.16), "Kazan, Tennessee Williams Reply to Spellman Attack on 'Baby Doll' " (1956.19), " 'Baby Doll' Garbed in Squalor" (1956.28), "Kennedy's Chain Bars 'Baby Doll' " (1956.63), "How to Police the Movies is under Debate Again" (1956.87), "Spellman Takes to Pulpit to Forbid 'Baby Doll' " (1956.88), "Should It Be Suppressed?" (1956.93), "Theatre in Albany Is Banned for Six Months for Scheduling 'Baby Doll' " (1956.100), "Tennessee Williams and His Po' White Trash" (1956.112), "Men and Dolls" (1957.1), "Aurora, Ill., Bans 'Baby Doll' " (1957.5), " 'Baby Doll' Ads Banned: Syracuse and Troy Newspapers Act against Movie" (1957.6), " 'Baby Doll' Censored" (1957.7), " 'Baby Doll' Ordered to Get License for Exhibition in Providence Theatre" (1957.9), "The Bitter Dispute over 'Baby Doll' " (1957.12), "Catholics in France May See 'Baby Doll' " (1957.20), "More on 'Baby Doll' " (1957.24), "Film Ban Assailed: Cultural Freedom Group Hits Boycott of 'Baby Doll' " (1957.33). And it is safe to say that such titles, multiplied many times over, fairly closely approximate the content of the articles they head.

Such an event as *Baby Doll* is what makes it so difficult to assess the critical reputation of Tennessee Williams. The popular press had more or less won back *its* Tennessee Williams. Once again, more considered criticism would have to stop, redirect its eye, almost apologetically, and find a means of "acquitting" Tennessee Williams, of relegitimizing him.

In a lengthy interview appearing in the *Educational Theatre Journal* in 1958 (1958.66), Arthur Miller addresses some of the issues that Williams criticism had already focused on and would, as the next few years unfolded, focus on all the more stridently. Miller compresses into a few words what Robert Brustein, Harold Clurman, and A. Alvarez would write more fully about: "Williams is a realistic writer.... I think Williams is primarily interested in passion, in ecstasy, in creating a synthesis of his conflicting feelings."

Within a year Brustein, writing about *Sweet Bird of Youth* (1959.23), shows how the attempt at realism in the play is a sham; he finds Williams using it as a flimsy pretext for what he calls his "hazy notions about . . . Sex, Youth, Time, Corruption." He complains forthrightly of Williams' sense of dramatic conflict being "fraudulent conflict," and he sanctions Williams for the unnecessary solipsism in the play, his inability to let it evolve to "a deeper subjective reality." Writing at the same time for *Encounter* (1959.22), again about the decade's last Williams play, *Sweet Bird of Youth*, the highly respected Brustein looks directly at *Sweet Bird* and finds it "the most baldly personal of a corpus of drama already unusual for its subjectivity." He doesn't stop with that, but adds an indictment that foreshadows the sort of excoriating criticism John Simon would take up in the decades to come: the play, "as dramatic art, is disturbingly bad—aimless, dishonest and crudely melodramatic." Further, he cites Williams' "ignorance of, and obsession with, himself," and he calls this the fundamental, main problem in his being able to write good plays.

Clurman, frequently Williams' most articulate popular press defender, writing at the same time as Brustein, identifies more merit in *Sweet Bird* (1959.33), but, in attempting to specify what's wrong with the play, offers the chilling observation: "What we suspect in 'Sweet Bird of Youth' is that Williams has become immobilized in his ideology." (Clurman's comment can be read now as unfortunately prophetic.)

As the decade closed, *Sweet Bird* would continue to receive mixed critical response, and *Orpheus Descending*, in its 1959 London production, would be praised by critics such as A. Alvarez (1959.2) who found it "extremely ingenious" although too close to the grain of what he saw as the glib Williams conceit, "his later sweatshirt realism." There was only one undisputed hit left for Williams (*The Night of the Iguana*);

it had already premiered in Spoleto, and it would come to Broadway at the end of 1961. Before that Arthur Miller would be interviewed again (1960.18) and, in a general overview of the decade just past, would touch only once on Williams. This time his comment doesn't hint at saying anything positive about his contemporary. In fact, what he offers is an indictment, and it's swift and corrosive: "The Fifties became an era of gauze. Tennesssee Williams is responsible for this in the main."

When the fifties began, the critics and the public were still reeling from the force of *A Streetcar Named Desire*. The impact of this play was soon intensified and generalized within the culture by its 1951 release as a well-received film. As the decade ended, the critical voice that had been almost exclusively the construct of the popular press had spread to the academic community. And in both the popular and the academic press there was more of a sense of debate about Williams than there had been previously. And beyond debate, there was evidence of deeper inspection of his plays, with harder questions being asked. For example, what had for almost ten years been acknowledged (and praised) as the bountiful originality of his themes was now cited as too predictable; it was argued that his themes were repeating themselves. It was said that his vision, worse than just "myopic" (as some were calling it), was focused on a mirror. The highly original and daring Williams was starting to be seen as self-conscious. Fortunately for Williams though, there would be at least one more blockbuster.

The Night of the Iguana premiered at New York's Royale Theatre on 28 December 1961. The unanimous critical praise of the popular press speaks for itself, and it is worth illustrating since it was the last time Williams would ever receive such notices. Chapman, in the New York *Daily News* (1961.13), called it "a beautiful play"; Freedley, in the *Morning Telegraph* (1961.27), said it "contains more of all Williams' gifts than any play since 'A Streetcar Named Desire'"; Kerr, in the *Herald Tribune* (1961.46), while considering the play "unsatisfactory," nonetheless thought it "the finest rough-work the contemporary theater is prepared to offer"; McClain, in the *New York Journal-American* (1961.57), called it "the most fruitful and versatile exercise by our best living playwright"; Nadel of the *New York World Telegram & Sun* (1961.59) found it "an awesome and powerful new drama"; Taubman, writing for the *Times* (1961.79), said it "achieves a vibrant eloquence"; Watts, in the *New York Post* (1961.99), while finding it a "surprisingly undramatic play," nonetheless celebrated its capacity to give us "insight into the author's dark and brooding mind." A year later, to no one's surprise, it won the Drama Critics' Circle Award.

The next time Williams would have a New York production of an original play would be at the end of the decade. Most of the New York dailies would have passed out of existence; his long-time lover, Frank Merlo, would have died; Williams would be heavily relying on (if not addicted to) drugs and alcohol; and his depression would become, by his own admission, "almost clinical." (As the famous anecdote goes, in the early seventies, Williams heard Gore Vidal refer to the sixties. "The sixties? I slept through the sixties," quoth Williams.)

While Williams slept, Hollywood filmed *The Fugitive Kind, Sweet Bird of Youth, Period of Adjustment, The Night of the Iguana, This Property Is Condemned*, and *Boom!* (and since *Suddenly Last Summer* was released in December of 1959, it too was a film of the sixties). Back and forth across the country, thousands of miles of celluloid carried Tennessee Williams to public notice. And since at least three of these films were successful, his "reputation," popularly speaking, continued to grow, abetted to be sure by reviews of the films in local newspapers and national magazines.

Also while Williams slept (and maybe precisely because he was sleeping), scholarly criticism became both more forthright and more abundant. At the start of the decade, Jacob H. Adler, who has written often and well about Williams, included comments on Williams in his essay in *South: Modern Southern Literature in Its Cultural Setting* (1961.3). His focus on Williams was unapologetically serious: What were the allegorical contexts of his work? How do ritual, religion, the grotesque correspond in actually defining culture in the South? Alan S. Downer, in the same year, would also give attention to Williams' place in the tradition (1961.20), and Signi L. Falk's often quoted, often praised (and, as of 1978, revised and updated and reprinted) *Tennessee Williams* (1961.26) plus Nancy M. Tischler's *Tennessee Williams: Rebellious Puritan* (1961.82) would set a precedent for books to follow—their studies were serious, they were intuitive, they were sensitive to probabilities. By no means of like significance, but still rewarding in its information, Benjamin Nelson's book on Williams (1961.60) saw publication the same year, making it, in sum, a year to begin a decade symbolically: concurrent with Tennessee Williams' going into repose, simultaneous with the last year of an unqualifiedly successful major play, the world of Tennessee Williams criticism within hard covers announced itself.

More organized statements on the dramatic influence Tennessee

Introduction

Williams was having beyond his own national borders began appearing in the early sixties with Horst Frenz (1961.28) and Fritz Andre Kracht (1966.42) addressing the impact of Williams' work in modern Germany. Seymour L. Flaxman, in *Comparative Literature Studies* (1963.18), refers to influence in the reverse geographic line, with a pointed tracing of the connection between Williams and "the two Scandinavian giants," Strindberg and Ibsen. The same year, Richard K. Barksdale in his essay in the *College Language Association Journal* (1963.1) wrote clearly of the Shakespeare-Ben Jonson-Miller-Williams connection.

Focusing primarily on the tradition of these shores, Esther M. Jackson, with her customary clean insight, draws the reader's attention (1960.64) to Williams' pivotal place in the formation of "an American dramaturgy." (She also discusses the conflict of his "popular acclaim" counterbalanced by "the censure of the academy.") Five years later, her important book, *The Broken World of Tennessee Williams* (1965.30), would use terms and argue premises that would forever dispatch any suspicion that Williams could get into the academy only by a back door. She analyzes—and praises—him "as the architect of form in the American drama," as the valid successor to O'Neill, as the progenitor of "an aspect of a second American Renaissance."

However serious these studies may be, they by no means fully characterize the decade in which they—and many other such works—appeared. The press was not immune to such mawkish books as Gilbert Maxwell's *Tennessee Williams and Friends* (1965.43) or Williams' mother's *Remember Me to Tom* (1963.68)—the less said the better. Similarly, the *New York Times* would open its pages to Hodding Carter and permit him to carp, "Yes, Tennessee, There *Are* Southern Belles" (1962.12). For every Gerald Weales, Kenneth Tynan, and Robert Brustein, there would be twenty triflers, attempting to set public taste by critical attitudinizing, most often in the popular—and sometimes in the scholarly—press.

The sixties would more or less be capped for Williams by an event that most likely was never intended to have the impact or consequences that it did. On 10 June 1969, *Life* magazine, then in its own death throes, ran a full-page ad in the *New York Times* (1969.29). In an attempt to show how gutsy, how astute, how unbent by sentiment it was, it insisted that it maintained the distinction of being honest even when it hurt. To wit, it featured Tennessee Williams in its ad, mentioning its upcoming Stefan Kanfer review of *In the Bar of a Tokyo Hotel* (1969.22), which review would pan the play. From this, *Life* went on to generalize

Williams' decay ("Tennessee Williams has suffered an infantile regression from which there seems no exit"), titling the whole ad "Played Out?" and patting itself grandly on the back.

The outcry against *Life*—and even more virulently against the *Times* for the un-"fit"-ness of running such an ad—was swift and ample. The premise of the many who wrote rebuttals (1969.9) was a direct one: a crass assault on an institution like Williams, so wanton in its intent and display, wouldn't be tolerated. Whether, despite its coarseness, *Life* magazine might have been correct, wasn't even really open to question. The sentiment appeared to be that Williams, even in his obviously debilitated physical and professional state, was a veritable national treasure. Aside from the fraternity of drama critics in newspapers and magazines, who had license to vilify him as they chose, no one else had the latitude even to look askance.

In 1971 Williams fired Audrey Wood. His *Memoirs* gives a detailed accounting of the break-up of their thirty-two-year relationship, and Williams ends up sounding both nostalgic and defensive. Into the void stepped Bill Barnes who, by virtue of working for what was then called International Famous Agency and having Raquel Welch as his other major client, knew how to give his clients public exposure, how to scrap with the fame brokers in the entertainment business, and how to make money. Under the mantle of Barnes' protection, encouragement, and, it would appear, pushing, Tennessee Williams arose from his somnolent sixties. He wrote and saw the production and failure of a string of mediocre plays whose titles read like a sad litany of creative might gone soft: *Small Craft Warnings, Red Devil Battery Sign, Out Cry, This Is (An Entertainment), Vieux Carre, Tiger Tail, Creve Coeur, Will Mr. Merriweather Return from Memphis?, Clothes for a Summer Hotel.* Interspersed were the publication of two works of fiction (*Eight Mortal Ladies Possessed* and *Moise and the World of Reason*), one collection of poems (*Androgyne, Mon Amour*), his selected essays (*Where I Live*), and his autobiography (*Memoirs*). And on top of that, as much through the energy and determination of Barnes as through their own readiness for it, several of his early plays saw important revivals: *Cat on a Hot Tin Roof, The Glass Menagerie, A Streetcar Named Desire.* By dint of its mass alone, the corpus of the seventies would indicate a conspicuous rejuvenation for the playwright.

The new plays and fiction, the revivals and autobiography, plus the significant publication by Donald Windham of *Tennessee Williams' Letters to Donald Windham* (1977.103) had the effect of once again

Introduction

putting Williams squarely before the scrutiny of the popular press. But whatever the volume of Williams' output and the corresponding volume of popular press response, the weighing of Williams' critical reputation in scholarly publications had enough of a foothold—and background—by now to become far more independent of the popular criticism than it was ten years earlier.

Leland Starnes, for example, writing in *Modern Drama* at the very start of the decade (1970.43), concerns himself with the issue of realism in the plays and the means Williams has found to disguise "the character-istic exaggeration and distortion of reality which permeates his entire canon." Two years later Nancy Tischler, in her *Mississippi Quarterly* essay (1972.55), focuses on the success-failure syndrome in Williams' productions; she argues that attention has to go all the way back to *Battle of Angels*, and that both *The Glass Menagerie* and *A Streetcar Named Desire* derive from that original early source. Her analysis is closely textual and free of the popular cant of less earnest criticism. Two years later still, S. Alan Chesler (1974.5) summed up the past twenty-five years of *A Streetcar Named Desire* criticism. His survey in *Notes on Mississippi Writers* organized the scholarly criticism, called attention to the prevailing focal elements in the criticism, and contrasted the more illustrious critics' estimates. His work was careful enough that it attained a stature all its own, but, by natural extension, it also lent a new stature to *A Streetcar Named Desire*, which was then having its major, much discussed Los Angeles, New York, and London revivals.

Augmenting Williams' reputation through the vehicle of his *Nation* column, the Williams loyalist Harold Clurman, at the time of the *Streetcar* revivals, wrote what will probably go on to be seen as one of the most seminal and attitude-producing essays to have appeared in the popular press (1973.15). Clurman takes on the timeworn but still pro-vocative debate of "who's the victim-who's the villain?" in *Streetcar*; his probing and uncompromising defense of Blanche over Stanley does what virtuous criticism has always had as its primary responsibility and end: it *illuminates* the play; it allows one to *see* it, to *read* it again, and to comprehend in a fresh way.

Within the same decade, Williams' reputation would necessarily suffer from the negative criticism which that decade's weak plays re-ceived—and more than likely deserved. But the castigation of Williams in this decade would reach a pitch of verbal abuse that rivaled the most scabrous criticism of the past thirty years as a whole. Ian Hamilton's *New Statesman* review of the London production of *Vieux Carre*

(1978.15) sought and found new reckless lows in its denunciation of Williams and his play: "Ninety minutes worth of wretched self-parody . . . and acting of a screeching falsity that only a writer as revered and talentless as this one could so fulsomely induce." While *Vieux Carre* was playing in London, *Creve Coeur* was premiering at the Spoleto Festival in Charleston, South Carolina, and while Hamilton was raking Williams in the *New Statesman*, John Simon was savaging him in the pages of *New York* magazine (1978.32) with a review so caustic and mean it is a critical indecency.

Just as indecent, but in entirely other ways, Clive Barnes, occupying the drama critic's chair at the *New York Times*, was writing his vapid, often simplistic reviews of Williams' work. His kind of criticism may have been more subtly injurious to Williams' reputation, precisely because it gave the impression that there was *nothing* to say, than Simon's and Hamilton's vicious denunciations which at least admitted there was a lot that *could* be said. Upon reviewing the *Cat on a Hot Tin Roof* revival in 1974 (1974.2), for example, Barnes would invoke the tired and fatuous aphorisms of stock play-reviewing: "a gripping and intensely moving play, a play that can hold its own with anything written in the post-O'Neill American Theater." And to cap his essentially disengaged review, he would add, Tennessee Williams "makes you care by showing you a world." Surely such a play deserved more of a statement than that. And it might be argued that Williams' reputation had to be negatively affected by the simple fact that the *Times*, with its capacity to sway—if not define—public taste, would even print such vacuous criticism.

Much in Williams' favor in the seventies was the publication of three collections of essays on his work. The year 1971 saw the release of Jordan Miller's *Twentieth Century Interpretations of A Streetcar Named Desire: A Collection of Critical Essays* (1971.19). Miller included reprints of reviews from the Boston try-out performance as well as Broadway premiere reviews. In addition, his collection gathered twenty other essays, ranging from a selection of notes from Elia Kazan's "Notebook for 'A Streetcar Named Desire'" to Signi Falk's 1961 essay, "The Southern Gentlewoman." In 1977, Stephen Stanton collected sixteen essays (all but one previously published) in his *Tennessee Williams: A Collection of Critical Essays* (1977.88). And quickly following Stanton in the same year, Jac Tharpe published his massive *Tennessee Williams: A Tribute* (1977.93) with fifty-three serious essays (only one of which was previously published). He divided the essays into seven categories: *Streetcar* criticism, criticism of the other plays as a group, "European Contexts," themes, prose and poetry, techniques, and assessment. The mass and general quality of the compendium make it difficult to single out any few for comment here. Rather, I would refer the reader to the elaborate annotations I provide in my 1977 chapter.

In mid-1978, Tennessee Williams and I spoke several times over the period of several days. In the lengthiest of the conversations, I tried numerous times to get him to address the issue of his critical reputation. No matter how I phrased the question, however, he continued to hear it as a question of his popular critical reputation alone: he talked of newspaper and popular magazine critics, he expressed his dismay over their treatment of "my recent work," he tried to discount their importance and their influence, he asked me whether I didn't agree that New York would not continue to remain the center of American theater. When I made it apparent that I was talking of critical reputation as an issue of scrutiny in the academy, he was simply dismissive—it seemed pointedly obvious that the issue did not interest him.

As far as Williams was concerned, his critical reputation would remain in the hands of those who gave him fame, those same critics against whom he railed for what he considered their provincialism, if not their conspiracy against him. The last time he spoke to me on the subject (and a bit of this is recorded in my *Washington Post* article [1978.25]), he relegated his *future* critical reputation to what would come from whoever his biographer might be. He made an intense plea for that person to rely heavily on his *Memoirs* and on his letters to Donald Windham. It was his impression that those two volumes contained all that was needed to appraise him well.

Later he somewhat disavowed his *Memoirs* and suggested there would be a thoroughly new version, under the title *Mes Cahiers Noirs*; the realization of how recklessly brutal Donald Windham's annotations to the *Letters* really are has indicated the need for extreme caution in working with that volume—the problem is one of separating the letters as letters from the tincture of Windham's characterization of them in the margin.

Whether Williams ever acceded to the need for a responsible weighing of his critical reputation or not, several things stand powerfully in the favor of whoever will eventually take the task on: James Laughlin of New Directions, Williams' faithful publisher since the days of *Glass Menagerie*, has made possible a fairly consistent stream of published plays and prose fiction; the Humanities Research Center of the Uni-

Williams, in 1963, began donat-
s a repository of a vast array
e place; the Theatre Collection
Center branch, inspired and
to keep remarkably thorough
disarray, gather in one place
logued items on Williams and
vey Wayne Gunn's bibliography
les critics to have an accurate
ention all the minute particulars
lays, filmscripts, fiction pieces,
ipated Andreas Brown primary
l add more particulars to what

ems is a simple one: the history
well enough to be considered
ailable, serious critics are freer

Abbreviations

TW	Tennessee Williams
AB	*American Blues*
AMA	*Androgyne, Mon Amour*
BA	*Battle of Angels*
BD	*Baby Doll*
BK	*Blood Kin*
Boom	*BOOM!*
CSB	*Cairo, Shanghai, Bombay*
CR	*Camino Real*
CAND	*Candles to the Sun*
CAT	*Cat on a Hot Tin Roof*
CSH	*Clothes for a Summer Hotel*
CC	*Creve Coeur*
DC	*Dragon Country*
EN	*The Eccentricities of a Nightingale*
8M	*Eight Mortal Ladies Possessed*
FGC	*The Frosted Glass Coffin*
FK	*Fugitive Kind*
GD	*Garden District: Something Unspoken* and *Suddenly Last Summer*
GM	*The Glass Menagerie*
GF	*The Gnädiges Fräulein*
HC	*Hard Candy*
HNM	*A House Not Meant to Stand*
ICI	*I Can't Imagine Tomorrow*
BAR	*In the Bar of a Tokyo Hotel*

Abbreviations

IWC	*In the Winter of Cities*
IR	*I Rise in Flame, Cried the Phoenix*
KE	*Kingdom of Earth*
KKK	*Kirche, Kuche, und Kinder*
KQ	*Knightly Quest*
LLL	*The Lady of Larkspur Lotion*
LSG	*The Last of My Solid Gold Watches*
LM	*Last of the Mobile Hot-Shots*
LDW	*Letters to Donald Windham, 1940–1965*
LBLL	*Lord Byron's Love Letter*
LTD	*Loss of a Tear Drop Diamond*
LSCC	*A Lovely Sunday for Creve Coeur*
MEM	*Memoirs*
MT	*The Milk Train Doesn't Stop Here Anymore*
MWR	*Moise and the World of Reason*
MK	*Moony's Kid Don't Cry*
M	*The Mutilated*
NI	*The Night of the Iguana*
OA	*One Arm and Other Stories*
OD	*Orpheus Descending*
OC	*Out Cry*
PAG	*Perfect Analysis Given by a Parrot*
PA	*Period of Adjustment*
PM	*Portrait of a Madonna*
P	*The Purification*
RED	*The Red Devil Battery Sign*
RSMS	*The Roman Spring of Mrs. Stone*
RT	*The Rose Tattoo*
7D	*The Seven Descents of Myrtle*
SST	*Slapstick Tragedy: The Mutilated* and *The Gnädiges Fräulein*
SCW	*Small Craft Warnings*
SML	*Some Problems for the Moose Lodge*
SC	*Something Cloudy, Something Clear*
SU	*Something Unspoken*
STR	*Stairs to the Roof*

Abbreviations

SND	*A Streetcar Named Desire*
SLS	*Suddenly Last Summer*
S&S	*Summer and Smoke*
SB	*Sweet Bird of Youth*
TTM	*Talk to Me like the Rain and Let Me Listen*
10B	*Ten Blocks on the Camino Real*
TIE	*This Is (An Entertainment)*
TPC	*This Property Is Condemned*
TT	*Tiger Tail*
27W	*27 Wagons Full of Cotton*
2CP	*Two-Character Play*
VC	*Vieux Carre*
WIL	*Where I Live*
WMM	*Will Mr. Merriweather Return from Memphis?*
YTM	*You Touched Me!*

Chronology

1911   26 March, Thomas Lanier Williams born in Columbus, Mississippi.

1918   Williams family moved to St. Louis, Missouri.

1927   First published work, his essay, "Can a Good Wife Be a Good Sport?" in *Smart Set.* It won third prize, $5.

1928   First story published, "The Vengeance of Nitocris," in *Weird Tales.*

1929   Entered University of Missouri.

1931   Worked for St. Louis shoe company.

1935   First play produced (in Memphis), *Cairo, Shanghai, Bombay.*

1936   Entered Washington University, St. Louis.

1937   *Candles to the Sun* and *Fugitive Kind* produced by Mummers of St. Louis. Entered University of Iowa.

1938   Graduated from University of Iowa.

1939   Won Group Theatre prize of $100 for *American Blues.* Received $1,000 Rockefeller grant.

1940   *Battle of Angels* produced in Boston.

1944   *The Glass Menagerie* produced in Chicago.

1945   *The Glass Menagerie* produced on Broadway.

1947   *A Streetcar Named Desire* produced on Broadway.

1948   *Summer and Smoke* produced on Broadway; *One Arm* published.

1950   *The Roman Spring of Mrs. Stone* published; film of *The Glass Menagerie* released.

1951   *The Rose Tattoo* produced on Broadway; film of *A Streetcar Named Desire* released.

1953   *Camino Real* produced on Broadway.

1954   *Hard Candy* published.

1955   *Cat on a Hot Tin Roof* produced on Broadway; film of *The Rose Tattoo* released.

1956   *In the Winter of Cities* published; film, *Baby Doll*, released.

1957   *Orpheus Descending* produced on Broadway.

1958   *Garden District* produced off-Broadway; film of *Cat on a Hot Tin Roof* released.

1959   *Sweet Bird of Youth* produced on Broadway; film of *Suddenly Last Summer* released.

1960   *Period of Adjustment* produced on Broadway; film of *Fugitive Kind* released.

1961   *Night of the Iguana* produced on Broadway; films of *The Roman Spring of Mrs. Stone* and *Summer and Smoke* released.

1962   Films of *Sweet Bird of Youth* and *Period of Adjustment* released.

1963   *The Milk Train Doesn't Stop Here Anymore* produced on Broadway.

1966   *Slapstick Tragedy* produced on Broadway; film of *This Property Is Condemned* released.

1967   *The Two Character Play* produced in London; *Knightly Quest* published.

1968   *The Seven Descents of Myrtle* produced on Broadway.

1969   *In the Bar of a Tokyo Hotel* produced on Broadway; film, *Last of the Mobile Hot-Shots*, released.

1972   *Small Craft Warnings* produced off-Broadway.

1973   *Out Cry* produced on Broadway.

1974   *Eight Mortal Ladies Possessed* published.

1975   *Red Devil Battery Sign* produced in Boston; *Moise and the World of Reason* and *Memoirs* published.

1976   *Letters to Donald Windham* published; *This Is (An Entertainment)* produced in San Francisco.

Chronology

1977   *Vieux Carre* produced on Broadway; *Androgyne, Mon Amour* published.

1978   *Where I Live* published.

1979   *A Lovely Sunday for Creve Coeur* produced off-Broadway.

1980   *Clothes for a Summer Hotel* produced on Broadway.

1981   *A House Not Meant to Stand* produced in Chicago; *Something Cloudy, Something Clear* produced off-Broadway. Williams celebrates seventieth birthday.

1983   24 February, Tennessee Williams dies at Hotel Elysée in New York City. (Pronounced dead 25 February.)

Writings about Tennessee Williams

1939

1 "Gossip of the Rialto." *New York Times*, 24 December, sec. 9, p. 1.
    TW mentioned as one of three recipients of Rockefeller Fellow-
    ships; he was sponsored by the Group Theatre.

2 "Naya Wins Play Prize." *New York Times*, 21 March, p. 26.
    Brief news release; highlights special $100 prize awarded to
    TW for *AB*; mentions the three sketches that constitute a full-
    length play.

1940

1 HASTINGS, MORRIS. "Miriam Hopkins Returns." *Boston Evening Tran-
    script*, 31 December, p. 14.
    Review of *BA*, Boston production. "Miss Hopkins by virtue
    of a spirited performance has turned an otherwise run of the mill
    melodrama into something to be richly enjoyed. But even she
    can do little for Mr. Williams' first professionally produced drama
    which, in its present stage, is a stumbling, pointless affair that . . .
    loses itself in deeper and deeper obscurity." No plot discussion.

2 "Miriam Hopkins at the Wilbur." *Boston Post*, 31 December, p. 8.
    Review of *BA*, Boston production. "Although New Year's Eve
    was still some twenty-four hours away many in the audience
    wondered if the happenings on the stage were not the aftermath
    of the glorious celebration in the imaginative brain of a genius

who celebrated gaily a little too well and was removed for quiet to that famous ward at the Bellevue Hospital." No plot discussion.

3   "New Playwright." *New York Herald Tribune*, 4 August, sec. 6, pp. 1, 2.

   Brief, one-paragraph biographical sketch of TW; refers to *BA*, as well as to *CAND* and *FK*.

4   Ross, George. "Tennessee Williams Has Yen for Moving; But Switch-board Operator Ties Him Down for Luncheon." *New York World-Telegram*, 30 November, p. 6.

   Brief gossip item; how he moved seven times in first few weeks in Manhattan.

5   "She Missed." *Boston Transcript*, 28 December, part 3, pp. 4, 5.

   Advance piece on *BA*; discusses the brewing dispute; gives background on TW.

6   "Stage Notes." *Daily Worker*, 10 February, p. 7.

   News item, brief. TW receives $1,000 Rockefeller award; will have first New York showing of his play, "The Long Goodbye," at the New School, with John O'Shaugnessey directing.

7   "Tennessee—He Roams." *Boston Post*, 22 December, p. 9.

   News and gossip piece about *BA* one week in advance of its Boston premiere; also focuses on TW: what his name means, his background, where he stays in New York.

8   "2 New Plays in Boston." *New York Times*, 31 December, p. 18.

   News item; *BA*, "by a 26-year-old Louisiana writer, Tennessee Williams," opens in Boston.

9   "Wilbur Theatre: 'Battle of Angels.'" *Boston Globe*, 31 December, p. 7.

   Review of *BA*, Boston production. "Taken as a whole, the play gives the audience the sensation of having been dunked in mire." Continues in same vein.

10 WILLIAMS, ALEXANDER. Review of *BA. Boston Herald*, 31 December, p. 10.

Boston production. "A mixture of poetry, realism, melodrama, comedy, whimsy and eroticism." Plot summary and comments on cast. Reprinted: 1978.19.

1941

1 "Boston Bars 'Delta Dirt' and Play by St. Louisan Closes." *St. Louis Post-Dispatch*, 7 January, sec. A, p. 3.

News item; refers to "Thomas L. Williams" arousing "censorship instincts" in Boston, and the consequent closing of *BA*; mentions police being called out to close it down.

2 "Boston by Wire." *New York Times*, 5 January, sec. 9, p. 1.

Surveys the *BA* issue in Boston; cites it as first Broadway-bound play by TW. "The reviewers were more impressed by the production . . . than the play."

3 "Gossip of the Rialto." *New York Times*, 7 September, sec. 9, p. 2.

"Hume Cronyn has taken an option on some ten one-act plays by Tennessee Williams, the scheme being to put on three or four for a Sunday evening program during the Winter. Mr. Cronyn will direct."

4 LIBBEY. Review of *BA. Variety*, 1 January, p. 45.

"The play is sordid, with little comedy relief." Summary of performance by cast.

5 NORTON, ELLIOT. " 'Battle of Angels' a Defeat, But No Disaster." *Boston Post*, 12 January, p. 25.

Discusses its closing in Boston, its need for rewriting, its being censored, its history before Boston. TW's "talent is most interesting."

6 "Play Must Have Lines Taken Out: 'Battle of Angels' Cut after Council Demands Probe." *Boston Post*, 7 January, p. 1.

Summary of Boston City Council and city censor actions, one

councillor observing, "This show is a crime to be permitted to run in the city of Boston."

7 "Rialto Gossip." *New York Times*, 9 March, sec. 9, p. 3.
    Text of apologies by Theatre Guild in Boston for producing *BA*.

1942

1 "T. Williams Revises Play." *New York Herald Tribune*, 25 January, sec. 6, p. 2.
    Brief news item; TW's intention to revise *BA* for a St. Louis production.

1943

1 "Gossip of the Rialto." *New York Times*, 17 October, sec. 2, p. 2.
    Review of *YTM*, Cleveland production. "Critics liked the play . . . [but] needs tidying up."

1944

1 CASSIDY, CLAUDIA. "Fragile Drama Holds Together in Tight Spell." *Chicago Daily Tribune*, 27 December, p. 11.
    Review of *GM*, Chicago production. "If it is your play, as it is mine, it reaches out tentacles, first tentative, then gripping, and you are caught in its spell." Detail about actors, characters, and plot.

2 "15 Creative Artists to Get $1,000 Each." *New York Times*, 27 April, p. 18.
    $1,000 grant awarded to TW for *BA* by American Academy and the National Institute of Arts and Letters; presentation on 9 May at Academy Auditorium.

3 MURDOCK, HENRY T. "'The Glass Menagerie' Has Light, Unique Fascination." *Chicago Sun*, 28 December, p. 11.
    Review of *GM*, Chicago production. "Translating this play by

Tennessee Williams into the quick paragraphs of a review is no simple task, because it has no straight lines of fact or philosophy." Extensive plot summary; each actor individually appraised.

4 POLLACK, ROBERT. "Cast, Staging Super in 'Glass Menagerie.'" *Chicago Times*, 27 December, p. 24.
   Review of *GM*, Chicago production. *GM* "is a curiously uneven affair. Williams' tragi-comedy . . . tackles some mighty big problems." Includes plot details and positive observations about characterization.

5 STEVENS, ASHTON. "Great Actress Proves It in Fine Way." *Chicago Herald American*, 27 December, p. 10.
   Review of *GM*, Chicago production. Emphasis on Laurette Taylor and her interpretation of Amanda. The play "has the courage of true poetry couched in colloquial prose."

6 "Tennessee Williams Comedy Would Bow New Repertory Troupe." *Variety*, 22 November, p. 40.
   Mentions *GM*'s scheduled Christmas opening at the Civic Theatre (Chicago). Briefly mentions *BA*.

1945

1 BARNES, HOWARD. "The Theaters." *New York Herald Tribune*, 26 September, p. 18.
   Review of *YTM*. "The theater is becoming literate and imaginative again. . . . [*YTM*] has heart and considerable eloquence; [it is] extremely satisfying."

2 BRON. Review of *YTM*. *Variety*, 3 October, p. 52.
   Regards *YTM* as too light for Broadway, few plot details. TW is referred to briefly along with Windham.

3 BROWN, JOHN MASON. "Miss Taylor's Return." *Saturday Review* 29 (14 April):34–36.
   Review of *GM*. "Has its high, shimmering virtues. . . . in this season it is outstanding, but not a masterpiece." Praises production. Reprinted: 1946.3.

4   "The Celluloid Brassiere." *New Yorker* 21 (14 April): 18–19.
Short biographical piece about TW's early days before establishing himself. Talks about his mother, his days as an usher, unsuccessful jobs.

5   CHAPMAN, JOHN. "'The Glass Menagerie' Is Enchanting Play, Truly Hypnotic Theatre." New York *Daily News*, 2 April, p. 25.
Review of *GM*. TW called "a dramatist who can show you four very unimportant, very undramatic people and make you live with them and feel for them." Suggests that only TW can explain the play's meaning.

6   _____. "'You Touched Me!' This Season's First Competent, Amusing Play." New York *Daily News*, 26 September, p. 41.
Review of *YTM*. "A play written by men who have a feeling for talk and character. . . . occasionally verges on the precious . . . [but] a delightful evening."

7   COTTER, JERRY. "Artificial Character Study." *Sign* 25 (November):26.
Review of *YTM*, brief. It fails to match quality of *GM*; "it abounds in dramatic cliche."

8   _____. "Play of the Year." *Sign* 24 (May):540.
Review of *GM*. GM "stands out as an event of far greater import than the achievement of mere technical perfection. . . . a tragedy that is haunting and beautiful . . . [with] a tremendous subterranean power and dramatic fire." Gives plot details; focuses on Laurette Taylor.

9   DAME. Review of *YTM*. *Variety*, 19 September, p. 52.
Boston production, dated 11 September 1945. Calls play "earthy, uproarious, and charming." Brief plot summary, praise for the players, no mention of TW; predicts a Broadway success.

10   "Donaldson Winners Listed for Awards." *New York Times*, 1 July, sec. 1, p. 19.
GM voted Best Play; awards also for Laurette Taylor and Anthony Ross of *GM* cast.

11   Freedley, George. "Added Comments on 'You Touched Me!' The Play Has Merits in Spite of Flaws." New York *Morning Telegraph,* 26 October, p. 2.
     Review of *YTM.* Sees problems mainly in direction and casting. . . . "definitely worth seeing."

12   ————. " 'The Glass Menagerie' Provides New York Season With Highest Moments." New York *Morning Telegraph,* 3 April, p. 2.
     Review of *GM.* Had TW "restrained himself more, . . . he would have written a better play. [TW] may not have written a great play, but he has certainly provided the New York season with its highest moment this year."

13   ————." 'You Touched Me!' Marred by Weak Direction, Miscasting of Leads." New York *Morning Telegraph,* 27 September, p. 2.
     Review of *YTM.* "Not . . . a perfect script." But whatever its merits, it's "butchered . . . in direction and in the casting. . . . the authors have written a choppy play."

14   Garland, Robert. "Laurette Taylor Stars in 'The Glass Menagerie.' " *New York Journal-American,* 2 April, p. 6.
     Review of *GM.* "A very fine play and a truly great performance." Looks for it to be "the outstanding production of the waning season of 1944–45, running off with the Pulitzer and Drama Critics' prizes." TW "is a playwright to be reckoned with. . . . [*GM*] is a masterpiece of make-believe."

15   ————. " 'You Touched Me!' Comes to the Booth." *New York Journal-American,* 26 September, p. 10.
     Review of *YTM.* "Too much going on." Not much beneath all "the talking, the acting, the storytelling, the gesticulating, the pausing for effect."

16   Gibbs, Wolcott. "Such Nice People." *New Yorker* 21 (7 April):40.
     Review of *GM.* "A very touching play. . . . Tennessee Williams has captured a brief but poignant period in four lives." Lavish praise for Laurette Taylor.

17   ————. "What They Say about Dixie." *New Yorker* 21 (6 October):48.

Review of *YTM*. "Proved so much better than anything that had preceded it this season . . . [still,] it wasn't much of a play. . . . [The authors] seem overconscientious." Refers to it as "an elaborate, intensely literary variation of 'Snow White.' "

18   GILDER, ROSAMOND. "Poetry, Passion and Politics." *Theatre Arts* 29 (November):618–21.

Review of *YTM*. "Break[s] the deadlock of inanity" on Broadway. Treats *actual* chronology of this with *GM*; refers to its "poetic realism."

19   ————. "Spring Laurels: The Sum of the Season." *Theatre Arts* 29 (June):325–27.

Review of *GM*. Includes plot details, and much praise for Laurette Taylor. TW's *GM* "proved once again what magic can be wrought when playwright, actor and artist meet on common ground."

20   "The Glass Hit." *Newsweek* 25 (9 April):86–87.

Review of *GM*. "An elegant . . . touching record of four people." *GM*'s quality is "at once evocative and elusive, not to be resolved by a synopsis of a simple, sentimental story." Praises production and cast, but insists the play is a superior piece that betters work by Saroyan.

21   " 'The Glass Menagerie.' " *New York Times Magazine*, 4 March, p. 28.

Advance press release; five photographs; brief quotes of main characters' lines.

22   " 'The Glass Menagerie' Is Best Play of Year, Drama Critics Decide." *New York Times*, 11 April, p. 18.

On first ballot, *GM* won Best American Play from New York Drama Critics' Circle. Citation: "To Tennessee Williams for his play 'The Glass Menagerie' and its sensitive understanding of four troubled human beings." Mentions eligibility for Pulitzer Prize; critics listed.

23   *GM*. *Theatre Arts* 29 (October):554.

Brief, illustrated mention of the play in New York City.

24 GOLDSMITH, THEODORE. "The Gentleman Caller." *New York Times*, 1 July, sec. 2, p. 1.
How Anthony Ross was cast in *GM*.

25 GUERNSEY, OTIS L. "The Theater at Its Best." *New York Herald Tribune*, 2 April, p. 10.
Review of *GM*. "A top-notch cast in an extraordinarily sensitive script by" TW. Discusses the "lack of action" and finds it to come to "no consequence" since all else is so good. Says the script "is so full of gentle hints at atmosphere and character."

26 HEWITT, BARNARD. Review of *GM*. *Players* 21 (September-October):5.
Considerable plot summary and description of the design of the sets; impressed with the humorous contents of what he thought would be "a play of frustration and futility."

27 IBEE. Review of *GM*. *Variety*, 4 April, p. 52.
Favorable with lengthy plot details and cast information.

28 "Inside Stuff—Legit." *Variety*, 4 April, p. 52.
Short biographical profile on TW with information on *GM* opening.

29 KRUTCH, JOSEPH WOOD. Review of *GM*. *Nation* 160 (14 April): 424–25.
Comments on the unusually positive response this "first" play has received: "After the final curtain had descended, the unfamiliar cry of 'Author! Author!' rang through the auditorium and next morning the reviewers staged what is commonly called a dance in the streets." TW's play is "powerful and arresting, if somewhat abruptly truncated." Plot details, praise for Laurette Taylor; says Amanda "is unforgettable."

30 ———. Review of *YTM*. *Nation* 161 (6 October):349–50.
Surveys the negative popular press response and calls most of the condemnation into question. Discusses the "confusions" in the plot and praises the performances of the leads. References to D.H. Lawrence.

31   "Laurette Taylor—Thirty Years a Star." *New York Times Magazine*, 15 April, p. 28.
     Photo of Laurette Taylor as Amanda in *GM*.

32   Lewis, Lloyd. "Memo from Chicago." *New York Times*, 14 January, sec. 2, p. 2.
     GM at Civic Center; "Laurette Taylor as great character actress."

33   MacBride, James. "Poet's Triumph on Broadway." *New York Times Book Review*, 2 September, p. 8.
     Book review of *GM*. Brief and positive.

34   "Menagerie Includes 18 Moles Toiling in Back-Stage Blackout." *New York Herald Tribune*, 2 December, sec. 5, p. 1.
     Brief news item; refers to backstage operations in Broadway production of *GM*.

35   "'Menagerie's' Author Calls Taxes Unfair." *New York Herald Tribune*, 4 April, p. 19.
     Brief news item. TW complains of unfairness of tax laws for playwrights; also mentions his "first fiasco," although he's now making $1,000 per week.

36   Morehouse, Ward. "Laurette Taylor Is Magnificent in a Vivid Play, 'The Glass Menagerie.'" New York *Sun*, 2 April, p. 10.
     Review of *GM*. "Great acting . . . a performance of such sustained skill and expressive force." Calls the play "fragile and poignant . . . a vivid, eerie and curiously enchanting play." Plot summary and lavish praise for Laurette Taylor.

37   _____. "'You Touched Me!' Presented at Booth, a Tenuous and Fragmentary Comedy." New York *Sun*, 26 September, p. 28.
     Review of *YTM*. "Comes forth as a tenuous and fragmentary comedy. . . . Its scenes don't hold together as a satisfactory play. . . . It goes its rambling way."

38   Nichols, Lewis. "Critics in a Menagerie." *New York Times*, 15 April, sec. 2, p. 1.

Comments on the voting of *GM* as Best Play by Drama Critics' Circle.

39 _____. "Drama in Print." *New York Times*, 9 September, sec. 2, p. 1.

Comments on the published version of *GM*, noting differences between print and stage.

40 _____. " 'Glass Menagerie.' " *New York Times*, 8 April, sec. 2, p. 1.

Cites "Laurette Taylor's great performance in Mr. Williams' new play"; mentions that TW "calls his drama a memory play."

41 _____. "The Play." *New York Times*, 26 September, p. 27.

Review of *YTM*. "It is, in short, a disappointment. . . . Every playwright is entitled to a slight fall from grace occasionally. 'You Touched Me!' is Mr. Williams'."

42 _____. "The Play in Review." *New York Times*, 2 April, p. 15.

Review of *GM*. Praises Laurette Taylor. *GM*, "like spring, is a pleasure to have in the neighborhood."

43 _____. "Two New Plays." *New York Times*, 30 September, sec. 2, p. 1.

Review of *YTM*. "The play is disappointing . . . has no sustaining quality and runs a course which is uneven."

44 PHELAN, KAPPO. "The Stage and Screen: 'The Glass Menagerie.' " *Commonweal* 42 (20 April):16–17.

GM is a mixture of "symbolism (the title), naturalism (the body of the piece), and fantasy (a number of theatrical effects)."

Argues that there is no sure time reference, too many anachronisms. "An exhibition of the art of playing and no play."

45 _____. "The Stage and Screen: 'You Touched Me!' " *Commonweal* 42 (12 October):623.

Mentions clichéd characters, illogical plot developments, good and bad acting by Gwenn and Clift, respectively; and finally wonders why the playwrights allowed the play to go into production.

46   "Plays Previously Reviewed." *Catholic World* 161 (June):263–64.
Collection of the past year's reviews in annotated form; however, that of *GM* is lengthy and carries an addendum explaining
that the Legion of Decency has rated *GM* on their white list as
Class A; in short—perfect entertainment suitable for all Catholics.

47   Preview, *GM*. *Theatre Arts* 29 (May):263.
Brief, one-paragraph announcement of cast and plot of *GM*.

48   RASCOE, BURTON. " 'The Glass Menagerie,' an Unforgettable Play."
New York World-Telegram, 2 April, p. 8.
Review of *GM*. "I never hope to see again, in the theater, any-
thing as perfect as Laurette Taylor's portrayal of [Amanda]. . . .
The play hurts you . . . hurts you all through. It arouses in you
pity and terror. . . . This play is an event of the first importance."

49   ————. Review of *YTM*. *New York World-Telegram*, 26 September,
p. 34.
Review of *YTM*. "Can recommend it [to] one and all . . . a work
of art, edification and entertainment . . . a vigorous and subtle
affirmation of the life-spirit."

50   Review of *GM*. *Life* 18 (30 April):81–83.
Discusses the audience's favorable, exultant reaction to opening
night. Briefly summarizes play, then singles out Laurette Taylor
for giving "one of the great performances of the last decade."

51   Review of *GM*. *Time* 46 (9 April):86, 88.
Review of *GM*. "As a piece of theater . . . it is appealing and
unusual." Praises Laurette Taylor's performance.

52   Review of *YTM*. *Time* 46 (8 October):77.
"A gallimaufry of didactic speeches and romantic flourishes."

53   "Speaking of Pictures." *Life* 18 (11 June):12–14.
GM: Twenty photos of Laurette Taylor playing Amanda; captions are lines from the play appropriate to each photo.

54   "To Honor Three Iowa Alumni." *New York Times*, 9 May, p. 27.
TW and two others honored by Iowa Alumni Association of
New York.

55 VAN GELDER, ROBERT. "Playwright with a Good Conceit." *New York Times*, 22 April, sec. 2, p. 1.

Profile on TW and career; quotes him on *BA* and *STR*; his Hollywood experiences.

56 WALDORF, WILELLA. " 'The Glass Menagerie' High Point of the Season So Far." *New York Post*, 2 April, p. 18.

Review of *GM*. Claims it's the best drama to have arrived that season; it's "full of wonderful comedy. . . . This is a subtle play of constantly shifting mood. . . . The drama and the comedy flow naturally out of the people involved."

57 _____. "Tennessee Williams Talks on Poetry in the Theatre." *New York Post*, 4 October, p. 33.

Refers to George Freedley's interview with TW, on radio station WNYC, on "The Role of Poetry in Modern Theatre." TW says we need noncommercial theater for that to happen.

58 _____. " 'You Touched Me!' Is Not as Touching as It Sounds." *New York Post*, 26 September, p. 38.

Review of *YTM*. "A confusion of tongues and a strange medley of dramatic styles." Contains "soap box orations and flights of romantic poetry."

59. "The Winner." *Time* 45 (23 April):88.

Announces Drama Critics' Circle Award for *GM*. Brief interview with TW and a few biographical notes. Reprinted: 1978.23.

60 WYATT, EUPHEMIA VAN RENSSELAER. "First Leaves Fall." *Catholic World* 162 (November):166–67.

Two-page summary of *YTM* with brief comments about "shifting symbolism" and theme. Attributes the basis of play to a story by D.H. Lawrence, which "hasn't really helped Williams."

61 _____. " 'The Glass Menagerie.' " *Catholic World* 161 (May): 166–67.

GM has "the haunting quality of an unhappy dream." Form is adapted from "Wilder's 'Our Town' . . ." and from "Van Druten's 'I Remember Mama.' " Finds difference between TW and

Saroyan to be that TW's characters find "any hope for a way out" through their own "imagination." Praise for all performers.

62   YOUNG, STARK. Review of *GM*. *New Republic* 112 (16 April):505.
     Review has much praise for Laurette Taylor's acting: "There is an inexplicable rightness, moment by moment, phrase by phrase, endlessly varied in the transitions. [Her] technique . . . is so overlaid with warmth, tenderness and wit that any analysis is completely baffled." Concerning the characters as written by TW: "All the language and all the motifs are free and true; I recognized them inch by inch, and I should know, for I come from the same part of the country . . . that Mr. Williams does." Reprinted: 1948.76, 1958.111.

63   ————. Review of *YTM*. *New Republic* 112 (8 October):469.
     Found *YTM* to be entertaining "for the most part." The play has too much talk, too many gestures, too little plot; the phrase "over-sexed" is not a correct description for the play.

64   " 'You Touched Me!' " *New York Times Magazine*, 23 September, pp. 28–29.
     Prerelease publicity; six photos with captions.

65   " 'You Touched Me!' " *Theatre Arts* 29 (December):680.
     Brief mention of the play in production; not a review.

66   ZOLOTOW, SAM. "Playwrights Prize Goes to Williams." *New York Times*, 6 June, p. 17.
     TW wins $1500 and Sidney Howard Memorial Award for *GM*. Quotes from citation.

1946

1   BENTLEY, ERIC. "Broadway Today." *Sewanee Review* 54 (Spring): 314–16.
     Reviews of *GM* and *YTM*. "Talented and earnest, Mr. Williams is the latest young writer to try to be an artist on Broadway. His 'Glass Menagerie' is a challenge. It abjures most of the tricks of the trade and presents, sincerely, rather bitterly, a little picture . . .

of a lower middle class home." Accuses TW of "sentimentalizing of the drama." "You may guess what the present state of Broadway is from the very fact that Tennessee Williams is the best playwright in town."

2 "Birthday Celebrants." *New York Times*, 31 March, sec. 2, p. 1.
    Photo of scene from *GM*; notes the play opened 31 March 1945.

3 BROWN, JOHN MASON. "Woman Who Came Back." In *Seeing Things*. New York: McGraw-Hill, pp. 224–30.
    Review of *GM*. Reprint of 1945.3.

4 "Eddie Dowling." *New York Times*, 2 June, sec. 2, p. 2.
    Photo of Eddie Dowling (Tom in *GM*); mention of *GM*'s five hundredth performance.

5 FREEDLEY, GEORGE. " 'The Glass Menagerie' after Year's Run Still Has Great Magic in Theatre." New York *Morning Telegraph*, 3 April, p. 2.
    Review of *GM*. Additional positive comments on its first anniversary on Broadway and after winning Drama Critics' Circle Award.

6 " 'Glass Menagerie' Will Close Aug. 3." *New York Times*, 23 July, p. 22.
    GM closes after 563 performances; arrangements for D.C. production; opens in Pittsburgh in September.

7 *GM. New York Times*, 27 January, sec. 2, p. 1.
    Photo of *GM* scene. Mentions "command performance" at National Theatre, Washington, D.C.

8 HOUGHTON, NORRIS. "Tomorrow Arrives Today: Young Talent on Broadway." *Theatre Arts* 30 (February):85–86.
    Brief biographical portrait of TW following opening of *GM*; mentions which plays were already written at that time.

9 KRUTCH, JOSEPH WOOD. "Tennessee Williams." *Nation* 162 (2 March):267–68.
    Book review of *27W*; claims the collection reveals an indis-

putable but very tentative talent. Praises "The Last of My Solid Gold Watches" and *TPC*. Discusses the "monotony" and "romantic pessimism" in TW's work.

10 NATHAN, GEORGE JEAN. "'The Glass Menagerie.'" In *The Theatre Book of the Year, 1944–45*. New York: Alfred A. Knopf, pp. 324–27.

Review of *GM*. Discusses it with reference to its producer (Dowling); then focuses on it as a play that is "rather less a play than a palette of sub-Chekhovian pastels brushed up into a charming semblance of one." Praises Laurette Taylor.

11 ————. "'You Touched Me!'" In *The Theatre Book of the Year, 1945–46*. New York: Alfred A. Knopf, pp. 87–96.

Review of *YTM*. Contrasts with *GM* which he says is "infinitely the better." Says "several passages in the play are fairly amusing . . . [but] the play itself is repetitious and . . . monotonous and static." Takes issue with TW's own (*New York Times*) printed comments about the play, and discusses other "strategies" the director might have chosen.

12 SUTCLIFFE, DENHAM. "Tennessee Williams." *New York Times Book Review*, 24 February, p. 8.

Book review of *27W*. Compares to *BA* and *LLL*; calls this collection "sentimental."

13 "To Aid Paralysis Fund." *New York Times*, 11 January, p. 17.

Brief news release. *GM* selected for benefit performance in Washington for National Foundation for Infantile Paralysis and to honor FDR's birthday.

1947

1 ATKINSON, BROOKS. "First Night at the Theatre." *New York Times*, 4 December, p. 42.

Review of *SND*. "Like 'Glass Menagerie' the new play is a quietly woven study of intangibles. But to this observer it shows deeper insight and represents a great step forward toward clarity. And it reveals Mr. Williams as a genuinely poetic playwright whose knowledge of people is honest and thorough, and whose sympathy is profoundly human."

2 _____. "Streetcar Tragedy." *New York Times*, 14 December, sec. 2, p. 3.
Review of *SND*. "Finest new play on the boards." Positive about all aspects of *SND*, including cast; briefly compares to *GM* and *S&S*. Reprinted: 1971.19.

3 _____. "Theatre in Dallas." *New York Times*, 10 August, sec. 2, p. 1.
Comments on "Theatre '47" in Dallas; calls *S&S* "finest play Tennessee Williams has ever written"; expects changes when play opens in New York.

4 BAILEY, CLAY. "Williams' One-Acter Ideas Broadly Based." *Dallas Daily Times Herald*, 20 November, sec. 4, p. 2.
Review of *LSG, PM, TPC*. "Good writing and excellent acting." Sees them containing "broadly based . . . situations and conditions of disturbing universality."

5 BARNES, HOWARD. "O'Neill Status Won by Author of 'Streetcar.'" *New York Herald Tribune*, 14 December, sec. 5, p. 1.
Review of *SND*. "A great new talent is at work in the theater to make one hope that the lean years are over. . . . Tennessee Williams more than justifies the promise of high dramatic imagination and craftsmanship. . . . [*SND*] has far more heroic dimensions than his earlier Broadway exhibit. There is a maturity about the offering . . . which is the product of discipline, integrity, and experience. . . . Williams is certainly the Eugene O'Neill of the present period on the stage. . . . Perhaps the chief distinction of a dramatist who must be counted right at the top of the heap in the contemporary theater is his resolute disregard for so-called social problems." Reprinted: 1971.19.

6 _____. "The Theaters." *New York Herald Tribune*, 4 December, p. 25.
Review of *SND*. "A savagely arresting tragedy . . . a work of rare discernment and craftsmanship." Refers to TW as "an artist achieving maturity."

7   BONE. Review of *SND*. *Variety*, 5 November, p. 60.
New Haven production, dated 30 October 1947; positive, with praise for all players; calls production "spotty as a checkerboard," and in need of eliminating the few superfluous elements. Lengthy plot summary with notes on the inadequate lighting.

8   BRAGGIOTTI, MARY. "Away from It All." *New York Post Magazine*, 12 December, p. 65.
Interview-commentary. TW goes into retreat the day after tremendous success of *SND*. TW discusses his pleasure with *SND*, southern women, introspection, marriage and artists, his early life.

9   BROWN, JOHN MASON. "Southern Discomfort." *Saturday Review*, 30 (27 December), 22–24.
Review of *SND*; "better, deeper, richer" than *GM*; praises TW as meticulous craftsman; praises the Kazan production. The play's "power is incontestable." Reprinted 1948.12, 1963.6, 1971.19.

10   CALTA, LOUIS. "Premiere Tonight for 'It Takes Two.'" *New York Times*, 3 February, p. 23.
TW protests *GM* at National in Washington for practicing discrimination.

11   CHAPMAN, JOHN. "'A Streetcar Named Desire' Sets Season's High in Acting, Writing." New York *Daily News*, 4 December, p. 83.
Review of *SND*. Calls TW "a young playwright who is not ashamed of being a poet." The play was given "a brilliant performance," and *SND* is "full-scale—throbbingly alive, compassionate, heart-wrenchingly human. It has the tragic overtones of grand opera." Plot and theme analysis (calls Blanche "a New Orleans Camille—a wistful little trollop"). Reprinted: 1971.19.

12   COLEMAN, ROBERT. "'Desire Streetcar' in for Long Run." New York *Daily Mirror*, 4 December, p. 38.
Review of *SND*. "Not . . . a top flight play . . . it is episodic and strangely static. . . . The characters that Williams has corralled in [*SND*] are a moronic, tedious and pathetic lot."

13   CURRIE, GEORGE. "'A Streetcar Named Desire' Is Fine Entertainment." *Brooklyn Daily Eagle*, 4 December, p. 8.

Review of *SND*. It's "excellent theater . . . I enjoyed it. But I
still wonder why." Sketchy plot details.

14 DURGIN, CYRUS. Review of *SND*. *Boston Daily Globe*, 4 November,
p. 7.
Boston production. Short sketchy plot and character details.
"A powerful play but don't expect to be amused and don't bring
the youngsters."

15 FREEDLEY, GEORGE. "Williams Writes a Brilliant, Moving Play in
'Streetcar.'" New York *Morning Telegraph*, 5 December, p. 2.
Review of *SND*. TW is "the most interesting young dramatist
in America." Finds *SND* "a drama of great and compelling honesty. . . . [TW] has really arrived as a dramatist of stature."

16 GARLAND, ROBERT. "Williams' New Play Exciting Theatre." *New
York Journal-American*, 4 December, p. 20.
Review of *SND*. Not sure if it's "a well-constructed play . . . [or]
a play at all . . . [still] an extraordinary exciting evening in
theatre . . . [TW's] latest draught of Southern Discomfort."

17 GIBBS, WOLCOTT. "Lower Depths, Southern Style." *New Yorker* 23
(13 December):50.
Review of *SND*. "A fine and deeply disturbing play, almost
faultless in the physical details of its production and the quality
of its acting . . . a strong, wholly believable play. . . . It is my suspicion that Mr. Williams has adjusted life fairly drastically to fit
his special theme. . . . [SND is] a brilliant, implacable play about
the disintegration of a woman, or, if you like, of a society."

18 "'The Glass Menagerie': Rome, Stockholm, Paris." *Theatre Arts* 31
(August):38–39.
Brief. *GM* is touring Europe, Africa, South America.

19 HAWKINS, WILLIAM. "'Streetcar' a Fine Play of Clashing Emotions."
New York World-Telegram, 4 December, p. 36.
Review of *SND*. "A terrific adventure in theater . . . his finished
art is harsh realism." Considerable plot summary.

20   HOPKINS, ARTHUR. "Mr. Hopkins Looks at the Theatre." *New York Times Magazine*, 2 March, pp. 18, 58.

Photo of scenes from *GM*. Plays like *GM* are content to be just what they are.

21   HUGHES, ELINOR. "Wilbur: 'A Streetcar Named Desire.'" *Boston Herald*, 4 November, p. 10.

Review of *SND*, Boston production. Tryout performance in Boston. "The most haunting new drama. . . . To compare [TW] with any current playwright is impossible, for he has a quality completely and uniquely his own—the ability to tell a pitiful, always believable and nakedly honest story in terms of moods, snatches of speech, emotions suggested." Praises Kazan, Tandy, Brando. Reprinted: 1971.19.

22   IBEE. Review of *SND*. *Variety*, 10 December, p. 68.

The "dramatic standout of recent seasons." Production needs minor cuttings; plot details, and much praise for stars Tandy, Brando, Hunter, Malden. "Kazan's many directive contributions are notable." " 'Streetcar' is all theatre."

23   KRUTCH, JOSEPH WOOD. Review of *SND*. *Nation* 165 (20 December):686–87.

Praises *SND* as "sure and sustained where [*GM*] was uncertain and intermittent." Now TW is beyond "all the distracting bits of ineffectual preciosity, all the pseudo-poetic phrases. . . . Everything is perfectly in key and completely effective." Discusses the frankness and pathology in the plot; and compares it specifically with *GM*. Praises Kazan and Tandy. Reprinted: 1971.19.

24   LEWIS, R.C. "A Playwright Named Tennessee." *New York Times Magazine*, 7 December, pp. 19, 67, 69–70.

Profile on TW, his background, and work to this point; "the author of 'A Streetcar Named Desire' seeks 'quiet truths' in a world lit by lightning."

25   MOREHOUSE, WARD. "New Hit Named 'Desire.'" New York *Sun*, 4 December, p. 44.

Review of *SND*. "A gaudy violent and fascinating study . . .

not a play for the squeamish . . . often coarse and harrowing. . . .
It is grequently [*sic*] some what jerky . . . [still] enormous gusto and
vitality and poignance."

26 NATHAN, GEORGE JEAN. "The Streetcar Isn't Drawn by Pegasus."
    New York Journal-American, 15 December, p. 14.
       Review of *SND.* Discusses the play's "unpleasantness" as op-
    posed to its being "disgusting." *SND* fails to "shock audience"
    into any "spiritual education." Reprinted: 1971.19.

27 "New Williams Play Opens in Pasadena." *New York Times,* 26 Feb-
    ruary, p. 35.
       Announcing the world premiere of *STR* at Pasadena Playhouse.

28 NORTON, ELLIOT. "Tennessee Williams Play Opens." *Boston Post,*
    4 November, p. 6.
       Review of *SND,* Boston production. *SND* "is a play of primitive
    power and fury, ugly as sin and lunacy can make it, lunging
    erratically along the line between melodrama and tragedy, grim-
    ly humorless, pitiless and sordid, yet as fascinating much of the
    time, as the evil it chronicles." Praise for Malden and Tandy.

29 PHELAN KAPPO. "The Stage and Screen: 'A Streetcar Named
    Desire.'" *Commonweal* 47 (19 December):254–55.
       "As was surely obvious in the earlier 'Glass Menagerie,' the
    author here again proves his dramatic imagination. . . . At first
    glance, it seems that Mr. Williams has conjured nothing more
    (nor less) than a melodrama, an especial Freudian case-history
    with all on stage only more or less diseased, the conflict being one
    of degree. And yet somehow the remembered lines do seem to
    indicate a further dimension. . . ." Praises Brando, and especially
    Malden, but not Tandy.

30 *PM. Dallas Morning News,* 23 November, Attraction sec., p. 1.
       Publicity photo and caption of *PM.*

31 Review of *SND. Time* 50 (15 December):85.
       "A fresh, vivid drama." Praises production and provides some
    biographical data on TW.

32   Review of *SND*. *Life* 23 (15 December):101–2, 104.
      Brief item praising text. TW "had written the season's best new play and was now a top U.S. dramatist." Numerous photos.

33   ROSENFIELD, JOHN. "Play by Williams Unveiled in Dallas." *New York Times*, 9 July, p. 18.
      Comments on opening of *S&S*, TW's writing style, its scenery. Brief synopsis of play.

34   "Scene from New Play by Tennessee Williams." *New York Times*, 1 August, p. 21.
      Production photo of *S&S*, plus short caption.

35   SHAW, IRWIN. "Masterpiece." *New Republic* 117 (22 December): 34–35.
      Review of *SND*. "A despairing and lonely play, in which the author . . . says that beauty is shipwrecked on the rock of the world's vulgarity." Calls attention to the attractive rhythms and imagery in the dialogue, which fall on the ear "like fresh rain water." *SND* is better than *GM* because it adds "the element of true tragedy to its other merits." Reprinted: 1971.19.

36   *SND*. *New York Journal-American*, 3 December, p. 20.
      Brief news item. *SND* to open that night.

37   STEVENS, VIRGINIA. "Elia Kazan." *Theatre Arts* 31 (December): 18–22.
      With three sketches by Jo Mielziner of the *SND* set. Lengthy profile of Kazan with little mention of *SND* and no mention of TW.

38   *STR*. *Theatre Arts* 31 (July):12.
      Photograph of production, with caption noting this as TW's third premiere at Pasadena Playhouse.

39   " 'A Streetcar Named Desire.' " *New York Times Magazine*, 23 November, p. 14.
      Preopening publicity photos, plus captions.

40 " 'Street Car Named Desire' Appears Geared for Long Broadway Run." *Variety*, 3 December, pp. 1, 7.
   Review of *SND*, brief. "Irene Selznick's managerial maiden effort on Broadway should be a real winner with Tennessee Williams' 'A Streetcar Named Desire.' " "Williams doesn't tell a pretty story of the characters in the poor quarter of New Orleans. . . . a triumph for Jessica Tandy." Brando called outstanding.

41 "Streetcar on Broadway." *Newsweek* 30 (15 December):82–83.
   Review of *SND*. "So much better than" *GM*; plot summary; praises cast and TW.

42 "Tennessee Tells All." *Cue* 16 (20 December):14–15.
   Interview two weeks after success of *SND* premiere. TW comments on his first name, his "morbid" imagination, his characters, *SND*, *GM*, southern women.

43 "Theatre Benefit Dec. 10." *New York Times*, 4 December, p. 41.
   News release. *SND* to be given as a benefit performance at Barrymore for the Speedwell Society.

44 WATTS, RICHARD, JR. " 'A Streetcar Named Desire' Is Striking Drama." *New York Post*, 4 December, p. 43.
   Review of *SND*. "A feverish, squalid, arresting and oddly touching study. . . . Mr. Williams is an oncoming playwright of power, imagination." Reprinted: 1971.19.

45 "The World and the Theatre." *Theatre Arts* 31 (September):11.
   Brief. *S&S* has been a success at Margo Jones's "Theatre '47" (Dallas).

1948

1 ADAMS, FRANK S. "Pulitzer Prizes Go to 'Streetcar' and Michener's Stories of Pacific." *New York Times*, 4 May, pp. 1, 22.
   SND wins 1948 Pulitzer Prize for best American play. Marks only second time Drama Critics' and Pulitzer went to same play.

2 ATKINSON, BROOKS. "At the Theatre." *New York Times*, 7 October, p. 33.
   Review of S&S. "Although Tennessee Williams writes in a gentle style, he has a piercing eye. In [S&S] . . . he looks again into the dark corners of the human heart, and what he sees is terrifying. . . . [It's] tremulous with beauty."

3 _____. "Everything Is Poetic." *New York Times*, 6 June, sec. 2, p. 1.
   Discussion in response to readers' remarks over a previous article by Atkinson on SND. Addresses the pain and poetry in SND.

4 _____. "Work of Art." *New York Times*, 17 October, sec. 2, p. 1.
   Review of S&S. "So far the season has yielded only one play that has the imagination of a work of art. Tennessee Williams' [S&S], . . . brings again into the theatre the gift of a poetic and creative writer for the stage."

5 BARNES, HOWARD. "The Theaters." *New York Herald Tribune*, 7 October, p. 16.
   Review of S&S. "There is little in [S&S] to make it recognizable as a work of one of the most gifted playwrights of our time." In this play TW is as "fumbling and obvious as he is trenchant and evocative in [SND]." S&S is "a pretentious and amateurish bore."

6 BARNETT, LINCOLN. "Tennessee Williams: A Dreamy Young Man with an Unconquerable Compulsion to Write Finds Himself at 33 the Most Important Playwright in the U.S. Theatre." *Life* 24 (16 February):113–14, 116, 118, 121–22, 124, 126–27.
   Biographical sketch of "Thomas Lanier Williams." Interview in which TW comments on SND, GM, his childhood, family, security ("a kind of death"), fulfillment. Reprinted: 1951.8.

7 BEYER, WILLIAM. "The State of the Theatre: A New Season." *School and Society* 68 (30 October):303–4.
   Review of S&S. Lavish praise for TW; plot details and theme analysis of this production; "Williams' discerning penetration of his characters, being sympathetic, has the poet's insight into the fertility of life itself." TW has work yet to do with S&S though; needs rounding out.

8 _____. "The State of the Theatre: Late Season." *School and Society*
   67 (27 March):241–43.
   Review of *SND*. Claims the American theater itself is richer
   for arrival of *SND*. Calls it "an engrossing, sensitive study. . . .
   [TW] has almost a clinical detachment in revealing the stages of
   Blanche's disintegration." Plot summary and character analysis.

9 "Broadway Tries Hard." *Life* 25 (25 October):102–3.
   Review of *S&S*. *S&S* is indicative of an honest effort on Broadway "to break away from stereotyped theatre," but the play
   "lacks voltage." However, "good acting" and "one of the handsom-
   est stage settings ever seen on Broadway" are the play's highlights.

10 BRON. Review of *S&S*. *Variety*, 13 October, p. 50.
   A "pale, disappointing facsimile of his [TW's] previous 'Streetcar' and 'Glass Menagerie.'" Brief plot and character details.
   "Melodramatic instances only serve to increase the impression
   of a weak play, sprawlingly presented."

11 BROWN, JOHN MASON. "People Versus Characters." *Saturday Review*
   31 (30 October):31–33.
   Review of *S&S*. Praises the play's structure; compares it to
   O'Neill. TW fails to expose the full intricacy of his characters."

12 _____. "Southern Discomfort." In *Seeing More Things*. New York:
   McGraw-Hill, pp. 266–72.
   Review of *SND*. Reprint of 1947.9.

13 CARROLL, SIDNEY. "A Streetcar Named Tennessee." *Esquire* 29
   (May):46.
   Interview, starting with premise, "He always disappoints the
   interviewers." Discusses his first name, speech habits, background
   as writer, autobiographical details in his plays, his current success.

14 CHAPMAN, JOHN. "'Summer and Smoke' a Talkative, Muddled Drama
   of Repressed Sex." New York *Daily News*, 7 October, p. 81.
   Review of *S&S*. "A juvenile and sadly delinquent effort . . .
   mawkish, murky, maudlin and monotonous."

15 CLURMAN, HAROLD. "Man with a Problem." *New Republic* 119 (25 October):25–26.

Review of *S&S*. Analyzes the faults in *S&S*—one of TW's fascinations is "with the opposition between the old Adam which tends to keep us mired in a kind of primitive inertia, and our impulse to transcend it. In 'Streetcar' this fascination led him almost unconsciously to a social theme: the 'animal' in that play as the 'ordinary' American. . . . In 'Summer and Smoke' so much time is given to a conscious exposition of theme that Williams loses the specific sense of his people . . . and our concern as spectators." Reprinted: 1958.17, 1974.8.

16 ————. "Night Life and Day Light: On Acting." *Tomorrow* 7 (February):51–54.

Review of *SND*. *SND* "stands high among the creative contributions of the American theatre since 1920. . . . It is virtually unique as a stage piece that is both personal and social and wholly a product of our life today. It is a beautiful play. . . . There are elements in the production—chiefly in the acting—that make for a certain ambiguity and confusion." Elaborate plot summary. Reprinted: 1958.17, 1961.41.

17 ————. Review of *S&S*. *New Republic* 119 (15 November):27–28.

Further review. Praises *S&S*'s "human speech on intimate matters."

18 COLEMAN, ROBERT. "'Summer and Smoke' Has a Searching Eloquence." New York *Daily Mirror*, 7 October, p. 36.

Review of *S&S*. "Reminiscent of Anatole France's 'Thais' in reverse. . . . [TW] . . . has no peer among modern dramatists in creating mood . . . though this is a verbose play, its verbosity is eloquent, searching and moving."

19 COTTER, JERRY. "The New Plays." *Sign* 27 (February):46.

Review of *SND*. TW "goes far down the ladder of human degradation for this latest probe of Southern decay," although the play does "exhibit the same brilliance shown in [*GM*]." Angered by TW's "predilection for the seamy side." Calls it a "well-acted tragedy."

20 CURRIE, GEORGE. "Tennessee Williams Returns with 'Summer and Smoke.'" *Brooklyn Daily Eagle*, 7 October, p. 6.
      Review of *S&S*. "For once Mr. Williams was not playing around with people of little chance. . . . With Tennessee Williams, it is now apparent one must take the bad with the good."

21 "Drama Mailbag." *New York Times*, 8 February, sec. 2, p. 3.
      In a letter to drama editor, theatergoer voices his objections to rudeness by the audience during *SND* performance.

22 "Drama Mailbag." *New York Times*, 13 June, sec. 2, p. 2.
      In a letter to drama editor, a reader takes issues with *SND*'s being called a tragedy.

23 "Drama Mailbag." *New York Times*, 24 October, sec. 2, p. 2.
      Three letters to drama editor. Two deal with TW's 3 October *New York Times* article, "Questions Without Answers"; one praises Paul Bowles' music in *S&S*.

24 DRUTMAN, IRVING. "Malden Owes 'Streetcar' Role to His 'Poor but Honest Face.'" *New York Herald Tribune*, 29 February, sec. 5, p. 4.
      Brief. Addresses Malden's career and the seemingly typecast roles he plays.

25 EATON, WALTER PRICHARD. "Across the Footlights." *New York Herald Tribune*, 29 February, sec. 8, p. 14.
      Book review of publication of *SND*. Praises it, contrasts it with A. Huxley's *Mortal Coils*.

26 FREEDLEY, GEORGE. "Tennessee Williams at His Best in 'Summer and Smoke.'" New York *Morning Telegraph*, 8 October, p. 2.
      Review of *S&S*. "The most important drama to be presented so far in the 1948–49 season. . . . [It's] considerably less sensational than [*SND*]." Many details on cast.

27 FUNKE, LEWIS. "News and Gossip Gathered on the Rialto." *New York Times*, 4 April, sec. 2, p. 1.
      Mentions *SND* as Critics' Circle choice for best play and sug-

gests that there may be too many prizes for plays. Notes Tandy,
Blanche in *SND*, as going on vacation.

28 GABRIEL, GILBERT W. "The Broadway Story." *Theatre Arts* 32
    (April):30.
        Brief review of *SND*. *SND* should be nominated for season's
    "most distinguished offering."

29 GARLAND, ROBERT. "Recasting Improves Play at Barrymore." *New
    York Journal-American*, 6 July, p. 12.
        Notes greater unity achieved in *SND* with cast changes.

30 _____. " 'Summer and Smoke' Unneeded Foreword to 'Streetcar'
    Theme." *New York Journal-American*, 7 October, p. 21.
        Review of *S&S*. Sees play as foreword to *SND*; "all the stock
    [TW] figures are up on the stage . . . pretty patches of highfalutin'
    writing."

31 GASSNER, JOHN. Review of *SND*. *Forum* 109 (February):86–88.
        Says *SND* confirmed the positive judgments made of TW be-
    cause of *GM*. *SND* "emerges as the most creative American play
    of the past dozen years. It is a play that needs no erudite exegesis,
    no coterie support, no apologetics to make it acceptable." Plot
    and theme analysis; discusses it as "a novel."

32 _____. Review of *S&S*. *Forum* 110 (December):351–53.
        Ties it in thematically with *SND*, *PM*, *BA*; claims it "does not
    quite materialize as drama. . . . In truth, I very much fear that
    'Summer and Smoke' only brings out the weaknesses I have sus-
    pected in its author for a long time—an insufficient exertion of
    intellect." Blames the failure here on "an inanition of the blood-
    stream that characterizes our generation."

33 _____. "Tennessee Williams: Dramatist of Frustration." *College
    English* 10 (October):1–7.
        Cites addendum to *BA*, from 1944, in which TW "affirmed his
    allegiance to the plastic medium of the theater," and traces his
    earliest history, up to the anticipated *S&S*. Analyzes the idioms
    TW works with, the "singularity" of his themes, going back to
    "Moony's Kid Don't Cry," which TW published in 1940. Talks

of eventually measuring him against Chekhov, Gorki, O'Neill, and Lorca. Says the judgment is yet to come.

34 GIBBS, WOLCOTT. "Smoke Gets in Your Hair." *New Yorker* 24 (16 October):51–52.
    Brief review of S&S. Has a "generally portentous air [but] has nothing especially interesting to say." Marred by "almost unendurable length."

35 GILDER, ROSAMOND. "The Playwright Takes Over." *Theatre Arts* 32 (January):10–11, 13.
    Review of SND. TW's characters "are as palpitatingly alive as Shakespeare's royal lovers whose downfall shook the world." Refers to "gigantic, tragic forces . . . implied, not stated." SND "gives renewed stature" to the theater.

36 HAWKINS, WILLIAM. "Tennessee 'Smoke' Smothers Its Fire." *New York World-Telegram*, 7 October, p. 14.
    Review of S&S. "A play so tenuous and so delicate that its title seems leaden by comparison to its content." Discusses the insufficiency of characterization.

37 "Haymarket Theatre: 'The Glass Menagerie.'" *Times* (London), 29 July, p. 6.
    Review of GM, London production. "Good acting in a play that is slow and sure in a very American way."

38 "Jessica Tandy Honored." *New York Times*, 18 May, p. 27.
    Tandy awarded silver ivy leaf by Twelfth Night Club for most distinguished performance as Blanche in SND. Audrey Wood representing TW will be guest of honor.

39 KRUTCH, JOSEPH WOOD. Review of S&S. *Nation* 167 (23 October): 473–74.
    Compares to SND; discusses character treatment. This one is "more varied and rapid in action" than SND. "A superlatively fine production brilliantly directed . . . and brilliantly acted."

40 "Lighting Up for 'Summer and Smoke.'" *New York Times*, 5 December, sec. 2, p. 7.

About lighting effects and how they were accomplished, with quotes by Jo Mielziner, lighting and set designer.

41 McCARTHY, MARY. "A Streetcar Called Success." *Partisan Review* 15 (March):357–60.
Starts off with ironic treatment of theme and plot; claims that except for "variation on the mother-in-law theme," *SND* is all "antimacassars." Further insists, "Acrimony and umbrage, tears, door-slamming, broken dishes, jeers, cold silences, whispers, raised eyebrows, the determination to take no notice, the whole classic paraphernalia of insult and injury is Tennessee Williams' hope chest." Suggests that had he restructured it a bit, "he might have produced a wonderful little comic epic, The Struggle for the Bathroom, an epic ribald and poignant." And other such observations. Reprinted: 1956.70, 1963.38.

42 McCULLERS, CARSON. Letter to Editor. *Life* 24 (8 March):16.
McCullers comments on Barnett's (16 February 1948) *Life* article on TW; praises Barnett's recognition of TW's "nobility of character and spirit."

43 " 'Menagerie' in London." *New York Times*, 29 July, p. 17.
GM receives moderately favorable reviews in London press; Helen Hayes praised as Amanda.

44 MERRITT, FRANCINE. "Staging 'The Glass Menagerie.' " *Dramatics* 20 (December):18.
Discussion of the suitability, plot, casting, and directing of the play itself relative to its use in school productions.

45 "Mississippi Mud." *Newsweek* 32 (18 October):88.
Review of *S&S*. It doesn't measure up to *GM* or *SND*; praises production.

46 MOOR, PAUL. "A Mississippian Named Tennessee." *Harper's* 198 (July):63–71.
Early biographical sketch, recounting the small magazines TW has published in, *GM*'s success, *BA*'s problems, TW's adolescence, his illness, his life in St. Louis, Audrey Wood, his speech habits, his methodology and work schedule, *SND* and *CR*.

47   MOREHOUSE, WARD. "Broadway after Dark—Little Town between the Rivers." New York *Sun*, 4 October, p. 10.
     Brief mention of three new Broadway plays about to open, one of which is *S&S*.

48   ———. "The New Play." New York *Sun*, 7 October, p. 28.
     Review of *S&S*. TW "combines metaphysics with realism and symbolism . . . a rueful and disturbing play. . . . the total effect is one sharp disappointment."

49   NATHAN, GEORGE JEAN. "'A Streetcar Named Desire.'" In *The Theatre Book of the Year, 1947–48*. New York: Alfred A. Knopf, pp. 163–66.
     Review of *SND*. Says a better title might have been "The Glans Menagerie." Rebuts critics of its premiere who found it "unpleasant." Claims in his defense that "Williams has managed to keep his play wholly in hand." But, taking exception, he asserts, "Williams seems to labor under the misapprehension that strong emotions are best expressed strongly only through what may delicately be termed strong language." Praises Kazan and cast (particularly cites Tandy "in the role of Forever Streetcar"). Reprinted: 1960.93, 1961.41.

50   ———. "Theater Week: The Menagerie Still Rides on the Streetcar." *New York Journal-American*, 18 October, p. 12.
     Review of *S&S*. Comparison-contrast of *S&S* with *GM*, *SND*, *BA*; "final result of this 'Summer and Smoke' is quite as unsatisfactory as that of his previous plays."

51   "Openings of the Week." *New York Times*, 3 October, sec. 2, pp. 1, 3.
     S&S mentioned; photo of Margaret Philips and Tod Andrews in leading roles.

52   "Personalities." *New York Times Magazine*, 25 July, p. 19.
     Photo of TW and Helen Hayes at *GM* rehearsal in London.

53   PHELAN, KAPPO. "The Stage and Screen: 'Summer and Smoke.'" *Commonweal* 49 (29 October):68–69.
     Plot summary and production details; cites the Freudian symbolism and anachronistic use of terms possibly not yet invented at the period of time TW describes.

54 POORE, CHARLES. "Books of the Times." *New York Times*, 9 December, p. 31.
    Brief allusion to TW's "Desire and the Black Masseur," and its appearance in *New Directions, 10*.

55 "Pulitzer Prize Awards." *Times* (London), 4 May, p. 3.
    TW announced as Pulitzer winner for playwriting; *SND* cited.

56 "Pulitzer Prizes." *New York Times*, 4 May, p. 24.
    Comments on Pulitzer Prizes; *SND* will be popularly received as drama choice.

57 REILEY, FRANKLIN C. "A Playwright Named Tennessee." *Palm* (March):6–7.
    Interest expressed in this fraternity journal in an ex–fraternity brother (TW) who "made good." Some biographical detail plus brief interview.

58 Review of *S&S*. *Time* 52 (18 October):82–83.
    The play is only a "lucid diagram." Generally negative about its structure.

59 SAROYAN, WILLIAM. "Keep Your Eye on Your Overcoat!" *Theatre Arts* 32 (October):21.
    Review of *SND*. Tries to determine what *SND*'s problems are. It's "easier to read than to see," but "it is perfect, and that is the reason its failure to satisfy is difficult to understand."

60 "Saroyan's Heir." *Time* 51 (7 June):85.
    Brief; mentions TW's recent awards.

61 "Sketches of Those Added by Columbia to the Roll of Pulitzer Prize Winners." *New York Times*, 4 May, p. 22.
    Brief profile on TW and other Pulitzer winners.

62 SMITH, HARRISON. "A Ferment at Work." *Saturday Review* 31 (25 December):9–10.
    Review of James Laughlin's *New Directions 10*, in which TW is referred to briefly.

63 *SND. Theatre Arts* 32 (February):35.
    Brief reference to cast and plot of Broadway production.

64 " 'Streetcar' Gets Best Play Honor." *New York Times*, 18 July, sec.
    1, p. 46.
    SND wins 5th Annual Donaldson Award for best play.

65 " 'Streetcar Named Desire' Captures Top Prize of Drama Critics'
    Circle." *New York Times*, 1 April, p. 29.
    SND voted best play by Drama Critics. Gives names of voters.

66 " 'Summer and Smoke.' " *New York Times*, 26 September, pp. 66–67.
    Prerelease photos of *S&S*, with captions.

67 TANDY, JESSICA. "One Year of Blanche DuBois." *New York Times*,
    28 November, sec. 2, pp. 1, 3.
    Tandy comments on how she feels as Blanche DuBois and how
    she got the part. Mentions her performance in *PM*.

68 TAYLOR, HARRY. "The Dilemma of Tennessee Williams." *Masses
    and Mainstream* 1 (April):51–56.
    Focuses closely on the style—and its devices—that TW creates
    for himself; explores some of the problems it causes for him.
    Cites "pessimism" as problem. Highlights *SND*, *TPC*, *GM*. Re-
    printed: 1961.41.

69 "Tennessee Williams' Detroit Press Stamps Author as Good Personal
    B.O." *Variety*, 22 September, p. 47.
    TW arrives in Detroit with *S&S* "an unknown" and leaves with
    "plenty of publicity." Refers to popular local press response.

70 "Tennessee Williams' Take Home Pay Now $7,500 Weekly." *Variety*,
    6 October, pp. 1, 62.
    Report on TW's royalty earnings, chiefly from *GM*, *SND*, and
    S&S.

71 TERRY, C.V. "Shock-Treatment for Thespis." *New York Times Book
    Review*, 1 February, p. 17.
    Book review of *SND*. Positive comments on *SND* publication,

noting that more drama like *SND* might improve the condition
of theater.

72 TREWIN, J.C. "Mother and Father." *Illustrated London News* 213
    (28 August):250.
        Brief review of *GM*, London production. Author discusses
    theme of motherhood in drama and invokes Amanda as illustra-
    tion; however, he doesn't specifically categorize her as a mother
    type.

73 WATTS, RICHARD, JR. "A Rather Gloomy Report on 'Summer and
    Smoke.'" *New York Post*, 7 October, p. 33.
        Review of *S&S*. TW "writes with sensitivity and probing in-
    sight ... [but] I found his new drama only intermittently satis-
    factory . . . less moving than [*GM*] and lacks the sense of pity
    and horror of [*SND*]."

74 WORSELY, T.C. Review of *GM*. *New Statesman* 36 (7 August):113.
        London production. Because TW is author of *GM* and "A Street-
    Car [sic] Called [sic] Desire," he is among America's "leading
    dramatists." *GM* can't sustain a reputation built on *SND*, and *GM*
    is bound to be disappointing. Cites lack of development in charac-
    ters and incidents as basis of its weakness.

75 WYATT, EUPHEMIA VAN RENSSELAER. Review of *S&S*. *Catholic World*
    168 (November):161.
        Acknowledges "some tragic-comic interludes," but finds the
    best parts of *S&S* to be the set design and the character of Alma,
    TW's "most tenderly drawn and the finest."

76 YOUNG, STARK. "'The Glass Menagerie.'" In *Immortal Shadows*.
    New York: Charles Scribner's Sons, pp. 249–53.
        Reprint of 1945.62. Reprinted: 1958.111.

77 ZOLOTOW, SAM. "Broadway to see O'Casey's Comedy." *New York
    Times*, 3 December, p. 32.
        News release. *SND*'s first anniversary to be celebrated at Barry-
    more; gives gross figure of box office takes; cites awards.

78 _____. "Sabinson Acquires New Trumbo Play." *New York Times*, 17 September, p. 29.

Brief news release. TW has let it be known that the first draft of an untitled new script is finished.

1949

1 ATKINSON, BROOKS. "Overseas Tornado." *New York Times*, 11 December, sec. 2, p. 3.

Discusses the controversy of *SND* in England plus differences between American and English theater.

2 _____. " 'Streetcar' Passenger." *New York Times*, 12 June, sec. 2, p. 1.

Announcing that Tandy, Brando, and Hunter are leaving cast of *SND*; some comparisons with new and old cast, especially Uta Hagen.

3 BENTLEY, ERIC. "Back to Broadway." *Theatre Arts* 33 (November):- 14.

Review of *SND*. Discusses going back to see *SND* again "because of interest in Uta Hagen's acting. Her performance is good enough to compel a reconsideration of the play." Refers to Brando as having been wrong for part of Stanley. Compares the two productions along lines of interpretation. Compares TW to Arthur Miller. Reprinted: 1953.3, 1961.41.

4 BROWN, RAY C.B. "Tennessee Williams: The Poetry of Stagecraft." *Voices* 138 (Summer):4–8.

"Among our contemporary playwrights, [TW] has aligned himself with the experimentalists, who are flouting the old conventions of structure and mounting. . . . The plays of Mr. Williams are static, more than less, and desperately in need of a movement uncompensated by the drive of the dialogue. . . . The poet in Mr. Williams is what the theatre needs." Discusses faults of *S&S*, *SND*. "Many as his technical ineptitudes are and numerous his errors in estimation of his material, one follows and applauds Mr. Williams for the courage of his convictions."

5 CALTA, LOUIS. "Abbot's Musical Will Bow Tonight." *New York Times*, 13 October, p. 33.

   C.K. Feldman confirmed acquisition of screen rights to *SND* for $350,000 plus percentage.

6 _____. " 'Clutterbuck' Set for Debut Tonight." *New York Times*, 3 December, p. 9.

   Brief announcement of second anniversary of *SND*. Number of performances and gross income noted; photo with caption.

7. DOWNER, ALAN S. "Mr. Williams and Mr. Miller." *Furioso* 4 (Summer):66–70.

   Starts with premise that TW and Miller are "completely dissimilar as men and as playwrights, . . . but alike as serious artists." Goes on to treat *SND, S&S*, plus *All My Sons* and *Death of a Salesman* separately and in contrast. Talks of such factors as "stage magic," "tragedy," and formulaic writing.

8 "Drama Mailbag." *New York Times*, 16 January, sec. 2, p. 2.

   In letter to drama editor, Herbert Morris expresses displeasure at closing of *S&S*.

9 "Drama Mailbag." *New York Times*, 30 January, sec. 2, p. 2.

   Letter to drama editor by playwright Joseph Hayes complains that comparing his play *Leaf and Bough* to work of TW was unjustified (22 January). Letter to drama editor by Robert Downing, responding to a previous letter by Morris (16 January) about *S&S* closing. Letter to drama editor by D. Loovis, commenting on TW's drawing on own experience.

10 "English Plays in Paris." *New York Times*, 9 July, p. 9.

   Announcement of the American Colony of Paris forming a company called the American Club Theatre—which opened with *LLL* and two one-acters by other writers.

11 FLEMING, PETER. Review of *SND*. *Spectator* (London), 183 (21 October):533.

   London production; many plot details; calls it a "synthetic and rather pretentious play." Claims mainly Leigh saves it; says Olivier's work is "masterly."

12 FUNKE, LEWIS. "Playgoers Fare." *New York Times Book Review*, 16 January, p. 20.
    Book review of *S&S*. Brief but generally positive; a "play that should endure."

13 GABRIEL, GILBERT W. "Playgoing." *Theatre Arts* 33 (January):10–11, 13.
    Brief review of *S&S*. Refers to the "battered spinsters" of *SND* and *GM*.

14 HOBSON, HAROLD. "Miss Vivien Leigh." *Sunday Times* (London), 13 November, p. 2.
    Contradicts the critical claim that *SND* is "a nasty and vulgar" play. Claims it "is strictly, and even puritanically, moral. . . . Mr. Williams, looking into Blanche with inflexible judgment but also with human pity, legitimately finds in her story many moments of touching beauty." Later observes, "The best thing I saw in America was Uta Hagen's performance as Blanche: Miss Vivien Leigh's is finer." Reprinted: 1971.19.

15 _____. "Tennessee Williams in London." *Christian Science Monitor*, 3 December, p. 4.
    Mentions *GM*'s not being a success in London; didn't draw large audiences; not same for *SND*; records outrage of some British critics over *SND*; compares *SND*'s technique to Ibsen's.

16 "Lawrence's Secret Test." *New York Herald Tribune*, 2 September, p. 11.
    Brief gossip item. Gertrude Lawrence screen testing for *GM* film.

17 "London Sees 'Streetcar.'" *New York Times*, 13 October, p. 33.
    News release about enthusiastic reviews received in London for *SND*.

18 "Mexican Streetcar . . ." *Theatre Arts* 33 (June):44.
    Brief. Mentions *SND* in Mexico; quotes Mexican critics.

19 NATHAN, GEORGE JEAN. "'Summer and Smoke.'" In *The Theatre Book of the Year, 1948–49*. New York: Alfred A. Knopf, pp. 114–21.

Review of S&S. Compares to *SND* and takes issue with initial popular critical response; discusses theme, setting, lighting, and TW's "legerdemain." Also calls attention to "Williams' character drawing" which he finds occasionally confusing.

20 "Paris Likes, Critics Dislike, 'Streetcar.' " *New York Times*, 19 October, p. 36.
Brief news release from Paris. Audience enthusiastic about *SND*; critics not ("denunciation whose thoroughness has been rarely seen in theatre criticism here"). Additional news that London *Evening Standard* announces publication of *SND* in serial form.

21 "Paris 'Streetcar.' " *Life* 27 (19 December):66.
Refers to the changes in stage business for Paris production: "a near-rape on the street, a sidewalk shooting, a naked belly-dance."

22 RICE, VERNON. "Helen Hayes Opens Rockland County's Season." *New York Post*, 18 July, p. 25.
Brief item announcing Hayes in *GM*.

23 SHANLEY, J.P. "2 Blind Actresses in Summer Stock." *New York Times*, 9 August, p. 21.
Two blind actresses in cast of S&S at Mountain Playhouse, Jennerstown, Pennsylvania.

24 SMITH, R.D. Review of *SND*. *New Statesman* 38 (22 October):451.
London production; defends the play against popular press attacks; ample plot details. Claims "the author's tone and intentions absolve him of any charge of vulgarity," and that "there is no exploitation of violence" for its own sake. Discusses the way TW "weakens and coarsens the pathos" in the play's last moments.

25 "Tennessee Williams Not Fired This Time." *New York Herald Tribune*, 18 September, sec. 5, p. 1.
Brief news item. TW in Hollywood rewriting screenplay for *GM*. Refers to previous presuccess dismissal from MGM.

26 "Tennessee Williams to Do Script." *New York Herald Tribune*, 7 January, p. 16.
Brief news item. TW leaves for Europe to work on two scripts.

27 "Tramway's Progress." *Time* 54 (31 October):54.
    London and Paris productions of *SND*; quotes reviews; mentions other European cities it's going on to.

28 TREWIN, J.C. "In the Fashion." *Illustrated London News* 215 (5 November):712.
    Review of London *SND*. Discusses popular, "fashionable" plays of both London and New York; generally regards *SND* as "two hours of tedium," but admits that "now and then good writing glimmers." Credits whatever longevity the play may have in London to Leigh's performance.

29 "Vivien Leigh Scores as 'Streetcar' Star." *New York Times*, 29 September, p. 38.
    Leigh considered excellent by London critics for role in *SND*.

30 "Williams' Snub Stirs Playgoers in Spain." *New York Times*, 12 December, p. 28.
    TW's refusal to allow *SND* to be performed in Spain causes controversy.

31 WORSLEY, T.C. "Theatre and State." *New Statesman* 38 (17 December):723–24.
    London production of *SND*; discusses problems arising from *SND*'s having been produced by nonprofit company, responsible for maintaining codes of Finance Act of 1946. Reviews the dispute and insists on a distinction between vigilance and censorship. Little comment on *SND* itself; considerable on the politics of the case.

32 ZOLOTOW, SAM. "'Happy Time' Lead to 13-Year-Old Boy." *New York Times*, 31 August, p. 27.
    Brief news release. TW traveling to Hollywood from Rome to assist in screen version of *GM*. He plans to attend London premiere of *SND*.

33 _____. "Muni Star of Play Due Here Tonight." *New York Times*, 16 February, p. 31.
    Brief item that TW's next play will not contain a "frustrated woman."

34 _____. "Pemberton Ready for Second Show." *New York Times*,
23 December, p. 16.
TW responds to Spain controversy noted on 12 December.

1950

1 ALPERT, HOLLIS. "Sex Fringed With Horror." *Saturday Review* 33
(30 September):18.
Book review of *RSMS*. "There seems to be a new school in
American fiction." Finds *RSMS* "skillful and sensitive. . . . As a
craftsman [TW] is superb."

2 ATKINSON, BROOKS. "At the Theatre." *New York Times*, 24 May, p. 36.
Review of *SND*. "Mr. Williams' characters are almost like
figures in an inhuman fantasy. . . . He does not move his pen
to one side or the other to help them." Original production seemed
to work better in the smaller Barrymore Theatre.

3 "Book Notes." *New York Herald Tribune*, 5 May, p. 17.
Brief mention that TW "has completed his first novel," *RSMS*.

4 "Book Notes: More Innocents Abroad." *New York Herald Tribune*,
7 August, p. 11.
Brief news item. Announcement of New Directions September
27 publication date for *RSMS*.

5 "Books and Authors." *New York Times*, 4 May, p. 25.
News item about TW completing *RSMS*.

6 BRADY, THOMAS F. "Hollywood Digest." *New York Times*, 22 January, sec. 2, p. 5.
Short gossip piece about Gertrude Lawrence concluding her
work in film of *GM*.

7 _____. "The Hollywood File." *New York Times*, 28 May, sec. 2,
p. 3.
Reporting on the filming of *SND* and the possible censorship
problems.

8. _____. "Loyalty Oath Issue Raised in Hollywood." *New York Times*, 27 August, sec. 2, p. 5.
News and gossip about censorship problems and Leigh and Brando during filming of *SND*.

9 CHAMBERLAIN, JOHN. "Meeting on an Island: International Congress for Cultural Freedom Convenes in Berlin." *New Leader* 33 (3 June):16–17.
Report on convocation on Western culture with TW and Arthur Koestler, Karl Jaspers, Aldous Huxley, Bertrand Russell, Andre Gide, and others in attendance; designed to investigate relationship between sciences and totalitarianism; between art(ists) and freedom.

10 CHAPMAN, JOHN. " 'A Streetcar' Pays Visit to City Center." New York *Daily News*, 24 May, p. 73.
Review of *SND*. "The play is there as splendid and touching as ever." Uta Hagen and Quinn are "first-rate."

11 COLEMAN, ROBERT. " 'Streetcar Named Desire' a Resounding Hit." New York *Daily Mirror*, 24 May, p. 39.
Review of *SND*. A "magnificent production . . . as exciting as watching the monkeys in a cage at the Central Park Zoo."

12 COOK, ALTON. " 'Menagerie' Is Faithful to Play." *New York World-Telegram & Sun*, 29 September, p. 26.
Review of film of *GM*. It's faithful in text, but without the "quality that made the play such a memorable experience."

13 CREELMAN, EILEEN. "Screen 'Streetcar' Gets Author's Nod." *New York World-Telegram & Sun*, 9 September, p. 4.
Details of TW and Kazan and the censorship problem with *SND*. TW commenting on the film and on *GM*.

14 CROWTHER, BOSLEY. "Handle with Care." *New York Times*, 8 October, sec. 2, p. 1.
Review of film of *GM*. Examines G. Lawrence's failings in her portrayal of Amanda; also considers the general shortcomings in the production; considers it to be in "battered condition."

15 DOWNING, ROBERT. "Streetcar Conductor: Some Notes from Backstage." *Theatre Annual, 1950* 8:25–33.
Written during the last week of the original Broadway run, describes the backstage goings-on at the Barrymore Theatre and every responsibility forced on the stage manager, who was R. Downing.

16 "Dreams in Glass." *New York Times Magazine*, 4 June, p. 58.
Photos from film of *GM*, with captions.

17 FREEDLEY, GEORGE. "Off Stage—and On." New York *Morning Telegraph*, 14 August, p. 2.
Book review of *RSMS*. Brief favorable note on its publication.

18 FUNKE, LEWIS. "News and Gossip Gathered on the Rialto." *New York Times*, 1 January, sec. 2, p. 1.
Items about expansion of *CR* and *27W*.

19 ————. "News and Gossip Gathered on the Rialto." *New York Times*, 29 October, sec. 2, p. 1.
Apparently M. Stapleton to play leading female role in *RT*.

20————. "Rialto Gossip." *New York Times*, 9 April, sec. 2, p. 1.
Gossip about Circle Critics voting, with brief mention of *GM* and *SND*. Also, *RT* will be presented by Cheryl Crawford.

21 GANNETT, LEWIS. "A Travesty of Tragedy." *New York Herald Tribune*, 6 December, p. 31.
Book review of *RSMS*. "Mr. Williams prettifies decay." The plot of *RSMS* is "almost . . . completely without human dignity. . . . His novella is a travesty of a tragedy."

22 GARLAND, ROBERT. " 'A Streetcar Named Desire': Tragedy Returns with a New Cast." *New York Journal-American*, 24 May, p. 22.
Review of *SND*. Focus on plot; assessment of new cast; prefers *GM*.

23 GEHMAN, RICHARD. "Guardian Agent." *Theatre Arts* 34 (July):18.
Influence of Andrey Wood on development of playwrights and directors of the era, TW among them.

24 GEISMAR, MAXWELL. "Tennessee Williams Fails in First Novel." *New York Post*, 15 October, p. M16.
    Brief book review of *RSMS*. "Failure ... in the dimensions of the literary scene."

25 GILBERT, JUSTIN. " 'Glass Menagerie' Strong as Movie." New York *Daily Mirror*, 29 September, p. 46.
    Review of film of *GM*. "A moving play transformed into an eloquent film." Plot summary.

26 *GM*. *New York Post*, 1 October, pp. M7–M13.
    Script of *GM* printed in supplement section.

27 GRIFFITH, RICHARD. "A Look at a Promise." *Saturday Review* 33 (14 October):32.
    Review of film of *GM*. Discusses *GM* in context of "American social dramas. Refers to its "surface accuracy ... [and] emotional truth."

28 HARTUNG, PHILIP T. "As Dreams Are Made on." *Commonweal* 52 (6 October):631–32.
    "Warner Bros. have made an excellent film [of *GM*]; perhaps it is too long and Irving Rapper's direction is at times on the slow and arty side ... but the production is so good ... and the script so fascinating, ... that you lose track of time and your own sense of reality." Praises the cast—Gertrude Lawrence, Arthur Kennedy, Jane Wyman—and the film for being "so full of compassion, that it ends a touch more hopefully than did Tennessee Williams' original play."

29 HATCH, ROBERT. "Damaged in Transit." *New Republic* 123 (23 October):22.
    Review of film of *GM*. "Patently a stage play with screen appendages. ... No movie can spend an hour and a half photographing what goes on in one small room and hope to survive as entertainment. . . . The quality of the performance was disappointing."

30 HAWKINS, WILLIAM. " 'Streetcar' Clangs into City Center." *New York World-Telegram & Sun*, 24 May, p. 40.

Review of *SND*. "One of the most fascinating plays of the generation." Focuses primarily on cast.

31   HAYES, ALFRED. "Another Williams Victim." *New York Herald Tribune Book Review*, 22 October, p. 14.
Brief book review of *RSMS*. Interprets theme; favorable.

32   "Jam of the Gods." *Time* 56 (30 October):109–10.
Book review of *RSMS*. "Written in the gutless, languid, pseudo-Jamesian manner." It makes TW "a member in good standing of the new school of decadence."

33   McCARTEN, JOHN. "Small Apartment, Teeming Valley." *New Yorker* 26 (30 September):60.
Review of film of *GM*. Praises cast's efforts; plot details for most part; says play translates adequately into film.

34   MacCOLL, RENE. "Laughter dans le Tramway." *Atlantic* 186 (July): 94–95.
Review of *SND*, French production. The production is described as tongue in cheek, "as uproarious as the Marx brothers." Reprinted 1971.19.

35   McCRARY, TEX, and FALKENBURG, JINX. "N.Y. Close-Up." *New York Herald Tribune*, 1 October, sec. 5, pp. 1–2.
Brief gossip item. TW going to California to write for MGM; refers to TW's comments on Ingrid Bergman and Garbo.

36   MACK. Review of *GM*. *Variety*, 8 March, p. 60.
Dublin production. Brief; mentions some difficulty with accents.

37   McLAUGHLIN, RICHARD. "A Streetcar Named Kitsch." *New Leader* 33 (30 October):23.
Book review of *RSMS*. Talks of TW's "full time predilection for the seamy side of life. . . . [*RSMS*] is deliberately meretricious, giving the impression of phoneyness." Refers to "the bad stench [of this] sordid tale."

38   MacMULLAN, HUGH. "Translating 'The Glass Menagerie' to Film." *Hollywood Quarterly* 5 (Fall):14–32.

GM "is not, in its theatrical form, suitable for film. It is essentially descriptive and without motion. . . . It relies, for its meaning, on basic, Ibsenesque symbols." Discusses particular script and cast difficulties in the adaptation; focuses on elements of mood, internal poetry, plot line. Details of the evolution of the film, its aesthetic integrity.

39 MILES, GEORGE. Review of *RSMS*. *Commonweal* 53 (3 November): 99–100.
Brief book review. "This is a cheap book. The idea is cheap, the treatment is cheap."

40 POPKIN, HENRY. "Bookshelf." *Theatre Arts* 34 (November):2, 4.
Book review of *RSMS*. Compares central character to other TW heroines; likes stage heroines better.

41 PRESCOTT, ORVILLE. "Books of the Times." *New York Times*, 29 September, p. 25.
Book review of *RSMS*. "Mr. Williams' first foray into fiction is, in the language of the theatre he knows so much better, a turkey. . . . [*GM* and *SND*] were unpleasant but wonderfully powerful and compassionate. This, his first novel, has none of their power or pity."

42 Review of film of *GM*. *Christian Century* 67 (22 November):1407.
Very brief. "A sensitive film probing the motivations and aspirations of frail human beings . . . movingly done."

43 Review of film of *GM*. *Time* 56 (2 October):74, 76–77.
"It does not live up to its stage success. Except for an 'upbeat' ending which Co-Scripter Williams reluctantly imposed on Playwright Williams at the urging of Hollywood, the film gives a reasonably faithful reading of the play." G. Lawrence "does a competent job, marred by some confusion of accents."

44 Review of *RSMS*. *Atlantic* 186 (November):101.
Brief book review, one paragraph. Plot summary plus: "*Roman Spring* is an accomplished reworking of rather stereotyped ingredients."

45

45   Review of *RSMS*. *New Yorker* 26 (25 November):149–50.
     Brief book review. "A swift moving, straightforward and com-
     pact piece of work."

46   ROLO, CHARLES J. "Life with Insulation Removed." *New York Times
     Book Review*, 1 October, p. 4.
     Book review of *RSMS*. "His novel is, in sum, readable and ad-
     mirably written, but in the final analysis rather pointless."

47   *RSMS*. *Newsweek* 38 (9 October):94.
     Brief note of publication of *RSMS*.

48   SHEAFFER, LOUIS. "Tennessee Williams' First Novel." *Brooklyn Daily
     Eagle*, 17 October, p. 8.
     Book review of *RSMS*; "Superior writing and a credit to his
     record." Plot summary.

49   ————. "Uta Hagen Excellent in 'Streetcar Named Desire.'" *Brook-
     lyn Daily Eagle*, 24 May, p. 12.
     Review of *SND*. "One of the two or three finest plays written
     in this country in the past decade.... [Now it's] as moving and
     powerful as ever ... was written with an irresistible combination
     of searching, scarifying honesty and endless compassion."

50   "'Streetcar' to Return to N.Y. for 2 Weeks." *Variety*, 8 March, p. 37.
     Announces return engagement scheduled for the spring at New
     York's City Center.

51   "Tale of 3 Cities." *Theatre Arts* 34 (January):35.
     Brief; refers to box office success of *SND*, and to furor in
     London and Paris when it opened there.

52   TINKLE, LON. "Tennessee Williams Turns Novelist." *Dallas Morn-
     ing News*, 1 October, sec. IV, p. 8.
     Book review of *RSMS*. "A lot more clinical than it is dramatic....
     shows an evolution in Mr. Williams as a thinker."

53   WATTS, RICHARD, JR. "That Streetcar Known as Desire." *New York
     Post*, 24 May, p. 71.
     Review of *SND*. It "once more prove[s] to be a drama of emo-

tional force and almost painful insight. . . . seems as skillful and powerful as it did when I first encountered it. . . . [But] its tragedy has a way of appearing to stem from the author's almost sadistic relish in tormenting his heroine."

54 YEATON, KELLY. " 'The Glass Menagerie' in the Arena." *Players* 26 (May):180–82.
Ideas on an in-the-round production of the play; light, blocking, designing elements. Specifically related to Penn State production.

55 ZOLOTOW, SAM. "Levin and Smith Plan Two Shows." *New York Times*, 10 May, p. 40.
Brief news item about *RT* being presented by C. Crawford, and *RSMS* being published.

56 ZUNSER, JESSE. "New Films on View: Tennessee Williams' Drama on Screen." *Cue* 19 (30 September):20.
Brief review of film of *GM*. Calls the project "Grade-A treatment." Talks of the altered ending.

1951

1 ALPERT, HOLLIS. "Double Bounty from Hollywood." *Saturday Review* 34 (1 September):28–31.
Review of film of *SND*. "Impressive production. . . . audiences will be unprepared for . . . the nearly overwhelming impact. . . . [The film is] even more poignant and forceful" than the play.

2 ATKINSON, BROOKS. "At the Theatre." *New York Times*, 5 February, p. 19.
Review of *RT*. Refers to TW's "respect for character and the quality of his writing." Considers TW to be "at the top of his form."

3 ———. "Don't Get Serious." *New York Times*, 27 May, sec. 2, p. 1.
Mentions *RT* as one of three serious plays that were successful during the season. Concludes that most successful plays were light and humorous.

4   _____. " 'The Rose Tattoo.' " *New York Times*, 11 February, sec. 2,
     p. 1.
        Review of *RT*. Brief synopsis; discussion of technique; praise
     for cast and script.

5   _____. "Tattooing." *New York Times*, 3 June, sec. 2, p. 1.
        Comments briefly on TW's changes to *RT*, then gives synopsis
     of play.

6   "Awards Given 'Rose Tattoo.' " *New York Herald Tribune*, 26 March,
     p. 12.
        Brief news item. Tony Award given to *RT*.

7   BARNES, HOWARD. " 'Rose Tattoo' Is Hailed as the Finest New Play."
     New York Herald Tribune, 11 February, sec. 4, p. 1.
        Review of *RT*. Calls it "the vaulting comic-tragedy." TW "has
     written [*RT*] with such imagination, depth of feeling and strange
     humor that his play now takes definite precedence over any new
     American play shown here this season." TW "has written a terrible
     'Pilgrim's Progress' in [*RT*] with a great deal of liturgical lore in
     the lines and situation." Talks of *RT* as inspired by T.S. Eliot's
     translation of "Anabasis."

8   BARNETT, LINCOLN. "Tennessee Williams." In *Writings on Life: Six-
     teen Close-Ups*. New York: William Sloane, pp. 243–61.
        Reprint of 1948.6.

9   BAUER, LEDA. "French Comedy—American Tragedy." *Theatre Arts*
     35 (July):36.
        Review of film of *SND*. "At least as effective on the screen as
     it was in the theatre. . . . production . . . of intelligence and taste."

10   BEAUFORT, JOHN. "Helen Hayes in 'Glass Menagerie.' " *Christian
     Science Monitor*, 18 September, p. 4.
        Announcement of "Theatre Guild on the Air" production of GM.

11   BEYER, WILLIAM. "The State of the Theatre: Hits and Misses."
     School and Society 73 (24 March): 181–83.
        Review of *RT*. "Williams at his best. Once more he has created
     stunning characters that vibrate with life. . . . The vitality of his

people and their emotional snarls...are of such intensity that they considerably overcome the play's foot-loose, rambling dramatic structure." Discusses the symbolism, its form as "folk comedy," its quality direction.

12 BOLTON, WHITNEY. "Tennessee Williams at His Best in 'The Rose Tattoo.'" New York *Morning Telegraph*, 6 February, p. 2.
      Review of *RT*. "A glowing, intelligent and unusual writing job.... [TW has] given the theater of N.Y. a prize.... He writes with singular power, and vast, sweeping compassion."

13 BROWN, JOHN MASON. "Saying It with Flowers." *Saturday Review* 34 (10 March):22.
      Review of *RT*. TW is "a wasteful writer who has no disciplined sense of form or structure." *RT* is "empty at its center." Reprinted: 1952.3.

14 CHAPMAN, JOHN. "'The Rose Tattoo' Affectionately Written and Admirably Staged." New York *Daily News*, 5 February, p. 37.
      Review of *RT*. TW has "out-Saroyaned" Saroyan in *RT*; "its mood is comic, not tragic, and its humor is first-rate.... [TW's] human insight is unimpaired and his ability to write vivid scenes is, as always, exceptional."

15 CLURMAN, HAROLD. "Tennessee Williams Rose." *New Republic* 124 (19 February):22.
      Review of *RT*. Concerned with it as a step in the development of TW's craft; praises the production.

16 COLEMAN, ROBERT. "'Rose Tattoo' Is Thorny, Much Too Earthy." New York *Daily Mirror*, 5 February, p. 23.
      Review of *RT*. TW, "in paraphrasing Eliot and Xenophon, has taken a journey downward to the very depths of human degradation.... [It's] a play that has moments of compassion, beauty and sheer nastiness ... episodes that can be construed as sacrilegious."

17 CRANDALL, NORMA. "Widow in Rome." *New Republic* 124 (22 January):20.
      Book review of *RSMS*. "A rather thin, somewhat mechanical, coldly analytical and detached novella."

18   CROWTHER, BOSLEY. "The Screen in Review." *New York Times*, 20 September, p. 37.

Review of film of *SND*. Considerable praise for V. Leigh. "Comments cannot do justice to the substance and the artistry of this film. . . . As fine as if not finer than the play."

19   _____. "Seen in Close-Up." *New York Times*, 23 September, sec. 2, p. 1.

Discussion of the "close-up" technique in making films; mention of *SND* as example.

20   DEMING, BEVERLY. " 'Streetcar' Author Readying New Play in Key West." *Miami Visitor*, 1951–1952 Winter Season, pp. 7, 42.

Chatty article discussing TW and his sports car, having his grandfather with him in Key West, his working on *CR* and a movie script.

21   " 'Dolls,' 'Tattoo' Get Perry Prizes." *New York Times*, 26 March, p. 20.

New item. *RT* and *Guys and Dolls* win Tony Awards for "outstanding contributions" to current season.

22   DOWNER, ALAN S. *Fifty Years of American Drama 1900–1950*. Chicago: Henry Regnery, pp. 102–5, 145–47.

"Of the younger writers, none has been more dedicated to theatrical symbolism than Tennessee Williams. . . . Though his themes are in possibility tragic, his plays are in actuality pathetic. Each of his characters passionately resists the moment of illumination. . . . [TW] chooses to give importance to the particular, the unique, rather than the universal." References to *GM*, *SND*, *S&S*.

23   "Drama Mailbag." *New York Times*, 4 February, sec. 2, p. 3.

In letter to drama editor, R. Sharp disagrees with article by TW (14 January).

24   "Drama Mailbag." *New York Times*, 1 April, sec. 2, p. 3.

Two letters to drama editor. First, by R.C. Boden, disagrees with *New York Times* critic's review of *RT*; second, by V. Conroy, suggests that TW may have "a morbid turn of mind" but that the letter writer enjoys TW's work.

25 DUPEE, F.W. "Theater Chronicle: Literature on Broadway." *Partisan Review* 18 (May):333–34.
Review of *RT*. Discusses its possible sources. TW "deepens [his native realism] by relying upon various novelists ... Caldwell, Anderson, Lawrence, and Steinbeck." Discusses plot of *RT* and its heroine and why it disintegrates.

26 FARBER, MANNY. Review of film of *SND*. *Nation* 173 (20 October): 334.
Claims that everything good about stage version "has been raped, along with poor Blanche Dubois [*sic*], in the Hollywood wood [*sic*] version." Calls it "all clamor, climax and Kazan." Kazan has "obliterated Williams's more delicate gradual revelation of the fact that Blanche is a rotten old Dixie apple fated for squashing."

27 GABRIEL, GILBERT W. "Tennessee Williams Tattoos His Bloom on Times Square." *Cue* 20 (17 February):18.
Review of *RT*. Calls it "this new Tennessee Williams hit." It contains "uneven but undoubted genius.... Flung in are such seeming opposites as complete funniness vs. total sadness.... You are ... arrested by the rage of warring values in Mr. Williams' own mind."

28 GIBBS, WOLCOTT. "The Brighter Side of Tennessee." *New Yorker* 26 (10 February):58–59.
Review of *RT*. TW "has abandoned the doomed, exhausted, and melancholy survivors of the Southern aristocracy.... he has also given up his old preoccupation with remorseless decay for what it is customary to describe as a note of hope." Calls attention to his "gift for lyric expression and his contempt for conventional plot structure."

29 GILROY, HARRY. "Mr. Williams Turns to Comedy." *New York Times*, 28 January, sec. 2, pp. 1, 3.
Preopening news, gossip, and anecdotes about *RT*; how TW came to write *RT*, plus quotes from TW about *GM*, *SND*, and *S&S*.

30 GUERNSEY, OTIS L., JR. "On the Screen." *New York Herald Tribune*, 20 December, p. 20.

Review of film of *SND*. "A darkly absorbing drama . . . a convincing and solid piece of movie work . . . something for its makers to take pride in, for movie audiences to experience."

31   ————. "Williams Tops the Season." *New York Herald Tribune*, 5 February, p. 10.
Review of *RT*. "An excellently written and brilliantly acted comedy-drama. . . . The new work shuttles between passion and humor." Notes its "erratic moments and weaknesses in construction, but . . . [still] the finest new American play of the season."

32 HARTUNG, PHILIP T. "Weep for Blanche." *Commonweal* 54 (28 September):596–97.
Review of film of *SND*. "Full of poignant situations that ought to move all viewers to compassion for Blanche DuBois." Yet the "lengthy" film oversteps the "bounds of good taste, contrary to [its] well-meaning intention," as it becomes "more suggestive than necessary." Brando and Leigh praised equally, but finds *SND* to be "a depressing film . . . you leave the film weeping for Blanche but not hopeful for mankind."

33 HATCH, ROBERT. "Old Hit, New Venture." *New Republic* 125 (8 October):21.
Review of film of *SND*. "It seems to me that Williams' great powers of observation are not matched by equivalent insights. . . . 'Streetcar' is less a tragedy than a depressant." But, "as a movie translation" it is "entirely successful." In fact, "screen translations from the more inventive arts can be no better than this."

34 HAWKINS, WILLIAM. "Williams Goes Comic in 'The Rose Tattoo.'" *New York World-Telegram*, 5 February, p. 10.
Review of *RT*. "Type—Comedy; Topic—Love; Virtue—Novelty; Debit—Talky; I find it—most unusual. . . . In its favor the play has atmosphere and warmth. . . . On the other hand the humor often seems glued to the surface."

35 ISAACS, HERMINE. "A Symposium on 'A Streetcar Named Desire,' I." *Films in Review* 2 (December):51–52.
"Tennessee Williams is a theatre magician. . . . What he says, it seems, must be true and good so poignantly does he say it. . . . He

has assumed the privileges of the realist and the poet without accepting the responsibilities of either. ... The result is conflict without resolution, tragedy without catharsis. ... If this was true in the stage play of 'Streetcar,' it is even truer in the film."

36 KAHN. Review of film of *SND*. *Variety*, 20 June, p. 6.
   Film portrays an "even more absorbing drama of frustration and stark tragedy" than does the play; "excellently produced and imparting a keen insight into a drama whose scope was, of necessity, limited by its stage setting." Detailed plot summary with plaudits for the cast and production crew.

37 KERR, WALTER. Review of *RT*. *Commonweal* 53 (23 February):492–94.
   "Tennessee Williams is the finest playwright now working in the American theatre." Praises the script and the production.

38 LERNER, MAX. "Letters from a Playwright." *New York Post*, 16 May, p. 44.
   Quotes a letter from TW in which he discusses the problem of being an American playwright, and the theater outside New York City.

39 "Lowering the Curtain." *New York Times*, 27 May, sec. 2, p. 1.
   RT mentioned as winner of Antoinette Perry Award.

40 "Lyric Theatre, Hammersmith." *Times* (London), 23 November, p. 2.
   Review of *S&S*, London production. Plot summary; first six scenes are "beautifully written." Praise for cast.

41 McCARTEN, JOHN. "Way down Yonder." *New Yorker* 27 (29 September):111–12.
   Brief review of film of *SND*. "A faithful translation to the screen." However, "it doesn't move about very much." General praise.

42 McCLAIN, JOHN. "Play Isn't Worthy of the Fine Acting." *New York Journal-American*, 5 February, p. 8.
   Review of *RT*. "The theme is thin, frequently offensive and

never sufficiently provocative. . . . Never before, to my knowledge, has a rather simple biological situation involved so many extraneous characters and so many words—or been so pretentiously elevated."

43 MARSHALL, MARGARET. Review of *RT*. *Nation* 172 (17 February): 161–62.
    Says Serafina is "free of the sadism that marked [TW's] dissection of Blanche." The first act is best; it's "vivid and humorous. . . . The play is good theater in the elementary sense." Gives attention to directing, lighting, acting. TW "is incapable of exercising the faintest critical judgment toward his own effusions."

44 "Menagerie of Managers on Williams Plays." *Variety*, 21 November, pp. 57–60.
    Brief. History of producers for TW's six Broadway productions.

45 MEZO. Review of *GM*. *Variety*, 10 October, p. 61.
    Lucerne production, brief. International Music Festival's choice of TW's *GM*, which was performed 25 September.

46 MITGANG, HERBERT. "A Familiar 'Streetcar' Passenger." *New York Times*, 9 September, sec. 2, p. 5.
    Profile of Malden and his role as Mitch in screen version of *SND*.

47 NASH, ELEANOR H. "A Symposium on 'A Streetcar Named Desire,' III." *Films in Review* 2 (December):54–55.
    SND "is better as a motion picture than as a play. . . . Just what was Mr. Williams trying to say? Just what was it all about?"

48 NATHAN, GEORGE JEAN. " 'The Rose Tattoo.' " In *The Theatre Book of the Year, 1950–51*. New York: Alfred A. Knopf, pp. 209–12.
    Reprint of 1951.49.

49 _____. "The Tattoo on Tennessee Williams' Brain." *New York Journal-American*, 12 February, p. 12.
    Review of *RT*. "I am disappointed at my continued disappointment in [TW]. . . . I had hoped . . . that with the passing of the years Williams might grow up a little and learn that sex, which seems to be his major obsession as it is that of other of our pro-

fessional genitalmen of letters, isn't such an innovation." Calls *RT* "his latest peepshow," and calls TW's [*New York Times*] essay on it "metaphysical twaddle . . . [and] rank dramatic presumption." Says that in reaction to *RT*, "Dr. Kinsey [is] laughing himself to death." Reprinted: 1951.48.

50 PATTERSON, FRANCIS TAYLOR. "A Symposium on 'A Streetcar Named Desire,' II." *Films in Review* 2 (December):52–54.
   "As a dramatist Tennessee Williams follows one of the methods of modern psychiatry: shock treatment. . . . It has been said that the play is a study in decadence. . . . The decadence is all on the side of Stanley. . . . Preoccupied with violence, Mr. Williams has let his previously shown talent for subtle characterization lapse."

51 "Playwright Wins Dispute over Royalties." *Dallas Morning News*, 22 August, pt. 2, p. 6.
   News item. TW wins dispute with Margo Jones of Dallas' Theatre '51 over royalties for *S&S*.

52 Review of film of *SND*. *Christian Century* 68 (28 November):1397.
   Extremely brief. "Emotions are set forth so rawly, the brutality is so unrelieved, that the film becomes a powerful document."

53 Review of film of *SND*. *Life* 31 (24 September):91–92, 95.
   Brief text praising Kazan, Brando, Leigh. Many photos.

54 Review of film of *SND*. *Newsweek* 38 (1 October):87–88.
   Refers to TW's sense of conflict being "overstressed by [his] lurid methods." Praises cast and TW's "exceptional dramatic force."

55 Review of film of *SND*. *Time* 58 (17 September):105–6.
   "A grown-up, gloves-off drama of real human beings." Comments on fidelity to original script, and refers to censorship problems.

56 Review of *RT*. *Newsweek* 37 (12 February):72.
   Brief. Plot summary and character analysis; mildly praising.

57 Review of *RT*. *Theatre Arts* 35 (April):16.
    Brief. Cast and production business. "Overall effect is ruined by
    Tennessee Williams' addiction to high falutin' language and
    feeble, muddled symbolism."

58 Review of *RT*. *Time* 57 (12 February):53–54.
    Brief. Mildly negative; plot and theme details.

59 SHANLEY, J.P. "'The Rose Tattoo' Due Here Tonight." *New York
    Times*, 3 February, p. 9.
    Preopening night news release about *RT* and cast.

60 SHEAFFER, LOUIS. "Williams' Lusty, Affectionate Story of Some
    Sicilian-Americans." *Brooklyn Daily Eagle*, 5 February, p. 7.
    Review of *RT*. "A healthy, vigorous feel of high noon to [*RT*] . . .
    with plenty of robust, earthy humor here, too." Not as good as
    SND, but "the high skill of its writing [is] unmistakable. . . . has a
    poetic flavor and the poetry of intense feeling."

61 "'A Streetcar Named Desire.'" *New York Times Magazine*, 22 July,
    pp. 34–35.
    Series of photos featuring Leigh and Brando as Blanche and
    Stanley, respectively, in film version of *SND*.

62 TYNAN, KENNETH. Review of *S&S*. *Spectator* 187 (7 December):772.
    London production. TW "has a nose for incompleteness." His
    characters are "wing-beating idealists," and puts Alma in this
    category along with Blanche and Amanda. TW is "an unsophisti-
    cated Chekhov," and his characters in *S&S* are "internally lame,"
    but the play contains "a great deal of brilliant and evocative hot-
    house writing."

63 WATTS, RICHARD, JR. "Mr. Williams among the Sicilians." *New York
    Post*, 5 February, p. 26.
    Review of *RT*. "Chief reaction to it is one of disappointment. . . .
    Some excellent individual scenes written with warmth, under-
    standing and a kind of lyric . . . simplicity. Unfortunately [TW]
    is not satisfied with his dramatic simplicity. [*RT*] is only inter-
    mittently satisfactory."

64 _____. "Sex, Sicilians and Mr. Williams." *New York Post*, 18 February, amusement sec. p. 12.
Review of *RT*. Refers to the varying popular critical response to premiere of *RT*; but most agree that TW "had fallen considerably from the heights reached by" *SND* and *GM*; thinks "the comedy and the happy ending are an afterthought"; talks of "the last act so filled with a sense of hasty improvisation."

65 "Williams to Key West." *New York Herald Tribune*, 16 February, p. 14.
Brief news item. TW leaves for Key West after major hit of *RT*.

66 WORSLEY, T.C. "Period Charms." *New Statesman* 42 (8 December):664.
Review of *S&S*, London production. "The play was a failure in America, though I must say I don't quite see why." Discusses its "succession of little haunting scenes" and says the work "seems very old-fashioned."

67 WYATT, EUPHEMIA VAN RENSSELAER. Review of *RT*. *Catholic World* 172 (March): 467–68.
"To hail [*RT*] as a 'folk-comedy' stamps it as a travesty of human decencies. . . . Act III is out of focus with any decent principles. . . . It is a real tragedy that a playwright who has such gifts of sympathy and human understanding as he has shown should have written any scenes so degrading as the closing ones of [*RT*]." Objects to the "full return to the lusts of paganism."

68 ZABE. Review of *RT*. *Variety*, 10 January, p. 60.
Chicago production. Describes play as uneven, with too long a first act and later acts "never being able to overcome the pedestrian pace set by the first." Praise for setting, music, and M. Stapleton. Suggests that first act be cut and rewritten, and the other acts tightened, with a stronger climax.

69 ZOLOTOW, SAM. "New Play by Luce in Need of Revision." *New York Times*, 23 November, p. 32.
News release. *S&S* opened in London. Received well.

70 _____. " 'Rose Tattoo' Closes Oct. 27." *New York Times*, 27 August, p. 16.

>After thirty-eight weeks at Martin Beck, *RT* to close; tour to start in Boston or Philadelphia; TW made "deal" for lower terms.

1952

1 ATKINSON, BROOKS. "At the Theatre." *New York Times*, 25 April, p. 19.

>Review of *S&S*, Circle-in-the-Square production. Positive comments on cast, generally. "You might fairly argue that [*S&S*] is a finer piece of literature [than *SND*]. The analysis of character is subtler and more compassionate. The contrasts are less brutish."

2 _____. "Second Chance." *New York Times*, 4 May, sec. 2, p. 1.

>Review of *S&S*. Pleased that *S&S* was revived, brief comparison with *SND* and positive comments on cast and production. "From every point of view [*S&S*] is a beautifully wrought drama. It cuts sharply into the essence of the truth."

3 BROWN, JOHN MASON. "Saying It with Flowers." In *As They Appear*. New York: McGraw-Hill, pp. 161–66.

>Review of *RT*. Reprint of 1951.13.

4 DARLINGTON, W.A. "Report on West End Stage Activities." *New York Times*, 10 February, sec. 2, p. 2.

>London production announcement about *S&S*; very brief.

5 DENT, ALAN. "All Sorts of Riff-Raff." *Illustrated London News* 220 (22 March):502.

>Review of film of *SND*. [The script] "is a low and alarming spectacle . . . but this film version certainly has its own superb peculiar fascination." Criticizes character of Blanche, because "there is no true pathos in her degradation." Film allows all characters to develop more fully than in stage version. Compares *SND* to something like a "tenement house on fire": "We despise ourselves for gazing," but cannot look away.

*6 FISHER, WILLIAM J. "Trends in Post-Depression American Drama: A Study of the Works of William Saroyan, Tennessee Williams,

Irwin Shaw, Arthur Miller." Ph.D. dissertation, New York University.

7 "14 Win Admission to Arts Institute." *New York Times*, 8 February, p. 18.
   Concerns National Institute of Arts and Letters addition of TW to their roster.

8 HAWKINS, WILLIAM. "Dana Andrews Scores Hit in 'Menagerie' Tour." *New York World-Telegram & Sun*, 11 July, p. 6.
   Note on summer tour of *GM*.

9 _____. "Tennessee's Play a Hit in the Village." *New York World-Telegram & Sun*, 7 May, p. 32.
   Review of *S&S*. Production has a "kind of illuminating authenticity.... There are facets of the play revealed in this run which no one would have guessed from the original production."

10 HEWES, HENRY. "Broadway Postscript." *Saturday Review* 35 (10 May):28.
   Brief review of *S&S*. Praises the Circle-in-the-Square production.

11 _____. "Broadway Postscript." *Saturday Review* 35 (21 June):32.
   Reports on TW standing to read a short story to audience at poetry reading; guesses at its future.

12 NISBET, FAIRFAX. "Williams' Grandfather for Films." *Dallas Morning News*, 3 January, pt. 1, p. 17.
   Report of TW's intent to use his 95-year-old grandfather for films of his short works.

13 "1:15 Matinee Is Tested." *New York Times*, 21 February, p. 23.
   RT was play featured at a test of 1:15 matinee in Omaha.

14 PRYOR, THOMAS. "Cooper Will Star in Michener Film." *New York Times*, 12 March, p. 32.
   News item. Warner Bros. announces an increase of prints of *SND* because of Academy Award nominations.

15   REISZ, KAREL. Review of film of *SND. Sight and Sound* 21 (April-June):170–71.
> Negative toward the transformation from stage to screen. "All the usual objections to stage adaptations apply." Negative about cast, except Brando.

16   SHEAFFER, LOUIS. "Circle-in-Square Hits Stride in Moving 'Summer and Smoke.'" *Brooklyn Eagle*, 28 April, p. 8.
> Review of *S&S*. "A fine, honest, moving performance, of a fine, honest, moving piece of theater. . . . [*S&S*] now appears to be a finer play than many of us had suspected when it was given on Broadway . . . a searching, probing play."

17   ———. "Tennessee Williams, Just Another American in Italy." *Brooklyn Eagle-Sun*, 13 January, pp. 23–24.
> Interview-commentary; TW discusses upcoming production of *CR*, others of his plays, the state of the theater.

18   TILLICH, PAUL. "Existentialism and the Courage of Despair." In *The Courage To Be*. New York: Yale University Press, pp. 145–46.
> A parenthetical mention of *SND* in reference to that play's "conditional negativity."

19   WEILER, A.H. "By Way of Report." *New York Times*, 4 May, sec. 2, p. 5.
> Gossip piece. Indications that *RT* is slated for a screen version.

20   WHITEBAIT, WILLIAM. Review of film of *SND. New Statesman* 43 (8 March):274.
> "Its realism is theatrical realism, it gilds violence with a thin wash of playwright's gab." Discusses its capacity to "excite." Praises the acting of Brando and Leigh, as well as Kazan's direction.

21   "Williams' Play in London." *New York Times*, 25 January, p. 13.
> News item. *S&S* opened in London, received well. Quote from W.A. Darlington of *Daily Telegraph*.

22   WYATT, EUPHEMIA VAN RENSSELAER. Review of *S&S. Catholic World* 176 (November):148–49.

This production is of less intensity because two characters, Alma and the minister, are considerably weaker as they are performed. Complaint about less effective set design (than that of original production in 1948).

1953

1 ATKINSON, BROOKS. " 'Camino Real.' " *New York Times*, 29 March, sec. 2, p. 1.
Review of *CR*. *CR* is TW's conception of life. Generally positive commentary on production, cast, and TW's talent as a writer. Reprinted: 1978.23.

2 _____. "First Night at the Theatre." *New York Times*, 20 March, p. 26.
Review of *CR*. "A sensitive, virtuoso writer, Mr. Williams knows how to create an intelligible world. As theatre, [*CR*] is as eloquent and rhythmic as a piece of music."

3 BENTLEY, ERIC. "Better than Europe?" In *In Search of Theater*. New York: Alfred A. Knopf, pp. 87–88.
Reprint of 1949.3. Reprinted: 1961.41.

4 _____. "Essays of Elia." *New Republic* 128 (30 March):30–31.
Review of *CR*. Dislikes script for what he calls its "non-genuine element." Notes that TW's strong point is his realistic, as opposed to fantastic, portraits. "In [*CR*], Tennessee Williams is not a dramatist but a librettist, a scenario writer." Reprinted: 1954.4, 1956.10, 1968.2.

5 BOLTON, WHITNEY. " 'Camino Real' Is Provocative, Compassionate and Never Dull." New York *Morning Telegraph*, 21 March, p. 3.
Review of *CR*. Contrasts it with "The Cocktail Party." "People will fang it savagely or embrace it heartily, according to their sensitivities and their own backgrounds. . . . [It's] written with imagination and vigor and often startling beauty."

6 "Boltons Theatre Club: A Double Bill." *Times* (London), 27 October, p. 10.

Brief review of *TPC*, London production. The heroine "sounds like a distracted parakeet." Generally negative.

7   BOOTH, SHIRLEY. "Concerning 'Camino Real.'" *New York Times*, 5 April, sec. 2, p. 3.

Letter to drama editor. Cites her own experience in plays that have closed; wants to add her congratulations to TW; would be a shame if people missed "this exquisite play."

8   BROWN, JOHN MASON. "The Living Dead." *Saturday Review* 36 (18 April):28–30.

Review of *CR*. TW's "most unconventional play." Details what he calls his "own unfavorable reaction." Refers to its "despair" and "melancholy." Ends by calling it "a flea circus."

9   CALTA, LOUIS. "Premiere Tonight for 'Camino Real.'" *New York Times*, 19 March, p. 34.

News release. Opening of *CR* in New York; names producers and assistants.

10   "Carl Zuckmayer's War Play." *Times* (London), 21 September, p. 10.

News item. *TPC* to be produced by the International Theatre Group at Boltons Theatre.

11   CHAPMAN, JOHN. "Symbols Clash in 'Camino Real.'" New York *Daily News*, 20 March, p. 63.

Review of *CR*. The play "induced in this observer an acute state of misery.... [It's] an enormous jumble of five-cent philosophy, $3.98 words, ballet symbolism, allegory, pretentiousness, lackwit . . . and overall bushwah." Forecasts its becoming "the darling of self-conscious intellectuals."

12   ———. "A Very Controversial Play." New York *Sunday News*, 29 March, sec. 2, p. 3.

Review of *CR*. Refers to its company with other "recent offbeat works" by T.S. Eliot, Anouilh, Sartre, and Giraudoux. TW "has not learned the first lessons that any artist or craftsman must master— self-discipline and self-criticism." Talks of its "excruciatingly fancy writing, pretentious philosophy and half-baked symbolism."

13 CLURMAN, HAROLD. Review of *CR*. *Nation* 176 (4 April):293–94.
CR "should be regarded as a work of the author's nonage.... [It] is immature ... less poetic than" *GM* or *SND*, "a fallible minor work of a young artist of important talent." Reprinted: 1958.17, 1974.8.

14 COLEMAN, ROBERT. " 'Camino Real' Will Please Some, Anger Others." New York *Daily Mirror*, 20 March, pp. 50, 51.
"Like Philip Barry before him, [TW] probably tired of making money from obviously successful scripts and decided to wrestle for a while with the gods." [*CR*] "is an arresting, vivid, kaleidoscopic, diffuse fantasy.... It is Williams' most ambitious, if least satisfying script." Quotes one theatergoer who observed: "[*CR*] is burlesque for Ph.D's."

15 "Drama Mailbag." *New York Times*, 3 May, sec. 2, p. 3.
In letter to editor, N. Poliakoff offers positive comments on *CR*; H. Clark says "nuts" to *CR*.

16 EATON, WALTER PRICHARD. "Short Plays." *New York Herald Tribune Book Review*, 8 November, p. 15.
Brief mention of publication of *27W*. It foreshadows his longer plays.

17 "Edinburgh Begins 7th Music Festival." *New York Times*, 24 August, p. 20.
GM revival is announced for Provincetown Playhouse, Greenwich Village.

18 ENCK, JOHN JACOB. "Memory and Desire and Tennessee Williams' Plays." *Transactions of the Wisconsin Academy of Sciences, Arts, Letters* 42:249–56.
Sets out to examine from where TW's fame derives and how his acclaim has come about so quickly. Discusses the "extensive similarities" of his early plays, TW's use of women ("who are not well") as leading characters, settings, memory (as "the nimbus enveloping the plays"), and diction. Also focuses on the "hazards" TW faces.

19 FREEDLEY, GEORGE. "'Camino Real' Brilliant, Provocative Job; Should
    Be Given Full Support." New York *Morning Telegraph*, 25 March,
    p. 3.
        Review of *CR*. "Certainly the finest play by the most outstand-
    ing American dramatist.... [It] gives encouragement to an adult
    theatre in America."

20 FULTON, A.R. "'It's Exactly Like the Play.'" *Theatre Arts* 37
    (March):78–83.
        Review of film of *SND*. Refers to difficulties in filming *SND*,
    among other non-TW works. Focuses on anticipated censorship
    problems, its not being "inherently cinematic," the critical re-
    sponse.

21 GASSNER, JOHN. "Realism and Poetry in American Playwrighting."
    World Theatre 2 (Spring):19–20.
        Brief reference to TW's *GM* and *BA*. Mostly biographical de-
    tails about TW at time of these early works. "Williams writes
    musically, poetically, and imagistically."

22 GIBBS, WOLCOTT. "Erehwon." *New Yorker* 29 (28 March):69–70.
        Review of *CR*. Compares it to Kafka; doubts TW's ability to
    handle it; considerable plot summary; praises acting; production
    "was adroitly arranged."

23 HAWKINS, WILLIAM. "'Camino Real' Is Pure Emotion." *New York
    World-Telegram & Sun*, 20 March, p. 28.
        Review of *CR*. A "brave and stimulating new play.... [TW] has
    composed his work in terms of pure emotions."

24 ————. "'Camino Real' Reaches the Printed Page." *Theatre Arts*
    37 (October):26–27, 96.
        Book review of *CR*. Praises the written script and attempts to
    explain discrepancy between that and the New York production;
    discusses audience problems; changes make it "more specific and
    less fleeting."

25 HAYES, RICHARD. "The Stage: 'Camino Real.'" *Commonweal* 58 (17
    April):51–52.
        Notes that in *CR*, TW has "sought a certain mobility and free-

dom of form, some strategy by which to circumvent the impasse of naturalistic theatre. But of the methods at his disposal, it seems that he has chosen the most disastrous to the positive distinctions of his talent. . . . In the last analysis, [TW] does justice to neither reality nor romance, the imagination nor the fact. . . . That our most distinguished playwright, one of our best directors and a large part of the intellectual audience should have conspired in so flagrant a dramatic abortion is, I should say, another tragic illustration of the malign state of our present cultural climate."

26   HEWES, HENRY. "The State of Denmark." *Saturday Review* 36 (10 October):32.
     Brief mention of TW's use of the Tivoli gardens in *CR*.

27   ————. "Tennessee Williams—Last of Our Solid Gold Bohemians." *Saturday Review* 36 (28 March):25–27.
     Review of *CR*. Attempts to reckon with play's meaning. Quotes TW as saying the play is "a prayer for the wild heart kept in cages." Additional TW quotes.

28   HOBE. Review of *CR*. *Variety*, 25 March, p. 72.
     Although it may be dramatic art, it is a "box office dud. . . . A diffusive, elusive fantasy. . . . most are likely to find it incomprehensible and unsatisfying." Suggests various interpretations of what the characters may represent, ending with notes on the actors and the staging.

29   HYMAN, STANLEY EDGAR. "Some Notes on the Albertine Strategy." *Hudson Review* 6 (Autumn):417–22.
     Discussing the problem of changing characters' gender to disguise homosexual intent—in fiction and drama. Focuses on TW's story "Rubio y Morena" (*Partisan Review*, December 1948). He finds the story's Amanda to be "in fact, a man, with only the most perfunctory disguise." Claims TW does the same in his plays, but doesn't specify.

30   "Inside Stuff—Legit." *Variety*, 24 June, p. 62.
     Brief. TW in Paris to catch *RT* before its closing; now working on *S&S*; plans for a French production of *CR*.

31   KAZAN, ELIA. "Notebook for *A Streetcar Named Desire.*" In *Directing the Play*. Edited by Toby Cole and Helen Krich Chinoy. Indianapolis and New York: Bobbs-Merrill, pp. 296–310.

The memoranda of Kazan's private notebook during *SND* production. Shows interest in Stanislavskian principles; highlights, in Blanche, for example, notions of romantic tragedy, contradictions within her. Production notes for "Marlon's objects . . . the things he loves and prizes." Revised and reprinted under title *Directors on Directing*, by the same editors, same publisher, 1963, with the Kazan "Notebook" appearing on pp. 364–79. Reprinted: 1958.53, 1971.19.

32   ————. "Playwright's 'Letter to the World.'" *New York Herald Tribune*, 15 March, sec. 4, pp. 1, 2.

Preopening (of *CR*) statement by the director; perhaps *CR* is a "masque, . . . is a plea for the individual 'soul,' is finally a step forward into an affirmation."

33   KERR, WALTER. "'Camino Real.'" *New York Herald Tribune*, 20 March, p. 12.

Review of *CR*. "It is . . . [this] reviewer's opinion that 'Camino Real' . . . is the worst play yet written by the best playwright of his generation. . . . [It's] hopelessly mired in . . . symbolism, . . . preoccupied with techniques for getting at truth."

34   ————. "'Camino' Symbols." *New York Herald Tribune*, 29 March, sec. 4, p. 1.

Review of *CR*. "Williams is now trying to construct plays in something of the same manner in which a lyric poet constructs images." *CR* is a "play of deliberate non-sequiturs." It's a failure: "an essentially verbal technique is a theatrical dead end." The play is TW's own glass menagerie.

35   KRUTCH, JOSEPH WOOD. "Modernism." In *Modern Drama*. Ithaca: Cornell University Press, pp. 126–30.

"In all his most striking plays [*GM, S&S, SND*] the chief character is obsessed, and in the last two the obsession takes a sexual form. Madness seems to interest the author more than anything else." Refers to TW's symbols, ambiguity, his interest in the past; compares to Miller. Reprinted: 1961.41.

36 LEWIS, THEOPHILUS. Review of *CR*. *America* 84 (4 April):25.
"The most serious writing [TW] has ever undertaken." Talks of "effort not excellence" on TW's part; he "did not make the grade."

37 ———. Review of *CR*. *America* 84 (11 April): 59–60.
Second of his reviews on premiere, more an analysis this time: "Since there is no moral conflict . . . the play falls far short of the stature of great drama. . . . A 'take-home' drama," one whose meaning only gradually becomes clear; calls *CR* TW's "version of what's wrong with God's world." Surveys some criticism from popular press.

38 McCLAIN, JOHN. "Williams' Play Baffling to Some." *New York Journal-American*, 20 March, p. 20.
Review of *CR*. TW "knocked himself out being oblique. . . . I would defy Mr. Williams to explain 'Camino Real' in less than a page of small print. . . . What is this all about? I dunno."

39 MITCHELL, JOHN D. "Applied Psychoanalysis in the Drama." *American Imago* 14 (Fall):263–80.
Brief, dealing with *CAT*. Plot summary plus analysis. "The author's censure of the unloving, remorseless, and aggressive female protagonist . . . was removed before the Broadway opening." Later, he notes, it was replaced, and shows this to be an attempt to satisfy the audience: "The stage has always mirrored the character of the audiences it entertained."

40 NATHAN, GEORGE JEAN. "American Playwrights, Old and New: Tennessee Williams." In *The Theatre in the Fifties*. New York: Alfred A. Knopf, pp. 109–12.
Review of *CR*. "The play . . . does not mean anything whatsoever. Its fault is that it has meaning only in very widely separated and isolated brief scenes. . . . The author's aim probably was a kind of philosophical, emotional, impressionistic, expressionistic, symbolic and poetical charade." (This review remotely parallels Nathan's *Theatre Arts* review of the same production [1953.42] but is by no means a reprint of it, as is claimed in some bibliographic listings of the piece.)

41   _____. "Delirium in X-Flat." *New York Journal-American*, 5 April,
      p. 18L.
          Review of *CR*. A "bewildered, high flown, exhausting minstrel
      show ... presided over by an interlocutor in the person of Williams
      whose too many ... drinks have gone to his head. ... It imperti-
      nently tries to pass off nonsense for sense."

42   _____. "Monthly Critical Review." *Theatre Arts* 37 (June):88.
          Review of *CR*. Only Kazan saves it; it's a "meaningless" play;
      TW has "undereducated himself in too many dramatic and literary
      directions."

43   "New York Stage Pulitzer Prize for 'Picnic.'" *Times* (London), (5
      May), p. 10.
          News item. *CR* received mixed reviews from critics.

44   POORE, CHARLES. "Books of the Times." *New York Times*, 14 Feb-
      ruary, p. 15.
          TW mentioned as being one of many authors contained in *New
      Directions 14*, edited by James Laughlin.

45   Review of *CR*. *Newsweek* 41 (30 March):63.
          "A grandslam of bafflement and boredom. ... A pretentious and
      misbegotten mixture of realism and fantasy, of masque and morbid
      morality."

46   Review of *CR*. *Time* 61 (30 March):46.
          CR is TW's "most agitated protest and least effective play. ...
      [It] uses the gaudiest of theater tricks." Refers to it as "lush, sensa-
      tional ... theatrical hootch," and claims it "sets out to convey the
      author's own revulsion."

47   RICE, VERNON. "The Talking Tennessee Williams." *New York Post*,
      18 March, p. 66.
          Interview. TW discusses forthcoming *CR*, its background.

48   *Saturday Review* 36 (4 July):28.
          Brief note that New Directions will publish *CR* in August.

49 SHEAFFER, LOUIS. "Mr. Williams' 'Camino Real,' a Boldly Imaginative Play." *Brooklyn Eagle*, 20 March, p. 8.
Review of *CR*. "The author is off on a binge of imagination.... [*CR* is] uncommonly absorbing, richly and boldly theatrical."

50 SITWELL, EDITH. "Concerning 'Camino Real.'" *New York Times*, 5 April, sec. 2, p. 3.
Letter to drama editor. Refers to *CR* as "this very great play.... Why are people who can see a little deeper to be deprived of a work which throws a blinding light on the whole of our civilization?"

51 STEINBECK, JOHN. "In Defense of 'Camino Real.'" *New York Post*, 10 April, p. 10.
Long letter to drama critic, defending *CR*. [I] "found in this one clarity and beauty ... a courageous and fine piece of work, beautifully produced and filled with excitement." Reprinted: 1975.46.

52 WATTS, RICHARD, JR. "An Enigma by Tennessee Williams." *New York Post*, 20 March, p. 62.
Review of *CR*. "Full of sound and fury, signifying very little.... [TW], growing studiously pretentious, pick[s] up his own drama and haul[s] it into oblivion ... an atmosphere reeking with ominous tragic symbolism ... a land of dogged determination to be as heavily symbolic as possible.... [*CR*] is an enigmatic bore."

53 _____. "The Gay Battle over 'Camino Real.'" *New York Post*, 12 April, amusement sec., p. 14.
Discusses the reactions to the play since its opening, particularly Edith Sitwell's letter in its defense in the *New York Times*, 5 April.

54 _____. "Worry about Tennessee Williams." *New York Post*, 29 March, amusement sec., p. 12.
Review of *CR*. TW should "curb his imagery a bit." Concerned about TW's "growing preoccupation with symbolism.... Mr. Williams has purposely made [*CR*] confused by giving simple, poetic ideas an air of pseudo-profundity ... moves toward sophomoric intellectual altitudinizing [sic] ... [it] finally becomes a bore."

55 WEILER, A.H. "Random Observations on Pictures and People." *New York Times*, 3 May, sec. 2, p. 5.

Gossip item. Hal Wallis is discussing movie rights with TW for *RT*. Anna Magnani may play leading role.

56 WHITE, STEPHEN. "A Few Unkind Words for Tennessee Williams Based on Two-Thirds of His Latest Play." *Look* 17 (5 May):17.

Review of *CR*. Generally negative, accusing TW, in writing *CR*, of "pure charlatanry" in trying to pass off this play as something of value.

57 WYATT, EUPHEMIA VAN RENSSELAER. Review of *CR*. *Catholic World* 177 (May):148.

CR "is not so much a play as a modern masque, a feverish dream." Summarizes play then arrives at judgment: "Out of the muck of the walled city, Williams send [*sic*] his three dreamers up into a cleaner life. Let us hope that the muck on the 'Camino Real' will be swept clean as Mr. Williams develops his finer talent." Praises cast, and extols Kazan's direction.

1954

1 ATKINSON, BROOKS. "Theatre: Williams and Giraudoux." *New York Times*, 29 May, p. 12.

Review of *P*, Dallas production. Positive comments on *P* as performed at "Theatre 54," with brief synopsis and praise for production.

2 ————. "Two of a Kind." *New York Times*, 6 June, sec. 2, p. 1.

Review of *P*, Dallas production. Analysis and comparison of *P* and "The Apollo Bellac" by Giraudoux; discussion of writing styles.

3 BEATON, CECIL, and TYNAN, KENNETH. *Persona Grata*. New York: G.P. Putnam's Sons, pp. 96–97.

"Tennessee Williams is a playwright with a nose for incompleteness. He sympathizes, passionately, with the worldly-weak and pure in heart and vision.... Williams seems convinced that life cannot fuse the real and the ideal."

4   BENTLEY, ERIC. Review of *CR*. In *The Dramatic Event: An American Chronicle*. New York: Horizon Press, pp. 107–110.
        Reprint of 1953.4.

5   FREEDLEY, GEORGE. *HC*. New York *Morning Telegraph*, 28 September, p. 2.
        Brief item. Mentions TW's work on short story form; refers to *HC*.

6   GASSNER, JOHN. "New American Playwrights: Williams, Miller and Others." In *The Theatre in Our Times*. New York: Crown, pp. 342–54.
        Based on a 1952 analysis of the state of American drama after WWII. Discusses TW along with Miller as the two Americans who "actually and deservedly aroused interest abroad." Gives history of TW's writing and career and discusses his "perennial avant-garde theatre of subjectivity and private sensitity," and how he "has a bohemian writer's 'art for art's sake' passion." Also, claims that "Williams has been suspicious of realism." Reprinted in abridged form: *On Contemporary Literature*, ed. Richard Kostelanetz (Freeport, N.Y.: Books for Libraries, 1964), pp. 48–63.

7   _____. " 'A Streetcar Named Desire': A Study in Ambiguity." In *The Theatre in Our Times*. New York: Crown, pp. 355–63.
        Claims that *SND* was the best play of its season (1947–48) and "the most indicative of the flexibility of realism." Cites its "stinging naturalistic detail" and its abounding in "poetic overtones." Analyzes distance between prose and poetry in TW's work (minimal) and relates the point to *GM*, *BA*, and *SND*; goes on to qualify TW's use of reality and how ambiguity fits in; claims TW "not only enriched but muddled his play with his ambiguities." Investigates means of *SND*'s successful staging, Kazan's role, *SND*'s possibilities as a novel.

8   JOHNSON, GRADY. "Key West, Playwright Get into 'Tattoo' Act." *New York Times*, 5 December, sec. 2, p. 9.
        Anecdotes and gossip about filming of *RT* in Key West.

9   McCORD, BERT. "Tennessee Williams Is Due Here Today with 2 Scripts." *New York Herald Tribune*, 13 April, p. 24.

Gossip item. TW expected from Memphis with two scripts for possible Broadway productions; both to have Mississippi delta as setting; *CAT* and *OD*.

10 PRYOR, THOMAS. "Play by Williams Planned as Film." *New York Times*, 13 December, p. 34.
      News release. Hal Wallis and TW have begun discussing *S&S* for film.

11 TYNAN, KENNETH. "American Blues: The Plays of Arthur Miller and Tennessee Williams." *Encounter* 2 (May):13–19.
      Begins by asserting they have little in common; says Miller "belongs to the thirties' tradition of social drama, while Williams looks ahead to a lyrical, balletic *Gesamtkunstwerk*." However, he claims they are linked by their affinity for "the bruised individual soul." His analysis of TW begins with premise that he "has no social commitments, but many aesthetic ones." Goes on to examine *GM, YTM, S&S, RT, SND, CR*, in brief. Reprinted: 1961.41, 1961.85.

1955

1 "All in One." *Theatre Arts* 39 (July):17.
      Brief synopsis of *27W*; cast list.

2 ASHTON, ROGER. "Correspondence." *New Republic* 132 (25 April):-23.
      A letter to editor taking issue with Eric Bentley for his opinions concerning *CAT* (*New Republic*, 11 April). TW is justified in writing the character of Brick as "vague"; states that Brick is not vague, but a multileveled personality. In a reply from Bentley, on same page, he states that TW may present vagueness "but he must not present it vaguely."

3 ATKINSON, BROOKS. "Theatre: 'Streetcar.'" *New York Times*, 4 March, p. 18.
      Review of *SND*. Brief comparative review between this production and the original. "Although Joanna Albus [director] has staged a thoroughly intelligible performance, there is no point

in pretending that the acting conveys the intricate mysteries of the script."

4 _____. "Theatre: Tennessee Williams' 'Cat on a Hot Tin Roof.'" *New York Times*, 25 March, p. 18.
Review of *CAT*. *CAT* "is Mr. Williams' finest drama. It faces and speaks the truth. . . . The play seems not to have been written. . . . It is the quintessence of life. It is the basic truth."

5 _____. "Theatre: 'Trouble in Tahiti,' Draper, '27 Wagons.'" *New York Times*, 20 April, p. 40.
Comments on *27W* as it appeared with two other plays in "All in One" at Playhouse; positive reaction.

6 _____. "Theatre: 2 By Williams." *New York Times*, 19 January, p. 23.
Review of *27W* and *LBLL*, New Orleans production. *27W* is cited as a good play with a faulty production; *LBLL* is praised as a play but its production is called "an artistic blunder."

7 _____. "A Triple Threat." *New York Times*, 24 April, sec. 2, p. 1.
Comments on *All in One*, three short plays at one theater—a short opera, a dance interlude, and *27W*. Praise for M. Stapleton.

8 _____. "Williams' 'Tin Roof.'" *New York Times*, 3 April, sec. 2, p. 1.
Review of *CAT*. "With the production of [*CAT*] Tennessee Williams has completed his first decade on Broadway. . . . He is not only a man of poetic sensibilities, he is a master dramatist with a terrifying knowledge of the secrets of the mind."

9 BEAUFORT, JOHN. "Tennessee Williams' *Cat*." *Christian Science Monitor*, 2 April, p. 36.
Review of *CAT*. TW "appears determined to continue as the contemporary American theater's poet laureate of degradation, decadence, and despair." *CAT* is a "descent into abnormality and wretchedness." Surveys acting and direction.

10 BECKER, WILLIAM. "Reflections on Three New Plays." *Hudson Review* 8 (Summer):268–72.

Review of *CAT*. "A really remarkable piece of work" and "the season's most solid dramatic success." Says it's based on "a curious dialectic of intense realism and rather eloquent fantasy." TW's "best play to date." Refers to its plot, dramatic method, complexities, problems of Kazan's interpretation.

11 BENTLEY, ERIC. Review of *CAT*. *New Republic* 132 (4 April):22.
    Review confines itself primarily to discussion of Kazan's methods of directing in this production.

12 _____. Review of *CAT*. *New Republic* 132 (11 April):28.
    Included with plot details is the reviewer's opinion that the production's intention is to "mislead" the audience by presenting a play "that might be called dirty" with attractive, wholesome actors and a sparkling-clean set. TW will find it hard to grow as a writer unless he begins to see "Truth and Sincerity" as things other than initially capitaled abstractions. Reprinted: 1968.2.

13 _____. Review of *27W*. *New Republic* 132 (2 May):22.
    "Williams at his best and worst." The "best" is another southern girl and the "worst" are the two men of the cast. Much praise for M. Stapleton.

14 BINGHAM, ROBERT. "Vittorio, Anna, and Tennessee." *Reporter* 13 (29 December):36–37.
    Review of film of *RT*. "The same burning intensity that Mr. Brando contributed to [*SND*] Miss Magnani has now brought to that author's [*RT*]." *RT* "noses out 'Marty' as the best picture of the year." Praises Magnani extensively.

15 BOLTON, WHITNEY. "'All in One' Often Stimulating Fare." New York *Morning Telegraph*, 21 April, p. 3.
    Review of *27W*. The play "can captivate those who nurture themselves on candidly and publicly stated obscenities." Demeaning of TW and his "aficionados."

16 _____. "Bringing Up a Point about Mr. Williams." New York *Morning Telegraph*, 28 April, p. 2.

"Mr. Williams has fallen into the low habit of writing dirty words on paper, instead of fences." Refers to *CAT* and *27W*.

17 _____. "Critics' Award to 'Tin Roof.'" New York *Morning Telegraph*, 13 April, pp. 1, 2.
Brief news item. Mentions Drama Critics' Circle Award to TW for *CAT*.

18 _____. "Powerful, Overwhelming New Drama by Tennessee Williams." New York *Morning Telegraph*, 26 March, p. 2.
Review of *CAT*. Refers to TW's "passion for truth . . . [and] miraculous ear. . . . Mr. Williams tears at his job."

19 "Book Notes: 'Cat on a Hot Tin Roof.'" *New York Herald Tribune*, 7 July, p. 19.
Brief mention of *CAT* being published.

20 BREIT, HARVEY. "In and Out of Books." *New York Times Book Review*, 3 July, p. 8.
Comments addressing TW's views on life; very brief.

21 CALTA, LOUIS. "Miss Roth Leaves 'Pleasure Dome.'" *New York Times*, 5 July, p. 36.
CAT voted best play for 1954–55 at Donaldson Awards.

22 _____. "Play by Williams Arrives Tonight." *New York Times*, 24 March, p. 39.
Brief preopening news release about *CAT*.

23 _____. "Theatre to Wrap 3 Bills 'All in One.'" *New York Times*, 19 April, p. 28.
27W to be one of three plays to be presented in one production.

24 *CR. New York Times*, 21 March, p. 21.
CR in West Germany fails to produce any positive comments from critics.

25 "'Cat on a Hot Tin Roof': Some Memorable Moments." *Theatre Arts* 39 (July):75–79, 96.

Pictorial essay. Cites TW's accomplishments; quotes TW on the play.

26 "'Cat on a Hot Tin Roof': Tennessee Williams' Play Probes into Nerve Racked Marriage." *Life* 38 (18 April):137–38, 140–42.
Photos and brief summary of who's who and what's what.

27 CHAPMAN, JOHN. "'Cat on a Hot Tin Roof' Beautifully Acted, But a Frustrating Drama." New York *Daily News*, 25 March, p. 65.
Review of *CAT*. "This time [TW] has outfrustrated himself by failing to remain in command of his own play.... [*CAT*] gets dull after three long acts.... a great deal of fine theatre ... but I wish there were more point and direction in the play."

28 COOPERMAN, STANLEY. Review of *OA*. *Nation* 180 (18 March):244.
Brief book review. Refers to its "luminous prose."

29 CROWTHER, BOSLEY. "Holiday Heapings." *New York Times*, 18 December, sec. 2, p. 3.
Review of film of *RT*. Comments that *RT* is worth seeing during holiday season. Praise for Magnani and Lancaster with details of basic story line.

30 ———. "Screen: Anna Magnani Triumphs in 'Rose Tattoo.'" *New York Times*, 13 December, p. 55.
Review of film of *RT*. Brief synopsis of plot; considerable praise for Magnani and Lancaster.

31 "Donates Pulitzer Cash." *New York Times*, 9 June, p. 33.
TW donates prize cash to Columbia University Graduate School of Journalism.

32 DOWNING, ROBERT. Review of film of *RT*. *Films in Review* 6 (December):527–28.
"In this picture the playwright's hopes for [Magnani] in the role are handsomely realized." Goes on to concentrate primarily on Magnani's performance.

33 "Drama Critics' Circle Makes Awards." *New York Times*, 16 May, p. 27.

Photo of TW with W. Kerr and caption announcing *CAT* as winner for best American play by Drama Critics' Circle.

34 "Drama Mailbag." *New York Times*, 3 April, sec. 2, p. 3.
Three letters to drama editor. Praise for *CAT* by A. Brooks and C.R. Luchsinger; negative letter from J. Fleming who calls it "Mouse on a Hot Tin Roof."

35 ENGLE, PAUL. "A Locomotive Named Reality." *New Republic* 132 (24 January):26–27.
Book review of *OA*. "Mr. Williams generally confines himself here to cruelty and its untrammeled expression. . . . [TW is] an interesting writer and a sensitive man. . . . Constant in Williams' work from the beginning has been the character who, ravaged with reality, retreats into fantasy. . . . Williams explores in fiction and the theatre the *true* world behind the apparent one."

36 "Final Score." *Time* 65 (23 May):54.
Details of *CAT*'s winning both Pulitzer Prize and Drama Critics' Circle Award.

37 "Finest of the Year." *Newsweek* 45 (4 April):54.
Review of *CAT*; refers to its "intellectual honesty and its attempt to whipsaw truth out of a resistant mass of humanity. . . . Far and away the finest play of the year."

38 FREEDLEY, GEORGE. "First Rate Volume of Short Stories by Tennessee Williams." New York *Morning Telegraph*, 13 April, p. 3.
Book review of *OA*. Refers to TW's "literary genius," his sense of "compassion." Brief.

39 ———. " 'Freud on Broadway' and Williams Comment; 'Cat' Is Discussed." New York *Morning Telegraph*, 11 April, pp. 2, 3.
Review of *CAT*. Relates TW to characterization of him in Sievers's book, *Freud on Broadway*; then draws the view out to an assessment of *CAT*.

40. ———. "Off Stage—and On." New York *Morning Telegraph*, 8 September, p. 3.
Brief mention of publication of *CAT*.

41   _____. " '27 Wagons' Highlights Pleasing Entertainment Program, All in One." New York *Morning Telegraph*, 6 May, p. 2.
> Brief review of *27W*. "The real thrill of the evening . . . a MUST show for Broadway playgoers."

42   FUNKE, LEWIS. "Gossip of the Rialto." *New York Times*, 3 April, sec. 2, p. 1.
> Reactions to *CAT* with quotes from other critics, W. Kerr, R. Watts, Jr.

43   GELB, ARTHUR. "News and Gossip Gathered on the Rialto." *New York Times*, 24 April, sec. 2, p. 1.
> Gossip. Burl Ives, appearing in *CAT*, will ride his motorcycle to work.

44   GERARD, ALBERT. "The Eagle and the Star: Symbolic Motifs in 'The Roman Spring of Mrs. Stone.'" *English Studies* 36 (August):145–53.
> Says publication of *RSMS* places TW "in the forefront of the movement in American fiction illustrated by such new-comers as Mr. Paul Bowles and Miss Elizabeth Pollett." Refers to Coleridge's theories on language as basis of its analysis; and claims *RSMS* "cannot by any means be considered a major work of art." Cites Mrs. Stone's shallowness and lack of "human significance." Accuses the novel of "oversimplifying." Thorough analysis of the character of Mrs. Stone and the symbolic devices used to illustrate her.

45   GIBBS, WOLCOTT. "Mixed Bag." *New Yorker* 31 (30 April):69–71.
> Review of *27W*. It's ambitious and "a comedy of almost matchless squalor and degradation." Compares it to *Tobacco Road*. "Written with amazing accuracy and gusto. . . . The production . . . is far less intelligent."

46   _____. "Something to Remember Us By." *New Yorker* 31 (2 April):68.
> Review of *CAT*. "An almost wholly admirable play . . . a piece of writing that is to be respected." Plot summary and analysis.

47 "Gifts to Columbia." *New York Herald Tribune*, 10 June, p. 12.
Brief news item. TW donates Pulitzer cash (for *CAT*) to
Columbia University's Graduate School of Journalism.

48 GRUTZNER, CHARLES. "Pulitzer Winners: 'Fable' and 'Cat on Hot
Tin Roof.'" *New York Times*, 3 May, p. 1.
Headline announcement of *CAT* as Pulitzer winner, plus names
of other winners.

49 HARTUNG, PHILIP T. "The Screen: Mourning Becomes Magnani."
Commonweal 63 (23 December):305.
"In writing the movie script [of *RT*], Tennessee Williams
cleaned up his original play somewhat, but it is still diffuse and
mainly a character portrait of a vain, superstitious woman who
is obsessed with sex." Praise for Magnani, without whom this
film "would not be worth the celluloid it's printed on."

50 HATCH, ROBERT. Review of *CAT*. *Nation* 180 (9 April):314–15.
Provides analysis of *CAT*'s themes. "I wish his plays weren't
so disagreeable." Felt like he'd "spent the evening with a group
of corpses."

51 _____. Review of film of *RT*. *Nation* 180 (7 January):18.
Brief. "Magnani is the most impressive female who has ever
appeared on the screen."

52 HAWKINS, WILLIAM. "Cat Yowls High on 'Hot Tin Roof.'" *New
York World-Telegram & Sun*, 25 March, p. 28.
Brief review of *CAT*. "The play functions like a snake charmer
... [it's] immensely effective."

53 HAYES, RICHARD. "The Stage: 'Cat on a Hot Tin Roof.'" *Commonweal* 62 (3 June):230–31.
Production is "full of a hard, richly-wrought and fluent poetry
of actuality, a vision of life arrested at the threshold of fantasy,
fixed in time yet extended out of reality into dream.... Here
we are at the center of Mr. Williams' moral universe: the chiaro-
scuro is most intricate, the dramatic surface infinitely plastic."

54 _____. "The Stage: A Modest Proposal." *Commonweal* 62 (10 June):255.
Review of "All in One," part of which was the play *27W*. Calls *27W* a "vicious, morbidly accomplished anecdote of Southern poor whites." Notes M. Stapleton's performance.

55 HENRY, W. BARKLIE. "Correspondence." *New Republic* 132 (18 April):22.
A letter to editor disagreeing with Eric Bentley's analysis (*New Republic*, 11 April) of *CAT*. Chides Bentley for not seeing the symbolism inherent in TW's work, and how TW's work compares to Strindberg's.

56 HERRIDGE, FRANCES. "Drama Notes." *New York Post*, 11 April, p. 38.
Brief item mentioning deletion of controversial lines in *CAT*.

57 HEWES, HENRY. "Broadway Postscript." *Saturday Review* 38 (14 May):26.
Review of *27W*. Brief; focuses on M. Stapleton's performance.

58 _____. "Critics on a 'Tin Roof.'" *Saturday Review* 38 (30 April)26.
Discusses awarding *CAT* the Drama Critics' Circle Award; how it should affect TW.

59 _____. "A Streetcar Named Mendacity." *Saturday Review* 38 (9 April):32–33.
Review of *CAT*. TW's "latest work is also disappointingly confusing and self-dissipating.... The action seems staccato and unfulfilling.... The resultant high level of theatrical excitement nevertheless leaves us with unanswered questions." Finds it "hot but indeterminate."

60 HOBE. Review of *CAT. Variety*, 30 March, p. 66.
TW's drama is "uncomfortably gabby and a bit obscure. It is an arresting, absorbing play." Notes "usual" emphasis on neurotics and sex, but suggests that play has "increasing interest in character and less in mere decadence." *CAT* "throbs with life and compulsion. Despite its vulgarity, prolixity, and opaqueness, it is undeniably engrossing."

61 "Inside Stuff—Legit." *Variety*, 13 July, p. 56.
      Concerns publication of *CAT*. Notes inclusion of famous "ele-
phant" story and omission of the "mendacity" scene. Also notes
that *CAT* was based on short story, "Three Players at a Summer
Game," by TW.

62 KASS, ROBERT. Review of film of *RT*. *Catholic World* 182 (De-
      cember):218.
      Brief. Says it's a showcase for Magnani. "The film is not with-
out serious shortcomings."

63 KEATING, JOHN. "Hot Afternoons Have Been in Mississippi." *Cue*
      24 (2 April):16.
      Review of *CAT*. "The sort of drama that ... belts you right
in the solar plexus. . . . [There is a] certain obscurity in its pattern, the author's seeming unwillingness to make his point
strongly and definite. . . . [But still it has] walloping dramatic
impact."

64 KELLEY, JAMES. "Madness and Decay." *New York Times Book Re-
      view*, 2 January, p. 5.
      Book review of *OA*. Notes shocking subject matter in "Desire
and the Black Masseur." Neutral review.

65 KERR, WALTER. " 'Cat on a Hot Tin Roof.' " *New York Herald
      Tribune*, 25 March, p. 12.
      Review of *CAT*. "A beautifully written, perfectly directed,
stunningly acted play of evasion. . . . Brilliant scenes, scenes of
sudden and lasting dramatic power."

66 ————. "A Secret Is Half-Told in Fountain of Words." *New
      York Herald Tribune*, 3 April, sec. 4, p. 1.
      Review of *CAT*. Questions the play's lack of clarity; re-pre-
sents the praise of his initial review; surveys significance of the
major characters; "Mr. Williams is naturally not unaware of
his own powers."

67 KINNAIRD, CLARK. "Literary Gems in Capsule." *New York Journal-
      American*, 9 October, p. 52L.
      Brief mention of publication of *CAT*.

68   KNIGHT, ARTHUR. "The Magnificent Magnani." *Saturday Review* 38 (10 December):25.
      Review of film of *RT*. TW "has written a screenplay of real substance and mature insight." Focuses primarily on Magnani, but praises TW and D. Mann for creating a movie worthy of the actress.

69   LEE, W. "Correspondence." *Reporter* 12 (30 June):4.
      Rebuttal of Mannes's *Reporter* (19 May) article. Focuses on nature of tragedy itself, violence, TW's optimism.

70   LEWIS, THEOPHILUS. Review of *27W*. *America* 93 (14 May):193.
      "A miniature 'Tobacco Road' without the social impact . . . , another play in which Mr. Williams prefers to be avenger rather than dramatist." Notes good performances by Myron McCormick and M. Stapleton.

71   McCARTEN, JOHN. "Adeste Fideles." *New Yorker* 31 (24 December):52.
      Review of film of *RT*; claims that Magnani was made for the role—lavish praise of her acting; brief reference to others in cast. Plot summary.

72   McCLAIN, JOHN. "Bad, Bawdy and Mixed-Up." *New York Journal-American,* 11 April, p. 17.
      Discusses TW's use of sex in *CAT*; analyzes the same in *Bus Stop*.

73   ————. "Drama Socks and Shocks." *New York Journal-American,* 25 March, p. 20.
      Review of *CAT*. More "compelling characters" than in previous plays. "But . . . the entire proceedings have a strange and somehow unsavory flavor; there is an absence of warmth and tenderness." Praises production.

74   ————. "Show's Prolific Cast: Bathtub Stranger." *New York Journal-American,* 13 May, p. 25.
      Brief mention of TW's travel plans and publication of *CAT*.

75 McCord, Bert. "Theater News: 'Cat' Gets Award of Critics' Circle." *New York Herald Tribune*, 13 April, p. 22.
   Brief announcement of *CAT* winning Drama Critics' Circle Award.

76 "The Magnificent Drab." *Life* 39 (28 November):139–40, 143–44.
   Review of film of *RT*. Praises Magnani: "she does ample justice to Williams' fine adaptation of his play." Brief text, many photos.

77 "Magnificent Magnani." *Newsweek* 46 (26 December): 65–66.
   Review of film of *RT*. Mainly a praise of Magnani's performance; the film prospers because of her; quotes popular criticism on her performance.

78 Mannes, Marya. "The Morbid Magic of Tennessee Williams." *Reporter* 12 (19 May):41–43.
   TW's "crises [are] never common"; he is "a theater magician" who can hold an audience in "a common trance." Claims the "emotional exhaustion" experienced after seeing his plays "is not catharsis" but "shock treatment." Focuses on *CAT*. Discusses TW's role as "poet," his fascination with nightmare. Reprinted: 1969.26.

79 "M-G-M Buys 'Cat on a Hot Tin Roof' as a Starring Vehicle for Grace Kelly." *New York Times*, 10 July, sec. 1, p. 52.
   News of purchase of film rights to *CAT*.

80 Mitgang, Herbert. "Burl Ives: Ballads to Big Daddys." *New York Times*, 17 April, sec. 2, p. 3.
   Profile on Burl Ives. References made to role in *CAT*.

81 "Mixed Fiction." *Time* 65 (3 January):76.
   Book review of *OA*. "This collection ... nears the scent of human garbage." Thoroughly negative, brief.

82 Nathan, George Jean. "Tennessee Williams and Sex." *New York Journal-American*, 2 April, p. 16.
   Refers to TW's "almost maniacal preoccupation with the more emphatic impulses and sensational aspects of sex ... [of his]

immaturity and torment." Focuses specifically on *CAT* in relation to this theory.

83 "A New Tennessee Williams Heroine." *New York Herald Tribune*, 20 March, sec. 4, p. 1.
    Publicity photos of *CAT*, focus on Barbara Bel Geddes.

84 "New York Drama Critics' Awards." *Times* (London), 22 April, p. 17.
    News item. *CAT* chosen as best play of the year in New York.

85 "New York: Stage for All the World." *New York Times Magazine*, 30 October, p. 29.
    Photo of Magnani in starring role in film of *RT*.

86 PEDEN, WILLIAM. "Broken Apollos and Blasted Dreams." *Saturday Review* 38 (8 January):11–12.
    Book review of *OA*. Mixed; some "have greatness," others seem "like dead mackerel." Finds "Portrait of a Girl in Glass" most moving.

87 "Pulitzer Prizes." *New York Times*, 3 May, p. 30.
    Brief news item on Pulitzer Prizes—mentions *CAT* as winner for drama.

88 "Pulitzer Prizes Awarded: Williams' 'Cat on a Hot Tin Roof' Wins." *New York Herald Tribune*, 3 May, pp. 1, 17.
    News item. Mentions *CAT*'s having previously won New York Drama Critics' Circle Award for 1954–55; chosen from field of thirty-five plays.

89 Review of *CAT. Theatre Arts* 39 (June):18–19.
    Brief; primarily a synopsis of play.

90 Review of *CAT. Time* 65 (4 April):98.
    "Shows again what potentialities its author has and demonstrates that power. But it remains a demonstration rather than an achievement. . . . His own feelings, often intemperate, work against him. . . . The play, closing on a lame, stagey note, lacks stature."

91 Review of *27W*. *Time* 65 (2 May):78.
    "For Tennessee Williams life had dirty fingernails from the outset." Praises cast; negative about play.

92 Review of *27W*. *Variety*, 27 April, pp. 64, 70.
    Brief; plot details and praise for M. Stapleton and McCormick.

93 "Rev. Walter E. Dakin." *New York Times*, 16 February, p. 29.
    Obituary for TW's grandfather.

94 " 'The Rose Tattoo.' " *New York Times Magazine*, 10 April, p. 47.
    Publicity photos, plus captions, of film of *RT*.

95 " 'The Rose Tattoo' in Key West." *Harper's Bazaar* 89 (February):124–25.
    Brief interview with TW. He discusses how Key West figures into the filming of the play *RT*.

96 ROTH, ROBERT. "Tennessee Williams in Search of a Form." *Chicago Review* 9 (Summer):86–94.
    Finds *OA* "embracing post-Freudian fables, psychotic fantasies, literal short stories, juvenilia, and resounding duds." Calls attention to its "vacillating formal experimentation with marvelously unique materials." Finds TW "remarkably unsure of himself in handling narrative," and notes "difficult aesthetic problems" caused by subject matter. Analyzes the stories' worth, use of heroes, "dark" qualities.

97 SIEVERS, W. DAVID. "Tennessee Williams and Arthur Miller." In *Freud on Broadway: A History of Psychoanalysis and the American Drama*. New York: Hermitage House; Toronto: George J. McLeod, pp. 370–88.
    "Of all the younger American playwrights, none is more characteristic of his generation, more psychoanalytic-oriented, or more provocative of popular controversy than Tennessee Williams." Discusses his background, his use of "sheltered Southerners," use of sex, violence, mental disorientation, God-images. Focuses on *GM, SND, IR, S&S, RT, CR*. Reprinted: 1961.41, 1971.19.

98   "16-mm. Festival Names Winners." *New York Times*, 7 April, p. 23.
     News item. Anecdote is deleted from *CAT*; rumor suggests
     avoidance of difficulties with Department of Licenses as reason.

99   SKELTON, B.J. "Stirring Drama of the Delta Told in Hit Play."
     Clarksdale (Miss.) *Press Register*, 23 July, p. 2.
     Book review of *CAT*. Relates the plot to a hometown (Clarks-
     dale) view.

100 "Sketches of the Pulitzer Prize Winners in Journalism, Letters
     and Music for 1955." *New York Times*, 3 May, p. 28.
     Biographical sketch of TW. Mentions *CSB* and *CAND* as TW's
     first productions.

101 "A Spade Is a Spade Is a Spade." *Variety*, 30 March, p. 63.
     Brief; announcing various critics' disapproval of the "salty"
     language used in *CAT*.

102 STAVROU, CONSTANTINE N. "The Neurotic Heroine in Tennessee
     Williams." *Literature and Psychology* 5 (February):26–34.
     Claims that all heroines, previous to *CR*, sustain a "disorder
     to the nervous system [which] results from some maladjustment
     of the superego-id balance." Finds Laura, Alma, and Blanche
     to be "obviously portraits of the same woman observed at differ-
     ent stages of her regressive neurosis." Notes similarity of tech-
     nique in Faulkner. Claims that Laura "remains the most tenuous"
     of Williams' characters. Also examines how "deliberate" Williams'
     use of neurotic heroines might be.

103 "Tennessee Williams's New Play." *Times* (London), 22 April,
     p. 16.
     News item. *CAT* scored "triumph" in New York.

104 "Theatrical Devices." *Times Literary Supplement*, 4 March, p. 130.
     Brief book review of *RT*. TW's "worst play to date . . . a glori-
     fication of sexual love in the person of a demented woman."

105 WALSH, MOIRA. Review of film of *RT*. *America* 94 (24 Decem-
     ber):362.
     Notes restraint placed on TW as scenarist, resulting in a film

better than original play: "it is a fact that blatantly uninhibited dialogue, while true to life, makes for bad art.... [*RT*] is probably the earthiest film ever to come out of Hollywood." Notes striking and convincing performance by Magnani, for whom TW wrote the play: "Magnani's performance is one of the greatest ever recorded on film."

106 WATERS, ARTHUR B. "Tennessee Williams Ten Years Later." *Theatre Arts* 39 (July):72–73, 96.

Interview-commentary. Attempts to trace the history of TW since *GM* of ten years earlier; TW discusses *GM, CAT, SND, YTM, OD*; his themes and aims.

107 WATTS, RICHARD, JR. "Elia Kazan, a Set and Some Actors." *New York Post*, 17 April, p. 24.

Brief item. Discusses Kazan's role in success of *CAT*.

108 _____. "The Impact of Tennessee Williams." *New York Post*, 25 March, p. 57.

Review of *CAT*. "The main impression that emerges ... is that of enormous theatrical power ... a grimly realistic play." Comments on its "exotic lyricism" maintained in midst of the "vulgar, morbid, neurotic and ugly."

109 _____. "Random Notes on This and That." *New York Post*, 17 May, p. 40.

Mention of deletion of lines in *CAT* production.

110 _____. "Returning to Tennessee Williams." *New York Post*, 10 April, p. 16.

Review of *CAT*. It's "not only exciting in the theater but provides food for contemplation that reviewers can argue over." Comments on Walter Kerr's finding it "elusive and ambiguous." Discusses its "sometimes frank and startling language."

111 _____. "Speaking of Tennessee Williams." *New York Post*, 3 April, p. 20.

Review of *CAT*. The play "has the driving power of a sledgehammer." Praises it as among the "few works of the modern stage that can be mentioned in the same class with it," but he is "discontented with its rather equivocal conclusions."

112 "Williams' Drama Cited by Critics." *New York Times*, 13 April, p. 33.
     CAT voted best American play by Drama Critics' Circle; brief comment on TW's background and list of judges and their votes.

113 WOOD, THOMAS. "Anna Magnani in Movie by Tennessee Williams." *New York Herald Tribune*, 23 January, sec. 4, p. 3.
     On *RT*; news item about filming in Key West.

114 "'World's Greatest Actress.'" *Time* 66 (19 December):94, 96, 98.
     Review of film of *RT*. Talks of its "sideshow" image; analyzes a few of its themes; considerable discussion of the Magnani performance.

115 "Wrong Track." *Newsweek* 45 (31 January):81.
     Review of *LBLL*. New Orleans staging of work as opera; "critics agreed it might better have remained a play."

116 WYATT, EUPHEMIA VAN RENSSELAER. Review of *CAT*. *Catholic World* 181 (May):147–48.
     CAT amounts to a "most approved nightmare," whose "power of an almost uncanny understanding of human nature ought to have been used for a nobler purpose.... The only thing of beauty and dignity ... is the set."

117 ————. Review of *27W*. *Catholic World* 181 (June):227.
     Deeply concerned with the suggestive and near-obscene content. Praises the production *only* for M. Stapleton's performance: "every word, every move, the awkward feet, the restless hands, the silly giggle are pertinent to the part."

118 ZINSSER, WILLIAM K. "Screen: 'The Rose Tattoo.'" *New York Herald Tribune*, 13 December, p. 20.
     Review of film of *RT*; plot summary; mentions TW wanting Magnani in original Broadway production of *RT*; "the film moves slowly, and its scenes seem disconnected."

119 ZOLOTOW, MAURICE. "The Season on and off Broadway." *Theatre Arts* 39 (June):22–23, 93.
Discusses TW as "a dramatist of greatness" and "his special vision of the world." Refers to *CAT* ("was written not by Tennessee Williams but by Stanley Kowalski"), Kazan's hand in it.

120 ZOLOTOW, SAM. " 'Cat' Drops Elephant." *New York Times*, 8 April, p. 18.
News item. Why elephant anecdote was deleted from *CAT*; also notice of TW going to Key West.

121 ⸺. "Williams Forms New Stage Team." *New York Times*, 28 October, p. 20.
News that TW will produce *OD* with Audrey Wood, under the name "Williams Wood."

1956

1 "Alan Directing Helen." *New York Herald Tribune*, 26 October, p. 14.
News item. Alan Schneider directing Helen Hayes in City Center revival of *GM*.

2 ATKINSON, BROOKS. "One Old: One New." *New York Times*, 2 December, sec. 2, p. 1.
Review of *GM*. Positive comments on *GM* revival with H. Hayes singled out positively. Praise for production and a wish the revival would last longer.

3 ⸺. "Theatre: Early Williams." *New York Times*, 22 November, p. 50.
Review of *GM*. Positive comments on revival of *GM* with brief comparison of TW's work in 1945 and his work in 1956. "Although Mr. Williams has written some overwhelming dramas since 1945, he has not written anything so delicate and perceptive.... To see it again is to see how much he has changed."

4 ⸺. "The Theatre: 'Streetcar' Is Revived." *New York Times*, 16 February, p. 24.

Comments favorably on *SND* revival with the exception that Bankhead was wrongly cast as Blanche.

5   " 'Baby Doll.' " *New York Times Magazine*, 22 April, p. 47.
    Publicity photos of filming of *BD* in Benoit, Mississippi.

6   " 'Baby Doll' Booked in 1,118 U.S. Cities." *New York Times*, 28 December, p. 17.
    Brief. Information as per title.

7   " 'Baby Doll' Cancelled." *New York Times*, 20 December, p. 36.
    News item; film of *BD* was canceled at a theater in Indianapolis.

8   BAKER, PETER. Review of film of *RT*. *Films and Filming* 1 (March):16.
    Brief. TW "has produced a masterly screenplay in which comedy and tragedy coexist. . . . Compared with the average run of pictures, this is a notable screen achievement."

9   BECKLEY, PAUL. "Three One-Act Plays Open at Cherry Lane Theater." *New York Herald Tribune*, 29 October, p. 10.
    Brief review of *TPC*. "Mr. Williams' poignantly bitter little offering."

10 BENTLEY, ERIC. "Camino Unreal." In *Dramatic Event: An American Chronicle*. Boston: Beacon Press, pp. 105–10.
    Reprint of 1953.4.

11 "Blunt and Banned." *Newsweek* 48 (17 December):106.
    Review of film *BD*. Notes the dispute with Legion of Decency and producers of *BD*; also, brief film review.

12 BOLTON, WHITNEY. "Saroyan Comes Off Best at Cherry Lane." New York *Morning Telegraph*, 30 October, p. 2.
    Review of *TPC*. "Mr. Williams, a fellow who likes to poke about in the middens of life and find some sort of meaning in the trash of existence."

13 "Book Notes: 'Baby Doll.' " *Reporter* 15 (20 September):48.
    Brief book review of *BD*. Tends toward negative.

14   "Books—Authors." *New York Times*, 4 June, p. 26.
     Announcement that *IWC* and original screenplay *BD* will be released as books; film of *BD* to be released by Warner Bros.

15   CALTA, LOUIS. "Williams Drama May Play Palace." *New York Times*, 23 August, p. 24.
     News item. Palace is being sought for production of *OD* with Magnani as star.

16   CAMERON, KATE. " 'Baby Doll' Risks Legion's Wrath." New York *Sunday News*, 2 December, sec. 2, p. 3.
     Details of censorship fight with Code Authority, Warner Bros., Kazan and Legion of Decency. Refers to filming and casting business.

17   "Cardinal Scores 'Baby Doll' Film." *New York Times*, 17 December, p. 28.
     News item. Cardinal Spellman denounces *BD* at St. Patrick's Cathedral. Quotes his sermon.

18   "Cardinal Spellman and 'Baby Doll.'" *New York Post*, 18 December, p. 31.
     Takes Spellman to task for his conjoining moral and "patriotic" duties.

19   CARR, WILLIAM H.A., and LOGAN, MALCOLM. "Kazan, Tennessee Williams Reply to Spellman Attack on 'Baby Doll.'" *New York Post*, 17 December, pp. 5, 42.
     Primarily Kazan's retort, but mentions TW's "criticiz[ing] those who set themselves up as censors."

20   "Carroll Baker: 'Baby Doll.'" *Look* 20 (25 December):95, 97–98.
     Pictorial review of film *BD*. Plot synopsis and briefest statement.

21   "Cat to Close." *New York Herald Tribune*, 10 November, p. 6.
     Brief news item. *CAT* ending its run on Broadway.

22   CHAPMAN, JOHN. " 'Glass Menagerie' Is Still Aglow with Rare and Tender Beauty." New York *Daily News*, 23 November, p. 60.

Review of *GM*. *GM* "is Tennessee Williams' finest play." The entire cast gives it a "tender and lovely performance. . . . This . . . is Williams' affectionate, compassionate and poetic nocturne. . . . Miss Hayes simply cannot do anything wrong on a stage."

23 _____. "Miss Bankhead Makes a Novelty Out of 'Streetcar Named Desire.'" New York *Daily News*, 17 February, p. 46.

Review of *SND*. Bankhead "can't quite manage to be the troubled and tremulous nymph whom the author created" in Blanche. Mentions other performances, but summarizes the play as being "a less exalted work than when I saw it first performed."

24 "Chapman Joins Cast." *New York Herald Tribune*, 6 November, p. 13.

Brief news item. Lonny Chapman cast in City Center revival of *GM*.

25 "City Center Season." *Theatre Arts* 40 (April):24.

Brief review of *SND*. Focuses on Bankhead performance (Blanche).

26 COLEMAN, ROBERT. "City Center Offers 'Glass Menagerie.'" New York *Daily Mirror*, 22 November, p. 28.

Review of *GM*. Disparages the character of Amanda, but admits that Hayes "etches . . . such a well-meaning bore (Amanda) that you feel sorry for her." *GM* "is a masterly study in frustration."

27 _____. "'Streetcar' Rolls Again with Talu at Helm." New York *Daily Mirror*, 17 February, p. 30.

Review of *SND*. "A dreary dramatic exercise" written in "pseudo-poetic terms." Praises Bankhead because "she satirized it [*SND*] unmercifully, stimulating gales of laughter." She brought "grand manner" to a "minor play." She wasn't Blanche DuBois; she was "Talu bent on spell-binding an audience."

28 COOK, ALTON. "'Baby Doll' Garbed in Squalor." *New York World-Telegram & Sun*, 19 December, p. 18.

Review of film *BD*. "A story harshly written . . . a striking achievement in acting, writing and direction." Plot summary.

29 CROWTHER, BOSLEY. "Screen: Streetcar on Tobacco Road." *New York Times*, 19 December, p. 40.
Review of film *BD*. Negative comments, but admits it was written "cleverly." Likes "pictorial composition."

30 "Daly Is Definite." *New York Herald Tribune*, 5 November, p. 20.
News item. James Daly will play in City Center revival of *GM*.

31 DAVIS, HELEN. "Gifted Aimlessness." *Mainstream* 9 (November):50–51.
Book review of *BD*. Praises the "interesting insight into the creative method of Tennessee Williams," but laments his "aimless artistic solutions."

32 DONNELLY, TOM. "Through a Glass, Not Darkly." *New York World-Telegram*, 23 November, p. 22.
Review of *GM*. Possible that Amanda "is [TW's] finest character creation," but cites a critical problem: Hayes "does not miss one of the humorous possibilities in the role, but she scarcely touches on any of the tragic implications." She "misses at least half of Mr. Williams' intention, and, unfortunately, the more significant half."

33 DOWNING, ROBERT. "From the Cat-Bird Seat." *Theatre Annual, 1956* 14:46–50.
On *CAT*. "It seems that what has been considered the playwright's theatre in America is becoming more and more frequently the theatre of the director and designer. Perhaps no production better illustrates this trend than" TW's *CAT*. Brief description of play with many details of the set design, staging, props, and designer Jo Mielziner.

34 _____. Review of *BD*. *Films in Review* 7 (December):534–35.
Review of the script as a book. Calls it "self-conscious, truncated, . . . another page from Williams' sordid album of bayou bavardage."

35 "Drama Mailbag." *New York Times*, 11 March, sec. 2, p. 3.
Letters (including one by T. Bankhead) concerning the TW

letter of previous Sunday's "Mailbag," (4 March), in which TW participated in the Bankhead-Blanche controversy.

36 ESTEROW, MILTON. " 'Baby Doll' in Dixie and Flatbush." *New York Times*, 26 February, sec. 2, p. 5.
    News and gossip about the filming of *BD* in Benoit, Mississippi.

37 "Festive Yuletide Saluted by Rabbi." *New York Times*, 23 December, sec. 1, p. 17.
    Lengthy article about Rabbi Dr. William F. Rosenblum, who mentions briefly the controversy surrounding *BD* and Cardinal Spellman's order to Catholics to avoid the film.

38 "Film Raises $40,000 for Actors Studio." *New York Times*, 19 December, p. 39.
    News item, brief. Premiere of *BD* raises money. List of celebrities who attended.

39 FITCH, ROBERT E. "La Mystique de la merde." *New Republic* 135 (3 September):17–18.
    Calls the mystique "a brand of piety . . . the deification of dirt, or the apotheosis of ordure . . . mud mysticism." Lumps TW with other authors; cites *CR* as primary example.

40 FITTS, DUDLEY. "Talking in Verse." *New York Times Book Review*, 8 July, p. 10.
    Book review of *IWC*. Generally negative, but admits some of TW's verse is good.

41 "Florida Premiere for New Tennessee Williams Play." *Theatre Arts* 40 (August):66–67.
    Preview notes on *SB*. Mentions its reception in Miami and TW's efforts to get it ready for Broadway.

42 FREEDLEY, GEORGE. "Freudians Both." *Players* 32 (March): 134–35.
    Discusses Inge along with TW, showing their similar interests and qualities as playwrights. "Tennessee Williams is the poet as he was when he began his scintillating writing career. . . . Since Eugene O'Neill, no American writer has so caught international theatre interest."

43 _____. "Williams 'Baby Doll' Authentic." New York *Morning Telegraph*, 1 October, p. 2.

Book review of *BD*. "One of the most sensuous pieces of writing that America's sensuous playwright has composed up to this time."

44 FUNKE, LEWIS. "Gossip of the Rialto." *New York Times*, 27 May, sec. 2, p. 1.

Gossip about TW and *SB*, with a one-sentence synopsis of play. Mentions production of *OD* being postponed because Brando not available.

45 _____. "Theatre: 3 Premieres." *New York Times*, 29 October, p. 34.

Positive comments on *TPC* with brief synopsis and praise for S. Kolb as star.

46 GEOR. "Three Premieres." *Variety*, 14 November, p. 74.

Mentions *TPC* as one of three one-acters not previously professionally produced in New York; "the audience is left sufficiently limp."

47 GIBBS, WOLCOTT. "Two Views of the South." *New Yorker* 32 (25 February):90, 92–93.

Review of *SND*. Emphasizes Bankhead performance ("one of this great woman's rare mistakes"); analysis of the Blanche character, as a character; assault of opening night audience.

48 *GM. New York Herald Tribune*, 19 October, p. 14.

Brief news item. Helen Hayes will play Amanda in City Center revival of *GM*.

49 *GM. New York Herald Tribune*, 1 November, p. 23.

Brief news item. Rehearsal information on City Center revival of *GM*.

50 *GM. New York Herald Tribune*, 12 November, p. 16.

Brief news item. Cast list for *GM* City Center revival.

51 HARTLEY, ANTHONY. "Poetry or Pistol." *Spectator* 197 (14 December):879–80.

Book review of *SND*, *27W*, *CAT*, *CR*, in one volume, at time
of their publication in England. Discusses TW's handling of
violence, sexuality, sadism, language ("the basic reason for Mr.
Williams's partial failure as a dramatist").

52 HARTUNG, PHILIP T. Review of film *BD*. *Commonweal* 65 (28 December):335.
Lengthy plot summary. Calls TW a "master of the perverse. . . .
Williams and Kazan work well together throughout—but to what
purpose? Who is the audience for this flaunting of traditional
morality, for this unrelieved study of decay? For whom was this
unhealthy film made?"

53 HATCH, ROBERT. Review of film *BD*. *Nation* 183 (29 December):567.
"Its dirtiness consists in the fact that it only teases with sex. . . .
For the picture, [TW] has complicated and 'humanized' the tale
[of *27W*]. . . . [It] betrays again Williams' infantile attitude toward sex." Does praise it, however, as a well-made film.

54 HAWKINS, WILLIAM. "Tallulah Brilliant in 'Streetcar' Role." *New
York World-Telegram & Sun*, 16 February, p. 20.
Review of *SND*. Singles out Bankhead for "one of the most
extraordinarily shattering performances of our time." Says nothing of the production or play, save for the character of Blanche
being "the most complex, tricky and demanding role in modern
dramatic literature."

55 ———. "Tallulah Hits 'Streetcar'—Head On." *New York World-
Telegram & Sun*, 11 February, p. 9.
Preopening announcement of the revival. Bankhead inter-
viewed about her role as Blanche.

56 "Hello from Bertha." *Theatre Arts* 40 (November):66.
Photo of TW plus caption. TW shown "attending the first play
he ever wrote" at a drama workshop in New York.

57 HEWES, HENRY. "The Boundaries of Tennessee." *Saturday Review*
39 (29 December):23–24.
Review of film *BD*. Companion piece to Arthur Knight's an-

alysis of the film in light of the controversy. Discusses TW's assets and faults; refers to his "greatness of outlook."

58   _____. "Helen of Sparta." *Saturday Review* 39 (8 December):29.
     Review of *GM*. Praises Hayes but states that the play "emerges less as a vehicle for a fabulous and unforgettable actress than as one of the truly marvelous works in our American dramatic album."

59   _____. "Off Their Trolleys." *Saturday Review* 39 (3 March):22.
     Brief review of *SND*. Praises Bankhead's performance in this revival production.

60   HIVNOR, MARY. Review of *CAT*. *Kenyon Review* 18 (Winter):125–26.
     Philosophic analysis of theme and plot. References to sinister qualities, silence, the charm of Brick, mendacity, loneliness. Claims *CAT* "is sensational *and* reverent." Says the Pulitzer Prize encouraged the finding of sensitive people as "awkward, crippled, or homosexual, and usually inarticulate besides."

61   HOUGHTON, NORRIS. "Off-Broadway Challenges Broadway." *New York Times Magazine,* 11 November, pp. 30–36.
     Several of TW's plays mentioned in article about growing prosperity of off-Broadway productions.

62   HUME, ROD. "New Baby." *Films and Filming* 2 (December):9.
     Review of film *BD*. Focuses on Baker and her performance. Plot details and information on its filming as well as Kazan's comments on its box office potential.

63   "Kennedy's Chain Bars 'Baby Doll.'" *New York Times*, 27 December, p. 21.
     BD banned by chain of twenty movie theaters owned by Joseph P. Kennedy.

64   KERR, WALTER. "'The Glass Menagerie.'" *New York Herald Tribune*, 22 November, p. 20.
     "The evening is entrancing on quite a few counts": Helen Hayes, the writing, A. Schneider. "In short, this is a beautiful production of a beautiful play, and what are you waiting for?"

65   _____. " 'Streetcar Named Desire.' " *New York Herald Tribune*,
      16 February, p. 14.
          Review of *SND*. Focus on Bankhead's performance—praise and
      criticism. Faults her chiefly for a lack of "self-deceit," because
      "Blanche . . . is a girl who deceives herself." Overall, a "far from
      satisfactory performance."

66   KNIGHT, ARTHUR. "The Williams-Kazan Axis." *Saturday Review* 39
      (29 December):22–23.
          Review of film *BD*. A companion piece to Henry Hewes'
      analysis of same movie, in light of its controversy. Praises Kazan
      and the project; sidesteps the controversy.

67   LOLLI, GIORGIO. "Alcoholism and Homosexuality in Tennessee
      Williams's 'Cat on a Hot Tin Roof.' " *Quarterly Journal of Studies
      on Alcohol* 17 (September):543–53.
          Physician's view of *CAT*, with quotes from Tillich, Buber, San-
      tayana, Russell, and Marcuse to substantiate the author's position.

68   LUMLEY, FREDERICK. "Broadway Cortege—Tennessee Williams and
      Arthur Miller." In *Trends in 20th Century Drama*. London: Ox-
      ford University Press, pp. 184–93.
          Cites TW's themes as embracing "a typically American pessi-
      mism, the result of a deliberate optimism *manque*." Finds TW
      "the poet who delights in language and symbolism and a non-
      naturalistic style of production," and that he and Miller both
      "are writing American folk tragedies of the twentieth century."
      Discusses TW's use of dream, symbols, theme of normality (and
      its contrary); refers to *GM, SND, CR, RT, CAT*. Frequent com-
      parison to Miller and the standard predecessors.

69   McCARTEN, JOHN. "Life among the Lintheads." *New Yorker* 32
      (29 December):59–60.
          Review of film *BD*. Discusses TW's "drollery" and the explora-
      tion of the humor resident in southern decay; TW "has produced
      a highly original mutation."

70   McCARTHY, MARY. "A Streetcar Called Success." In *Sights and
      Spectacles, 1937–1956*. New York: Farrar, Straus, & Cudahy, pp.
      131–35.
          Reprint of 1948.42. Reprinted: 1963.38.

71 McClain, John. "Amiable Time Provided by One-Act Trio." *New York Journal-American*, 29 October, p. 10.
Brief review of *TPC*. Comments limited to plot summary.

72 _____. "Tallu Gives a Sunday Try." *New York Journal-American*, 16 February, p. 18.
Review of *SND*. Praises Bankhead; *SND* "suffered somehow through the passage of time. . . . perhaps we've had too many people, including Tennessee Williams, trying to write like Tennessee Williams, with very little success."

73 _____. "Williams' Gem Brilliantly Led by Miss Hayes." *New York Journal-American*, 23 November, p. 22.
Review of *GM*. Praises Hayes as giving "a fierce force to the author's words which was never there before." TW has talent for "both forthright and forceful writing and [a] preoccupation with symbolism. . . . A fine production."

74 McCord, Bert. "Maureen Stapleton Set for Williams' New Play." *New York Herald Tribune*, 2 November, p. 12.
Casting notice for *GM* revival at City Center.

75 _____. "Williams Will Produce His Own Play." *New York Herald Tribune*, 29 August, p. 12.
News item. TW and Audrey Wood to produce *OD*; casting news; history of *OD* traced back to *BA*.

76 Marcorelles, Louis. Review of film *BD*. *Sight and Sound* 26 (Winter):150–51.
Analysis of character Baby Doll as a symbol of "wanton sexuality." Synopsis of script. Comments on Kazan's filming techniques.

77 Marowitz, Charles. Review of *BD*. *Village Voice*, 12 September, pp. 9, 10.
Brief book review. Praises the accomplishment.

78 Nathan, George Jean. "Williams on a Hot Tin Dollar Sign: Reflections after the Curtains Fall." *Esquire* 45 (April):47–48.
Discussses TW's "talent," his "genius," and "his poetic gift."

79 "Old Play in Manhattan." *Time* 67 (27 February):61.
    Review of *SND*. Focuses negatively on Bankhead's perfor-
    mance as Blanche in this revival.

80 PEPER, WILLIAM. "Tennessee Does a Quick Switch." *New York
    World-Telegram & Sun,* 24 May, p. 20.
    News item, about shelving *OD* and work on *SB*. Also writing
    screen adaptation of *S&S*.

81 PHELPS, ROBERT. *B.D. National Review* 2 (15 September):20.
    Brief book review of *BD*. "Tricks, tricks, tricks; and not a
    shred of honest feeling."

82 "Pike Backs Right to See 'Baby Doll.'" *New York Times,* 24 De-
    cember, p. 14.
    Bishop James A. Pike, dean of St. John's, replies to Cardinal
    Spellman that *BD* should not be suppressed, but its issues an-
    swered.

83 "A Play in Progress: Mr. Tennessee Williams's New Work." *Times*
    (London), 11 August, p. 10.
    News item. TW is revising *SB* for next season on Broadway.

84 PRATLEY, GERALD. "Recorded Filmusic." *Films in Review* 7 (April):
    182–83.
    Discusses the style of the music used in the film of *RT*. Relates
    to various parts of the film's theme.

85 "The Production Code and 'Baby Doll.'" *America* 96 (29 Decem-
    ber):367.
    Describes the "streamlining" of the movie code, and lists
    passages from the code specifically concerning *BD*. Seems to ap-
    prove code revision, but asks what this or any other code means
    in practice.

86 PROUSE, DEREK. Review of film of *RT. Sight and Sound* 25 (Spring):
    194–96.
    Focuses on the sexuality portrayed in the film. *RT* is "clearly
    the work of a superior craftsman." Praises Magnani.

100

87 PRYOR, THOMAS. "How to Police the Movies Is Under Debate Again." *New York Times*, 23 December, sec. 4, p. 8.
Concerning the issue of censorship within the film industry in addition to pressure from outside groups. *BD* and Cardinal Spellman are cited as main examples.

88 QUINT, BERT. "Spellman Takes to Pulpit to Forbid 'Baby Doll.'" *New York Herald Tribune*, 17 December, pp. 1, 15.
Summation of Cardinal Spellman's position on *BD*. Also contains text of Spellman's sermon; Kazan's reply; TW's reply.

89 "A Quiz for Kazan." *Theatre Arts* 40 (November):30–32, 89.
Interview with Elia Kazan. Discusses making *BD*, TW's appeal, TW's feeling for films.

90 Review of film *BD*. *Time* 68 (24 December):61.
"Just possibly the dirtiest American-made motion picture." Mentions Catholic furor; refers to its "pica-risque comedy."

91 ROSSELLI, JOHN. "A Moral Play." *Spectator* 196 (2 March):284.
Review of *CAT*, at time of its publication in England. "This is Mr. Williams's best play and his most moral yet." Says that the Lord Chamberlain would ban it in England; plot details; TW has "grown up" from what was his status in writing *SND*. Refers to Big Daddy as a "Homeric figure" and that TW's handling of him is "Ibsen like." Additional reference to the Broadway (Kazan) production.

92 SELDIN, JOEL. "Tennessee Williams' 'Baby Doll': Legion of Decency Says Film Censors Break Code." *New York Herald Tribune*, 27 November, sec. 4, pp. 1, 19.
Report on dispute between Catholic censors and MPA Production Code Authority on *BD*.

93 "Should It Be Suppressed?" *Newsweek* 48 (31 December):59.
Review of film *BD*; deals with Cardinal Spellman's denunciation of *BD*, and Bishop Pike's counter charges.

94 SKELTON, B.J., and ABERNATHY, HARRY. "Tennessee Williams Turns to Film Writing, Poetry." Clarksdale (Miss.) *Press Register*, 1 September, p. 5.

Book review of both *BD* and *IWC*. *BD* treated favorably, but its inconsistencies cited; *IWC* looked at positively, with attention going to its *dramatic* impact.

95   "Sobering Thoughts?" *Theatre Arts* 40 (June):11.
Brief. Discusses TW's coming to Bankhead's defense on her performance in *SND*; refers to variou⁚ letters to NYC newspapers, and Bankhead's response.

96   "Some Notes on 'Baby Doll.'" *America* 96 (15 December):320.
Brief mention and endorsement of Legion of Decency's condemnation of the film: "We strongly recommend that all decent people of all faiths avoid 'Baby Doll.'"

97   "Starmaker's New Star Shines Bright in 'Baby Doll.'" *Life* 40 (11 June):111–14, 117, 118.
Pictorial report of C. Baker in *BD*.

98   "Tennessee's World." *Time* 67 (25 June):94.
Book review of *IWC*. "Their interest derives from the way they help explain the roiled and vaporous innards of the tortured little man who is rated the nation's No. 1 playwright."

99   "Tennessee Williams Comedy." *Times* (London), 1 September, p. 8.
News item. *YTM* to be televised by BBC, 9 September. Will be first performance in England.

100 "Theatre in Albany Is Banned for Six Months for Scheduling 'Baby Doll.'" *New York Times*, 30 December, p. 24.
Brief. Information as per title.

101 TYNAN, KENNETH. "Valentine to Tennessee Williams." *Mademoiselle* 42 (February):130–31, 200–203.
Lengthy article describing the (then) current status of TW's private life in contrast with his more well-known plays. "As we shall see, much of what has happened to them [his characters] has also happened to him. He is the most personal of playwrights. Incomplete people obsess him—above all, those who, like himself, have ideals too large for life to accommodate." Included in

piece: biographical details that lay the foundation for his future work, and details concerning the production of *GM*, *SND*, and *CAT*. Reprinted: 1961.92.

102 WATTS, RICHARD, JR. "Fine Revival of a Beautiful Play." *New York Post*, 23 November, p. 66.
Review of *GM*. "It is the miracle of TW, and of the theater's alchemy that, out of the materials of frustration, bitterness, and resentment, he could bring such tender beauty, such oddly gentle and forgiving compassion." This revival "recaptures all the warmth, sadness, humor and poignancy of one of the memorable works of American dramatic art." Praises H. Hayes.

103 _____. "Tallulah Bankhead in 'Streetcar.'" *New York Post*, 16 February, p. 15.
Review of *SND*. Bankhead's performance "compelling and dynamic." *SND* "a drama of pity and cruelty that brings his quality of dark poetry to a realistic theme . . . one of the finest works of recent American theatre." Brief mention of other performances by supporting cast.

104 WHITEBAIT, WILLIAM. "Magnani the Magnificent." *New Statesman* 51 (3 March):192–93.
Review of film of *RT*. Praises the film as a Magnani vehicle. She remains the focus of the review.

105 "Williams Play Opens." *New York Times*, 17 April, p. 27.
Announcement of production of *SB*, a "work in progress" in Coral Gables; TW quoted as calling it "an examination of what is really corrupt in life."

106 WYATT, EUPHEMIA VAN RENSSELAER. Review of *SND*. *Catholic World* 183 (April):67.
A "very unpleasant story." Finds the play's only merit to be Bankhead's "intelligent and moving performance." Hopes "that I will never have to sit through [*SND*] again."

107 YOUNG, VERNON. "Social Drama and Big Daddy." *Southwest Review* 41 (Spring):194–97.
Comparison of Chekhov's *Three Sisters* and TW's *CAT*. Hav-

ing just seen the New York production, he analyzes its merit and theme. Suggests "the Total Subject (I make so bold) seems to be the obscenity of being human." Goes on to contrast with Chekhov's *Three Sisters*; characterizes TW, through *CAT*, as sympathizing with "the uncouth views of his leading character." Generally negative about entire production.

108   ZINSSER, WILLIAM. " 'Baby Doll.' " *New York Herald Tribune*, 19 December, p. 17.

Review of film *BD*. Plot summary; discusses quality of its direction; little reference to TW.

109   ZOLOTOW, SAM. "New Comedy Role for Don Ameche." *New York Times*, 19 October, p. 22.

Helen Hayes to star in *GM* at City Center.

110   _____. "Song Bill Tonight by Judy Garland." *New York Times*, 26 September, p. 28.

OD to begin rehearsal; Magnani not to star, and production not at Palace—as originally planned.

111   _____. "Williams Writes a Poetic-Tragedy." *New York Times*, 13 April, p. 21.

Announcement of new play, *SB*, by TW and that performances will begin immediately in Florida.

112   ZUNSER, JESSE. "Tennessee Williams and His Po' White Trash." *Cue* 25 (22 December):8.

Review of film *BD*. Mostly plot summary; reports on the censorship strife; praises the production.

1957

1   ANDERSON, LINDSAY. "Men and Dolls." *New Statesman* 53 (5 January):13–14.

Review of film *BD*. "Another excursion into the airless fantasy world of Tennessee Williams. . . . In the hands of another director, the script might have been translated into a briskly, bitterly funny film, but Kazan's touch is a trifle heavy for comedy." Attacks Cardinal Spellman's attack.

2 ATKINSON, BROOKS. "Theatre: Capital Arena." *New York Times*, 1 April, p. 21.
Review of *PM*. Brief synopsis of play with positive comments on play and cast.

3 _____. "Theatre: Rural Orpheus." *New York Times*, 22 March, p. 28.
Review of *OD*. "Mr. Williams is in a more humane state of mind than he has been in several years.... There are streaks of his special genius all through his [*OD*]."

4 _____. "Virtuoso Theatre." *New York Times*, 31 March, sec. 2, p. 1.
Review of *OD*. Synopsis of play with kind remarks for TW, but insists that *OD* is not up to TW's normal excellence.

5 "Aurora, Ill., Bans 'Baby Doll.'" *New York Times*, 30 January, p. 33.
News item. Mayor of Aurora telegraphs Illinois governor requesting ban on *BD* to be made statewide.

6 "'Baby Doll' Ads Banned: Syracuse and Troy Newspapers Act against Movie." *New York Times*, 1 January, p. 19.
Brief. Information as per title.

7 "'Baby Doll' Censored." *New York Times*, 6 January, sec. 1, p. 86.
Providence, Rhode Island, theater runs cut version of *BD* despite lawsuit threats.

8 "'Baby Doll' Observed." *New York Times*, 20 January, sec. 2, p. 5.
Four letters to screen editor. Agreement and disagreement with *BD* furor.

9 "'Baby Doll' Ordered to Get License for Exhibition in Providence Theatre." *New York Times*, 5 January, p. 11.
News item. One local Providence, Rhode Island, theater gets movie license to show *BD*, only if film is cut in accordance with

"suggestions" made by the License Investigation Squad of the Providence, Rhode Island, Police Department.

10   *BD. Look* 21 (12 March):124.
      Photo and caption mentioning *Look*'s award for best original screenplay going to *BD*.

11   BINGHAM, ROBERT. "Movies: A Child Bride, A Wide-Screen Globe Trotter." *Reporter* 16 (24 January):36.
      Review of film *BD*. Generally negative; opposes both Cardinal Spellman's and Kazan's views.

12   "The Bitter Dispute over 'Baby Doll.'" *Life* 42 (7 January):60–65.
      Many photos, brief summary of censorship trouble.

13   BOLTON, WHITNEY. "On Doubtful Merits of 'Baby Doll.'" New York *Morning Telegraph*, 18 February, p. 2.
      Review of film *BD*. "A noisesome nothing. . . . It is simply trash." Refers to clergy dispute.

14   ———. "Williams' 'Orpheus' Has Its Moments." New York *Morning Telegraph*, 23 March, p. 2.
      Review of *OD*. "A curious unevenness . . . scenes of power . . . scenes of vagueness and loose writing." TW seems "to have become tired and to have borrowed ideas and devices from himself. . . . [There are] several moments of great beauty and definite tragedy."

15   BROOK, PETER. "Portrait Gallery: A Provocative Playwright." *Sunday Times* (London), 7 April, p. 3.
      Profile of TW published on eve of his arrival in London for *CR*'s opening. TW is "an insignificant, unexciting, deeply endearing man." Refers to the South, *CR*.

16   BUTCHER, MARYVONNE. "Realism on the Screen." *Commonweal* 67 (22 November):202–4.
      Cites *BD* as "deflected from tragedy into sensation. . . . Its danger lies . . . in its despair. . . . Its impact is contrived. . . . There must be . . . some basic demand in the American public for this kind of overstatement."

17 CALLAHAN, EDWARD F. "Tennessee Williams' Two Worlds." *North Dakota Quarterly* 25 (Summer): 61–67.
Examines tetralogy of *GM*, *SND*, *S&S*, *RT*, as illustration of TW's "progress from the formulation of an ethical problem to a solution of it in terms of his particular frame of reference: man in a dichotomized world of matter opposed to spirit.... This series of four plays envisions the problem of man in the modern world as an extension of the traditional conflict of appearance and reality."

18 "'Camino Real' in London." *New York Times,* 9 April, p. 41.
News item that TW did not thrill British critics with *CR*.

19 "'Camino Real' to be Withdrawn: High Running Cost." *Times* (London), 17 May, p. 3.
News item. International Playwrights' Theatre to close *CR* because of high expenses of paying cast, technicians, and stage management.

20 "Catholics in France May See 'Baby Doll.'" *New York Times,* 7 January, p. 29.
French Catholics are not prevented from seeing *BD*; also, the U.S. Army has banned *BD* from all of its movie theaters in Europe.

21 CHAPMAN, JOHN. "'Orpheus Descending' Has Fiery Scenes and Acting, But it Misses." New York *Daily News,* 22 March, p. 52.
Review of *OD*. "The play is an oddly fragmentary affair which never quite comes to grips with itself.... more like random samples of all Williams' dramas and all his characters than it is a theatrical work with a satisfying singleness of purpose."

22 "City Center Season." *Theatre Arts* 41 (February):24.
Brief review of *GM*. It has "evocative beauty and haunting, dreamlike quality he has never again approximated." This revival shows that "the play has lost none of its magic."

23 CLURMAN, HAROLD. Review of *GD*. *Nation* 186 (25 January):86–87.
Treats mainly *SLS*. Analyzes meaning; defends TW against attackers. However, finds that the two works "represent marginal efforts by a leading dramatist."

24   COGLEY, JOHN. "More on 'Baby Doll.'" *Commonweal* 65 (1 February):465.

An editorial against the Catholic Church's boycott of *BD*, asserting that "the Church loses its meaningful influence to the degree that it hides its own bridal identity behind swagger and cockiness." The Church in effect is egregiously involved "in a case of naked economic pressure, a display of sheer power ... the candid use of nonspiritual power to achieve a worthy spiritual goal."

25   ————. "The 'Baby Doll' Controversy." *Commonweal* 65 (11 January):381.

Defends Cardinal Spellman's insistence that people, above all Catholics, should not patronize the film. Carefully explains the text of Spellman's attack, saying that Spellman acted "properly both as a Bishop and an American ..." in line with the Church that has "the right to act in accordance with its own understanding of itself." Does not necessarily agree with Spellman's view that film is "morally repellent"; merely a defense for Spellman's proper rights and duty.

26   COLEMAN, ROBERT. "Williams' 'Orpheus' Not for Squeamish." New York *Daily Mirror*, 22 March, p. 32.

Review of *OD*. "Clurman has staged this dance of death with a sure hand. ... [*OD* is] an exploration into the depths of depravity, should turn the Martin Beck into a veritable mint for Producers' Theatre. ... [TW's] brutal rhythms exert the fascination of a cobra."

27   CROWTHER, BOSLEY. "The Proper Drama of Mankind." *New York Times*, 6 January, sec. 2, p. 1.

Comparison between *BD* and foreign films (especially *La Strada*). Generally negative about *BD*; "What 'Baby Doll' lacks is ... compassion for the weaknesses and sadnesses of man."

28   DENT, ALAN. "A Blaze of Gloom." *Illustrated London News* 230 (12 January):80.

Review of film *BD*. Disparages the characters calling them "curiously similar" to all his other characters. Virtually dismisses the plot, but "as drama ... you must call it compelling, disturbing, and not a little frightening ... singularly well done. ... As film-making, it is undeniably superb."

29 DONNELLY, TOM. "A Lost Landscape and a Lost Lady." *New York World-Telegram & Sun*, 1 April, p. 10.
Review of *OD*. "A curiously synthetic effort, hackneyed in its essentials, eccentric in its details, and empty in its pessimism." However, if *OD* is a failure, "Mr. Williams is not."

30 _____. "Tennessee Williams Loses Round Two of His Battle." *New York World-Telegram & Sun*, 22 March, p. 22.
Review of *OD*. "Least characteristic of the author's plays and communicates virtually no sense of the artist's personal vision." Compares it to *BA*; "indulge[s] in various deviltries without any dramatically comprehensible motive."

31 "Dublin Bars 'Rose Tattoo.'" *New York Times*, 24 May, p. 31.
RT canceled at small Dublin theater because of police objections.

32 DYER, PETER JOHN. Review of film *BD*. *Films and Filming* 3 (February):21–22.
Focuses on Kazan's talent as a director; elements of plot and theme discussed. "It is a tough script, all scarecrow lyricism and tense non-sequitur. ... Kazan has mistaken messy profusion for crystal-clear imagination."

33 "Film Ban Assailed: Cultural Freedom Group Hits Boycott of 'Baby Doll.'" *New York Times*, 4 January, p. 19.
News item. The American Committee for Cultural Freedom criticizes attempts to suppress *BD*.

34 FINLEY, JAMES FENLON, C.S.P. "The Children's Hour." *Catholic World* 185 (April):62–63.
Says those who patronized *BD* are "blameworthy." Claims that audience immaturity catered to its success.

35 _____. Review of film *BD*. *Catholic World* 184 (January):302.
TW "has canned some more of his refuse heapings." Calls it "long day's journey into this garbage dump."

36 FREEDLEY, GEORGE. "Of Books and Men." New York *Morning Tele-graph*, 1 April, p. 2.
    Review of *OD*. Brief mention of opening; "one of [TW's] most endearing" plays.

37 GELB, ARTHUR. "News and Gossip of the Rialto." *New York Times*, 15 December, sec. 2, p. 3.
    An explanation with quotes from TW why *GD* is to be off-Broadway.

38 ————. "Play by Williams Arrives Tonight." *New York Times*, 21 March, p. 36.
    Preopening news release on cast and producer and plot of *OD*.

39 GIBBS, WOLCOTT. "Well, Descending, Anyway." *New Yorker* 33 (30 March):84, 86.
    Review of *OD*. "The trouble with [*OD*] is that the people in it aren't terribly interesting.... In [*OD*] I could see nothing but purposeless ruin.... I don't believe [TW] has turned out a coherent play." Does admit though that it's "beautifully produced."

40 GREEN, WILLIAM. "Significant Trends in the Modern American Theatre." *Manchester Review* 8 (Autumn):65–78.
    In his survey of the history of American theater, he makes reference to the "current generation" and refers to TW. Discusses structure in *GM*, *SND*, *S&S*, *RT*, and *CAT*. "In all these plays of Williams it will be noted how he has brought his poetic imagination to heighten essentially realistic character portrayals."

41 HALL, DONALD. Review of *IWC*. *Yale Review* 46 (Winter):297–98.
    Quotes Bentley's phrase: "'Mr. Williams' besetting sin is fake poeticizing....'" Goes on to add, "The faults which undermine the plays are the faults of which the poems are entirely composed.... When he writes verse, he is awkward and technically primitive. Most fundamental is his inability to use the line as a unit of rhythm."

42 HALL, PETER. "Tennessee Williams: Notes on the Moralist." *Encore* 4 (September-October):16–19.
    "Williams is the victim of his own great fame. This most moral

of writers has become synonymous with violence, sadism and sex. . . . He believes in happiness and the peace which we can give each other. . . . Williams is not a great thinker. He has . . . a Shakespearean lack of thesis."

43 HARPER, MR. "Morpheus Ascending." *Harper's* 214 (May): 76–77.
Review of *OD*. Calls TW "a major artist who insists, by deliberate choice, on writing minor works." Classifies *OD* as minor, "a shiny package [made out of] a shopworn product. . . . An attractive and repulsive transparency." Also indicts it for "undercut[ting] Mr. Williams' view of the south."

44 "Harrington Finds Morality in 'Baby Doll' But Not in Film of 'Ten Commandments.'" *New York Times*, 4 February, p. 22.
News item-interview. Rev. Donald Harrington expresses his opinion on the two films mentioned in title.

45 HART, HENRY. Review of film *BD*. *Films in Review* 8 (January):32–33.
A "culturally worthless and socially debasing film . . . 'Baby Doll' is not realism. It is merely a literary trick, whereby the more complicated and degenerate kinds of smut are covered over with pseudo-social significance."

46 HATCH, ROBERT. Review of *OD*. *Nation* 184 (6 April):301–2.
OD is "discursive, indecisive, awkward as to its machinery." Praises cast.

47 HAYES, RICHARD. "The Tragic Pretension." *Commonweal* 66 (26 April):94–97.
"The authority to which Tennessee Williams aspires in *Orpheus Descending* is visibly that of tragic statement. . . . Nothing is here of logic, of strict psychology or plausible assumptions: The drama is rather closer in texture to the dark, indolent, keening lyricism of Mr. Williams' poems and stories." It evokes "that crawling moral unease. . . . Mr. Williams confirms the mythic overtones of his title."

48 HEWES, HENRY. "Tennessee Revising." *Saturday Review* 40 (30 March):26.

Review of *OD*. Refers back to *BA*. *OD* "runs into trouble when it attempts to fly its poetry through a conventional stage thick with gossiping old ladies.... [TW's] poetic notions and symbolism tend to emerge as too obvious or too unrelated to the action."

49   HOBE. Review of *OD*. *Variety*, 27 March, p. 66.

"A sort of melodramatic tone-poem tragedy in the Orpheus-Eurydice pattern.... What he seems to be saying is that purity and integrity are corrupted when dreamers and idealists descend to the reality of life." Notes that show will not be as popular as other TW plays, but might make an excellent film if skillfully adapted.

50   KAUFMAN, BORIS. "Filming *Baby Doll*." *American Cinematographer* 38 (February):92–93, 106–7.

Describes lighting devices, sets, location work, technical details in filming of *BD*; brief plot outline.

51   KEATING, JOHN. "Tennessee Williams' New Play a Moving Drama." *Cue* 26 (30 March):8–9.

Review of *OD*. Refers to its similarity to Inge's *Picnic*. "The shape and substance of tragedy are here ... [but] extensive revisions ... may have overbalanced the play. [It's] head and shoulders above the usual Broadway offering.... exciting, absorbing theatre."

52   KERR, WALTER. "Failures of Williams." In *Pieces at Eight*. New York: Simon and Schuster, pp. 125–41.

Begins with premise "The failures of Tennessee Williams are worth talking about.... [TW] sees and writes as an artist and a poet.... [TW] is all flesh and blood." Cites problems in *RT*—the implausibility of using sex as the resolution, and the "sentimentality about sex ... a kind of humorless dedication." Even *GM* and *SND* have "escape-hatch endings." *CR*, "that fresh, clear picture, that stabbingly felt emotion—never emerges." Faults Williams' "own imaginative equipment," among other things, for problems in *CR*.

53   _____. " 'Orpheus Descending.'" *New York Herald Tribune*, 23 March, p. 12.

Review of *OD*. *OD* "seems to me a make-believe play." The passions of the play "are postures, devices, excuses for handsome big scenes. . . . There is an essential artifice at the very heart of this reworking of Mr. Williams' first-produced play, 'Battle of Angels,' . . . a serious loss in sustained power."

54 _____. " 'Orpheus': Winged Purity." *New York Herald Tribune*, 31 March, sec. 4, pp. 1, 2.
Review of *OD*. Refers to TW's "steadily hardening philosophical commitment," but questions his "drift." Provides an interpretation of the play's meaning.

55 KESTING, MARIANNE. "Tennessee Williams." *Hochland* 50 (December):171-74.
Discusses TW as southern writer—in company of Faulkner and Wolfe; analyzes themes and settings in *GM, SND, RSMS, CAT, CR.*

56 KRUTCH, JOSEPH WOOD. *The American Drama since 1918: An Informal History.* New York: George Braziller, pp. 324–32.
Closes out his study with TW. Williams' plays "are also what Shaw would have called 'unpleasant plays.'" Traces history of the earlier plays, citing their themes and plots; frequent comparisons to Miller and O'Neill. The most obvious interpretations put [TW] among the despairing explorers of pathological states of mind just as the obvious interpretations put Miller among the sociological naturalists."

57 KURNITZ, HARRY. "Tennessee Williams' 'Baby Doll.' " *Holiday* (February), pp. 93, 103.
"As vicious a movie as you are likely to encounter from here on in . . . a very exciting piece of work. . . . Some of it becomes faintly absurd." Plot summary and details on acting.

58 " 'Lewd Play' Allegation: Dublin Director Given Bail." *Times* (London), 25 May, p. 4.
News item. A. Simpson, codirector of *RT* in Dublin, appeared in court charged with "producing for gain an indecent and profane performance."

59 LEWIS, THEOPHILUS. Review of *OD*. *America* 97 (27 April):148–50.
"A drama of anguish and frustration"; discusses sex in play,
M. Stapleton's performance, the choices open to TW in devising
plot.

60 "Liberties Union Hits Theatre Ban." *New York Times*, 3 January,
p. 28.
Brief. Information as per title, pertaining to ACLU and *BD*.

61 LOWE. Review of *OD*. *Variety*, 27 February, p. 58.
Washington production. "Tennessee Williams has again mined
the bitter passionate slag heap that is his particular corner of the
South and has come up with another hit in *Orpheus Descending*."
Brief plot description; cites this production as "the fifth writing
and third naming of the play."

62 McCLAIN, JOHN. "'Orpheus' Raises Williams' Stature." *New York
Journal-American*, 22 March, p. 18.
Review of *OD*. "The author has done a masterful job of getting inside [his] characters. . . . It reinstates the author's position
in the modern theatre."

63 "Man Named Tennessee." *Newsweek* 49 (1 April):81.
Interview-commentary; TW discusses his pessimism, his characters, his limitations.

64 MANNES, MARYA. "Mr. Williams and Orpheus." *Reporter* 16 (18
April):43.
Review of *OD*. "In many ways, this is the most compassionate
play Williams has written. But it is also a very loose and very
contrived play." Commenting on the characters, she says, "The
more we know of these people, the less interesting they become."
The play demonstrates "the one recurrent weakness in the art of
Tennessee Williams"—he doesn't deliver on the promise the play
seemed to offer.

65 MAROWITZ, CHARLES. "Movies: 'Baby Doll.'" *Village Voice*, 23
January, p. 6.
Review of film *BD*. Liked the idea for the film on paper, but
not the film, which has lost much in the translation. Faults the

director, who takes the "tough steak of the play" and turns it into "minced meat."

66 MARSHALL, MARGARET. "Orpheus in Dixie." *New Republic* 136 (8 April):21.
    Review of *OD*. Relates it to other plays (*GM, SND*) and emphasizes characters. Suggests rewriting.

67 "Mike Wallace Asks Tennessee Williams 'What Makes You Angry?'" *New York Post*, 30 December, p. 28.
    Report of interview. TW discusses honesty, communication, *GD, OD, CAT*.

68 MOREHOUSE, WARD. "Keeping up with Kazan." *Theatre Arts* 41 (June):21–22, 90–91.
    Brief references to Kazan's work with *SND* and *BD*.

69 "Movie Banned in Gary." *New York Times*, 24 January, p. 34.
    News item. Theater owners face arrest if they show *BD* in Gary, Indiana. However, Grand Rapids, Michigan, theater owners may show the film there with no trouble.

70 "New Ban on 'Baby Doll.'" *New York Times*, 10 March, sec. 1, p. 76.
    In Philadelphia, three suburban movie theaters and one in the city have canceled plans to show *BD*; no official ban imposed.

71 PATTERSON, NANCY MARIE. "Patterns of Imagery in the Major Plays of Tennessee Williams." Ph.D. dissertation, University of Arkansas.
    Concerns the tracing of imagery in the setting and the characters in the plays *BA, GM, YTM, SND, S&S, RT, CR,* and *CAT*. Concludes that TW does not use an abundance of images, but that he uses one thematic image around which he builds his plays. (*DA* 17:2014.)

72 "Pike Theater: 'The Rose Tattoo.'" *Times* (London), 14 May, p. 3.
    News item. *RT* performed in Dublin. Synopsis of play with comments.

73 "Play Continues in Dublin: Detectives See Performance: Director in Court." *Times* (London), 25 May, p. 6.
    News item. Police threaten to arrest cast of *RT* if play is produced; it was and they were not.

74 "Plays Coming to London: Something to Look Forward to." *Times* (London), 7 November, p. 3.
    News item. In an article about future theatrical productions, *CAT* is announced to be scheduled for Comedy Theatre.

75 POWERS, HARVEY M., JR. "Theatrical Convention: The Conditions of Acceptability." *Bucknell Review* 7 (May):20–26.
    Concerned with the differentiation between, and the conditional justification of, "dramatic convention" and "scenic convention." Using *CAT* as an example, he states that the "emphasized void" of the play's set did not further the story; and since it did nothing to help the audience accept a play steeped in realism as being more real, the scenic convention of a near-empty set did nothing to enhance the drama and was therefore unnecessary.

76 PRYOR, THOMAS M. "Of Local Origin." *New York Times*, 25 May, p. 25.
    Notice from Kazan that *BD* would gross $5 million from the first-run release, despite the censorship controversy.

77 QUIGLY, ISABEL. "Testy Babe." *Spectator* 198 (4 January):22.
    Review of film *BD*. "The most spectacular of Tennessee Williams' circular studies of frustration; one that almost bridges the short but important gap between horror and tragedy.... The style and content of the film are so fused" that we can't separate Kazan from Williams.

78 "Reflections on a Condemned Film." *America* 96 (5 January):386.
    Editorial on prospect of *BD*'s being judged an " 'artistically' fine though 'morally' bad film." Tries to define art as having a "rational appeal," one that does not "view as acceptably pleasurable such things as brutality, perversion, degeneracy."

79 REID, DESMOND. "Tennessee Williams." *Studies* 48 (Winter):431–46.
    Biographical details; discusses TW as an "enduring controversy

which his plays continue to whip up. . . . The main point at issue is the predominance of 'sex,' and sexual aberration, in his work." Focuses on the two aspects of the argument: whether he's "bold and bawdy [and] . . . indecent," or whether he's "a sincere artist." Survey of themes and characters in *SND, RT, S&S, GM, PM,* and *TPC.* Questions whether TW's aim "to reflect reality" is accomplished; says he "exaggerates the universality and aloneness of suffering humanity." Refers to TW's theological stance. Reprinted: 1961.41.

80 Review of *OD. Newsweek* 49 (1 April):81.
Brief. TW is "unable to write bad theater"; claims *OD* takes its place with *Long Day's Journey into Night.*

81 Review of *OD. Theatre Arts* 41 (May):20.
Brief. Praises cast but says characters "remain commonplace"; still, audience can "become engrossed with them." Plot summary; mentions its similarity to *BA.*

82 Review of *OD. Time* 69 (1 April):61.
Focuses on the "objectionable" elements; refers to TW's "garish orchestrating."

83 "Revival of 'Glass Menagerie.'" *New York Times*, 7 March, p. 24.
Brief announcement of *GM* revival.

84 "'The Rose Tattoo.'" *Times* (London), 9 July, p. 6.
News item. Producer of *RT*, Alan Simpson, appeared in Dublin District Court, charged with "producing for gain an indecent and profane performance."

85 "'The Rose Tattoo' 'Obscene': Submission in Dublin Court." *Times* (London), 5 July, p. 14.
News item. Details of trial of Alan Simpson, codirector at Pike Theater, charged with producing an indecent play, *RT.*

86 ROSS. DON. "Williams in Art and Morals: An Anxious Foe of Untruth." *New York Herald Tribune*, 3 March, sec. 4, pp. 1–2.
Interview-commentary. TW discussed "sordid" characters, *CAT*, characters in general, life itself, *RT.*

87 "Shorter Notices." *Times* (London), 24 January, p. 11.
    News item. One sentence announcing publication of film
    script of *BD*.

88 " 'Tattoo' Producer Arrested in Dublin." *New York Times*, 25 May,
    p. 24.
    News item. Dublin producer arrested for presenting produc-
    tion of *RT*. The play was called "indecent and obscene" by author-
    ities.

89 "T. Williams Descending." *America* 97 (6 April):4.
    Surveys a sampling of critical responses to premiere of *OD*.
    There's "something about Mr. Williams' work which cannot ring
    utterly true." Quotes TW's attitude toward what's true.

90 "Tennessee Williams to Present First Creative Film Awards." *Vil-
    lage Voice*, 23 January, p. 6.
    Notes TW as guest of honor in ceremonies of Creative Film
    Foundation.

91 "Theatre Director Arrested: Action after Dublin Police Warning."
    Times (London), 24 May, p. 10.
    News item. A Simpson, director of Pike Theater Club in Dub-
    lin, arrested for presenting *RT* after police warned him not to.

92 THESPIS. Review of *CR*. *English* 11 (Summer):186.
    London production. Refers to the line "Humankind cannot bear
    very much reality," as setting a T.S. Eliot-like tone and motif
    in the play; plot details; claims "the dramatist's vision of mankind
    alternates between disgust, weary amusement, and a compassion."

93 TREWIN, J.C. "A Tale of Three Nights." *Illustrated London News*
    230 (27 April):702.
    Review of *CR*, London production. Calls it "a chaotic piece";
    cites the play's lack of "lucidity," and claims TW is intent on
    demonstrating his "powerful command of atmospherics." Calls
    Peter Hall's production "a sensuous, horrific ballet."

94 "The Trouble with 'Baby Doll.' " *Time* 69 (14 January):100.
    Report on the public furor, police action. Comments on the
    reaction in Britain.

95 WATT, DAVID. "Outward Bound." *Spectator* 198 (12 April):488.
Review of *CR*, London production. Plot and theme details;
"a gigantic parade of brilliance and bathos." Its language is "an
infuriating mixture of the 'shocking' and 'poetic,' and marvel-
lously effective." Praises Peter Hall's production.

96 WATTS, RICHARD, JR. "The World of Tennessee Williams." *New
York Post*, 22 March, p. 60.
Review of *OD*. "Another searing look at the dark and tor-
mented world of [TW].... Splendidly acted and staged...a
drama of notable power, grim poetic insight and disturbing fascination."

97 "Week by Week." *Commonweal* 65 (11 January):371–72.
Defense of Spellman's right to condemn *BD* and warn Catholics to stay away from it. Attacks public for crying out against
censorship, which article says is *not* Spellman's intent. Claims
Hollywood "had no right" to advertise *BD*, and "even the most
innocent movies, so luridly."

98 WEILER, A.H. "By Way of Report." *New York Times*, 28 July, sec.
2, p. 5.
News item that TW has been working on original screenplay
entitled *The Loss of a Teardrop Diamond*.

99 WILLIAMS, TENNESSEE. "A Talk with Tennessee Williams." *New
York Post*, 17 March, p. 4M.
TW authors piece in form of an interview playing both roles.
Discusses *GM*'s success; reading notices; tension, anger, violence;
central message; "corruption" as involuntarily chosen major alle-
gorical theme of his plays as a whole; his theory about people.

100 WINN, JANET. "The Crass Menagerie." *New Republic* 136 (21 January):21.
Review of film *BD*. Disparages the film on a schedule of six
categories, ranging from subject matter to costumes and sets.
Quite negative.

101 WOODS, JOHN. "Tennessee Williams as a Poet." *Poetry* 90 (July):
256–58.

Book review of *IWC*. Refers to his "personal language, suggesting at times the surrealism of Pablo Neruda," his "gorgeousness of imagery." Quotes from several poems and observes, "What I miss in most of these poems is that singing tension between formal and conversational rhythms."

102   WORSLEY, T.C. "Puzzle Corner." *New Statesman* 53 (13 April):473.
Review of *CR*, London production. "A very odd, very rum sort of allegory whose meaning . . . completely and absolutely eluded me." Says the play belongs to "the obverse side of [TW's] remarkable talent." "I hardly remember in the last ten years seeing a production which was so assured, masterly, and certain of itself."

103   WYATT, EUPHEMIA VAN RENSSELAER. "The Duchess of Malfi; 'Orpheus Descending.'" *Catholic World* 185 (June):226–27.
"Savagery is . . . the note of" *OD*. The play "shows a Saroyan influence but Saroyan gone very sour." Praise for Cliff Robertson, Lois Smith, and Joanna Roos. "Mr. Williams' sensitive dramatic sense and the validity of his dialogue give life to a second-rate play (because of specious music and a last act that is purely melodrama) as savage as the 17th C. tragedy but without its dignity. Nobility is an adjective lacking in Mr. Williams' vocabulary."

1958

1   ALPERT, HOLLIS. "Fixed Cat." *Saturday Review* 41 (13 September):58.
Review of film of *CAT*. "Much of the time [it] seems directionless, like a hurricane without an eye." Maintains the removal of the element of homosexuality makes dealing with film awkward and untenable, making the plot "rudderless."

2   ASTON, FRANK. "Williams Has a Strong Pair." *New York World-Telegram & Sun*, 8 January, p. 32.
Review of *GD*. "It is fierce, furious theater, and it leaves you

all pulled apart. . . . Mr. Williams pulls savagery and tumult out of sheer talk . . . some excellent writing."

3 ATKINSON, BROOKS. " 'Garden District.' " *New York Times*, 19 January, sec. 2, p. 1.
Review of *GD*. Brief synopsis of *SLS* with many comments on violence and repugnance of TW's writing.

4 _____. "Theatre: 2 by Williams." *New York Times*, 8 January, p. 23.
Review of *GD*. Synopsis of *SU* and *SLS* with praise for TW's powerful and shocking writing.

5 "Author's 'Frontier Post': 'Camino Real' at the A.D.C." *Times* (London), 28 November, p. 8.
Review of *CR*, London production. Brief; generally positive with plaudits for cast.

6 BAKER, PETER. Review of film of *CAT*. *Films and Filming* 4 (November):21.
Begins with premise: "Richard Brooks and James Poe have been kind to Tennessee Williams in their adaptation of his play. Almost too kind." Claims the film "is too close to the stage original," and calls the script "a kind of old-fashioned melodrama laced with hysteria." Discusses thematic elements, varying acting angles, homosexuality, marriage.

7 BECKLEY, PAUL V. " 'Cat on a Hot Tin Roof.' " *New York Herald Tribune*, 19 September, p. 17.
Review of film of *CAT*. "A powerful film . . . a conscientious and honest expression of all that is most important in [TW's] extraordinary play." Compares film and play in their "fundamental moral[ity]." General survey of acting and directing.

8 BOLTON, WHITNEY. "Of Tennessee and the Sheriff." New York *Morning Telegraph*, 1 July, p. 3.
Gossip item. Audrey Wood tells about TW buying a car and being arrested in Florida for no legal ID.

9 _____. "Williams Twin Bill at York Theatre." New York *Morning Telegraph*, 9 January, p. 2.

Review of *GD*. TW is "a brilliant, powerful playwright. . . . [He] has a blazing talent for surging use of the English language." Balks at tone and subject matter; hopes TW won't "continue to add to his growing gallery of monsters and perverts." Disturbed at "such torrents of degeneracy."

10   BRIEN, ALAN. "A Shock in the Dark." *Spectator* 201 (26 September):401–2.

Review of *GD*, London production. "It's hard to imagine a Tennessee Williams play which isn't about Sex with a capital S." Claims that most people go to his plays to see the work of a "bedding specialist." "He writes of love-making like a teetotaller writing of drunkenness." These two plays show TW's interest in a "pedagogic approach to pederasty." Thinks *SLS* is "more ambitious" than *SU*.

11   "British See U.S. Play." *New York Times*, 17 September, p. 44.

Brief news item. British unenthusiastic about *GD*.

12   BRUSTEIN, ROBERT. "America's New Culture Hero: Feelings without Words." *Commentary* 25 (February):123–29.

Calls attention to the popularization of the "inarticulate hero" who "clearly finds his immediate origin in Tennessee Williams' Stanley Kowalski as interpreted by Marlon Brando." Traces origins back to O'Neill's *Hairy Ape*. "If Williams created an ignoble rather than a noble savage, how do we explain the spectacular success of Brando and the extensive influence his playing of Stanley has had?" Reprinted: 1969.5.

13   CALTA, LOUIS. " 'Firstborn' to get Bernstein Songs." *New York Times*, 22 February, p. 8.

News that TW has added new scene to *SLS*.

14   ———. "Opening of Play Set Back Five Days." *New York Times*, 25 September, p. 30.

TW has requested, and the producers agreed, that the *SND* production that features black actor be postponed. TW's concern is with its "proximity in time to a new play" that is scheduled for a winter Broadway run; play's title: *SB*. (Title of article does *not* pertain to these plays.)

15   " 'Cat on a Hot Tin Roof': Mr. Tennessee Williams's Play at the Comedy Theatre." *Times* (London), 31 January, p. 3.
     Review of *CAT*, London production. Pro and con; synopsis of play. "Play is exciting to watch but leaves the audience empty."

16   CHAPMAN, JOHN. "New Williams Play Chock Full of Nuts." New York *Daily News*, 8 January, p. 52.
     Review of *GD*. "Both [*SLS* and *SU*] are weird ventures into psychopathology and neither is dramatic." Characters are "leftovers" from *GM* and *SND*.

17   CLURMAN, HAROLD. "Tennessee Williams." In *Lies like Truth*. New York: Macmillan Co., pp. 72–86.
     Reviews of original productions of *SND*, *S&S*, and *CR*. Reprint of: 1948.15, 1948.16, 1953.13. Reprinted: 1961.41.

18   COPPOLA, JO. "The View from Here." *New York Post*, 17 April, p. 30.
     Brief mention of Kraft TV Theatre doing three of the one-acts from *27W*.

19   "Could Not Come." *Stage*, 18 September, p. 1.
     Four-line news item. Sunstroke prevents TW from attending premiere of *GD* in London.

20   "Critical Views on Unlicensed Play: Mr. Wanamaker Urges Censorship Change." *Times* (London), 6 June, p. 6.
     News item. Controversy on production of unlicensed plays at theater clubs is blamed on censorship. Resolution is urged to change censorship laws. Mixed views reported on production of *CAT*.

21   CROWTHER, BOSLEY. "Southern Accent." *New York Times*, 21 September, sec. 2, p. 1.
     Review of film of *CAT*. Notes similarities in the settings of film of *CAT* and a play called *Hot Spell*.

22   ————. "Screen: The Fur Flies in 'Cat on a Hot Tin Roof.' " *New York Times*, 19 September, p. 24.
     Review of film of *CAT*. "As a straight exercise in spewing

venom and flinging dirty linen on the line, this fine . . . production . . . would be hard to beat."

23   DAVIS, HELEN. "Burden of Concern." *Mainstream* 11 (April):55–57.
       Book review of *OD* (with *BA*). Comparison of the two "versions." Mentions TW's introduction. Plot summary and suggestion of interest in the "critical question which has plagued Mr. Williams' work."

24   DENNIS, PATRICK. "Tennessee off Broadway." *New Republic* 138 (27 January):20.
       Review of *GD*. With this duo, TW has "something to offer once again." Calls *SLS* "the heavy artillery" of the pair. "Exquisitely directed and performed."

25   DONY, NADINE. "Tennessee Williams: A Selected Bibliography." *Modern Drama* 1 (May):181–91.
       Checklist of critical works, popular and scholarly.

26   DOWNING, ROBERT. Review of film of *CAT*. *Films in Review* 9 (October):454–55.
       "Richard Brooks has done a superior job of rewriting and directing Tennessee Williams' sprawling and disorganized script." Praises Elizabeth Taylor.

27   "Drama Bookshelf." *New York Times*, 25 May, sec. 2, p. 1.
       News of publication of *SLS* by New Directions.

28   "Drama Mailbag." *New York Times*, 31 August, sec. 2, p. 3.
       Letter to drama editor. Members of Pike Theatre Fund request contributions for defense fund over closing of theater in Ireland for producing *RT*.

29   DRIVER, TOM F. "Accelerando." *Christian Century* 75 (29 January):136–37.
       Focuses on *SLS*, and discusses—at length—the emotional effects; compares to *CAT*; "The play as a whole is too nervous to make a dramatic statement and must settle for a sensual wallop."

30   "Dublin Booking of Play Cancelled: Advice to Management." *Times* (London), 5 June, p. 16.

News item. *CAT* production is canceled in Dublin because of impending court case over production of *RT*.

31 FALK, SIGNI. "The Profitable World of Tennessee Williams." *Modern Drama* 1 (May):172–80.
   Raises question of whether TW's "work has not been obscured by brilliant productions." Surveys TW's comments on himself and his work, as recorded in interviews and prefaces he wrote to plays. Discusses TW as a "sentimentalist," as shown by the "types of characters he favors, his taste for escapism, the range of his wisdom." Reprinted: 1961.41.

32 FREEDLEY, GEORGE. "Of Books and Men." New York *Morning Telegraph*, 16 January, p. 2.
   Brief review of *GD*. TW "has enhanced his own considerable reputation with" *GD*.

33 ———. "Of Books and Men." New York *Morning Telegraph*, 6 August, p. 2.
   Brief note of publication of *OD* (with *BA*).

34 ———. *SLS*. New York *Morning Telegraph*, 20 May, p. 2.
   Brief positive note of publication of *SLS*.

35 GELB, ARTHUR. "Negroes Slated for 'Streetcar.'" *New York Times*, 14 July, p. 16.
   Permission granted by TW to have desegregated production.

36 ———. "Williams Revises Plot of New Play." *New York Times*, 30 June, p. 23.
   News that *SB* has been revised and ready for rehearsal; revision is not as violent as original.

37 GIBBS, WOLCOTT. "Oddities, Domestic and Imported." *New Yorker* 33 (18 January):66, 68.
   Review of *GD*. *SLS* is "an impressive and genuinely shocking play." With *SU*, TW "seems again to be in sharp and deadly control of his material."

38 GLICKSBERG, CHARLES I. "Depersonalization in the Modern Drama." *Personalist* 39 (Spring):158–69.

Starts with assertion: "The twentieth century may well be called the Age of Freud, an age which encompasses such recurrent and familiar psychic states as anxiety, irrationality, dissociation, masochism, sadism, and neurotic behavior of all kinds." Then relates twentieth-century dramatists to the thesis: Strindberg, Chekhov, Pirandello, O'Neill, Eliot. Brief reference to TW: "In Tennessee Williams' dramas, too, the interest is centered on the tragedy of the interior life."

39 _____. "The Modern Playwright and the Absolute." *Queen's Quarterly* 65 (Autumn):459–71.
   Examines moral and intellectual nihilism in drama, surveying dramatists from Chekhov to TW; considers the dire consequences of a drama without an ontological footing; references to *CR*; finds it an example of the work of a dramatist who is "striving to transcend the horror" of absurdity.

40 GOULD, JACK. "T.V. Tennessee Williams." *New York Times*, 17 April, p. 63.
   TW introduced the plays *MK*, *LSG*, *TPC*, remarking that since they were written in the 1930s, he had difficulty realizing he was their author.

41 HARTUNG, PHILIP T. "Through a Glass Darkly." *Commonweal* 68 (26 September):637.
   Praises the film of *CAT*. Claims that "Williams states well, perhaps better than any other living dramatist, the great problem of man's loneliness and inability to communicate with his fellow men. . . . Williams presents his argument with stinging force. . . . Although it is rather talky for a movie, the dialogue is undeniably interesting and the story moving."

42 HATCH, ROBERT. Review of film of *CAT*. *Nation* 187 (11 October):220.
   "By screen standards [it's] uncommonly good. . . . Much of this excellence is directly attributable to [TW]. . . . [It is] melodramatic with tension."

43 HAYES, RICHARD. "An Infernal Harmony." *Commonweal* 68 (30 May):232–33.

Refers to "the charismatic intensity" of *SLS*; "yet there are failures, of thinness as well as deliberate evasion: the strident jungle overtones are indulgently reiterated. . . . What is new is a fresh security of poetic resource—'Suddenly Last Summer' is often close to Lorca's theater poetry in the savage ceremony of images, all of color, with which it concludes. . . . There is an equation between intention and effect in this production."

44 HEWES, HENRY. "Boundaries of Tennessee." In *The Passionate Playgoer.* Edited by George Oppenheimer. New York: Viking Press, pp. 250–54.
    Reprint of 1958.45.

45 ———. " 'Sanity' Observed." *Saturday Review* 41 (25 January):26.
    Review of *SLS*. Play called, at that time, "Suddenly One Summer." Traces the plot, its themes, autobiographical elements. Reprinted: 1958.44.

46 HOUSTON, PENELOPE. "Shouting Match." *Observer* (London), 12 October, p. 19.
    Review of film of *CAT*. "Not, certainly, the easiest of plays to put on the screen." Discusses the alterations to the script needed to make the film; negative criticism.

47 HYMAN, STANLEY EDGAR. "Some Trends in the Novel." *College English* 20 (October):1–9.
    Refers to the Albertine strategy he discussed in his *Hudson Review* (Autumn 1953) article; furthers the point with references to *RSMS*, among others' work; reference is only incidental.

48 INGLIS, BRIAN. "Contemporary Arts: Eugene and Tennessee." *Spectator* 200 (7 February):174.
    Review of *CAT*, London production. "There is no delicacy, no depth in the work. . . . There is never the feeling, as there is in even the worst Ibsen, that the writer is deeply interested in the riddle of human behaviour for its own sake." However, he claims it "is undeniably effective theatre. . . . Peter Hall stages it as melodrama."

49 ISAAC, DAN. "In Defense of Tennessee Williams." *Religious Education* 53 (September-October):452–53.

Comments on demeaning remarks made about TW at a religious convention. "That Tennessee Williams is basically a sen-
sationalist I would vehemently deny. True, there is a steady
stream of decay, corruption, and sex in his works. But these are
the building blocks of his plots. . . . His particular genius lies
neither in the realm of philosophy nor polemics."

50 JACKSON, ESTHER MERLE. "The Emergence of a Characteristic Contemporary Form in the Drama of Tennessee Williams." Ph.D.
dissertation, Ohio State University.
    Identifies the rise in this century of an anti-Aristotelian drama,
parts of which are the works of French philosophical playwrights
and the American psychological playwrights, which include TW;
goes on to deal with the synthetic properties of TW's plays, referring to the fundamental internal antagonism of *GM*, *SND*,
S&S, and *CR*. (*DA* 19:3053–54).

51 JOHNSON, ALBERT. Review of film of *CAT*. *Film Quarterly* 12 (Winter):54–55.
    Brief synopsis; praise for production and cast.

52 KAUFFMANN, STANLEY. "The Outer Edges." *New Republic* 139 (29
September):21–22.
    Review of film of *CAT*. A film of TW's "least worthy long
play. . . . [TW] abuses a license he has earned by past work."
Claims that the film emphasizes the play's worst parts. Reprinted:
1966.39.

53 KAZAN, ELIA. "Notebook for *A Streetcar Named Desire*." In *The
Passionate Playgoer: A Personal Scrapbook*. Edited by George
Oppenheimer. New York: Viking Press, pp. 342–56.
    Reprint of 1953.31.

54 KERNAN, ALVIN B. "Truth and Dramatic Mode in the Modern
Theatre: Chekhov, Pirandello and Williams." *Modern Drama* 1
(May):101–14.
    Discusses poetic drama and realistic plays and relates modern
dramatists to the thesis. TW "cannot, as Pirandello and Chekhov
do, simply deny the validity of the realistic perspective." In TW
"symbolism is poised against realism." Treats *SND* thoroughly

and discusses, among other things, setting. "For Williams, reality is the naturalistic setting of the urban jungle."

55 KERR, WALTER. "A Poetic Horror Story by Tennessee Williams." *New York Herald Tribune*, 19 January, sec. 4, pp. 1, 4.
Review of *GD*. Comments on poignancy of *SLS* and *SU*, how their drive "constitute[s] the whole truth about the universe." Refers to TW's movement toward "holocaust . . . pure horror."

56 _____. "Williams' 'Garden District' Presented at York Theater." *New York Herald Tribune*, 8 January, p. 16.
Review of *GD*. *SLS* "is a compelling . . . a serious and accomplished work to be seen. . . . [*SU*] is less vigorous as a piece of theater . . . decidedly minor Williams."

57 LAMBERT, J.W. "Theatre." *Sunday Times* (London), 23 March, p. 11.
Review of *GM*, Stratford production. Brief positive review of *GM* production at Theatre Royal, Stratford's revival.

58 LEWIS, THEOPHILUS. "Freud and the Split-Level Drama." *Catholic World* 187 (May):98–103.
Examines Freudian influence in drama. Shows consequence in audiences' perception levels—"two levels of intention, the apparent and the latent." Specifically relates this theory to *SND*.

59 "License Sought for 'Rose Tattoo.'" *Times* (London), 3 November, p. 7.
News item. Sam Wanamaker, director of New Shakespeare Theatre Club, has applied for license for public performance of *RT* in Liverpool.

60 "Liz 'The Cat.'" *New York Times Magazine*, 31 August, p. 34.
Short series of photos of Elizabeth Taylor as Maggie of *CAT*.

61 "London Sees 'Cat': Opinion Is Divided." *New York Times*, 31 January, p. 24.
News item stating reactions to *CAT* in London.

62 M., A. "Tennessee Williams—Leucotomy, Cannibalism." *Stage*, 18 September, p. 11.

Review of *GD*, London production. It "extends his morbid range." Plot details; "powerfully acted"—praises P. Neal.

63   MANNES, MARYA. "Something Unspeakable." *Reporter* 18 (6 February):42–43.

Written as a dramatic dialogue between Mannes and TW. Derisive and demeaning of TW; pivots on premise that TW wants nothing more than to appall and that his stock-in-trade is "frightful vision."

64   McCARTEN, JOHN. "Cotton-Belt Bedlam." *New Yorker* 34 (27 September):163–64.

Review of film of *CAT*. Talks of the monotonous aspects of the script; provides data on cast and directing.

65   McMANIGAL, ROD. Review of film of *CAT*. *Sight and Sound* 28 (Winter):36.

Responds negatively to film version of *CAT*; Elizabeth Taylor is unconvincing as Maggie. Script has been altered to "avoid offense." Critical of camera work.

66   MILLER, ARTHUR. "Morality and Modern Drama." *Educational Theatre Journal* 10 (October):190–202.

Interview conducted by Philip Gelb. "Williams is a realistic writer. . . . I think Williams is primarily interested in passion, in ecstasy, in creating a synthesis of his conflicting feelings." Refers to the authenticity of TW's view of the South, and how much it can be held to question.

67   ———. "The Shadows of the Gods: A Critical View of the American Theater." *Harper's* 217 (August):35–43.

Shows TW, in *SND*, carrying on tradition, as it was understood in Chekhov's work. Refers to *CAT* as having striking similarity to numerous other plays of its own period. Goes on to discuss *CAT*'s theme: "Williams has a long reach and a genuinely dramatic imagination." Also refers to TW's interest in "causation."

68   MILSTEAD, JOHN. "The Structure of Modern Tragedy." *Western Humanities Review* 12 (Autumn):365–69.

Claims that contemporary dramatists have "three approaches
to tragedy," and lists them as mythic, insisting on tragedy while
"denying tragic values," and retrieval of station for man. Analyzes place of "spiritual values" in a drama that is basically
naturalistic and realistic; cautions against excessive "self-con-
sciousness" on part of dramatist. Claims TW "sees man as trapped
by his environment and bedeviled by his own self-defeating ignorance."

69   "No Four-Letter Words." *Newsweek* 52 (1 September):56.
        Review of film of *CAT*. Criticizes "the practically plotless
     story"; calls it "adult film fare." Praises the acting, particularly
     Newman and Taylor.

70   NORTON, ELLIOT. "Williams' Career Nearly Ended at its Start Here."
     Boston Daily Record, 13 January, p. 40.
        Refers to TW's history in Boston, the controversy with *BA*;
     discusses upcoming opening of *CAT*.

71   "Off-Broadway Triumphs." *Newsweek* 58 (20 January):84.
        Review of *GD*. Praises *SLS* as showing TW's "unerring sense
     of theater. . . . Playwright Williams at his shattering best."

72   "People at Top of Entertainment's World." *Life* 45 (22 Decem-
     ber):165.
        Photo of TW and caption; refers to his "shattering power."

73   POWELL, DILYS. "Thin Ice on a Tin Roof." *Sunday Times* (London),
     12 October, p. 21.
        Review of film of *CAT*. "It is essentially heartless." The film
     leaves out the TW moral judgment implication in the play, mak-
     ing "a weakness at the center of the film." But "it is splendidly
     played."

74   PRICE, ROBERT. "A Man Named Tennessee." *New York Post*, 21
     April, sec. 2, pp. 1–2.
        A series of twelve pieces, beginning on this date and continu-
     ing until 4 May; interview-commentary format. TW discusses:
     OD; Audrey Wood; *RT*; violent events in his life; the South;
     newspapers; his childhood; early writing; college years; frater-

nity and wrestling team; first jobs; first theatrical productions in St. Louis; going to Iowa and New Orleans; going to California and New York; his first successes; writing for Hollywood; how success is changing him; how to find peace; *SND*'s success; his influence on American theater; McCullers; influence of D.H. Lawrence, Hart Crane, Chekhov, Rilke. Series continues according to following arrangement: 22 April, sec. 2, p. 2; 23 April, sec. 2, p. 2; 24 April, sec. 2, p. 2; 25 April, sec. 2, p. 2; 27 April, sec. 2, p. 2; 28 April, sec. 2, p. 2; 29 April, sec. 2, p. 2; 30 April, sec. 2, p. 2; 1 May, sec. 2, p. 2; 2 May, sec. 2, p. 2; 4 May, sec. 2, p. 5.

75   "Profile—Tennessee Williams." *Observer* (London), 26 January, p. 5. "Not since D.H. Lawrence has any writer provoked the British public to so many of its famous fits of morality.... His appearance and personality are, perhaps, willfully enigmatic.... he has a great mistrust of comfort, both physical and spiritual." Refers to *CAT* being banned in London.

76   PRYOR, THOMAS M. "New Movie Role for Miss Taylor." *New York Times*, 31 October, p. 33.
    News item. Elizabeth Taylor to star in film of *SLS*.

77   ————. "Play by Williams Coming to Screen." *New York Times*, 2 April, p. 36.
    News item. *OD* will be filmed with Magnani and A. Franciosa as stars.

78   ————. "Serling to Write Script for Film." *New York Times*, 1 December, p. 35.
    News item. Parts for film of *OD* offered to Brando and Magnani.

79   QUIGLY, ISABEL. Review of film of *CAT*. *Spectator* 201 (17 October):516.
    "A photographed stage play.... The play has been bowdlerised a bit.... The emphasis altered here and there." Through it all, TW "burns like a blow-lamp, a presence and a voice."

80   Review of film of *CAT*. *Time* 72 (15 September):92.

It's a minor piece relative to the play; analyzes themes and their interpretation by the cast; it "sits static."

81 Review of film of *CAT. Variety*, 13 August, p. 6.
Refers to it as "hard hitting and not watered-down." Praises the acting, the screenplay, the sets, and the color.

82 Review of *GD. Theatre Arts* 48 (March):13.
TW has "descended with a vengeance" in *SLS*; questions "its propriety as subject matter."

83 Review of *GD. Variety*, 15 January, pp. 74, 79.
SU "is replete with hushed psychological pressures that never quite burst out of their bounds." *SLS* "is chockful of overt hate, vindictiveness and shock."

84 RICHARDS, STANLEY. Review of *GD. Players* 34 (March):136–37.
Dismisses *SU*, but mildly praises *SLS* (it "is in the typical Williams vein: a probing study of decadence"). Praises the acting.

85 ROBINSON, ROBERT. "Cobweb Armour." *Spectator* 200 (28 March): 389–90.
Review of *GM*, London production. "Of all Mr. Williams's plays this comes nearest to establishing an independent circulatory system." Refers to this revival as "a somewhat dogged production."

86 ————. "Here Be Cannibals." *New Statesman* 56 (27 September):407.
Review of *GD*, London production. "For Mr. Tennessee Williams the world is a place in which we become aware of others only in so far as they stimulate our awareness of ourselves. . . . Mr. Williams is a doggedly minor artist, unable to distinguish between the usual and the odd. . . . His attitude to this world? Regret, but also fascination."

87 " 'The Rose Tattoo.' " *Times* (London), 21 November, p. 16.
News item. After five-year period of negotiations, Sam Wanamaker, director of New Shakespeare Theatre Club, was granted a license for public performances of *RT* in Liverpool.

88 " 'The Rose Tattoo' Judgment: Dublin Producer Discharged." *Times* (London), 10 June, p. 6.

News item. A. Simpson, director of *RT* production in Dublin, freed of charges of "producing for gain an indecent and profane performance" of *RT*. There was no statute legislated in Ireland that censored theater, only English common law.

89 SHANLEY, JOHN P. "Tennessee Williams on Television." *New York Times*, 13 April, sec. 2, p. 13.

Quotes by TW with regard to television and censorship. Preshowing interview in which he discusses upcoming airing of *LSG, TPC, MK*.

90 "State of Tennessee." *Theatre Arts* 42 (May):10–11.

Refers to Mike Wallace TV interview, with TW discussing his resistance to writing comedy, fame, being religious.

91 STAVROU, CONSTANTINE N. "Blanche DuBois and Emma Bovary." *Four Quarters* 7 (March):10–13.

Refers to Krutch's view that Flaubert and TW "are on the side of cynicism and realism." Claims they both avoid indictment: "Their depiction of reality does not imply, let alone constitute, a negation of said reality in the manner of the cynic, the misanthrope, the nihilist. . . . They are incorrigibly 'romantic.' " Focuses on the heroines Emma and Blanche; says both are "rebuffed and mauled by the Anti-romantic," and that both "are consigned to defeat."

92 "Storm over Theatre's Choice Of Play: Public Given Chance To Question Experts." *Times* (London), 2 June, p. 7.

News item. *CAT* produces controversy in Liverpool, which spurs theater to have public meeting on the subject of promoting unlicensed play. Public may question a panel of doctors, social welfare workers, and members of cast.

93 " 'Suddenly,' by Stages." *Theatre Arts* 42 (May):10.

History of *SLS* and its rewritings.

94 "Tennessee Williams Discussed." *Stage*, 16 October, p. 14.

GD discussed by panel in London on 8 October; panel consisting of Henry Adler, Ellen Pollock, Charles Marowitz. Emphasis on his "poetic quality" and his "personality in relation to [*GD*]."

95 "Tennessee Williams's Double Bill for London." *Times* (London), 4 August, p. 10.

News item. American producer (Herbert Machiz) to stage *GD* in London with British cast. Biography of Machiz.

96 "Two by Two." *Time* 71 (20 January):42.

Review of *GD*. *SLS* gets most attention: "a vivid display of Williams' unique virtues and persisting excesses."

97 VOWLES, RICHARD B. "Tennessee Williams and Strindberg." *Modern Drama* 1 (May):166–71.

Begins with Krutch's remark "Strindberg is ... directly or indirectly the strongest literary influence upon the currently admired" TW. Vowles traces possible influence through several plays: *YTM, GM, S&S, CR*. In sum, says he's "not so much interested in establishing a case of outright influence, as I am in determining the lineal descent of Williams from Strindberg."

98 _____. "Tennessee Williams: The World of His Imagery." *Tulane Drama Review* 3 (December):51–56.

Assesses reasons for "slight critical approbation" in literary press: too successful on Broadway; his "moral world"; the South itself. Reference made to *BA, CR, CAT*.

99 WALKER, DANTON. "Broadway." New York *Daily News*, 8 January, p. 51.

Gossip item. On *GD*: all the characters are "sick, sick, sick."

100 WALLACE, MIKE. "Tennessee Williams." In *Mike Wallace Asks: Highlights from 46 Controversial Interviews*. Edited by Charles Preston and Edward A. Hamilton. New York: Simon & Schuster, pp. 20–23.

Interview. TW discusses analysis, "infantile omnipotence," comedies, friendship, *BD* and Spellman's attack, religion.

101 WALSH, MOIRA. Review of film of *CAT*. *America* 99 (27 September):679.

TW "seems to outdo himself in devising exacerbated relationships for a Deep South family." Gives plot details; calls it "an improvement over the play."

102 ———. Review of film of *CAT*. *Catholic World* 188 (November):153–54.
    Brief. "A strong, well-acted drama." Its theme "has a tragic pertinence for many contemporary audiences." Discusses its theme of "lovelessness."

103 WASHBURN, BEATRICE. "Tennessee Williams: Mankind Is Doomed." *Miami Herald*, 28 January, sec. G, pp. 1, 6.
    Interview-commentary. TW discusses living and working in Miami, divorce rate, juvenile delinquency, hostility, corruption. "I think Armageddon really is at hand."

104 WATTS, RICHARD, JR. "The Magic of Tennessee Williams." *New York Post*, 19 January, p. 21.
    Justifies TW's gloomy and foreboding characters in light of O'Neill and Dostoyevsky; "he is a simply stunning writer for the theatre." Refers to *SLS* and *OD*.

105 ———. " 'Orpheus' Ascending." *Theatre Arts* 42 (September):25–26.
    Discusses *OD* and its failure on stage; calls it "a fine and darkly beautiful drama that deserved far more than the rather bleak reception" it got; attempts to determine its structural problems.

106 ———. "Two Dramas by Tennessee Williams." *New York Post*, 8 January, p. 64.
    Review of *GD*. "They weave a haunting spell that is virtually hypnotic in its compelling power."

107 "Way Down Yonder in Tennessee." *Time* 71 (3 March):72, 74.
    Interview. Focuses on his psychoanalysis; TW discusses his reaction to it, its effect on his work; plays' themes.

108 WEIGHTMAN, J.G. "Out and About: Varieties of Decomposition." *Twentieth Century* 164 (November):461–63.
    Review of *GD*, London production. Claims he prefers to con-

sider Americans "as our [Britishers'] imperial heirs—big strong men thinking confidently in global terms"—and therefore finds the "moist swell of rotting Southerners" in TW's *GD* particularly distasteful. Says it "would win a prize at any Satanic show." Disparages the plays but remains "convinced of Mr. Williams's cleverness."

109 "Williams Not Exportable?" *Variety*, 26 November, p. 1.
　　U.S. denies right to sell films *SND, CAT, BD* to certain countries.

110 WYATT, EUPHEMIA VAN RENSSELAER. Review of *GD*. *Catholic World* 186 (March):469–70.
　　"*Something Unspoken* is a trite little sketch." Regarding *SLS*: "uncannily deft in writing, unexcelled in horror. One leaves the theatre in a daze. . . . Dante's hell seems the Milky Way compared to Williams' garden."

111 YOUNG, STARK. "Stark Young Reviews 'A Glass Menagerie.'" In *Passionate Playgoer*. Edited by George Oppenheimer. New York: Viking Press, pp. 588–91.
　　Reprint of 1945.62, 1948.76.

112 ZOLOTOW, SAM. "Mankiewicz Play Interests Fonda." *New York Times*, 14 May, p. 37.
　　News item. Change of cast for *GD* postpones closing.

113 ZUNSER, JESSE. "The 'Off-Broadway' Phenomenon: Tennessee Williams et. al. Discuss and Analyze It, Praise and Hail It as 'Theatre of Tomorrow.'" *Cue* 27 (11 January):10, 15.
　　Discussion of the York Theatre, showing *GD*. TW cites problems with Broadway theaters.

1959

1 "All Palpitating with Life: Sick Obsession Overcome." *Times* (London), 15 May, p. 6.
　　Review of *OD*, London production. "An obsession with cor-

ruption appears to be growing on Mr. Tennessee Williams." Generally positive, but considered to be "longwinded."

2   ALVAREZ, A. "Hurry on Down." *New Statesman* 57 (23 May):721–22.
Review of *OD*, London production. Traces its compositional history; says it contains TW's "early romanticism and later symbolism, the poeticisms of his Rose (Tattoo) period and his later sweatshirt realism." Says it parallels most of TW's work by being "a myth retold in modern terms," and on that basis is "extremely ingenious." Says TW resembles Anouilh. Mixed review on production.

3   "Arletty and Babilee Star in 'Orpheus Descending.'" *Times* (London), 3 April, p. 14.
News and review of production in Paris of *OD*. Generally positive, with comments about the French translation. Praise for cast.

4   "As It Should Be." *Newsweek* 54 (28 December):64.
Review of film of *SLS*. "The script...is beautiful....An absorbing, original and often moving film." Criticizes its sometimes being bogged down by too much fascination with its own material.

5   ASTON, FRANK. "'Bird of Youth' Stormy Drama." *New York World-Telegram & Sun*, 11 March, p. 30.
Review of *SB*. "A magnificently theatrical storm of passion, bigotry and tolerance." Cast and plot details.

6   _____. "Enthused Cast Revives 'Orpheus Descending.'" *New York World-Telegram & Sun*, 6 October, p. 20.
Brief review of *OD*. Calls TW's style of drama "raw entertainment." Positive about production.

7   _____. "Tandy and Cronyn Win with Snappy 'Triple Play.'" *New York World-Telegram & Sun*, 16 April, p. 22.
Review of *PM*. "It is, briefly, typical of Williams: garrulous, creepy, clinical, understanding."

8   ATKINSON, BROOKS. "'Bird of Youth.'" *New York Times*, 22 March, sec. 2, p. 1.

Review of *SB*. Analysis of techniques, how play unfolds, and how characters develop. Praise for cast and TW as a writer.

9 ————. "The Theatre: Portrait of Corruption." *New York Times*, 11 March, p. 39.
Review of *SB*. "Despite the acrid nature of its material [SB] is Mr. Williams in a relaxed mood as a writer. He seems to have made some sort of peace with himself."

10 ————."Theatre: Triple Play." *New York Times*, 16 April, p. 28.
Review of *PM*. Positive comments on play and acting; *PM* as one of three plays presented in one show entitled *Triple Play*.

11 ————. " 'Triple Play.' " *New York Times*, 26 April, sec. 2, p. 1.
Review of *PM*. "On paper and on stage [PM] is a flawless gem. Although Mr. Williams has written several more powerful plays, he has not written anything so dainty, poignant and merciful since [GM]."

12 BALCH, JACK. "Kazan Rehearses Williams' 'Sweet Bird of Youth.' " *Theatre* 1 (March):22–23.
Newsy short piece; where they rehearse, how they look, and similar concerns.

13 ————. " A Profile of Tennessee Williams." *Theatre* 1 (April):15, 36, 40.
Profiles TW in St. Louis, Boston, Chicago; cites reactions to him from associates; discusses "whether Mr. Williams is more typically American than Mr. Miller."

14 BOLTON, WHITNEY. "Cronyns Make Most of 'Triple Play.' " New York *Morning Telegraph*, 17 April, p. 2.
Review of *PM*. Comments most on *PM*'s being a forerunner of *SND*. Brief.

15 ————. Interview with TW. New York *Morning Telegraph*, 26 January, pp. 1, 2.
TW discusses violence and shocking tactics in *SLS*; Kazan.

16 _____. "New York Theatre." New York *Morning Telegraph*, 16
    March, pp. 1, 2.
        Review of *SB*. About TW "speaking for himself through his
    young man [Chance]." Talks of the kinds of characters he creates
    and why.

17 _____. " 'Sweet Bird of Youth' Is a Brutal Drama." New York
    Morning Telegraph, 12 March, p. 2.
        Review of *SB*. Shows "that odd, personal, distinctive genius
    for a magic flow of words that is particularly and peculiarly the
    Williams trademark. . . . It has power . . . dimension."

18 _____. "Williams Talks on Violence." *Philadelphia Inquirer*, 1
    February, amusement sec., pp. 1, 4.
        Interview-commentary. TW discusses his house on E. 65th St.,
    champagne, Havana, Kazan, violence, torment and torture.

19 BRIEN, ALAN. "Noddy in Little Rock." *Spectator* 202 (22 May):
    725–26.
        Review of *OD*, London production. Plot, theme details; faults
    in production are more Tony Richardson's (director) than TW's,
    although he claims TW's world is seen "through the distorted
    magnifying eye of a brilliant child—a world full of mysterious
    obscenities, motiveless violence." Refers to its "dreamy, slow,
    doom-laden naturalism."

20 _____. "Shades of the Prison-House." *Spectator* 202 (23 January):
    103, 105.
        Review of *RT*, London production. TW is a romantic "during
    the decadence of romanticism"; he "is obsessed with himself
    at the age of puberty." Claims *RT* is "another [TW] commer-
    cial for the therapeutic value of sex." The writing is bad, and
    it's a "flawed production."

21 BROOKS, CHARLES. "The Comic Tennessee Williams." *Quarterly
    Journal of Speech* 44 (October):275–81.
        Traces the history of TW's use of comedy, claiming that in
    RT, for example, comic contrast produces "perhaps the most
    effective line." Attempts to illustrate his "comic evaluations" of
    various dimensions in the plays, including "cultural illusions" and
    religion. Cites examples in *BD*, *SND*, *RT*, *CAT*.

22 BRUSTEIN, ROBERT. "Sweet Bird of Success." *Encounter* 12 (June): 59–60.

Claims *SB* is "the most baldly personal of a corpus of drama already unusual for its subjectivity," and asserts that "the play is interesting primarily if you are interested in its author," but that "as dramatic art, it is disturbingly bad—aimless, dishonest and crudely melodramatic." Claims TW's "ignorance of, and obsession with, himself" is his main problem in writing good plays. Refers to his Freudian influences and his "pseudo-Lawrencian affirmations."

23 _____. "Williams' Nebulous Nightmare." *Hudson Review* 12 (Summer):255–60.

Review of *SB*. Maintains that the dramatic action itself is only a pretext for TW's "hazy notions about . . . Sex, Youth, Time, Corruption. . . . [SB], in consequence, contains the author's most disappointing writing since *BA*." Says it's unnecessarily solipsistic, both in how the characters are drawn and in various actors' (productions') interpretations. Contrasts with Strindberg and says TW's "nightmare does not penetrate to a deeper subjective reality." Refers to Christian context in the play, its pagan implications, the central theme, its "fraudulent conflict."

24 CALTA, LOUIS. "Actor Gets Rights to Business Play." *New York Times*, 7 January, p. 28.

News item. Opening date set for *SB;* touring rights for *GD* acquired by V. Rubber, F. Ackerman.

25 _____. "Play by Williams on ANTA Double Bill." *New York Times*, 15 April, p. 30.

News item. *IR* presented as one of two plays by American National Theatre and Academy; pro and con analysis with praise for cast.

26 _____. "The Theatre: 'Orpheus Descending.'" *New York Times*, 6 October, p. 45.

Review of *OD*. Brief compliments for cast, with brief synopsis of plot for this revival.

27 CARPENTER, CHARLES A., JR., and COOK, ELIZABETH. "Addenda to Tennessee Williams: A Selected Bibliography." *Modern Drama* 2 (December):220–23.

Additions to the Nadine Dony check list in May 1958 *Modern Drama* (1958.25).

28 CHAPMAN, JOHN. "Tandy, Cronyn and 'Triple Play' Add Up to a Diverting Evening." New York *Daily News*, 16 April, p. 77.
Review of *PM*. "A beautifully made, very moving portrait of a batty old spinster." Traces relationship to *SND*.

29 ———. "Williams' 'Sweet Bird of Youth' Weird, Sordid and Fascinating." New York *Daily News*, 11 March, p. 65.
Review of *SB*. TW "is a greatly-gifted, extraordinarily original and dirty minded dramatist who has been losing hope for the human race . . . [he] has an odd and curious strength . . . [he] cannot be ignored . . . [he] has written [in *SB*] of moral and physical decadence as shockingly as he can."

30 CLURMAN, HAROLD. "Is Off-Broadway On or Really Off?" *New York Times Magazine*, 22 March, pp. 26, 61–62.
GD mentioned briefly as example in article about off-Broadway productions.

31 ———. "The Neon Sickness." *Observer* (London), 17 May, p. 19.
Profile of TW. At time of *OD* being produced in London, TW talked of as a romantic and social playwright.

32 ———. *OD*. *Nation* 188 (20 June):563.
Brief. News of the Paris production *La Descente d'Orphée*.

33 ———. Review of *SB*. *Nation* 188 (28 March):281–83.
SB "interested me more as a phenomenon than as a play." Analyzes themes; focuses on problems in characterization in Chance; praises cast. "Its place in the author's development and its fascination for the audience strike me as more significant than its value as drama. . . . What we suspect in [*SB*] is that Williams has become immobilized in his ideology." Reprinted: 1966.14.

34 COLEMAN, ROBERT. " 'Sweet Bird of Youth' Is Sure Fire Hit." New
York *Daily Mirror*, 11 March, p. A–1.
Review of *SB*. TW is "again dealing with the abnormal and
frustrated. . . . [It's] hypnotic theatre."

35 ———. " 'Triple Play' Proves a Winner." New York *Daily Mirror*,
16 April, p. 25.
Review of *PM*. "A touching cameo." Very brief on TW.

36 COTTER, JERRY. "The New Plays." *Sign* 38 (May):55.
Brief review of *SB*. Cites the sordid realm of TW's "despair and
despondency and degeneracy." TW "dissipates his talent."

37 CRIST, JUDITH. " 'Orpheus Descending' in Revival at Gramercy Arts."
New York Herald Tribune, 6 October, sec. 2, p. 6.
Review of *OD*. "A lesser Tennessee Williams work . . . in the
hands of a less than inspired cast." Refers to the conditions
upon which TW allowed the revival.

38 CROWTHER, BOSLEY. "The Screen: 'Suddenly, Last Summer.' " *New
York Times*, 23 December, p. 22.
Review of film of *SLS*. "Direction is strained and sluggish, as
is, indeed, the whole conceit of the drama. It should have been
left to the off-Broadway stage."

39 "Drama Mailbag." *New York Times*, 22 March, sec. 2, p. 3.
Five letters to editor commenting on *SB*, four positive and one
negative.

40 DRIVER, TOM F. "Epistle from the Thespians." *Christian Century*
76 (15 April):455.
SB is "the boldest kind of theatrical experimentation, certainly
the most daring and probably the most haunting thing he has
ever written." Would be hard "to explain why, deeply opposed as
it is to Christianity, it is Williams' most religious play."

41 ———. "Epistle from the Thespians." *Christian Century* 76 (17
June):726.
Examines "the question of sexual morality" in *SB*, how TW
and T.S. Eliot (in *The Waste Land*) "took a similar starting

point. . . . [SB] is to be regarded as profoundly un-Christian. But it retains the pagan religious seriousness."

42 _____. "Tennessee Williams' Best." *New Republic* 140 (20 April):21–22.
   Review of *SB*. TW has related his "dream . . . with daring and power unequaled in his previous work." Praises Kazan. Philosophic about meaning.

43 DUPREY, RICHARD A. "Tennessee Williams' Search for Innocence." *Catholic World* 189 (June):191–94.
   SB "leaves one limp with a revelation of overwhelming evil. . . . [It's] deistic in concept." Compares to *OD*; praises TW for showing "at least a hunger for truth."

44 FUNKE, LEWIS. "News and Gossip Gathered on the Rialto." *New York Times*, 6 December, sec. 2, p. 5.
   News-gossip item. TW returns from global tour with four playscripts: *PA, NI, MT, PT*.

45 _____. "Rialto Gossip." *New York Times*, 8 March, sec. 2, p. 1.
   Announcement that TW will attend premiere of *SB*, then off to Key West to work on *PA*.

46 GASSEL, SYLVIA. "Sex, Sin and Brimstone in Tennessee Williams." *Village Voice*, 24 June, pp. 8–9.
   Review of *SB*. Refers to TW and his "ultra-conservative view of life. . . . [TW] is a dyed-in-the-wool Puritan, Southern variety, and as such does nothing at all to disturb our conventional attitude toward sex." Illustrates the position by discusssing the fate awaiting his female characters in *SND* and *RT*.

47 GASSNER, JOHN. Review of *SB*. *Educational Theatre Journal* 11 (May):122–23.
   "A genuinely theatrical imagination enables Tennessee Williams to project his theme and story with frequently stunning effect. . . . [An] excellent portrait on the stage." Refers repeatedly to "the power" of the composite of script, staging, and acting: ". . . admirable atmospheric evocativeness in the author's writing."

48 GEIER, WOODROW AUGUSTUS. "Images of Man in Five American Dramatists: A Theological Critique." Ph.D. dissertation, Vanderbilt University.

Concerns the theological aspects in the works of TW and four other American dramatists. Also addresses the concepts of individuality and Incarnation-Resurrection and how they relate to the playwrights' work. (*DA* 20:1463–64.)

49 GELB, ARTHUR. "Portman Named by Kim Stanley." *New York Times*, 23 March, p. 27.

PM to replace play *I Spy* by J. Mortimer in a triple-bill show called *Triple Play*.

50 ———. " 'The Purification' by Williams Is Staged." *New York Times*, 9 December, p. 57.

Review of *P*. "Underscored by the haunting music of guitar and the dolorous chanting of a chorus, it has a somber unity and beauty that soar beyond the limits of our earth-bound contemporary theatre."

51 ———. "Williams Booed at Film Preview." *New York Times*, 8 December, p. 58.

Gossip. After a preview showing of *FK*, TW was recognized and booed. His explanation was given.

52 GRAY, PAUL. "Alteration at No Extra Charge." *Saturday Review* 42 (18 April):29.

Letter to editor responding to H. Hewes (28 March) review of *SB*. Rebuttal from Hewes follows on same page.

53 HAYES, RICHARD. Review of *SB*. *Commonweal* 70 (24 April):102.

Brief. "An ultimate technical bravura marks Tennessee Williams' latest—last?—parable of violation. . . . [*SB*] has a lyric unity, too." Praises both Page and Newman, but singles out the latter as the actor "who extends the play into a macabre poetics."

54 HERRIDGE, FRANCES. " 'Orpheus' Returns with Full Impact." *New York Post*, 6 October, p. 66.

Brief review of *OD*. Refers to TW's world of "terrifying power of evil and doom . . . [which] comes vividly to life."

55 HEWES, HENRY. "Mr. Menotti's Expensive Hobby." *Saturday Review*
      42 (1 August):30.
        Review of *NI*. Discusses *NI*'s premiere at Spoleto, Italy. "The
      play has interesting characters."

56 _____. "Tennessee's Eastern Message." *Saturday Review* 42 (28
      March):26.
        Review of *SB*. "Has more wonderful sights in its landscape
      than any American play this season.... [Its] speeches [are]
      fashioned with the great playwright's special brand of poetic
      imagery ... rare euphemistic humor, and a simultaneous recog-
      nition of the ecstatic wonder and degraded terror of life."

57 _____. "Tenstrikes." *Saturday Review* 42 (25 April):23.
        Review of *IR*. TW's "purest piece of dramatic writing" dis-
      cusses D. H. Lawrence source; praises production.

58 HIGHET, GILBERT. "A Memorandum." *Horizon* 1 (May):54–55.
        Disguised as a memo to TW from Seneca: "I must express my
      admiration for your work.... But I have a bit of advice for you
      about a special dramatic effect in which you have almost rivaled
      me: horror.... You have a marvelous dramatic sense, but you are
      in danger of blunting it and wasting your creative energy."

59 HOBE. Review of *SB*. *Variety*, 18 March, p. 90.
        A "pulsating restatement of the familiar Williams theme of
      the corrupting influence of time on the sweet innocence of
      youth." Praise for Newman and Page, and includes quotes
      from the play. "Its sheer power holds an audience spellbound."

60 _____. "'Triple Play.'" *Variety*, 22 April, p. 78.
        "Triple Play"—a triple bill that included TW's *PM* (which is
      noted as possible basis for *SND*). *PM* "is a taut, potent and
      touching drama that demonstrates anew the unmistakability of
      a genuine artist." Praises Tandy "who has never done anything
      finer."

61 "Human Conflicts." *Times Literary Supplement*, 19 June, p. 370.
        Book review of *GD*, British publication. Praises the dramatic
      effort and accomplishment, but says TW "has written a play

with catastrophe and no denouement," and that "in play after play this dramatist has been running down a backstreet full of noisome human garbage, decadence, depravity, squalor."

62 HYAMS, JOE. "Tennessee Williams Turns Critic." *New York Herald Tribune*, 23 December, p. 13.
   Interview. At time of release of film of *SLS*, TW discusses what he thinks about the films based on his plays; refers to *FK*, *SLS*, *RT*, *GM*, *SND*, *CAT*.

63 Interview. *Daily Express* (London), 5 May, p. 10.
   TW discusses shock therapy, sympathy, hatred, vulgarity, prejudice, love, snobbery. All these addressed personally as well as matters of his drama.

64 "Into Purgatory Again." *Newsweek* 53 (23 March):75–76.
   Review of *SB*. "Once again Williams is involved with humanity in the purgatorial reaches of decadence and despair." Calls it "triumph for Tennessee." Adds brief interview with TW; he discusses *SB* ("the toughest one I've ever done"), how he works, his asthma, *PA*.

65 JAMPEL, DAVE. "Tennessee Williams Touring Orient, Working in Mornings on Four Scripts." *Variety*, 30 September, p. 1.
   Brief news item. TW on first visit to Orient, has four drafts of four plays.

66 JONES, ROBERT EMMET. "Tennessee Williams' Early Heroines." *Modern Drama* 2 (December):211–19.
   Starts with premise that "critics have generally agreed that the heroines of [TW] are his finest creations," and then goes on to analyze the "two types of women in the plays": "[1] relics of the moribund tradition of gentility . . .; and [2] the healthy, uncultured, basically sensual women, usually of Latin origin." Relates theory to Alma, Cassandra, Blanche, and Amanda, among others. Maintains that "there is little that is tragic about the early Williams heroines." Reprinted: 1961.41.

67 JUSTICE, DONALD. "Unhappy Fate of the 'Poetic.'" *Poetry* 93 (March):402–3.

Brief book review of *OD, BA, SLS*. Chastises works for "typical Williams image of the poetry of life; contrived out of memories of the past." *OD* is "a key work to the understanding of Williams."

68 KERR, WALTER. "Another Fierce Drama by Tennessee Williams." *New York Herald Tribune*, 22 March, sec. 4, pp. 1, 2.
Review of *SB*. Praises its "independent mastery.... The authority this restless, howling, defiant work exercises over us is wholly its own.... [It's] thrilling."

69 _____. "Does Our Stage Mirror Our World? Yes, but the Image Has False Whiskers." *New York Herald Tribune*, 6 September, sec. 4, p. 1.
Review of *SB*. "I am by no means certain that the exotic flavor of 'Sweet Bird of Youth' [is] wholly without value as a contemporary sounding board." Relates *SB* to *J.B.* and *A Raisin in the Sun*.

70 _____. "First Night Report: 'Sweet Bird of Youth.'" *New York Herald Tribune*, 11 March, p. 16.
Review of *SB*. "A succession of fuses, deliberately—and for the most part magnificently—lighted.... This is the noise of passion, of creative energy, of exploration and adventure... enormously exciting." Reprinted: 1963.32.

71 _____. "First Night Report: 'Triple Play.'" *New York Herald Tribune*, 16 April, p. 14.
Review of *PM*. "Minor Tennessee Williams... a minor evening." Traces relationship to *SND*. Brief.

72 _____. "In 'Bird,' a Jolt; Next, Tragedy?" *New York Herald Tribune*, 17 May, sec. 4, pp. 1, 2.
Review of *SB*. "The biggest, most exhilarating jolt we've had all season.... [It] shake[s] the theater with its vitality." Talks of wanting *more* from TW, "want[ing] tragedy. Mr. Williams seems capable of it but not yet ready to reach for it."

73 LANDWEHR, SHELLY. "Manhattan Tips." *Theatre* 1 (December):10.
Photo of TW and Magnani dining in Boboli.

74 "Legion Labels Film." *New York Times*, 4 December, p. 36.
News item. National Legion of Decency has given film version of *SLS* a separate classification.

75 "Legit & Followup." *Variety*, 23 December, p. 56.
Review of *SB* nine months after its Broadway premiere. "One of Williams' most provocative theatrical expressions, a poetic fable of our time."

76 Letters to the Editor: "Driver and Williams." *Christian Century* 76 (22 July):854.
Three letters to editor about Driver's TW reviews of *SB*: two accuse him of missing the point; one praises him.

77 Lewis, Theophilus. "Theatre." *America* 101 (4 April):55–56.
Review of *SB*. TW "seems to think that sex is the elixir of life.... Beneath the noisome scum, however, there is shrewd observation of character and at least the germ of moral homily."

78 "Lisbon Critic Pans 'Cat.'" *New York Times*, 23 October, p. 23.
News item. Portugal critics give negative review to *CAT*.

79 "Lovers in Quest of Youth." *Life* 46 (20 April):71–73.
On *SB*, brief. Mentions the roles of Page and Newman, and refers to the play's moral. Several photos.

80 M., A. "Smooth Minutia." *Village Voice*, 6 May, p. 8.
Brief review of *PM*. "A lesser Williams... which strangely works eventually, in spite of itself."

81 McClain, John. "The Cronyns Score a Clean Two-Base Hit." *New York Journal-American*, 16 April, p. 20.
Review of *PM*. "Sheer and horrendous Williams.... The piece amounts almost to a demented monologue."

82 _____. "Excellent Job by Gifted Cast." *New York Journal-American*, 6 October, p. 15.
Review of *OD*. It "remains one of Tennessee Williams' most powerful and persuasive offerings.... [Has a] mood of loneliness and despair as only Mr. Williams can display it."

83 _____. "Hot *Bird* Flies to Town." *New York Journal-American*,
   8 March, p. 27L.
      Advance notice of *SB*'s opening. Refers to Kazan and TW,
   Newman, the plot, TW's method of writing.

84 _____. "Williams' Best—and Maybe Best of Year." *New York
   Journal-American*, 11 March, p. 21.
      Review of *SB*. " 'Power' ... best expresses this latest effort by
   our brightest scripter. ... The writer's technique is as unconventional as it is unsure. ... Bold and brilliant theatre."

85 McCullers, Carson. "The Flowering Dream: Notes on Writing."
   Esquire 52 (December):162–64.
      Comments on her own writing relative to TW, Hemingway,
   and Faulkner.

86 Mannes, Marya. "Sour Bird, Sweet Raisin." *Reporter* 20 (16
   April):34.
      Review of *SB*. *SB* is a record of "depravity, sickness, and deg-
   radation"; chides critics and audiences who like it. Claims, nonetheless, that "it is without a doubt one of the decade's finest
   productions," and that "it is the nature of the excitement that
   disturbs me deeply: a violence of corruption and decay in which
   all natural appetites are diverted—and perverted." Praises Page
   and Kazan.

87 Marriott, R.B. "Tennessee Williams Loves Tenderness—but Brutality Makes Better Copy." *Stage*, 21 May, p. 8.
      Interview-commentary. TW discusses *OD*, tenderness, brutality,
   the South. Commentary focuses on his arrival in London for
   opening of *OD*.

88 Michelfelder, William F. "Tennessee Williams, Sensitive Poet,
   Still Searches for Serenity." *New York World-Telegram & Sun*,
   11 March, p. 17.
      Review of *SB*. "An aesthetic fulfillment." Refers to TW saying,
   "I am poisoned by success."

89 "Mr. Tennessee Williams Writes Another Powerful Play." *Times*
   (London), 10 April, p. 4.

Review and brief synopsis of New York production of *SB*. Generally positive: "bears a certain resemblance to the film 'Sunset Boulevard.'"

90 NASON, RICHARD. "'Fugitive' Is Shot." *New York Times*, 5 July, sec. 2, p. 5.
Brief news item. A day in the filming of *FK*.

91 NEDI. Review of *OD*. *Variety*, 21 October, p. 82.
A "dark tragedy in search for truth." Describes production as having added dimension that the earlier Broadway production lacked.

92 "Paris Sees Arletty in Play by Williams." *New York Times*, 18 March, p. 44.
Semipositive reviews given to French version of *OD* with enthusiasm for actress Arletty.

93 Review of *SB*. *Theatre Arts* 43 (May):21–22.
Brief. Praises it; talks of its "poetic-symbolic overlay."

94 Review of *SB*. *Time* 73 (23 March):58.
Refers to "the sex violence, the perfumed decay" in the play. It's "very close to parody, but the wonder is that Williams should be so inept at imitating himself.... In essence, *Bird* copies *Cat*." Demeans the positive reviews in New York City's dailies.

95 RODO. "Bird in Book Form." *Variety*, 2 December, p. 77.
Announces publication of the "acting" version of *SB* complete with pertinent production credits.

96 ROSS, DON. "'Sweet Bird of Youth' Violent in Tennessee Williams Style." *New York Herald Tribune*, 8 March, pp. 1, 9.
Interview-commentary during week previous to premiere of *SB*. TW discusses Broadway hits, money, big business, luridness, security, psychiatric care, drinking.

97 SHIPLEY, JOSEPH T. "Tennessee Williams' Unsweet and Unsoaring Bird of Youth." *New Leader* 49 (30 March):26.

Brief review of *SB*. Its art is "stifled [in] the marsh fire of melodrama."

98   STURDEVANT, JOHN. "Tennessee Williams." *American Weekly*, 21 June, pp. 12–15.
Interview at time of "current *Sweet Bird*." Discusses his success through the years, his fondness for *Streetcar*, his dominant themes.

99   " 'Sweet Bird of Youth': In Unmeditated Flight." *Esquire* 51 (April):24.
Mentions the simultaneous publishing and opening of the play; some details of the play's background and TW's reactions to aspects of its Broadway production. (Complete text of *SB* in same issue, pp. 114–55.)

100   TALLMER, JERRY. "Mr. Williams' New Play." *Village Voice*, 18 March, p. 9.
Review of *SB*. Finds little quality except for Page's performance; refers to the play's two divisions as "unrelated" and causing problems in the production.

101   T[ALLMER], J[ERRY]. Review of *P*. *Village Voice*, 16 December, p. 8.
Notes its having been written originally for Margo Jones' Theatre in Dallas; plot summary. "It is Mr. Williams that Mr. Williams is writing about here, in close relation to" *SLS*.

102   ———. Review of *OD*. *Village Voice*, 14 October, p. 9.
"A beautiful, soft-burning, thrilling production ... [with] tenderness, richness of spirit, affirmation in negation and lyric attainment of fused anger."

103   "Tennessee Laughter." *Time* 73 (12 January):54, 56.
Review of *PA*, Miami production. Refers to the "grimly bizarre comedy." Mentions TW's attempt to direct the production, his return to playwriting after "well-advertised long-term leave on the psychiatrist's couch." "Williams is still undecided about taking [PA] to Broadway."

104   "Tennessee Sez He's Finished Scripting Pix; Hates to Re-Create." *Variety*, 4 November, p. 23.

In Tokyo, TW says he'll do no more screenplays; talks of *OD* and his displeasure with film of *CAT*.

105 "Theatre: ANTA Matinee." *Village Voice*, 22 April, p. 7.
Review of *IR*. "An exquisite fragment by Tennessee Williams, receiv[ing] its ideal production." Refers to it as "this beautiful effort."

106 THESPIS. Review of *RT*. *English* 12 (Summer):184.
Brief; original British production. Ample plot analysis; calls it "a typical Tennessee Williams portrait of physical obsession." Praises the acting.

107 " 'Triple Play.' " *Theatre Arts* 43 (June):9.
PM is "interesting principally in an academic sense.... 'Portrait of a Madonna' is, indeed, the short play out of which *Streetcar* grew."

108 TYNAN, KENNETH. "A for Effort, O for Obstinacy." *New Yorker* 35 (25 April):82–83, 85.
Review of *PM*. Links the central character to Blanche of *SND*. Plot summary.

109 _____. Review of *SB*. *New Yorker* 35 (21 March):98–100.
Almost everything except Page's performance "dismayed and alarmed" him. Plot summary, commentary, and analysis; refers to disregard for "laws of dramatic structure." Reprinted: 1961.91.

110 VIDAL, GORE. "Love, Love, Love." *Partisan Review* 26 (Fall):613–20.
"I save any further defense of Williams for another occasion, since my intention in these notes is entirely destructive."

111 WATTS, RICHARD, JR. "The Magic of Tennessee Williams." *New York Post*, 22 March, p. 11.
Review of *SB*. "His most fascinating work ... staged close to perfection.... You are not only interested [in the characters] as curious specimens of decay, but concerned with them as human beings."

112 _____. "Tennessee Williams Does It Again." *New York Post*, 11 March, p. 78.
Review of *SB*. "Written with enormous dramatic drive. . . . [*SB*] proves that Mr. Williams has lost none of his force as a poet of evil. . . . Always this author's amazing power and candor are what emerge so unforgettably." Complains only "of a number of loose ends, the lack of complete fulfillment of several characters."

113 _____. "Three Dramatists in Minor Moods." *New York Post*, 16 April, p. 26.
Review of *PM*. "Distinctly minor accomplishment . . . given to monotony." Only important as draft for *SND*.

114 _____. "Williams and O'Casey and Chekhov." *New York Post*, 26 April, p. 14.
Review of *PM*. It's important, but a "decidedly lesser achievement. . . . [Its] fascination . . . is due to the evidence to be found in it that it served as a laboratory exercise for the final scene of [*SND*]." Also compares some speeches to those in *SLS* and *SB*.

115 "Williams' 'Orpheus' in London." *New York Times*, 15 May, p. 23.
News item. *OD* received politely but generally unenthusiastically by British critics.

116 WOLF, MORRIS PHILIP. "Casanova's Portmanteau: A Study of *Camino Real* in Relation to the Other Plays of Tennessee Williams, 1945–1955." Ph.D. dissertation, University of Georgia.
Twenty-five plays and twenty-one stories published from 1945–1955 are used as background in this examination of *CR*; discusses characters from *CR* in relation to corresponding characters from other TW works. (*DA* 20:2817.)

117 WYATT, EUPHEMIA VAN RENSSELAER. Review of *SB*. *Catholic World* 189 (May):158–59.
Lists all the characters with focus on their corruptness, how much, and why. Singles out Newman for best performance, and says, "Mr. Williams writes of evil with horrifying candor and power. . . . When will Mr. Williams write as cogently of the spirit as of the flesh?"

118 ZOLOTOW, SAM. "Williams' Drama Attracts Throng." *New York Times*, 12 March, p. 26.
News item. Success of *SB*; MGM acquires screen rights.

1960

1 ALPERT, HOLLIS. "In a Messel Garden." *Films and Filming* 6 (January):8, 32.
Review of film of *SLS*. Discusses the sets used in the London filming ("certainly one of the most lavish and astonishing ever created for a movie"). Numerous details on means and attitude in construction of the Venable garden set.

2 ————. "Orpheus Descended." *Saturday Review* 43 (23 April):28.
Review of film of *FK*. "A portentous movie. . . . [We're] up against some of the windiest writing Mr. Williams has ever perpetrated."

3 ASRAL, ERTEM. "Tennessee Williams on Stage and Screen." Ph.D. dissertation, University of Pennsylvania.
Examines the plays that have become films, the essential differences of each medium. (*GM*, for example, cited as illustration of how visual—as opposed to verbal—properties can change the character of a story.) References to *CAT*, *S&S*, *SND*. (*DA* 22:1169–70.)

4 ASTON, FRANK. "Williams Play at the Hayes." *New York World-Telegram & Sun*, 11 November, p. 16.
Review of *PA*. "Does little more than exhibit an ineptitude for sentence tossing. . . . Three acts of carefully planted comery [*sic*], tenderness, ruckuses, odd-ball cracks, doubts."

5 ATKINSON, BROOKS. "'Camino Real.'" *New York Times*, 29 May, sec. 2, p. 1.
Review of *CR*. Positive comments and analysis of *CR*; negative comments concerning some actors not being heard.

6 ————. "The Theatre: Black Phantasmagoria." *New York Times*, 17 May, p. 42.

Review of *CR*. General comments about *CR* revival at St. Marks Playhouse, neither pro nor con.

7   "Bad Dream Come True." *Newsweek* 55 (25 April):115.
      Brief review of film of *FK*. Refers to pretentious performances by Magnani and Brando; finds the plot laborious.

8   BAKER, PETER. Review of film of *SLS*. *Films and Filming* 6 (June):21.
      Claims the film gives the critic problems; praises dialogue, acting, "imaginative production." But claims, "It is false, phoney, and utterly lacking in human values." Plot details; says it "does not hold water. . . . [It] is exactly the kind of film that causes the East (not without justification) to brand the West as decadent. Only one truth stands out from it. Mr. Williams doesn't give a damn for the people he's writing about."

9   BECKLEY, PAUL V. " 'The Fugitive Kind': An Important Film." *New York Herald Tribune*, 24 April, sec. 4, pp. 1, 6.
      Review of film of *FK*. "One of the most important American films so far this year. . . . In this work Williams sees life in a sort of tragic vision."

10   ————. "New Movie." *New York Herald Tribune*, 15 April, p. 9.
      Review of film of *FK*. TW "has created a poetic but terrible vision. . . . This is strong meat." Refers to TW's "special feeling" for victims.

11   BOGDANOVICH, PETER. "The Fate of 'Camino Real.' " *Village Voice*, 21 July, pp. 7, 8.
      Review of *CR*. Praises it as a script, *not* as a production.

12   BOLTON, WHITNEY. "Affectionate Touch in Williams Reveals Flair for Comedy." New York *Morning Telegraph*, 28 November, p. 2.
      Review of *PA*. TW can "find the comedy frailties that lie in a human being"; relates it to a Chaplin concept of the comedic.

13   ————. " 'Camino Real' Still Has Spotty Flavor." New York *Morning Telegraph*, May 18, p. 2.
      Review of *CR*. This revival is "no more disciplined [than in

1953] but [TW's] philosophies seem much less capricious." Praises direction.

14 ————. "New Williams Play Has Its Moments." New York *Morning Telegraph*, 12 November, p. 2.
   Review of *PA*. TW's "bemused exploration into the crises of marriage. . . . some scenes with brilliant invention and almost firework use of the comedy principle."

15 ————. "Tennessee Williams' First Comedy Has 'Humor,' Not Jokes and Gags." New York *Morning Telegraph*, 3 October, p. 2.
   Interview-commentary. TW discusses *PA*, *NI*, Bette Davis, Castro and Cuba, his mother.

16 BOYLE, ROBERT. "Williams and Myopia." *America* 104 (19 November):263–65.
   Response to *America*'s 30 July "Is Williams' Vision Myopia?" Takes exception to previous assessment. Argues that TW "see[s] ultimates and express[es] them." Compares him with Hopkins; discusses concept of artistic vision; makes reference to *CAT*, *SLS* in his defense.

17 BRADY, LEO. "The Showcase." *Critic* 19 (August-September):61, 78.
   Furthers the Marya Mannes-TW debate; reviews both sides and relates the point ("violence, aberration and decay") to ancient theatrical tradition, maintaining, "Theatrical tradition comes to our aid also in trying to understand the kind of play Williams writes."

18 BRANDON, HENRY. "The State of the Theater: A Conversation with Arthur Miller." *Harper's* 221 (November):63–69.
   Offhanded comment by Miller on TW: "The Fifties became an era of gauze. Tennessee Williams is responsible for this in the main."

19 "Broadway Stage: Tennessee Williams's New-Found Optimism." *Times* (London), 23 November, p. 15.
   Review of *PA*. Limited to synopsis and general positive statements; examines the use TW makes of comedy.

20 BROOKING, JACK. "Directing 'Summer and Smoke': An Existentialist
    Approach." *Modern Drama* 2 (February):377–85.
        Invokes Clurman as basis for his argument that S&S lends it-
    self to new direction techniques. Surveys the abiding questions
    that the text prompts, the ways of answering them. Discounts
    the traditional moral standard of good and evil as devices for
    this play; says the play "takes on form and unity" when examined
    existentially. Focuses mainly on Alma and John as "types." Postu-
    lates this method as valuable for "unraveling . . . other modern
    plays."

21 "Brother's Eye-View of Tennessee Williams." *Variety*, 30 March,
    pp. 1, 79.
        Paulist Press addresses TW's spiritual life, as reported by his
    brother.

22 BRUSTEIN, ROBERT. "Disputed Authorship." *New Republic* 143 (28
    November):38–39.
        Review of *PA*. Calls it a "bourgeois psychodrama written to
    formula by a Broadway hack insufficiently schooled in his
    trade. . . . Williams never bored us like this before. . . . [He] has
    momentarily run out of autobiographical material. . . . This is the
    worst." Reprinted: 1965.7.

23 BURM. " 'Camino Real.' " *Variety*, 1 June, p. 72.
        Review of off-Broadway production. "Individual scenes have
    theatrical effectiveness, but the parts do not make a unified
    whole. . . . his message often remains too personal."

24 "Catholic Sheet Raps Williams." *Variety*, 27 July, pp. 2, 127.
        Brief news item. Notes Catholic papers' attacks on TW's "sub-
    standard values" and warning readers not to see his summer
    stock productions.

25 CHAPMAN, JOHN. "Period of Adjustment for Dramatist." New York
    Sunday News, 20 November, sec. 2, p. 1.
        Review of *PA*. TW "has strengthened his position as one of
    our foremost practicing dramatists" with this production. Dis-
    cusses the humor in *RT*, *SB*, and remains obviously pleased with
    this change toward humor in TW.

26 _____. "Williams' 'Period of Adjustment' Is an Affectionate Little Comedy." New York *Daily News,* 11 November, p. 60.

Review of *PA.* The play "shows Williams' interest in people and his ability to create them for the stage.... [It is a] rather charming little domestic comedy."

27 "Circle in Square to Add a Revival." *New York Times,* 5 April, p. 43.

News item. *CR* to be presented at Circle-in-the-Square.

28 CLAYTON, JOHN S. "The Sister Figure in the Works of Tennessee Williams." *Carolina Quarterly* 11 (Summer):47–60.

Attempts to "direct attention to the poet's truth rather than the historian's in Williams' autobiographical fiction." Cites TW's sister as "the central element of [his] past." Points out that TW "remained the physically delicate child who did not send away for the barbells, the bullied son who did not fetch Pap a clout alongside the head"—and other such observations. Applies his observations to the stories and plays accordingly.

29 _____. "Themes of Tennessee Williams." D.F.A. dissertation, Yale University.

Examines works of TW in an attempt to reveal a definite thematic pattern of character development. Characters identified are the Mother, the Father, the Sister, and the Son. Additional characters are the Delicate Lady, the Husband, the Salesman, the Artist, and the Natural Man. (*DAI* 30:718A.)

30 CLURMAN, HAROLD. Review of *PA. Nation* 191 (3 December):443, 44.

Brief. "The lightest and slightest of [TW's] plays." Plot summary; praises cast.

31 COLEMAN, ROBERT. "'Period' Is Touching Comedy." New York *Daily Mirror,* 11 November, p. Al.

Review of *PA.* "Packed with laughs, and they are often tender and touching.... [TW] garners chuckles that have a warm glow. He serves notice that he can handle comedy as well as drama with a shock in it.... It proves that Williams can make you laugh as well as cry."

32   CRIST, JUDITH. "Revival of 'Camino Real' at St. Mark's Playhouse."
     New York Herald Tribune, 17 May, p. 22.
          Review of *CR*. "A major accomplishment in a revival." It
     merits attention because of direction and cast, "but for little else."

33   CROWTHER, BOSLEY. "Screen: 'Fugitive Kind.'" *New York Times*,
     15 April, p. 13.
          Review of film of *FK*. Positive comments with brief synopsis
     and praise for cast.

34   _____. "Williams' Fugitives." *New York Times*, 24 April, sec. 2,
     p. 1.
          Review of film of *FK*. Positive comments, with plot summary
     and analysis of its themes. Some comparison to previous TW
     works.

35   DENT, ALAN. "Two Haunting Films." *Illustrated London News* 237
     (17 September):494.
          Review of film of *FK*. The script, with "so contrived a plot,"
     is highly predictable. The characters, "who ought, by all the laws
     of nature, to be inarticulate because their actions speak so much
     louder than words turn out to be picturesquely articulate after
     all." Praise, though reserved, for Brando; dismissal for Wood-
     ward.

36   "Dixie Proud of, Not Mad at Tennessee: 'No Beef on Williams'
     View of South.'" *Variety*, 20 April, p. 5.
          Refers to success of films of *SLS* and *CAT* as indicative of his
     being favored in South. Estimates given of box office takes on the
     two films.

37   "Double Bill Opens the Season: London University Drama Society."
     Times (London), 3 November, p. 16.
          News item. *SU* one of two plays produced by London Uni-
     versity Drama Society.

38   DRIVER, TOM F. Review of *PA*. *Christian Century* 77 (28 Decem-
     ber):1536.
          Considerable plot summary; reviewer found himself "utterly
     bored." Cites subject matter as cause.

39   DUSENBURY, WINIFRED L. "In the South." In *The Theme of Loneliness in Modern American Drama.* Gainesville: University of Florida Press, pp. 134–54.
Lillian Hellman, Paul Green, TW, and other Southern writers are examined with a view to their emphasis on the changing social and economic structure as the basis for "a kind of personal near-annihilation of those Southern aristocrats who cannot adapt themselves to changing conditions."

40   ELLIS, BROBURY PEARCE. " 'The True Originall Copies.' " [*The Glass Menagerie*]. *Tulane Drama Review* 5 (September):113–16.
Notes the problem of "at least four important texts" of *GM*; surveys the most pronounced differences and similarities, and calls attention to the critical problems arising from the confusion.

41   FOSTER, FREDERICK. "Filming *The Fugitive Kind.*" *American Cinematographer* 41 (June):354–55, 379–82.
Details include brief plot outline, technical problems, and difficult shots. One particular shot, one of the last ones of Magnani, is explained in detail.

42   FREEDLEY, GEORGE. "Of Books and Men." New York *Morning Telegraph*, 27 December, p. 2.
Brief mention of publication of *PA*.

43   ———. Review of *CR*. New York *Morning Telegraph*, 23 May, pp. 2, 10.
Brief. Calls the revival "too rough" a production.

44   GALLAWAY, MARIAN. Review of *SB*. *Players* 37 (November):42–43.
Brief. Praises it as a significant piece in the career of TW; minor theme analysis.

45   GARDINER, HAROLD C. "Is Williams' Vision Myopia?" *America* 103 (30 July):495–96.
Notes exchange of arguments printed in the *New York Times* between TW and Marya Mannes (Mannes' article and TW's rebuttal). Questions TW's point of view, his "vision," saying that to call TW a liar, that he does not see the things he describes, would be beyond the limits of valid criticism. Argues that while

TW *does* see what he describes, it is a warped, or incomplete, vision.

46 GASSNER, JOHN. Review of *CR*. *Educational Theatre Journal* 12 (October):227.

In an overview of Broadway season, Gassner refers to the Quintero revival of *CR* as lacking "provocativeness," that even though TW "apparently simplified" the script from its original production, there was no "true excitement" in the revival. Praises Quintero's "finely-spun, more moderate style of staging." Reprinted: 1968.14.

47 _____. "Tennessee Williams: 1940–1960." In *Theatre at the Crossroads*. New York: Holt, Rinehart & Winston, pp. 77–91.

Focuses on TW's early "embrace" of the audience, starting with *BA*, traces its consummation in *GM*, and discusses his career as it advanced from that point. Gives considerable biographical and show-biz data surrounding composition and production of the plays, calls attention to primary sources of influence (Chekhov, Lawrence, Faulkner); illustrates themes and technique in the little-discussed shorter plays; calls attention to dimensionality in his characterizations.

48 _____. "Tennessee Williams' 'Summer and Smoke': Williams' Shadow and Substance." In *Theatre at the Crossroads*. New York: Holt, Rinehart & Winston, pp. 218–23.

Says Quintero's production at Circle-in-the-Square (1952) brought *S&S* "a Rembrandtlike imagination," and claims it to be "a better play" than it was in 1948 primarily "because it gave excellent theatrical realization to the shadow rather than to the substance of the play." Discusses use of effects in achieving this quality. Contrasts fully and specifically with aspects of Broadway production.

49 _____. "Tennessee Williams; Williams' Descent: 'Orpheus Descending.'" In *Theatre at the Crossroads*. New York: Holt, Rinehart & Winston, pp. 223–26.

"One of the most chaotic contemporary works of genius" of the season. Finds TW "scatter[ing] the largesse of his invention and pessimism all over the stage." Says "the immediacy of his wild tale" obscures TW's efforts in the play; calls attention to attempt made "to present two of his major themes conjointly: the tragic isolation of the artist in the hell of modern society and the crucifixion of the pure male on the cross of sexuality."

50   _____. "Williams' Garden." In *Theatre at the Crossroads*. New York: Holt, Rinehart & Winston, pp. 226–28.

Dismisses *SU*, and calls *SLS* "a work of perversely overwhelming power." Refers later to the play as "the sensational expression of his most nihilistic mood," and questions whether there might be "an old-fashioned romanticism" in TW's work.

51   _____. "Williams' 'Sweet Bird of Youth.'" In *Theatre at the Crossroads*. New York: Holt, Rinehart & Winston, pp. 228–31.

Asserts that "Williams' picture of the deep South was no more inviting than the bleakest of Faulkner's Southern Gothic landscapes." Highlights Kazan's role in producing its intensity, and discusses several reasons for its early popularity. Encourages TW to become more serious about the convention of tragedy itself.

52 GELB, ARTHUR. "Williams and Kazan and the Big Walkout." *New York Times*, 1 May, sec. 2, pp. 1, 3.

Brief news item. Explanation of why Kazan walked out of production of *PA*. Quotes by TW and Kazan. Some gossip, some facts. TW admits he will probably never do another production with Kazan.

53 GRIFFIN, JOHN. Review of *PA*. *Theatre* 2 (December): 18, 45.

"Mr. Williams hasn't really changed so very much . . . [he hasn't] been entirely honest about this play." Concerned with "what must surely be Mr. Williams' real message."

54 GROSS, JESSE. "Williams' Rap for Film Version." *Variety*, 30 March, pp. 69, 75.

Regarding film of *SB*, a planned Spanish version; but plans are indefinite because of dislike of TW in Spain since he linked Spain to the cannibal scene in *SLS*.

55 HART, HENRY. Review of film of *SLS*. *Films in Review* 11 (January):39–41.

Suggests TW's motivation for writing the original play was that a psychiatrist told him "he had better stop denigrating normality and begin exposing the evils in homosexuality and its allied forms of vice." Claims this film "exposes clearly the foremost cause of male homosexuality." Ample plot summary; praises K. Hepburn.

56   HARTUNG, PHILIP T. "Encroaching Jungle." *Commonweal* 72 (29 April):127.
     Review of film of *FK*. "A mixture of styles and confusion of themes ... not very well planned to start with."

57   _____. "The Screen: The Voice of the Turtles." *Commonweal* 71 (1 January):396.
     Review of film of *SLS*. Lengthy plot summary and analysis, calling it a study in evil reminiscent of James' *The Turn of the Screw*. "One doesn't really believe *SLS*; but one does not quite disbelieve it—and the total effect is like that of a frightening nightmare that one can't fully shake off."

58   HATCH, ROBERT. Review of film of *SLS*. *Nation* 190 (16 January):59.
     The film has "a serial thriller tone" and becomes a "coldly fabricated melodrama." Emphasis on plot.

59   HERRIDGE, FRANCES. "Controversial 'Camino' Is Back." *New York Post*, 17 May, p. 66.
     Review of *CR*. TW's "most comprehensive vision of life—his farthest excursion into poetic and allegorical drama. ... Still Williams' most provocative play."

60   _____. "Sweet Bird Is Still Flying High." *New York Post*, 22 January, p. 50.
     Brief news item. Torn replacing Newman in role of Chance hasn't altered attendance.

61   HEWES, HENRY. "Snowflakes in Tennessee." *Saturday Review* 43 (26 November):28.
     Review of *PA*. "A deceptively merry new play ... a comic-strip view of the absurdities of modern marital discord. ... [TW] has

also seen the pathos in his characters." Discusses the charge that
TW "lean[s] a little too much on the psychosexual" elements.

62 HOBE. Review of *PA. Variety*, 16 November, p. 70.
Despite different tone, the new play is unmistakably TW—preoccupied with sexual maladjustment and explicit dialogue. "The
new play seems a juvenile treatment of a threadbare subject.
The laughs are there, but the play is shallow and forced."

63 "In the Gutter." *Time* 75 (11 April):76.
Analysis of contemporary decadence in theater. Quotes critics
and refers to the "disastrous influence" TW and others have had
on American stage.

64 JACKSON, ESTHER M. "The Problem of Form in the Drama of
Tennessee Williams." *College Language Association Journal* 4
(September):8–21.
Calls attention to "the argument between the 'ancients' and
the 'moderns'" regarding form. Applies the argument to TW.
Calls him "the most important writer in the American theatre,
the pivotal figure in a school of theatrical art which is largely
responsible for the development of an American *dramaturgy*."
Notes that "he has gained popular acclaim without substantial
critical acceptance. The censure of the academy has been, char-
acteristically, directed against his failure to conform to the traditional 'laws' of dramatic construction." Traces this rebellion in
other writers' work, and then examines TW's plays particularly.
Focuses on the realistic and antirealistic guises, "imaginative for-
mations," TW's "'plastic theatre,'" his "mythic perspectives," his
"popular language."

65 JACOBS, JAY. "Putting the Bite on Sebastian." *Reporter* 22 (4 February):37–38.
Review of film of SLS. "Mr. Williams's most hysterical view
thus far of what he seems to consider a bitch-eat-dog world." Plot
analysis.

66 JOHNSON, ALBERT. Review of film of SLS. *Film Quarterly* 13
(Spring):40–42.
Praise for cast and brief synopsis of each character's role.

67   KARSH, YOUSUF. "Tennessee Williams." *Coronet* 48 (May):62–63.
     One paragraph biographical sketch, plus photo.

68   KAUFFMAN, STANLEY. "Arty Horror, Straight Suspense." *New Republic* 142 (18 January):20–21.
     Review of film of *SLS*. "Basically a foolish unrewarding work but it could not have been conceived or written except by a dramatist of extraordinary talent." Examines plot problems, its "unresolved motivations." Reprinted: 1966.39.

69   _____. "The Tennessee Williams Cycle." *New Republic* 142 (2 May):21–22.
     Review of film of *FK*. Contains "a suspicion of bankruptcy of material." Examines its themes (and TW's history); TW's "name has become a trademark of sweaty sexuality." Praises Brando and Magnani. Reprinted: 1966.39.

70   KERR, WALTER. "Comic Muse of Williams Echoes Own True Sound." *New York Herald Tribune*, 20 November, sec. 4, p. 2.
     Review of *PA*. Plot summary and interpretation; calls it "not a conventional comedy" and refers to "Mr. Williams' slightly dark humor."

71   _____. "First Night Report: 'Period of Adjustment.'" *New York Herald Tribune*, 11 November, p. 10.
     Review of *PA*. "Nearly everything is made funny and touching as Dr. Williams ascends to the chair of human wisdom.... It's a believable evening, it's probably even a wise one." Discusses the humor at the heart of the play.

72   KLEP. "Show Out of Town." *Variety*, 19 October, p. 60.
     Review of *PA*, Wilmington production. TW "makes transition from serious drama to comedy with apparent ease.... The playwright is still concerned with human foibles, but from a different angle than in previous plays. There is a new warmth in his approach."

73   KNIGHT, ARTHUR. "Eating People Is Wrong." *Saturday Review* 43 (2 January):31.
     Review of film of *SLS*. Discusses its themes and their effect

on the future of "adult" films in U.S.A. "A wholly admirable rendering into film of a work that is at once fascinating and nauseating."

74 KUHN, HELEN W. Review of film of *FK*. *Films in Review* 11 (May):290–92.
"A mess of technical incompetence and psychopathic misrepresentation ... a disgrace to U.S. culture.... It derives from one of the last scraps ... at the bottom of Tennessee Williams' barrel of degenerate plays.... Tennessee Williams has unscrupulously tried to give this bilge social significance."

75 LARY. Review of *NI*. *Variety*, 31 August, p. 54.
Miami stock production. "Needs plenty of revision before being ready for Broadway. It lacks plot development, despite TW's normal quota of shock-lines."

76 LEJEUNE, C.A. "Deep in the Heart of Tennessee." *Observer*, 15 May, p. 21.
Review of film of *SLS*. Discusses its sensational aspects; generally negative.

77 LEWIS, THEOPHILUS. Review of *CR*. *America* 103 (2 July):422–24.
Brief. "We see his significance as a dramatist" more clearly here than in his other plays. "We see Williams, perhaps more richly endowed with imagination than any playwright since Shaw, led astray by the social and psychological fallacies of his age, trying to find a meaning in life." Lengthy description of the plot, noting that the drama ends on an affirmative note.

78 ————. Review of *PA*. *America* 104 (17 December):410–11.
Brief. Refers to TW's "mellow mood"; "most mature and amusing comedy of the season."

79 McCARTEN, JOHN. "Meagre Merriment." *New Yorker* 35 (9 January):74–75.
Review of film of *SLS*. "A preposterous and monotonous potpourri of incest, homosexuality, psychiatry, ... cannibalism." Plot summary.

80 _____. "Orpheus with a Hot Guitar." *New Yorker* 36 (23 April): 147–48.

Review of film of *FK*. Mostly plot summary; admits "Mr. Williams' muse is beyond my grasp." Calls *FK* "corn-pone melodrama."

81 _____. "Tennessee Tries a Tender Pitch." *New Yorker* 36 (19 November):93–94.

Review of *PA*. TW is "loquacious" and "has adopted a serio-comic attitude.... Unfortunately his attempts at comedy are all too often aimless or vulgar.... He advances ideas that are hopelessly banal."

82 McCLAIN. JOHN. "'Camino Real' Still Has Power." *New York Journal-American*, 17 May, p. 15.

Review of *CR*. A "contentious piece of puzzlement...Mr. Williams had to get out of his system." Refers to its "high-flown meanderings."

83 _____. "Tennessee at His Best." *New York Journal-American*, 11 November, p. 11.

Review of *PA*. "It is, quite simply, a resounding success.... The secret of its brilliance...is the author's exceptional artistry with the language....[TW] has come full cycle, from the diffuse and dissolute, to the comedy."

84 McHARRY, CHARLES. "'Camino Real' Revived, It's Loud but Obscure." New York *Daily News*, 23 May, p. 39.

Brief review of *CR*. Calls the revival "murky," and suggests TW was not sufficiently aware of his subject matter.

85 MALCOLM, DONALD. "Off Broadway." *New Yorker* 36 (28 May): 92, 94.

Review of *CR*. Attempts serious analysis of its fantasy properties. Finds faulty structure: "The plain fact is that Mr. Williams does not submit his fantasy to any order at all."

86 MANNES, MARYA. "Just Looking." *Reporter* 23 (22 December):35.

Review of *PA*. Says she regrets she urged TW to turn "his great talents away from the drama of shock and perversion" if this is the result. Calls it "an attenuated one-acter." Derides the whole intent and achievement: "the kind of colloquial squalor that passes for comedy."

87 _____. "Plea for Fairer Ladies." *New York Times Magazine,* 29 May, pp. 16, 26–27.
TW is heavily criticized for too much violence in drama.

88 MARKEL, LESTER. "One on the Aisle." *New York Times,* 7 August, sec. 2, pp. 1, 3.
In a criticism of stage and theater, TW is mentioned as a powerful writer but not the solution to the problems of theater.

89 MEKAS, JONAS. Review of film of *FK. Village Voice,* 20 April, p. 6.
Brief, somewhat negative. States that only two scenes in the film are worth seeing.

90 MOK, MICHAEL. "Tennessee Williams Writes Off Boredom." *New York World-Telegram & Sun,* 17 November, p. 17.
Interview. TW discusses *PA, SND* ("I think it's my best play"), his work generally.

91 "More Tennessee Williams Films." *Times* (London), 12 August, p. 5.
News item. Three more TW plays to be filmed—*SB, S&S, RSMS.*

92 NATANSON, WOJCIECH. "American Plays on Polish Stages." *Polish Review* 5 (Winter):86–89.
Mentions anxiety about how Polish audiences would deal with Stanley of *SND;* however, "no prejudicial generalizations were involved here; that the issue . . . is in the nature of a philosophical and . . . poetical metaphor." Refers to and quotes from Polish reviewers; focuses on their interest in the "subconscious-conscious" properties and problems in *SND.*

93 NATHAN, GEORGE JEAN. "Tennessee Williams." In *The Magic Mirror: Selected Writings on the Theatre.* Edited by Thomas Quinn Curtiss. New York: Alfred A. Knopf, pp. 238–42.
Reprint of 1948.50.

94   "The New Pictures." *Time* 75 (11 January):64, 66.
     Review of film of *SLS*. Treats the awkward themes and situa-
     tions; plot analysis; refers to the director's "considerable skill
     and taste."

95   "New Play on Broadway." *Time*, 76 (21 November), 75.
     Review of *PA*; refers to TW as "Broadway's master of violence."
     The play "seems somehow unsatisfying. . . . [*PA*] has Broadway's
     laureate of sex writing what for him is virtually light verse. . . .
     [TW is] trading claws for Santa Claus."

96   *PA. Theatre Arts* 44 (October):16.
     Photo of TW and brief mention of *PA*.

97   PEARSON, KENNETH. "Worlds of Violence." *Sunday Times Magazine*
     (London), 26 June, p. 40.
     Discusses TW as a "decadent Southerner" and refers to his
     use of violence.

98   POPKIN, HENRY. "The Plays of Tennessee Williams." *Tulane Drama
     Review* 4 (March):45–64.
     Discusses *SND* among other of TW's works, illustrating how
     Williams devises archetypal patterns that feature the healthy,
     handsome man (Adonis) and the decaying older woman (Gar-
     goyle). Refers to *SLS, SND, RSMS, RT*.

99   _____. "Williams, Osborne, or Beckett?" *New York Times Maga-
     zine*, 13 November, pp. 32–33, 119, 121.
     Attempts to show inherent differences in American, British,
     and French theater (and each with its corresponding nationality)
     by using TW, Osborne, and Beckett among others as examples.
     U.S. drama deals with psychology, British with social rebellion,
     and French with experimental themes.

100 POWELL, DILYS. "Way Down with Tennessee." *Sunday Times* (Lon-
     don), 4 September, p. 35.
     Review of film of *FK*. "One of the more likeable of the Ten-
     nessee Williams films." Details on acting and production.

101 PROUSE, DEREK. Review of film of *FK*. *Sight and Sound* 29 (Sum-
     mer):144–45.

Brief. Poor camera work and script; praise for Magnani and Brando.

102 PYRO. "The Fugitive Kind." *Variety*, 13 April, p. 6.
Review of film of *FK*. "Not basically one of Tennessee Williams' better works. . . . The general level of the production reflects professional competence, but as an entertainment experience 'The Fugitive Kind' is a disappointment."

103 QUIGLY, ISABEL. "Mumble-Jumble." *Spectator* 205 (9 September): 372–74.
Review of film of *FK*. "Mr. Lumet is one of the best directors to tackle Tennessee Williams: less visually exciting than **Kazan**, he uses darkness and junk with effect." Praises cast but says TW "seems more and more to parody himself."

104 ———. "Neither Here nor There." *Spectator* 204 (20 May):736–38.
Review of film of *SLS*. *SLS* "seems to me not so much moral or immoral as simply a caricature; not admirable or deplorable, but absurd. . . . I found [*SLS*] hollow, unproductive, unalive, and above all stagy: not cinematic. . . . To me, the film's great and only pleasure lay in the presence of Katharine Hepburn, infinitely stylish and remote."

105 Review of *FK*. *Time* 75 (18 April):81.
Quotes about the play from TW; plot summary; "like all of Williams' plays, 'The Fugitive Kind' is aswarm with symptoms and symbols for amateur psychiatrists to figure out and snigger at."

106 ROBERTS, MEADE. "Williams and Me." *Films and Filming* 6 (August):71.
TW is one of the few writers who invariably works on screenplays of his own plays.

107 ROSS, DON. "A Williams Play Ends Happily." *New York Herald Tribune*, 6 November, sec. 4, pp. 1, 3.
Interview-commentary. TW discusses "happy" aspects of *PA*;

"my work reflects what's going on in the world only obliquely";
NI and *MT*.

108   SAGAR, K.M. "What Mr. Williams Has Made of D.H. Lawrence."
      Twentieth Century 168 (August):143–53.
      Calls readers' attention to TW's acknowledgement of D.H.
      Lawrence as "the greatest writer of our time," and goes on to
      investigate "Lawrentian themes and characters" in TW's works.
      Refers to *BA, OD, CR*, among others, and elements of "purity,
      of sacredness in sex, or in human life" as it figures in the work
      of both authors.

109   *SB. New York Morning Telegraph*, 19 January, p. 2.
      Brief note on closing of *SB* and its anticipated publication.

110   "So They Say." *Variety*, 11 May, p. 54.
      Small item. References made by G. Page to similarities in TW
      plots and Shakespeare plots.

111   "So They Say." *Variety*, 27 July, p. 123.
      Small gossip item. Quote of TW that "all artists are eccentrics."

112   "So They Say." *Variety*, 3 August, p. 56.
      Two-line gossip notice: John Chapman's question on title
      of *PA*.

113   "So They Say." *Variety*, 31 August, p. 56.
      Brief item concerning TW's habit of writing an essay for the
      New York Times the Sunday before a play opens and how diffi-
      cult this is.

114   "State of the Drama: Debate Continued." *New York Times Maga-
      zine*, 26 June, pp. 16, 38–39.
      Letters to editor in response to articles written by TW and
      Mannes, the violence debate (*New York Times*, 29 May).

115   "Sunny Stuff." *Newsweek* 56 (21 November):79.
      Review of *PA*. "Irresistibly comic"; praises it fully.

116   T[ALLMER], J[ERRY]. "Atop a Chasm." *Village Voice*, 24 November,
      p. 9.

Review of *PA*. "It is inhabited, not by people, characters . . . but by amusing nonentities." It's not "a theatre piece of any substantial dimension."

117 TALLMER, JERRY. Review of *CR*. *Village Voice*, 25 May, p. 7.
    This revival production is "a failure. . . . The failure is in the play not in [the director]." Refers to its "catchall anarchy of styles and tones."

118 TAUBMAN, HOWARD. "Hospital Ward." *New York Times*, 20 November, sec. 2, p. 1.
    Review of *PA*. Brief synopsis. Considers characters to be thin, but states that TW is consistent in his writing about world ills.

119 _____. "Theatre: Serious Comedy by Williams." *New York Times*, 11 November, p. 34.
    Review of *PA*. Comments that play is neither especially funny nor serious. Praise for cast. This not TW at his usual best.

120 "Tennessee Williams Loses Kazan." *Times* (London), 3 May, p. 16.
    News from New York. TW and Kazan end their long partnership. Kazan announced he would not direct *PA* because of schedule conflict.

121 "That Sweet Bird." *Time* 75 (11 April):76–77.
    Presents TW's brother's (Dakin's) views of TW. Refers to themes of specific plays.

122 "Two Duologues from U.S.: Early Tennessee Williams Piece." *Times* (London), 26 August, p. 5.
    Review of *TPC*, London production. "Disappointing" but not the author's fault. Audience had a hard time understanding "the speech of a small Mississippi town."

123 TYLER, PARKER. Review of film of *FK*. *Film Quarterly* 13 (Summer):44–49.
    Brief. Analyzes plot and themes; generally negative about story.

124 "Unbeastly Williams." *Newsweek* 55 (27 June):96.
    Interview-commentary. TW discusses *PA*, his "black" plays, bestiality, drugs.

125   "Vidal Admires Tennessee—But." *Variety*, 24 August, p. 55.
      "Tennessee Williams is the best of American playwrights, but he has gone overboard."

126   WALSH, MOIRA. Review of film of *FK. America* 103 (30 April):201.
      Refers to the "substitution of irrational fate and obscure religious symbolism for rational human motivation" in this adaptation of *OD*. Brief plot and character sketches. Notes that characters and TW seem to be "looking for something better, but ... are looking too far down and not finding enough."

127   ————. Review of film of *SLS. America* 102 (9 January):428–29.
      Talks of TW's "pervasive and perhaps perverse vision of evil ... never more graphically and powerfully conveyed than in" this film. Also discusses critical response in popular press; praises production.

128   WATTS, RICHARD, JR. "Charm and Tennessee Williams." *New York Post*, 11 November, p. 54.
      Review of *PA*. "A warm-hearted and charming romantic comedy ... brightly winning. ... Its status as a comedy arises from its philosophical point of view. ... [TW] looks at the world with surprisingly tolerant humor."

129   WEISSMAN, PHILIP. "Psychopathological Characters in Current Drama: A Study of a Trio of Heroines." *American Imago* 17 (Fall):271–88.
      Starts with reminder of the "parental heritage" that Freud's psychoanalysis has cast upon the "current period," and goes on to present Freud's "comments on the psychopathological drama." Ties TW's characters in for examination, calling TW "the Toulouse-Lautrec of New Orleans." Refers to audience response to TW's work, his heroines, his ambiguity, the "necessarily regressed ego of the author." References to *SND, LLL, TPC*. Reprinted: 1965.73, 1971.19.

130   WHITEBAIT, WILLIAM. "No Fun Intended." *New Statesman* 60 (10 September):336.
      Review of *FK*, London production. There isn't much humor intended in many of TW's "contrived" plot structures—including, especially, *FK*.

131 ————. "Aftermaths." *New Statesman* 59 (21 May):753.
Review of film of *SLS*. "If we wanted a parody of [TW]
where should we go but to [TW]? [*SLS*] provides this . . . a film
that is all cats on hot roofs and hysteria whooped up, with a
torch of anthropology for the kick. . . . The plot is so absurd that
one couldn't seriously set it down on paper."

132 WHITEHALL, RICHARD. "Poet . . . but Do We Know It?" *Films and
Filming* 6 (August):8, 32.
Review of film of *FK*. Attempts to categorize TW as either
slick or moral; surveys his past films, referring to *BD*, *SND*, *SLS*;
claims: "There is no great original philosophy in Williams'
work." Interested in TW's "revelation of motives which lie . . .
beneath human behaviour. . . . The appetite for shock tactics . . .
is the most suspect element in his work. There is [also] an increasing willingness to use sentimental or sensational twists of
situation." Discusses the themes and uses of myth in *FK*; "in
many ways *Fugitive Kind* is the first Beat film."

133 WILLIAMS, WALTER DAKIN. "Is Tennessee Williams a Catholic Play-
wright?" *Information* (April):2–7.
Reviews the comments of some who call TW's plays "dirty."
Contends they are "morality plays"; invokes St. Paul to explain
Stanley Kowalski, for example.

134 WINSTEN, ARCHER. "The 'Fugitive Kind' in Dual Bow." *New York
Post*, 15 April, p. 19.
Review of *FK*. "This weird and woeful view of life is presented rather brilliantly. . . .[It's] picture making in the best
big style."

135 ZOLOTOW, SAM. "Brian Moor Play Ready for Stage." *New York
Times*, 25 August, p. 24.
Brief news item. *GM* to be one of three plays to make world
tour on behalf of U.S. State Department.

136 ————. "Play by Costigan for Julie Harris." *New York Times*,
11 March, p. 19.
News item. TW and Kazan to produce *PA* together.

137 _____. "Williams Drama Due Next Winter." *New York Times*,
27 December, p. 23.
News item. *NI* will be staged on Broadway after sixteen-
week tour. Brief history of play to date.

1961

1 "Acting Their Age." *Time* 78 (29 December):57.
Review of film of *RSMS*. "Was a rather limp novel, and this
is sometimes a rather limp picture." Talks of Leigh's performance.

2 "'Adjustment' Has a $40,000 Profit; Extends 2 Weeks." *Variety*, 22
February, pp. 71, 76.
Notice concerning the gross profits accrued by TW and anyone
else connected with this production of *PA*.

3 ADLER, JACOB H. "The Rose and the Fox: Notes on Southern Drama." In *South: Modern Southern Literature in its Cultural Setting*. Edited by Louis D. Rubin, Jr. and R.D. Jacobs. Garden
City, N.Y.: Dolphin, pp. 349–75.
"By almost any standards—literary, dramatic, commercial, or
national identification with the South—the first among Southern
playwrights is" TW. Discusses "the pastness, the allegorical form,
and allegorical context of" *S&S* as it illuminates the South. Lists
elements of withdrawal, ritual, religion, grotesqueness as they
course through the play and further illustrate the South. Also
focuses on *GM*, *SND*, *RT*, and *CAT*, bringing into the discussion
elements of power, class, and culture itself as further devices for
"defining" the South. Reprinted in revised form: 1977.1.

4 BECKLEY, PAUL V. "Catching the Feel of South." *New York Herald
Tribune*, 19 November, sec. 4, p. 4.
Review of film of *S&S*; *S&S* "could be considered a modern
parallel to Marvell's seventeenth century poem, 'A Dialogue Between Body and Soul.' ... Mr. Williams' lines, particularly in
Miss Page's mouth, provide poetry." Refers to Harvey and rest
of cast.

5_____. "The New Movie: 'Summer and Smoke.'" *New York Herald Tribune*, 17 November, p. 15.

Review of film of S&S. "The study of a mordant struggle between body and soul...a passionate insight into the genesis of...Blanche DuBois of [*SND*].... Certainly one of the best film interpretations of a Williams play."

6 _____. Review of film of *RSMS*. *New York Herald Tribune*, 29 December, p. 9.

"Slightly sweet smell of decay hovers over everything in [*RSMS*].... [It has] a rather self-consciously literary quality... occasionally a trifle stuffy.... Does tend to grow too languorous."

7 "Belfast Welcomes New Theatre." *Times* (London), 20 April, p. 8.

News item. Enthusiastic crowd at new Arts Theatre enjoy *OD*.

8 "Berlin Acclaims U.S. Stage Troupe." *New York Times*, 1 May, p. 35.

News item. Theatre Guild American Repertory Company is successful in Berlin. *GM* is one of several plays presented.

9 "Brussels Hails Repertory Unit." *New York Times*, 20 March, p. 32.

News item. *GM* and other plays were well received in Brussels, as presented by Theatre Guild American Repertory Company.

10 BURKS, EDWARD C. "New York Repertory Troup Is Praised in Buenos Aires." *New York Times*, 29 July, p. 8.

SB and *SLS* were received well when presented in Buenos Aires. Plays by Edward Albee were also staged during tour.

11 CAMERON, KATE. "'Summer and Smoke' Casts a Subtle Spell." New York *Daily News*, 17 November, p. 66.

Review of film of S&S. Praises the "performances of fine calibre." Examines the plot and cites good direction.

12 _____. "Tennessee Williams' Story of an Aging Beauty and Gigolo." New York *Sunday News*, 17 December, sec. 2, p. 3.

Background piece on making film of *RSMS*; discusses plot and notes casting troubles.

13   CHAPMAN, JOHN. "Williams Is at His Poetic, Moving Best with 'Night of the Iguana.'" New York *Daily News*, 29 December, p. 44.

Review of *NI*. "It will haunt you . . . with things said and unsaid . . . with its beauty." Calls it "a beautiful play" and praises its cast and direction.

14   COLEMAN, ROBERT. "Williams at 2nd Best in 'Iguana.'" New York *Daily Mirror*, 29 December, p. 28.

Review of *NI*. "A harrowing and often touching play. Some of the dialogue is deeply moving while much of it is unnecessarily sordid." Although TW has "a touch of the poet," *NI* is still "second rate Williams."

15   CROWTHER, BOSLEY. Review of film of *S&S*. *New York Times*, 19 November, sec. 2, p. 1.

S&S has lost its mood in the film because of its colorful production; it is compared with "Flower Drum Song" and "Susan Slade."

16   ————. "Screen: 'Roman Spring.'" *New York Times*, 29 December, p. 11.

Review of *RSMS*. Praise for Leigh, plus plot outline; negative comments about Beatty's performance.

17   ————. "The Screen: 'Summer and Smoke.'" *New York Times*, 17 November, p. 41.

Review of film of *S&S*. Generally negative comments on film and its production.

18   CUNNINGHAM, MILES. "Tennessee Williams Talks to the Press: 10 Minute Interview with Playwright." *Rochester Times-Union*, 4 November, sec. A, p. 14.

Interview-commentary on opening night of Rochester (N.Y.) pre-Broadway production of *NI*. TW, in a stormy mood, discusses American theater generally, *NI*, dislike of reporters.

19   DAVE. "Shows Out of Town: 'The Night of the Iguana.'" *Variety*, 8 November, p. 75.

Review of *NI*, Rochester production. *NI* offers "another of the author's compassionate combinations of beset characters and earthy lines. The play is skillfully cast, but will presumably undergo considerable revision before its opening on Broadway." Notes details of plot, staging, and scenery.

20 DOWNER, ALAN S. *Recent American Drama*. University of Minnesota Pamphlets on American Writers. Minneapolis: University of Minnesota Press, pp. 28–33.

"At the far end of the dramatic spectrum from William Inge is Tennessee Williams, the most daring, spectacular, and fecund of the postwar dramatists." Traces the history of his work from *BA* through 1960. Williams "senses the dangerous nature of his chosen subject matter."

21 ———. "The Two Worlds of Contemporary American Drama: Tennessee Williams and Arthur Miller." *Princeton Alumni Weekly* 62 (20 October): 8–11, 17, 20.

Analyzes the nature of drama itself, and how TW and Arthur Miller can satisfy that taste. Cites essential differences between them as based on "the worlds they reflect." Discusses use of gothic detail, psychology, aspects of tragedy, and what he calls "Williams' Ultimate Theme." References to *CAT, SLS, SND*.

22 "Dublin Theatre Festival Gets Off to a Good Start." *Times* (London), 14 September, p. 16.

News item. Preparations for Dublin Theatre Festival; refers to TW's "Hello from Bertha" at Pocket Theatre.

23 DUGAN, GEORGE. "Cleric Discounts 'Religious' Films." *New York Times*, 7 February, p. 40.

News item. In speech by Rev. Malcolm Boyd, *CAT* cited as reflecting more basic religion than "Ten Commandments."

24 DUPREY, RICHARD A. Review of *PA*. *Catholic World* 192 (January): 255–56.

Attacks the work's thematic level, and calls its language "conversation that belongs ... in a G.I. latrine."

25 DUSENBERRY, WINIFRED. " 'Baby Doll' and 'The Ponder Heart.' " *Modern Drama* 3 (February):393–95.

Relates the script of *BD* to TW's *27W* and *Long Stay Cut Short*. Describes the metamorphosis of the script as TW devised it, and then ties it into Welty's story, suggesting "The Ponder Heart" as a tenable source.

26 FALK, SIGNI L. *Tennessee Williams*. New York: Twayne. Revised and updated: Boston: Twayne, 1978, 194 pp.
    "Attempts to present an objective analysis of the drama and the fiction that comprise the considerable literary accomplishment of Tennessee Williams." Gives attention to "his early poems, stories, and short plays: a close record of his personal experience, but also a basis for his later work." Presents information on TW's "view of the world," play summaries that "attempt to elucidate the meaning . . . a wide sampling of critical comment." Mentions that her "final chapter is yet to be written." Addresses his place in the "Southern Renaissance," his own psychology and its function in his work, the issue of "the Southern Gentlewoman" and "Southern wenches," along with the issue of heroes and artists. Her final chapter, "The Literary World of Tennessee Williams," focuses on his preoccupation with sex, his work as "Screenwright," his use of idiomatic language, as well as the place of comedy, evil, and therapy in his work. Chapter 3 reprinted: 1971.19.

27 FREEDLEY, GEORGE. " 'Night of Iguana' Eloquent, Moving." New York *Morning Telegraph*, 30 December, p. 2.
    Review of *NI*. "Contains more of all [his] gifts than any play of his since" *SND*. Refers to "this new and lovely play . . . a play of pity. . . . [It] enthralled me . . . and moved me profoundly."

28 FRENZ, HORST. "American Playwrights and the German Psyche." *New Statesman* 10 (April):170–78.
    Discusses the effect of eastward movement of theater from U.S.A. to Germany. Brief reference to TW. Notes the critics in Germany finding *SND* to be redolent of Strindberg and Ibsen, "but modernized by the injection of psychoanalysis."

29 FUNKE, LEWIS. "News of the Rialto." *New York Times*, 5 March, sec. 2, p. 1.
    GM is to be one of a cross section of American plays to be presented in Europe, sponsored by U.S. State Department.

30 _____. "News of the Rialto: Renunciation." *New York Times*,
   5 November, sec. 2, p. 1.
   Gossip item. TW may not write any more plays for Broadway,
   but he might for off-Broadway.

31 GILL, BRENDAN. "High Spirits and Low." *New Yorker* 37 (25 Novem-
   ber):205–6.
   Review of film of *S&S*. TW "is surely the last of the romantic
   Victorians." Maintains the film sustains structural problems.

32 GRANDE, LUKE M., F.S.C. "Metaphysics of Alienation in Tennessee
   Williams' Short Stories." *Drama Critique* 4 (November):118–22.
   The short stories are "particularly illuminating, for in them
   Tennessee Williams' essential vision is evident even more clearly
   than in his dramas; the themes are simplified, sharpened, reduced
   to almost painful clarity." Discusses his choice of subjects, his
   attitude toward his characters' pursuit of happiness, and the
   place of the "fugitive." Cites TW's work as picturing "all men's
   restless vigil at the windows of the soul."

33 HALE, WANDA. "Vivien Leigh Stars in Capitol's Drama." New
   York *Daily News*, 29 December, p. 48.
   Review of film of *RSMS*. "Movie is slow and weighted down
   with words . . . [but] has its compensations."

34 HANDLER, M.S. "U.S. Actors' Visit Hailed in Vienna." *New York
   Times*, 21 April, p. 29.
   News item. Report on success of Theatre Guild American Repertory Company tour. High ticket demand resulted in matinee
   and evening performance of *GM*.

35 HARTUNG, PHILIP T. "Roman Stone Gathers No Moss." *Commonweal*
   75 (29 December):365–66.
   Review of film of *RSMS*. "A sad and grim vignette. . . . [It]
   fails even to make [the original story] interesting."

36 _____. "Varieties of Americana." *Commonweal* 75 (1 December):259.
   Review of film of *SLS*. "Rather pretentious. . . . The padding
   [of original script] shows. [It's] talky, static and repetitive."

37   HARVEY, LAURENCE. "Following My Actor's Instinct." *Films and Filming* 8 (October):22–23.
Harvey discusses his film career. Refers to TW as "just about my favorite playwright barring Shakespeare.... I chose 'Summer and Smoke' because there's always an aura of importance to a film adapted from a Tennessee Williams play."

38   HATCH, ROBERT. "Human Beings and Substitutes." *Horizon* 3 (March):102–3.
Review of *PA*. Says it's "skillfully written... [but] dulls the spirit." Sees TW's being "driven from within" as causing problems for the play.

39   HAWK. "Venice Film Fest Reviews: 'Summer and Smoke.'" *Variety*, 6 September, p. 6.
Review of film of *S&S*. "Producer Wallis and director Glenville have fashioned a distinguished motion picture from the latest of Tennessee Williams' plays to be adapted to the screen." Notes that performances are "uniformly excellent," especially G. Page, repeating her Broadway role.

40   HAYES, RICHARD. "The Contemporaries." *Commonweal* 74 (2 June): 255.
Brief review of *PA*. Calls *PA* TW's "most *coherent* work." Praises its "dramatic wit."

41   HURRELL, JOHN D. *Two Modern American Tragedies: Reviews and Criticism of "Death of a Salesman" and "A Streetcar Named Desire."* New York: Charles Scribner's Sons, pp. 89–145.
Collects significant criticism on *SND*. Reprints of 1948.16, 1948.50, 1948.68, 1949.3, 1953.3, 1953.35, 1954.11 (1961.81), 1955.98 (1971.19), 1957.79, 1958.17, 1958.31, 1959.66.

42   HURT, JAMES R. "'Suddenly Last Summer': Williams and Melville." *Modern Drama* 3 (February):396–400.
Refers to the New York popular periodical response to *SLS* when it premiered. Follows that with: "It is my thesis that the theme of the play may be clarified by taking as a starting point the Melville allusion in the first scene and tracing its implications through the play." References to Sebastian's vision of evil, the play's ironies, the enchanted isle motif, the use of whiteness.

43   "Israel Acclaims American Troupe." *New York Times*, 11 April,
     p. 43.
        News item. *GM* is presented by Theatre Guild American Rep-
     ertory Company as one of several plays on tour. All plays are
     successful despite illnesses of several actors.

44   KAUFFMANN, STANLEY. "About Williams: Gloom and Hope." *New
     York Times*, 6 March, sec. 2, p. 1.
        Review of *SST*. Considers the similarities between *SST* and
     other plays; praises humor; and hopes TW will write more
     comedy.

45   _____. "Macbeth in Japan, Stale Smoke in Dixie." *New Repub-
     lic* 145 (27 November):18, 20.
        Review of film of *S&S*. "The years have dealt unkindly with
     the play." Calls film "pedestrian."

46   KERR, WALTER. Review of *NI*. *New York Herald Tribune*, 29 De-
     cember, p. 8.
        "I find myself very much moved by an unsatisfactory play."
     Sees it as sketches lacking center, but "the sketches in them-
     selves are the finest rough-work the contemporary theater is pre-
     pared to offer."

47   KNIGHT, ARTHUR. "A Dissertation on Roast Corn." *Saturday Re-
     view* 44 (11 November):32.
        Review of film of *S&S*. "Verges perilously close to 'corn.' . . .
     [It's] a distended production. . . . [The characters'] agonies seem
     as arbitrary, contrived—and prolonged—as those of . . . the after-
     noon soap operas."

48   _____. "Romans in the Gloamin'." *Saturday Review* 44 (9 De-
     cember):28.
        Review of film of *RSMS*. Makes comparison with "La Dolce
     Vita." "It remains cold and unmoving."

49   KRUTCH, JOSEPH WOOD. "Why the O'Neill Star Is Rising." *New
     York Times Magazine*, 19 March, pp. 36, 108, 111.
        TW is mentioned in article about popularity of Eugene O'Neill;
     he is compared to O'Neill briefly.

50   "Law Engages a Playwright." New York *Daily News*, 2 September, p. 23.
     Brief news item. Court trial scheduled for man apprehended trying to cash a TW check with a TW credit card in Saks Fifth Avenue.

51   LEE, M. OWEN. "Orpheus and Eurydice: Some Modern Versions." *Classical Journal* 56 (April):307–13.
     Cites the historic popularity of the myth and traces modern adaptations; focuses on *OD* and *FK*. Claims the use of Orpheus in the title of *OD* is a pretense and a charade since it "has no connection whatsoever" with the myth.

52   LEMON, RICHARD. "Cinderella Descending." *Saturday Review* 44 (16 September):6.
     Very brief *sui generis* piece; a parody of TW's style.

53   LYONS, LEONARD. "The Lyons Den." *New York Post*, 20 September, p. 19.
     Gossip item. TW has stopped going to his psychoanalyst.

54   ———. "The Lyons Den." *New York Post*, 19 October, p. 37.
     Gossip item. TW seeing "The Caretaker" in New York City.

55   McCARTHY, MARY. "Americans, Realists, Playwrights." *Encounter* 17 (July):24–31.
     Considers Miller, Inge, Rice, O'Neill and TW. Says TW is "pledged to verisimilitude," and questions whether his "authenticity" might be only regional; claims his characters are "offered as samples to the audience's somewhat voyeuristic eye." Refers to *BD* and Kazan. Reprinted: 1963.37.

56   ———. " 'Realism' in the American Theater." *Harper's* 223 (July): 45–52.
     Names TW as one of the "American realist playwrights." Says he "is fascinated by the refinements of cruelty, which with him become a form of aestheticism, and his plays, far from baring a lie that society is trying to cover up, titillate society like a peep show."

57 McCLAIN, JOHN. "Brilliant Cast Adds to Great Williams Play." *New York Journal-American*, 29 December, p. 9.

Review of *NI*. "In many respects the most fruitful and versatile exercise by our best living playwright." Calls the play "this searing pastorale." Praises cast, director.

58 MIANO, LOUIS S. Review of *NI*. *Show* 1 (December):33.

Gives history of its composition and pre-Broadway productions; news of cast, producer's comments on TW and the play.

59 NADEL, NORMAN. "'Iguana' Unleashed at the Royale." *New York World Telegram & Sun*, 29 December, p. 10.

Review of *NI*. "An awesome and powerful new drama vividly laced with strident comedy." There's "a tortured beauty to this play."

60 NELSON, BENJAMIN. *Tennessee Williams: The Man and His Work.* New York: Obolensky; London: Peter Owen, 262 pp.

States his intent to be to gain "an understanding of the life and work of Tennessee Williams . . . to discuss and analyze his major work for the themes, techniques and basic beliefs." Ample details on early developmental biography, especially as it pertains to and influences TW's writing; details pertaining to preparation for and opening of major plays, both in New York and on the road; references made to critical response, more the popular than the scholarly; eventually questions the next possible direction of TW's work. *PA* and *SB* are last works considered.

61 "'Orpheus' in Moscow." *New York Times*, 28 August, p. 21.

News item. *OD* is very successful in Moscow according to TASS, Soviet Press.

62 PECK, SEYMOUR. "Rehearsal Time, Rehearsal Problems." *New York Times Magazine*, 29 October, pp. 34–35.

Discussion of rehearsal problems, and photos of rehearsals of *NI* with captions.

63 ———. "Williams and 'The Iguana.'" *New York Times*, 24 December, sec. 2, p. 5.

Interview-commentary. Notes the pressures on TW prior to

Broadway opening of *NI* and discusses the setting of the play. TW provides explanation of *NI*.

64   "Plays by U.S. Repertory Troupe Win Warm Response in Athens." *New York Times*, 1 April, p. 11.

News item. *GM* described as an "unqualified success" in Athens as one of several plays presented by Theatre Guild American Repertory Company.

65   PRYCE-JONES, ALAN. "Alan Pryce-Jones at the Theatre." *Theatre Arts* 45 (January):57–58.

Review of *PA*. Traces the basis of its humor; praises TW's leaning toward comedy.

66   QUINTERO, JOSE. "The Play's the Thing." *Films and Filming* 8 (October):19, 37.

Interview with Gordon Gow. Quintero discusses filming of *RSMS*, the things that influenced him in the interpretation, his "subjective treatment."

67   RICHARDS, STANLEY. Review of *PA*. *Players* 37 (April):161.

Brief. The production deserves "respect" and it's not getting it. Plot summary.

68   SCHUMACH, MURRAY. "Author Changes 'Sweet Bird' Play." *New York Times*, 27 October, p. 27.

News item. TW makes radical changes to *SB*. Brief description of changes. Gossip about film version.

69   _____. "Hollywood Trial." *New York Times*, 29 January, sec. 2, p. 7.

Gossip item about the technical problems encountered in filming a play by TW so as to capture the mood.

70   _____. "Muted Hollywood." *New York Times*, 27 August, sec. 2, p. 7.

Gossip item. The filming of *SB* is clothed in secrecy and author attempts unsuccessfully to find reason.

71 SIMON, JOHN. Review of *PA*. *Hudson Review* 14 (Spring):83–85.
    Refers to *PA* as "boring," "untruthful," "cowardly." It's one
    truth is "clinical truth."

72 "A Small Thing but His Own." *Time* 78 (1 December): 76.
    Review of film of *S&S*. TW "writes like an arrested adolescent
    who disarmingly imagines that he will attain stature if . . . he
    loads enough manure in his shoes. . . . Yet Broadway's bad boy
    has his sweet-mouthed moments." The film has "sincerity" and is
    "faithful generally to the play."

73 SMITH, MILBURN. Review of film of *S&S*. *Theatre* 3 (September):
    20–21.
    Focuses on G. Page's performance; finds her repeating her
    1952 off-Broadway revival performance.

74 "Stockholm Reviews Are Mixed in Reaction to U.S. Stage Troupe."
    New York Times, 19 May, p. 22.
    Theatre Guild American Repertory Company receives mixed
    reviews during tour in Sweden. *GM* was well received but con-
    sidered not to be as good as it should have been.

75 "Story of Two Uneasy Marriages: Mr. Tennessee Williams's Comic
    Gift." *Times* (London), 5 September, p. 15.
    Review of *PA*, London production. "The evening proves one
    of unexpectedly uncomplicated delight."

76 "Suddenly, This Summer—Check Casher Sees Light." *New York
    Post*, 1 September, p. 48.
    News article on check cashed at Saks Fifth Avenue by thief
    of TW's checkbook and credit cards.

77 TAUBMAN, HOWARD. "Not What It Seems." *New York Times*, 5
    November, sec. 2, p. 1.
    CAT is mentioned in article concerned with homosexuality
    infiltrating the themes of American drama.

78 _____."Theatre: American Repertory Group." *New York Times*,
    6 March, p. 30.
    News item; *GM* is one of several American plays on tour in

Europe and Mideast. News on production and problems encountered.

79 _____. "Theatre: 'Night of the Iguana' Opens." *New York Times*, 29 December, p. 10.
Review of *NI*. Play is slow paced at first but "achieves a vibrant eloquence." Gives synopsis.

80 "Tennessee Williams Manuscript Comes to Auction Block." *New York Herald Tribune*, 10 December, p. 50.
News item. "Featured item is Tennessee Williams' original draft of 'Glass Menagerie,' the first of his major manuscripts to be offered at public sale."

81 "Theatre Abroad: 'This Rotted World.'" *Time* 78 (1 September):52.
Comments on the Brazil furor over *SB*, their attacking the TW "spirit."

82 TISCHLER, NANCY M. *Tennessee Williams: Rebellious Puritan*. New York: Citadel Press, 319 pp.
Begins with premise: TW "is a latter day romantic. Both his writings and his life follow the pattern of the romantic nonconformist." Goes on to deal "with his plays, stories, poems, and articles as these have mutually reflected and influenced his life, and with the audience and critical reactions to them as these have mutually reflected or influenced his work and the social acceptance of new themes." Explores this theory through plays up to *SB*, heavily relying on and using his autobiography ("The mother Williams has chosen to write about in *GM* was, naturally, his own"). Concludes with an assessment of TW's possible future—as much an illustration of his evolving aesthetics as of probable directions.

83 "Trying, as It Were." *Newsweek* 58 (20 November):106.
Review of film of *S&S*. Denounces G. Page's performance and her role: "clogged, studied and repetitious." Sees Harvey as relieving the "tediousness."

84 "Two by Tennessee." *New York Times Magazine*, 16 April, pp. 72, 74.
Photos, with captions, of films of *RSMS* and *SLS*.

85   TYNAN, KENNETH. "American Blues: The Plays of Arthur Miller and
     Tennessee Williams." in *Curtains: Selections from the Drama
     Criticism and Other Writings*. New York: Atheneum, pp. 257–66.
     Reprint of 1954.11. Reprinted: 1961.41, 1967.31.

86   _____. "At the Theatre." *Observer* (London), 17 September,
     p. 26.
        Brief review of *PA*, London production. Refers to its "hollow
     sentimentality. . . . The real trouble with the play is its narrow-
     ness of vision."

87   _____. "The Broadway Dilemma." In *Curtains: Selections from
     the Drama Criticism and Other Writings*. New York: Atheneum,
     pp. 365–75.
        Quotes TWs' 1944 evaluation of Broadway and moves forward
     to 1959, assessing the change in TW's attitude during the span;
     sees TW as a "tycoon." Examines *SB* briefly, along with other
     plays on the Broadway circuit at the time.

88   _____. " 'The Entertainer,' by John Osborne at the Royal Court;
     'Camino Real,' by Tennessee Williams at the Phoenix; 'Comedy
     in Music' at the Palace." In *Curtains: Selections from the Drama
     Criticism and Other Writings*. New York: Atheneum, pp. 173–76.
        Review of *CR*. "The author's simple thesis: . . . purity can sur-
     vive corruption as long as it gets the hell out." Finds TW's world
     view placing him among those who "recommend withdrawal,"
     therefore aligning himself "with the saints, the hermits, the junk-
     ies, and the drunks."

89   _____. " 'Garden District' by Tennessee Williams, at the Arts
     Theatre, London." In *Curtains: Selections from the Drama Criti-
     cism and Other Writings*. New York: Atheneum, pp. 278–80.
        Review of *GD*, London production. *S&S* seems like a short
     story told on stage in the mood of a recital abruptly ended.
     Concerning *SU*: what was done to this play "is nobody's business
     except perhaps that of Mr. Williams and his lawyers."

90   _____. " 'The Iceman Cometh,' by Eugene O'Neill, at the Arts;
     'Cat on a Hot Tin Roof,' by Tennessee Williams, at the Comedy."

In *Curtains: Selections from the Drama Criticism and Other Writings*. New York: Atheneum, pp. 202–4.
Brief review of *CAT*. A magnificent play marred by "inadequate direction and amateur acting."

91 ————. " 'Sweet Bird of Youth' by Tennessee Williams." In *Curtains: Selections from the Drama Criticism and Other Writings*. New York: Atheneum, pp. 306–7.
Reprint of 1959.109.

92 ————. "Valentine to Tennessee Williams." In *Curtains: Selections from the Drama Criticism and Other Writings*. New York: Atheneum, pp. 266–71.
Reprint of 1956.101.

93 UNDERWOOD, PAUL. "Belgrade Critics and Audiences Hail Guild Repertory Company." *New York Times*, 28 March, p. 40.
News item. Belgrade audiences give warm reception to touring U.S. actors; *GM* among the works presented.

94 "U.S. Actors Find Rome Receptive." *New York Times*, 31 May, p. 28.
News item. *GM* and other plays presented by Theatre Guild American Repertory Company receive standing ovations.

95 "U.S. Stage Troupe Is Blasted in Rio." *New York Times*, 21 August, p. 18.
News item. New York Repertory Company deletes *SB* and *SLS* from its performances in Rio because of "savage" reviews received after first performance. Quotes from critics.

96 "U.S. Troupe Plays at Fete in Paris." *New York Times*, 16 June, p. 27.
News item. Theatre Guild American Repertory Company is held over for two extra performances with much praise for Helen Hayes in *GM*.

97 WALD, RICHARD C. "Quintero on Set: A Cat with Cream." *New York Herald Tribune*, 1 January, sec. 4, p. 9.
Gossip piece about Quintero working on filming of *RSMS*.

98 WALSH, MOIRA. Review of film of *S&S*. *America* 106 (25 November):308–10.
Discusses themes and TW's handling of plot; says TW does his task with "skill and passionate conviction"; "a fine piece of screencraft."

99 WATTS, RICHARD, JR. "Reveries of Tennessee Williams." *New York Post*, 29 December, p. 20.
Review of *NI*. "One of [TW's] saddest, darkest and most contemplative plays.... The important interest of the play lies in the insight it gives into the author's dark and brooding mind.... a surprisingly undramatic play."

100 WATTS, STEPHEN. "'Roman Springs' Season in a London Studio." *New York Times*, 15 January, sec. 2, p. 7.
Gossip about cast and filming problems of *RSMS*.

101 WHARTON, FLAVIA. Review of film of *S&S*. *Films in Review* 12 (December):621.
"Without Geraldine Page 'Summer and Smoke' would merely be more of Tennessee Williams' pathologic preoccupation with the negative and evil aspects of human nature.... As for the rest ... it is as confused and meaningless as the title."

102 "Williams Draft of Play Brings $6,000 at Auction." *New York Herald Tribune*, 13 December, p. 18.
News item. Sale of original manuscript of *GM*.

103 WINSTEN, ARCHER. "'Roman Spring' at Two Theaters." *New York Post*, 29 December, p. 25.
Review of film of *RSMS*. "An experience of a perfection to be expected when Tennessee Williams looks at upper-class society in Rome.... This is a picture of characters so fully rounded and well packed that they are immune to adverse notice."

104 ————. "'Summer and Smoke' at the DeMille." *New York Post*, 17 November, p. 59.
Review of film of *S&S*. "One of the earlier, simpler, more normal of Tennessee Williams' visions." Mostly production details.

1962

1   "Acting up a Storm." *Newsweek* 59 (2 April):86.
Review of film of *SB*. "A forceful, often devastating piece of work" Praises cast: G. Page "gives as vivid a portrait of conscious egomania as the screen has ever offered."

2   "Actress Comes Back to Tennessee Williams." *Times* (London), 2 October, p. 18.
News item. Elizabeth Shepherd returns to part of Isabel in London production of *PA*.

3   ADLER, JACOB H. " 'Night of the Iguana': A New Tennessee Williams?" *Ramparts* 1 (November):59–68.
Analysis of TW's work up to *NI*. Specific analysis of method in *NI*; comparison of *NI* to strategies of earlier TW work.

4   ALBEE, EDWARD. Letter to editor. *Time* 79 (16 March):7.
Comments on *Time*'s 9 March cover story on TW; on same page, TW's three-line letter of thanks.

5   ALPERT, HOLLIS. "Tennessee, Anyone?" *Saturday Review* 45 (31 March):26.
Review of film of *SB*. "Richard Brooks ... has applied himself diligently to the cinematic problems inherent in [*SB*] and has succeeded, for the most part, in surmounting them." Brooks has preserved "the author's sadness over the world's misuse of youth and beauty."

6   "The Angel of the Odd." *Time* 79 (9 March):53–56, 59, 60.
Long cover story piece. Traces his career; compares him to contemporaries; discusses themes of his plays and autobiographical elements in them; refers to his moral attitudes and symbols, plus his introspection.

7   BAKER, PETER. Review of film of *S&S*. *Films and Filming* 8 (May): 31–32.
Claims that although TW always writes "good theatre ... I find increasingly less appeal in the content of his work." Discusses

TW's "distorting mirror" in *S&S*; but praises the film's "immaculate design and fine photography."

8   BECKLEY, PAUL V. "The New Movies: 'Period of Adjustment.'" *New York Herald Tribune*, 1 November, p. 13.

Review of film of *PA*. "This film wrestles with what was apparently felt to be the extraordinary difficulties of making a Williams comedy funny. . . . It is boring . . . deadening."

9   ———. "The New Movies: 'Sweet Bird of Youth.'" *New York Herald Tribune*, 29 March, p. 15.

Review of film of *SB*. Its best sequences are those "which stay closest to Williams' original." General praise for Newman and G. Page.

10   BROUSSARD, LOUIS. *American Drama: Contemporary Allegory from Eugene O'Neill to Tennessee Williams*. Norman: University of Oklahoma Press, pp. 111–16.

"Williams, the sensual realist who had produced in rapid succession plays like *A Streetcar Named Desire* and *The Rose Tattoo*, had not prepared anyone for a play quite like [*CR*]." Discusses critical response to *CR*, its method and theme. *CR* "becomes the playwright's prescription for the character failures presented in his other plays."

11   BRUSTEIN, ROBERT. "A Little Night Music." *New Republic* 146 (22 January):20, 22–23.

Review of *NI*. "Much too aimless, leisurely, and formless. . . . The play seems tired, unadventurous, and self-derivative." Provides analysis of structure. Reprinted: 1965.7.

12   CARTER, HODDING. "Yes, Tennessee, There *Are* Southern Belles." *New York Times Magazine*, 7 October, pp. 32–33.

Discusses Southern women; takes issue with the way that TW describes them in his plays; goes on to focus on famous Southern women.

13   CHAPMAN, JOHN. "Tennessee Williams' Most Mature Drama." New York *Sunday News*, 14 January, sec. 2, p. 1.

Review of *NI*. "The best American play of the season to date."

Provides plot summary and calls the work "quite beautifully written."

14   CLURMAN, HAROLD. Review of *NI*. *Nation* 194 (27 January):86.
"Gives us an idea of how Williams sees and judges himself." The writing is "lambent, fluid, malleable." Praises cast. Reprinted: 1966.14.

15   ————. Review of *PA*. *Nation* 195 (11 August):59.
London production. Considers its effect on English audiences; mentions TW's "pok[ing] fun at the sexual timidity, frustration, psychic impotence, gingerliness of the average (Puritan) American."

16   COFFEY, WARREN. "Tennessee Williams: The Playwright as Analysand." *Ramparts* 1 (November):51–58.
Critical analysis of TW's work. Parallels TW to Edgar A. Poe, especially on level of the psychology explored.

17   COLEMAN, JOHN. "Conversations." *New Statesman* 63 (20 April): 570.
Review of film of *S&S*. One sentence.

18   ————. "The Marienbad Game." *New Statesman* 63 (23 February):273.
Review of film of *RSMS*. Describes TW as slightly less sympathetic than Arthur Miller; the film does not "touch the heart."

19   "Comedy by Williams in London Premiere." *New York Times*, 14 June, p. 24.
News item. Pro and con quotes by London critics on *PA*'s London run.

20   COMERFORD, ADELAIDE. Review of film of *PA*. *Films in Review* 13 (December):627.
Brief. "When Tennessee Williams isn't writing about sex degenerates or other psychopaths his ignorance of life is boringly patent." Refers to entire production as an "ineptitude."

21   "Critics Pick 'Iguana.'" New York *Daily News*, 11 April, p. 66.
News item. Drama Critics' Circle Award goes to *NI*.

22   CRONIN, MORTON. "Desolate Victories." *National Review* 12 (27 February):137.
     Review of film of *SB*. Analyzes themes; it "ends in the general waste of spirit with which a Williams play on this theme evidently must end." Compares TW to Fitzgerald, Hemingway, Faulkner, Salinger, MacLeish—"they have all delivered the Williams message. And they are all sick unto death."

23   CROWTHER, BOSLEY. "Screen: 'Period of Adjustment' Opens." *New York Times*, 1 November, p. 34.
     Review of film of *PA*. "Much better, we would say, than it was on the Broadway stage." Praises cast and the production generally.

24   _____. "Screen: 'Sweet Bird of Youth' Opens." *New York Times*, 29 March, p. 28.
     Review of film of *SB*. Brief synopsis of screenplay with praise for acting and screen graphics. Calls the happy ending "implausible and absurd."

25   _____. "Wronging Writing." *New York Times*, 8 April, sec. 2, p. 1.
     TW's writing tends to be unsuitable for "translation to the screen" because the violence needs to be toned down. Refers to *PA, NI, CAT, SLS, SB*.

26   CUTTS, JOHN. Review of film of *SB*. *Films and Filming* 8 (June):35.
     "In cold print, the effect of [TW's] dramatic deluge was overwhelming; . . . on film, its effect is perhaps more immediately satisfying and less wholly so." Discusses which parts of plot are "banal" and which lend themselves to film. But calls the whole an "emotional extravagance, beautifully mounted."

27   DENT, ALAN. "A Circe's Odyssey." *Illustrated London News* 240 (3 March):346.
     Review of film of *RSMS*. Primarily centered on character of Mrs. Stone, as played by Leigh, who gives "surely her best performance since [SND]. . . . Considerable ingenuity" in the plot, but little else said about either the writing or production.

28   DOWNER, ALAN S. "Experience of Heroes: Notes on the New York

Theatre 1961–1962." *Quarterly Journal of Speech* 48 (October): 261–70.

"The Reverend Lawrence Shannon, current entry from the stud-farm of Tennessee Williams, in *The Night of the Iguana*, is a kind of transvestite Blanche DuBois. . . . His fate is determined by Mr. Williams' hypothesis, his sex by the necessity for a new look in an over-exposed myth." Gives analysis of main characters; concludes that TW "is content to lead his audience . . . where he has taught them to want to go."

29 DRIVER, TOM F. "Self-Transcending Realism." *Christian Century* 79 (7 February):169.

Review of *NI*. TW's realism "has always been something more than mere naturalism." Surveys his past themes; gives plot summary of *NI*; "not notable as a message play." Talks of its "spiritual yearning."

30 FEDDER, NORMAN JOSEPH. "The Influence of D.H. Lawrence on Tennessee Williams." Ph.D. dissertation, State University of New York.

Compares their personal backgrounds, their attitudes toward sexual fulfillment, Freud, and civilization as it exists; their relative faith and basic sympathy for human failure also developed. (*DA* 24:742–43.)

31 "Festivals: Milk Run." *Time* 30 (20 July):40.

Review of *MT*, Spoleto production. Brief summary-style review of world premiere, pre-Broadway run.

32 FOREMAN, CARL. "Major and Minors." *New Statesman* 63 (22 June):917.

Review of *PA*, London production. Explores minor deficiencies in the production: the characterization is "as counterfeit as a II-shilling note." Their diction is chaotic, the stage sets are paltry. "It is a very brave piece for Mr. Williams to write, for it is bound to upset many of his admirers."

33 FORREY, ROBERT. Review of *NI*. *Mainstream* 15 (August):62–64.

Calls *NI* "a play of considerable impact." Numerous plot details. Claims that TW "is a spokesman for the insulted and humiliated, a poet of suffering and distress."

34   FREEDLEY, GEORGE. "Publication of Plays Profitable; Williams' 'Iguana' a Top Drama." New York *Morning Telegraph*, 22 March, pp. 2, 8.
    Brief note of publication of *NI*. Quite positive.

35   FUNKE, LEWIS. "News of the Rialto, Williams." *New York Times*, 4 November, sec. 2, p. 1.
    News item. Announces the opening of *MT* at the Morosco; gives names of cast and some of production crew.

36   FUNKE, LEWIS, and BOOTH, JOHN E. "Williams on Williams." *Theatre Arts* 46 (January):16–19, 72–73.
    Interview. TW discusses upcoming *NI*, poetic plays, playwrights he favors, future work, cynicism in theater, his restlessness.

37   GANZ, ARTHUR. "The Desperate Morality of the Plays of Tennessee Williams." *American Scholar* 31 (Spring):278–94.
    Examines TW as a moralist with respect to his work—in which "sinners" are punished, the corrupt are destroyed—and how in plays like *CAT*, TW's mind is confused and cannot tell whether the central characters are guilty or innocent. Reprinted in *American Drama and Its Critics: A Collection of Critical Essays* (Chicago: University of Chicago Press, 1965), pp. 203–17. Reprinted in revised form: 1977.88.

38   GASCOIGNE, BAMBER. "Strictly for the Bees." *Spectator* 208 (22 June):823, 26.
    Review of *PA*, London production. A "serious comedy." Traces theme through plot. Refers to its "oversimplification" of marriage. The play is "saved by Williams' most reliable talent: he can write superb lines for actors."

39   GASSNER, JOHN. "The Influence of Strindberg in the United States." *World Theatre* 11 (Spring):21–29.
    Traces Strindberg's influence in work of Saroyan, O'Neill,

Barry, Anderson, Inge, Miller, and TW. Compares heroine of *Craig's Wife* with Blanche.

40 "Germans Hail Williams Play." *New York Times*, 3 January, p. 25.
     News item. *PA* received warmly in Germany; critics cited.

41 GILL, BRENDAN. "Family Matters." *New Yorker* 38 (10 November):234–35.
     Review of film of *PA*. The original play has been "boldly and attractively hoked up in a screenplay by Isobel Lennart.... a cheerful, harmless trifle."

42 ———. "Hard Times." *New Yorker* 37 (13 January):97–98.
     Brief review of film of *RSMS*. "The movie version is lamentably faithful to the original.... [It's] a painful assault on love."

43 ———. "Men in Trouble." *New Yorker* 38 (7 April):148–50.
     Review of film of *SB*. Calls TW "the mad surgeon of dramaturgy" and *SB* "a revolting play ... [that] appears to have marked the end of Dr. Williams quack-medical phase." In the film, "the subject matter has been tubbed and damp-dried to the point of being practically ladies'-magazine material.... Still shocking, ... but shocking in a fashionable way.... The picture is even more unbelievable than the play."

44 GILMAN, RICHARD. "Williams as Phoenix." *Commonweal* 75 (26 January):460–61.
     Review of *NI*. Surveys TW criticism generally, and the popular criticism of this play specifically; discusses its themes. Reprinted: 1971.11.

45 GLICKSBERG, CHARLES I. "The Lost Self in Modern Literature." *Personalist* 43 (Autumn):527–38.
     In the midst of the "Being and Nothingness" conceit and the existentialist drift of the century, he shows TW (in a brief reference) depicting the homosexual. "At odds with himself and his society, the invert retreats into fantasy, unable ... to come to terms with social reality."

46 GRIFFIN, HILARY. Review of *NI*. *Catholic World* 194 (March):380–81.

Although *NI* "is about God," it "does not make his play great, but it does show that his pen is pointing in the right direction." The [play's] result "is a peculiar sort of weightlessness for the characters and a phantasmagorical quality for the play." Mood is TW's strength: "He can weave a spell and conjure visions as no other playwright alive. . . . [TW] is at the heart of the tortured human condition."

47   HARTUNG, PHILIP T. "Confused Reflections in a Mirror." *Commonweal* 76 (30 March):18.

     Review of film of *SB*. "The screenplay and direction are good." Praises G. Page's performance over the others.

48   ————. "The Ins and the Outs." *Commonweal* 77 (14 December):315.

     Brief review of film of *PA*. "A little too slapstick for my taste." Generally favorable.

49   HEWES, HENRY. "El Purgatorio." *Saturday Review* 45 (20 January):36.

     Review of *NI*. TW is working here "with the same style, humor, and sensitivity that make him the foremost American playwright of his time." Refers to *CAT* and *SB*; *NI* "preserves Mr. Williams' unique and inspired vision, and would appear to be the best new American play of the season."

50   HOBE. "Shows on Broadway: 'The Night of the Iguana.' " *Variety*, 3 January, p. 56.

     "The underlying theme of the drama is tender and the quality of much of the writing is exalted." Details of plot and staging; actors Leighton, Davis, and O'Neal generously praised. "Although 'Iguana' is not one of Williams' most distinguished plays, when it holds the audience in enthralled silence, it is emotionally rewarding."

51   HURLEY, PAUL J. "Tennessee Williams: Critic of American Society." Ph.D. dissertation, Duke University.

     Attempts to show that TW's characters and the events in his dramas reveal his attitude toward his country; *RSMS, SB, S&S, CAT, SND, CR*, and *OD* cited as examples. Further attempts to show that his plays consistently champion certain moral values and condemn others. (*DA* 24:2034–35).

52   KAUFFMANN, STANLEY. "Truth Will Out—Sometimes." *New Republic* 146 (16 April):28.

Review of film of *SB*. The play "was an embarrassment." Goes on briefly to discuss the film's technical flaws. Reprinted: 1966.39.

53   KEATING, EDWARD M. "Mildew on the Old Magnolia." *Ramparts* 1 (November):69–74.

Critical analysis of TW's "decadent" writing. Establishes the premise that TW's greatest talent is to show pain; relates the theme to the canon.

54   KERR, WALTER. "'Iguana': True Tone." *New York Herald Tribune*, 7 January, sec. 4. pp. 1, 3.

Review of *NI*. In-depth assessment of the play's controls: the demon in the characters' wills. *NI* is "a dream of immobility from which the dreamers never wake. . . . Mr. Williams . . . reminds us what it is to watch poetry in the process of finding itself."

55   KNIGHT, ARTHUR. Review of film of *PA*. *Saturday Review* 45 (10 November):77.

Isobel Lennart "shape[s] and sharpen[s] a lesser play of Williams until it seems it should have been written for the screen in the first place. . . . One of the most winning adult entertainments of the year."

56   LABADIE, DONALD W. Review of film of *SB*. *Show* 2 (March):30.

"Bears a stronger surface resemblance to the original Broadway version than most adaptations." Quotes G. Page: "I think people forget how funny [TW] really is." Proceeds to interview Page.

57   LEWIS, ALLAN. "The American Scene: Tennessee Williams, Arthur Miller." In *The Contemporary Theatre*. New York: Crown Publishers, pp. 282–303.

Cites O'Neill's 1920 *Beyond the Horizon* as "the coming of age of the American theatre," and Wilder, TW, and Arthur Miller as "noteworthy successors" to the tradition of O'Neill. Discusses TW as "absorbed with the instinctive and the behavioral, the cry for emotional freedom"; he paints his characters as "lost in a struggle against the sadism of the insensitive." Refers to *BA, GM, SND, SB,* and the influence of Lawrence, among others.

58 LEWIS, THEOPHILUS. Review of *NI. America* 106 (3 February):604.
   Brief. Refers to TW's "uncanny flair for creating vivid characters ... at long last he has discovered the world is not wholly populated by neurotics, nymphomaniacs and degenerates."

59 LITTLE, STUART W. "Tennessee Williams Play in Rehearsal." *New York Herald Tribune,* 14 November, p. 21.
   Advance comments and notes for Broadway opening of *MT.* Comments on TW's work in preparing it.

60 LYONS, LEONARD. "The Lyons Den." *New York Post,* 5 October, p. 43.
   Gossip item. Elia Kazan asks TW to write a play for the new Lincoln Center.

61 MCCARTEN, JOHN. "Lonely, Loquacious, and Doomed." *New Yorker* 37 (13 January):61.
   Review of *NI.* "Tennessee Williams' genius for making assorted bizarre types believable is in evidence but our interest in them is aroused only sporadically." Considerable plot summary.

62 MACDONALD, DWIGHT. Review of film of *SB. Esquire* 57 (June):56, 58.
   Generally negative; criticizes production, writing, acting.

63 MANNES, MARYA. "Just Looking." *Reporter* 26 (1 February):45.
   Review of *NI.* TW "grants his human beings stature and his audience the privilege ... of admiration." Plot details; calls TW's writing "tender and luminous"; the play "has moments of suspended belief."

64 "Marriage Comedy at Its Best." *Times* (London), 11 July, p. 13.
   Brief comment on *PA.* Discusses plot and compares it to *BD.*

65 MEKAS, JONAS. Review of *RSMS. Village Voice,* 1 February, p. 11.

Review of film of *RSMS*. "Remarkably dull, academic, and colorless."

66 " 'Menagerie' Is Banned by Williams." *New York World Telegram & Sun*, 20 September, p. 17.
Audrey Wood announces TW's refusal (temporarily) to allow future professional productions of *GM* because it's "been over-exposed to the point of weariness."

67 NEWMAN, DAVID. "The Agent as Catalyst: [Part II]." *Esquire* 58 (December):217–18, 261–64.
Discusses TW's relationship with his agent, Audrey Wood; makes reference to her influence over TW generally, her hand in *SND, GM, BA, NI*; biographical data.

68 "No More Southern Belles." *Times* (London), 1 August, p. 12.
News item. Press conference with TW in England to defend production of *MT* at Spoleto.

69 "People." *Time* 80 (10 August):26.
Brief gossip item. TW talking of not wanting to write anymore about Southern belles; "I have so little money it scares me."

70 "The Prize Winners on Broadway." *New York Times*, 20 May, sec. 2, p. 1.
News item. Critics' Circle cites *NI* as best American play.

71 "Putting on the Cat." *Time* 80 (30 March):83.
Brief review of film of *SB*. "A fast, smart, squalid melodrama." Praises cast.

72 QUIGLY, ISABEL. "Between Two Worlds." *Spectator* 208 (23 February):242.
Review of film of *RSMS*. "The direction is so insipid and stagy that we get no feeling of place." The film presumes a "myopic or somnolent audience."

73 RHODE, ERIC. Review of film of *S&S*. *Sight and Sound* 31 (Spring):95.

Sees sexual guilt as a theme in TW's plays. Story is spoiled by "parade of symbolism." Praise for G. Page and camera work.

74 RICHARDS, STANLEY. Review of *NI*. *Players* 38 (April):218–19.
Brief. The play "is one of the author's finest"; praises Leighton's performance. Refers to *NI*'s being "a Chekhovian exercise in dramatic probing."

75 ROTHSCHILD, ELAINE. Review of film of *SB*. *Films in Review* 13 (April):233–34.
"Do not allow Williams-disgust to keep you from seeing Geraldine Page as a debauched and fading movie star in 'Sweet Bird of Youth.' " Plot summary and cast details.

76 SCHLESINGER, ARTHUR, JR. "Movies: Love Sacred and Profane." *Show* 2 (March):98.
Review of film of *S&S*. "Hard to say what went wrong with [*S&S*] . . . the trouble begins . . . with [TW]." His characters are "vivid and arresting, but not credible."

77 SCHUMACH, MURRAY. "Hollywood Plays." *New York Times*, 4 November, sec. 2, p. 9.
Notes the decline of Broadway and rise of film industry as a major source of "adult" entertainment to combat television. *SND* was labeled "adult" by Warner Bros.

78 SHARP, WILLIAM. "An Unfashionable View of Tennessee Williams." *Tulane Drama Review* 6 (March):160–71.
Sees current criticism as simplifying TW too much, making him a "sensation monger." Criticizes Falk and Popkin, particularly; the most important thing is that TW "is a writer of tragedy." Cites numerous works to defend thesis, relative to tone, characterization, and situation.

79 SIMON, JOHN. Review of *NI*. *Hudson Review* 15 (Spring):120–21.
It's "not vintage Williams." Provides plot summary and character analysis.

80 ———. Review of *NI*. *Theatre Arts* 46 (March):57.
NI is "preferable to all his plays since 'Streetcar.' " Considerable interpretation of plot.

81 "Sneaky Tweaker." *Newsweek* 60 (12 November):96.
    Review of film of *PA*. "Best American comedy of the year."
    Praises TW and Fonda.

82 SORELL, WALTER. "The New Tennessee Williams." *Cresset* 25
    (March):21.
    Review of *NI*. "A masterpiece of a play without plot. ... In
    its Chekhovian mood, the whole play seems to sear with wounds
    and yet to soar to heights of human greatness." Emphasizes
    TW's capacities as a poet.

83 "Spoleto Gets a New Play from Tennessee Williams." *Times* (Lon-
    don), 14 July, p. 4.
    Review of *MT*, Spoleto production. Brief, surface comments.

84 "Suddenly, Last Spring." *Newsweek* 59 (1 January):53.
    Brief review of film of *RSMS*. Praises the cast for whatever
    success the film achieves; considerable plot analysis.

85 " 'Sweet Bird of Youth.' " *New York Times Magazine*, 14 January,
    pp. 62, 65.
    Photos with captions from production of *SB*.

86 TALLMER, JERRY. "The Lizard's Skin." *Village Voice*, 4 January,
    p. 9.
    Review of *NI*. It "earns the most terrible of all condemnations."
    Sees TW as a "past master." Still, "there is much poetry within
    individual fragments." Contrasts TW's internal and external dar-
    ing.

87 TAUBMAN, HOWARD. "Changing Course." *New York Times*, 7
    January, sec. 2, p. 1.
    Review of *NI*. Cites *NI* as a change of direction for TW:
    "Rarely has Tennessee Williams written with more perception
    or with greater beauty." Praise for cast.

88 "Tennessee in Mexico." *Newsweek* 59 (8 January):44.
    Review of *NI*. Refers to TW's "clinical compassion ... and
    comic passion." Praises cast.

89 "Tennessee's All Over in Boston Next Week." *Variety*, 5 December, p. 55.
    Brief notice of three TW works in Boston: *MT*, film of *PA*, a few one-acters.

90 "Tennessee Williams Farce Subtly Played." *Times* (London), 14 June, p. 6.
    Review of *PA*. Short synopsis of plot plus slight analysis.

91 "Tennessee Williams May Desert 'Southern Belles' for Mysticism." *New York Times*, 2 August, p. 16.
    Gossip item. TW seeking new topics, possibly mysticism; TW has been in Italy for premiere of *MT*.

92 "Tennessee Williams Work Has Premiere at Spoleto." *New York Times*, 12 July, p. 19.
    News item. World premiere of *MT* receives "cordial reception" in Spoleto, Italy.

93 "Tough Angel of Mercy." *Life* 52 (13 April): 67–70.
    Review of *NI*. Calls it TW's "best play in many seasons." Regards Hannah as the character who "drives home—more explicitly than any of his characters ever has—the heart of his writing."

94 TUBE. " 'Period of Adjustment.' " *Variety*, 31 October, p. 6.
    Review of *PA*. " 'Period of Adjustment' is lower case Tennessee Williams, but it also illustrates that lower case Williams is superior to the upper case of most modern playwrights." Lengthy plot details; note on players who do adequate jobs all around.

95 TYNAN, KENNETH. "The Outer Circle Comes to Life." *Observer* (London), 17 June, p. 23.
    Review of *PA*, London production. "Lends itself . . . to inadvertent self-parody."

96 "The Violated Heart." *Time* 79 (5 January):53.
    Review of *NI*. "Perhaps the wisest play he has ever written." Discusses "Williams' perverse conviction that evil is overwhelmingly strong and will prevail."

97   VON DORNUM, JOHN HOWARD. "The Major Plays of Tennessee Williams, 1948–1960." Ph.D. dissertation, University of Southern California.

Cites *GM, SND, CAT* specifically; concludes that unless TW can learn to give his "overspecialized characters and situations" some profound human relevance, he will not be an important part of American drama. (*DA* 23:1371–72).

98   WALSH, MOIRA. Review of film of *RSMS*. *America* 106 (13 January):481.

Brief. Negative about plot and filming.

99   WATTS, RICHARD, JR. "A Somber Lyric Vision of the Lost." *New York Post*, 14 January, amusement sec., p. 21.

Review of *NI*; "It is possible to divide the plays of Tennessee Williams roughly into two groups . . . the violent so-called 'block busters' . . . and the quieter, more leisurely works." *NI* fits into the second category; its "effect is undeniably something of a disappointment. . . . [It's] a drama of mood" featuring "the dark, brooding lyricism of the author."

100   WEALES, GERALD C. "Tennessee Williams' *Fugitive Kind*." In *American Drama Since World War II*. New York: Harcourt, Brace & World, pp. 18–39.

Focuses on TW's characters who are "fugitives," the outsiders who seek "freedom." "The one thing that all of them seem to have in common is the combination of sensitivity and imagination with corruption—physical, spiritual, sexual disability. From the beginning, the plays have suggested that the heroes are abnormal and that there is something damnable about normality."

101   WEILER, A.H. "By Way of Report." *New York Times*, 11 February, sec. 2, p. 7.

Gossip item. Seven Arts Productions acquire film rights to *TPC*.

102   "Wholesome Williams." *Time* 80 (16 November):97.

Brief review of film of *PA*. Pleased with TW's gentler themes; plot summary.

103   "Williams Cancels Bids for 'Glass Menagerie.'" *New York Times*, 21 September, p. 35.

News item. TW feels *GM* has been "overexposed" and has "withdrawn permission for production."

104 "Williams 'Rests' Play." *New York Herald Tribune*, 21 September, p. 11.

News item. TW withdrawing permission for future productions of *GM*; also notes closing of *NI* on Broadway.

105 "Williams's 'Night of the Iguana.'" *Times* (London), 11 January, p. 14.

Review of *NI*. Compares the New York production with *CAT, OD, SB, S&S*; generally negative about cast.

106 WINSTEN, ARCHER. "'Period of Adjustment' in Dual Bow." *New York Post*, 1 November, p. 20.

Review of film of *PA*. The film is "edging over into farce." It's a departure for TW since it is "a major step out of his utterly degraded view of the wicked world."

107 ————. "'Sweet Bird of Youth' in Dual Bow." *New York Post*, 29 March, p. 26.

Review of film of *SB*. Talks of its departures from TW's script and speculates on why TW would have permitted it.

108 ZOLOTOW, SAM. "'Iguana' Is Cited by Critics Circle." *New York Times*, 11 April, p. 46.

News item. New York Drama Critics' Circle cites *NI* as best American play. Names voters.

109 ————. "Tennessee Williams Gives Play to Actors Studio." *New York Times*, 12 April, p. 43.

News item. TW to give *TTM* to Actors Studio to help establish them as permanent theater company. Mentions TW's *CAT, SND, GM, NI* as prize winners, and *MT* as one of his next plays.

1963

1 BARKSDALE, RICHARD K. "Social Background in the Plays of Miller and Williams." *College Language Association Journal* 6 (March): 161–69.

Compares Miller to Ben Jonson and TW to Shakespeare; TW "is the practising, hard-writing, critically inarticulate writer that Will Shakespeare apparently was to his age." Goes further to suggest that "dark moods and violent deeds haunt certain of Williams' plays just as insanity and sadism haunt certain of Shakespeare's plays." Reviews critical estimate of TW and focuses on setting in *SND, CAT*, and *OD*, citing them as being of particular interest for their use of the American South.

2   BLUEFARB, SAM. *"The Glass Menagerie:* Three Visions of Time." *College English* 24 (April):513–18.
    The play is examined with regard to the element of time— Amanda representing the past, Tom the future, and Laura standing somehow outside the change of time, always in the present. Time is described as having these three faces, each looking toward a separate fragmented vision.

3   BOLTON, WHITNEY. " 'Milk Train' Change of Pace for Williams; Arresting Play." New York *Morning Telegraph*, 18 January, p. 2.
    Review of *MT.* "An intellectual and at times mystic study. . . . [It] is a dissertation in beautifully written language of the whole mystique of death. . . . Mr. Williams [is] on a morally more lofty level than has been the case before."

4   BRADBURY, JOHN M. *Renaissance in the South: A Critical History of the Literature, 1920–1960.* Chapel Hill: University of North Carolina Press, pp. 192–95.
    "Tennessee Williams' development . . . has been an almost uninterrupted movement from compassion and poetry to harshly dramatic exposure of twisted and perverted lives." Surveys his "sense of dramatic form" in *GM, S&S, SND, RT, CR, PA, NI, CAT, SLS.*

5   BROWN, ANDREAS. "Tennessee Williams by Another Name." *Papers of the Bibliographic Society of America* 57 (Third Quarter): 337–78.
    Locates eleven of TW's early contributions to periodicals written under his real name.

6 BROWN, JOHN MASON. "Southern Discomfort: Tennessee Williams' Streetcar." In *Dramatis Personae: A Retrospective Show.* New York: Viking Press, pp. 89–94.
Reprint of 1947.9.

7 BRUSTEIN, ROBERT. "A Buccaneer on Broadway." *New Republic* 148 (2 February):26–27.
Review of *MT*. Brief and extremely negative; refers to it as "unadventurous" on TW's part. Reprinted: 1965.7.

8 BUELL, JOHN. "The Evil Images of Tennessee Williams." *Thought* 38 (Summer):167–89.
Starts with the "fact that Williams writes about certain moral and psychological horrors" and that popular response to him has a lot to do with that. Refers to the "certain malaise that can be found in [his] plays and their effect." TW, among the other modern tragedians, has "one prominent characteristic: . . . dealing in unresolved mental breakdown, incipient or final, neurotic or psychotic." Discusses the critical problem of separating the "art itself" from the decadent aspects in it. Starting with *Oedipus Rex*, goes through an historic analysis of TW's work, covering his use of realistic and nonrealistic structures, myth, and applicable critical theories.

9 "The Cast Menagerie." *Time* 82 (8 November):69.
Gossip item about filming *NI* in Mexico. Refers to TW's involvement, his not wanting a happy ending tacked on.

10 CHAPMAN, JOHN. Review of *MT. New York Theatre Critics' Reviews* 24:391–94.
(Review intended for publication in the striking New York *Daily News*, 17 January.) *MT* is TW's most arresting drama—fascinating in its technique, and both profoundly searching and mercilessly cruel. . . . Once again, Williams gives the theatre great excitement."

11 CLURMAN, HAROLD. Review of *MT. Nation* 196 (2 February):106.
TW "should have waited and allowed the material to crystallize beyond its crude and amorphous state."

12 COLEMAN, JOHN. "First Night." *New Statesman* 65 (25 January):
    134.
        Review of film of *PA*. "A Sixties lightweight of sorts, [that]
    draws its fun from a much closer acquaintance with reality. . . .
    The sense of Mr. Williams pacing cosily around a calamitous
    marriage bed is certainly nothing new."

13 DAVIES, BRENDA. Review of film of *PA*. *Sight and Sound* 32
    (Spring):93.
        Brief. Synopsis and generally positive comments on production.

14 DUKORE, BERNARD F. "The Cat Has Nine Lives." *Tulane Drama
    Review* 8 (Fall):95–100.
        Refers to the two most scenic elements in *CAT*: "liquor cabinet
    and a bed." Also mentions TW's use of animal images, homo-
    sexuality, mendacity, procreation.

15 DUPREY, RICHARD A. "The Battle for the American Stage." *Catholic
    World* 197 (July):246–51.
        Describes the differences between the "epic" theater and the
    "avant-garde." Details about almost every major playwright, in-
    cluding TW. "In addition to trends there are always individual
    writers either bucking the stream or writing in so unique a
    manner as to stand . . . apart from it. . . . Such a writer is Ten-
    nessee Williams. . . . [His] moral symbolism, cast into his own
    smoky manner of twentieth century morality play . . . is so much
    a unique phenomenon that he establishes no drift, no current
    but his own."

16 ———. "Where Are Our Playwrights?" *America* 108 (5 January):
    10–12.
        "Williams never managed to stumble out from the jungle of
    his own confusion. He gave us grotesque wonders to marvel at,
    but he has been so saddled by his sentimentality . . . that he has
    never been able to spread the wings of the great and fearful
    vulture he has stuffed before us."

17 EVANS, PETER. "Tennessee Wants to Unsweeten Ava." *New York
    World-Telegram & Sun*, 24 October, p. 12.
        Interview-commentary, focusing on film of *NI*. TW says, "The

script is better constructed than my play ever was," but wants it to remain a tragedy. His argument with Huston: TW wants no happy ending. TW has written five different endings for the film. He goes on to observe, "Death is my best theme.... I'm a tortured man and vain and self-centered."

18   FLAXMAN, SEYMOUR L. "The Debt of Williams and Miller to Ibsen and Strindberg." *Comparative Literature Studies* (Special Advance Issue):51–60.
     Proposes to trace the influence of "the two Scandinavian giants" on Miller and TW. Mainly interested in "similarities in characters, themes, and dramatic technique." Illustrates pointed influence of Strindberg's *The Father* on *YTM* and *NI*, as well as on *SND*; shows *Miss Julie* strains in *CR*, *GM*; *Ghost Sonata* shown to influence *GM*, *SND*, *S&S*, and *SB*. Finally questions whether Miller or TW has indeed gone beyond the tradition of Strindberg or Ibsen. "They have made no real innovations in dramatic structure or technique."

19   FREEDLEY, GEORGE. Review of *MT*. New York *Morning Telegraph*, 25 January, pp. 2, 7.
     "The least effective of his plays with the possible exception of 'Period of Adjustment.' ... The first Williams play that lacks heart."

20   GILLIATT, PENELOPE. "Films." *Observer*, 20 January, p. 25.
     Brief review of film of *PA*. "One of the most disconcerting films I have ever seen."

21   GILMAN, RICHARD. "The Drama Is Coming Now." *Tulane Drama Review* 7 (Summer):27–42.
     Brief reference to TW: "The American drama is itself almost mindless; we weep for the intellectual deficiencies of Miller and Williams."

22   ————. "Mistuh Williams, He Dead." *Commonweal* 77 (8 February):515–17.
     Review of *MT*. TW "has had it and I have had it too." Refers to his "creative suicide." Substantial analysis of the structure. Reprinted: 1971.11.

23   GLOVER, WILLIAM. "Back Stage with Tennessee Williams." *Christian Science Monitor*, 7 January, p. 11.

Interview prior to opening of *MT*. TW discusses bringing *MT* to New York from Spoleto, decadence, his work, going to India.

24   GOBNECHT, ELEANOR ALBERTA. "A Descriptive Study of the Value Commitments of the Principal Characters in Four Recent American Plays: *Picnic, Cat on a Hot Tin Roof, A Long Day's Journey Into Night*, and *Look Homeward, Angel*." Ph.D. dissertation, University of Southern California.

Attempts to identify the values to which the characters in the titled plays are committed. Big Daddy is mentioned specifically. (*DA* 24:433–34.)

25   GRANDE, LUKE M., F.S.C. "Tennessee Williams' New Poet-Prophet." *Drama Critique* 6 (Spring):60–64.

MT is a "fascinating drama"; it shows a new "progression" in TW's work and the movement toward the "poet-prophet" conceit. Compares to Inge, Albee.

26   GRAY, PAUL. "The Theatre of the Marvelous: From the Director's Prompt Books." *Tulane Drama Review* 7 (Summer):143–45.

Discusses Kazan's notes on *SND*, the use of "inscape" in the play, the set and lighting in the play, "the world of Blanche DuBois."

27   HEWES, HENRY. "Gradually This Summer." *Saturday Review* 46 (2 February):20–21.

Review of *MT*. *MT* "is perhaps his most ambiguous and subliminal" work; assumes TW was not "interested in fulfilling the dramatic potential of his play. . . . The evening tinkles with the great playwright's special brand of humor and poetic insight. . . . [It's] worthy of our respect and any future attention its author may find it possible to give it."

28   HOBE. "Show on Broadway: 'The Milk Train Doesn't Stop Here Anymore.'" *Variety*, 23 January, p. 72.

Generally negative review of Broadway opening. TW "has come up with a muddled, dull play, poorly presented, and a doubtful project for Broadway, picture or even stock."

29 "Hotted-up Humanity." *Times Literary Supplement,* 12 July, p. 510.
   Book review of London publication of *NI*. A survey of his
   previous works' themes. In *NI*, "corruption, and the methods of
   resisting it are his theme." Many plot details.

30 Johnson, Mary Lynn. "Williams' 'Suddenly Last Summer,' Scene
   One." *Explicator* 21 (April): item 66.
   Brief item suggesting "Shakespearean origin of their [Violet
   and Sebastian] names." Cites *Twelfth Night.*

31 Kennedy, Paul P. "John Huston's 'Iguana.'" *New York Times,*
   1 December, p. 5.
   News and gossip concerning the filming of *NI* in Mexico.

32 Kerr, Walter. "Mr. Williams." In *The Theatre in Spite of Itself.*
   New York: Simon & Schuster, pp. 247–55.
   Reprint of 1959.70.

33 Kirk, Don. "White House Library Loses a Writers' Poll." *New
   York Post,* 18 August, p. 16.
   TW comments on "decision barring living writers of fiction
   from the new White House library."

34 Lewis, Theophilus. Review of *MT. America* 108 (30 March):449.
   Brief. Discusses *MT* in terms of characters' integrity.

35 Lyons, Leonard. "The Lyons Den." *New York Post,* 22 July, p. 23.
   Brief gossip item. Filming business on *NI* in Mexico.

36 McCarten, John. "Slow Death in Italy." *New Yorker* 38 (26 January):72.
   Review of *MT*. TW is "at his most arcane" in this play. It's
   "made up of shreds and patches of the author's other works."

37 McCarthy, Mary. "American Realists, Playwrights." In *Theatre
   Chronicles 1937–1962.* New York: Farrar, Straus, pp. 209–29.
   Reprint of 1961.55.

38 ———. "A Streetcar Called Success." In *Theatre Chronicles
   1937–1962.* New York: Farrar, Straus, pp. 131–35.
   Reprint of 1948.42, 1956.70.

39   MAGID, MARION. "The Innocence of Tennessee Williams." *Commentary* 35 (January):34–43.

     TW "is not our best, but our only playwright since O'Neill. His imagination . . . is a kind of fever chart of our national ailments." Says his plays "cannot be talked about except in their performance." Then discusses production of *SND* and Kazan's influence. Discusses "reasons why a successful Williams play in full regalia does not seem written and produced so much as masterminded; it is more like a perfect crime than an artistic undertaking." Refers to his heroes, his use of sexuality, theme control, images of manhood, his vision. Reprinted: 1971.19.

40   MANNES, MARYA. "The Half-World of American Drama." *Reporter* 28 (April):48–50.

     Brief review of *MT*. Discusses the play as an illustration of how "'love' never transcends sexuality." Emphasis on Flora and her predicament, as well as on Chris as a Savior figure.

41   "'Milk Train' Gets a Second Chance." *New York Times*, 18 September, p. 32.

     News on the revised opening of *MT* with brief outline of story and plans for touring.

42   MILLHAUSER, MILTON. "Science Literature, and the Image of Man." *Humanist* 23 (May–June):85–88.

     Surveys conventions of post-Darwinian literature; brief reference to TW and the issue of the "audience's recognizing that homosexuality might disguise itself as aggressive maleness"—in defense of which he cites *CAT*.

43   "Mr. Tennessee Williams's Two Steps Back." *Times* (London), 6 February, p. 13.

     Review of *MT*, London production. Compares briefly to *OD* and *NI*.

44   "No Time Like the Present." *Esquire* 59 (April):58–59.

     A collection of excerpts from fourteen *Time* magazine reviews of TW's films and plays (from 1945 to 1962); reviews of *YTM*, *SND*, *S&S*, *RSMS*, *RT*, *CR*, *OA*, *CAT*, *GD*, *PA*, *SB*.

45 "Peggy Wood to Act in Chicago." *New York Times*, 12 November, p. 46.
    News item. Wood to be star of *GM* in Chicago.

46 PRIDEAUX, TOM. "Tennessee's Mistake." *Life* 54 (1 February):14–15.
    Brief review of *MT*. "Motionless, shallow, brackish ... Williams' intent, as usual, is anything but shallow."

47 Review of *MT*. *Theatre Arts* 47 (February):66.
    Brief. Attempts to explain difficulties in plot and characterization.

48 RIDDEL, JOSEPH N. " 'Streetcar Named Desire'—Nietzsche Descending." *Modern Drama* 5 (February):421–30.
    Says *SND* fails "not ... in its subthemes, ... but in its overabundant intellectualism." Claims that TW is as much Nietzschean as he is neo-Lawrentian. Says " 'Streetcar' ... borrows from Nietzsche in great chunks." Among the ways he cites: "contradiction between intellectual design and the militant primitivism of the theme"; its "metaphysical tension"; the setting of *SND* ("combination of raw realism and deliberate fantasy"); its "violence and reconciliation." Reprinted: 1971.19.

49 SCHMIDT, SANDRA. "Theatre: Williams in Workshop." *Village Voice*, 1 August, p. 12.
    Review of *MK*. "Amateurish effort by Tennessee Williams." Refers to "Mr. Williams' awful wordiness."

50 SIMON, JOHN. Review of *MT*. *Hudson Review* 16 (Spring):87–89.
    It's "abortive ... the characters are either wooden or preposterous. The plot could not involve one less, the dialogue ... [is] a barren waste." Mocks TW's attempts at producing a Christ-figure. Reprinted: 1975.45.

51 SMITH, MICHAEL. Review of *MT*. *Village Voice*, 24 January, p. 20.
    "At its best, 'Milk Train' is a profoundly cynical, corrupt, disgusted play. ... [TW] gives us only decoration, the glittering surfaces of empty people in an empty world. ... As a theatre experience the play is extremely unsatisfactory."

52 "Stars Fell on Mismaloya." *Life* 55 (20 December):69–76.
    News and gossip piece about filming of *NI* in Mexico. Refers to
    cast, salaries, location work, and TW ("who just laughed and
    laughed"). Many photos.

53 STUTZMAN, RALPH W. "The Sting of Reality: The Theology of
    Tennessee Williams." *Unitarian Universalist Register-Leader*
    (April), pp. 11–13.
    Using *SLS* and *NI* as examples, cites the theological ideas in
    TW's fiction: God depicted as senile, cruel, or dead at the hands
    of those He created. Using the image of the sea turtles being
    devoured by flesh-eating birds as a model for human existence,
    the writer states that the survivors will be responsible for taking
    the place of the destroyers.

54 SUTTON, HORACE. "Golden Cities of the Gold Coast." *Saturday Re-
    view* 46 (16 February):39–40, 50–52.
    Article on Florida. Brief mention, at end, of TW's home in
    Key West.

55 TAUBMAN, HOWARD. "Theater: Tennessee Williams 'Milk Train.'"
    New York Times, 18 January, p. 7.
    Review of *MT*. Generally favorable but considers *MT* disap-
    pointing for a TW work; brief synopsis.

56 "Tennessee Williams Play Re-Written." *Times* (London), 28 Sep-
    tember, p. 12.
    News item. *MT* has been rewritten and slated for production
    at Royal Court Theatre.

57 "Tennessee Williams Tabus South African Segregation." *Variety*,
    7 August, p. 64.
    Letter from Audrey Wood about TW's refusal to permit per-
    formances of any of his plays in South Africa's segregated
    theaters.

58 THOMAS, BOB. "Long Absent Ava Returns to the Scene." *New York
    Post*, 24 October, p. 21.
    Brief news item. TW and Ava Gardner in Puerto Vallarta for
    filming of *NI*.

59 TISCHLER, NANCY M. "Tennessee Williams' Bohemian Revision of Christianity." *Susquehanna University Studies* 7 (June):103–8.
A speculation on TW's "religious idiosyncrasies," focusing on *MT*, *NI*, and *BA*. Treats TW's use of Christ-figures, and concludes that he believes "Christianity needs renovation." Also examines the relation of his use of sex in this plan and the presence and influence of autobiography. Concludes that "the Williams Christ is still a gentle god . . . , a kindly therapist, a good friend, a compassionate listener rather than a real force."

60 "To a Mountain Top." *Time* 81 (25 January):53.
Review of *MT*. "His first unequivocally symbolic and undeviatingly religious allegory." Praises mostly the attempt he makes.

61 "Unwieldy Williams." *Newsweek* 61 (28 January):79.
Review of *MT*. "Curiously indecisive drama," saved only by TW's "theatrically gripping gimmick."

62 VON DREELE, W. H. "All Aboard for Allegory." *National Review* 14 (9 April):291, 293.
Comments on *MT*, upon its closing in New York City. Surveys criticism from popular press; plot summary; says it "was great fun." Cites TW's "optimistic view toward sex and the senior citizen."

63 WALSH, MOIRA. Review of film of *PA*. *America* 108 (19 January): 119.
Brief. Says she "cannot get as enthusiastic over this comedy" as other critics have; TW is trifling—yet she still finds room for praising his attempt here.

64 WARREN, CLIFTON LANIER. "Tennessee Williams as Cinematic Writer." Ph.D. dissertation, Indiana University.
Cites the movie versions of *SND*, *GM*, *RT*, and the film *BD* as examples of melodrama. Most of TW's work is in a melodramatic vein and therefore easily translatable to the screen. (*DA* 25:489–90.)

65 WATT, DOUGLAS. " 'Milk Train' on 2d Trip." New York *Daily News*, 19 November, p. 50.
Advance notice of revival of *MT*.

66   WEST, ANTHONY. "One Milk Train, One Scandal." *Show* 3 (April): 40–41.

Review of *MT*. "Involuntary self-parody . . . the saddest thing of all is that [in *MT*] one hears Mr. Williams more and more frequently rattling the dry bones of old speeches from old plays together to try to strike a spark." The work is an "aberration."

67   WILLIAMS, EDWINA DAKIN. "Remember Me to Tom." *Show* 3 (February):60–63, 103–5.

Editor's claim: "A famous playwright's mother tells a story as stormy and pathetic as a Tennessee Williams melodrama." Her book of the same title would expand the contents here.

68   WILLIAMS, EDWINA DAKIN and FREEMAN, LUCY. *Remember Me to Tom.* New York: Putnam, 255 pp.

Memoirs of TW's mother. Begins with suggestion that TW's dramas fill out a childhood statement, his "trying to discover where the devil lives inside all of us," and she asserts that "it's time to tell the truth." Goes through details of TW's childhood, his siblings, his youth (which "explain[s] . . . his deep interest in and sympathy with people trapped in emotional tragedy"); the development of his writing and university experience. She includes letters that reflect his attitude and feelings at given stages, gives substantial biographical detail relating to premieres of early plays.

69   "Williams Gives Scripts to Texas University Library." *Variety*, 20 February, p. 63.

Mentions donation of manuscripts to University of Texas: *SND, CAT, NI, GM, S&S, RT, CR, BD, OD, SB, PA, SLS*.

70   "Williams to Give Papers to Texas U." *New York Times*, 23 January, p. 5.

News item. TW gives original manuscripts to University of Texas. Includes plays, movies, poems, stories, and essays. (Included are *SND, CAT, NI, GM, S&S, RT, CR, OD*.)

71   WOOTEN, CARL. "*The Country Wife* and Contemporary Comedy: A World Apart." *Drama Survey* 2 (Winter):333–43.

Refers briefly to *BD*. Plot and theme analysis, showing it to be parallel in some ways to elements of Wycherley's play.

72 ZOLOTOW, SAM. "Playwright Picks West Side Setting." *New York Times*, 10 September, p. 47.
News item. TW has revised and expanded *MT*; will open in Abingdon, Virginia.

73 ⸻. "Williams Offers Two Short Plays." *New York Times*, 27 November, p. 33.
News item. *SST* to be performed by Actor's Studio Theater; quotes TW regarding new version of *MT*.

1964

1 BOLTON, WHITNEY. "New Version of 'Milk Train' with Tallulah No Improvement." New York *Morning Telegraph*, 3 January, p. 2.
Review of *MT*. "The play is still a failure." The failure "was inherent in the play itself."

2 "Books Received." *Times Literary Supplement*, 29 October, p. 985.
Brief book review of *MT*. "An oddly broken-backed piece."

3 CALVERY, CATHERINE ANN. "Illusion in Modern American Drama: A Study of Selected Plays by Arthur Miller, Tennessee Williams, and Eugene O'Neill." Ph.D. dissertation, Tulane University.
Treats TW's *SND* and *GM* in light of their main characters who escape an awareness of time through their illusions, Amanda's nostalgic grasp of the past, Blanche's self-protective stepping back into a "beautiful" past. Focus on the way the present is categorically avoided. (*DA* 25:6111–12.)

4 CHAPMAN, JOHN. "Miss Bankhead Lacks Steam in Second Run of 'The Milk Train.'" New York *Daily News*, 2 January, p. 55.
Review of *MT*. "A simplified and awkwardly stylized version of the drama which was presented a year ago." In an effort to clarify the play, TW has "lessened its emotional appeal."

5 COOK, ALTON. "Big Day for 'Night of the Iguana.'" *New York World Telegram & Sun*, 8 August, p. 15.

News item prior to opening (the private one and the public one) of film of *NI*. Discusses the script variations of the play, the cast, the director.

6   CRIST, JUDITH. "Plain Talk and Fancy Sex." *New York Herald Tribune Magazine*, 1 July, p. 15.

Discusses "The Carpetbaggers" and *NI* in relation to sex and language. Calls *NI* "a drama of content and subtlety derived from Williams' play, with a tight dramatic line and superb cinematic values."

7   ———. "Two of the Best: 'Night of the Iguana.'" *New York Herald Tribune*, 1 July, p. 14.

Review of film of *NI*. "Screenplay has departed from the Tennessee Williams stage play for valid cinematic purpose." It's better than the "relatively static original.... Compassion is the keynote and maturity the hallmark."

8   CROWTHER, BOSLEY. "Screen: Travelers Down Mexico Way." *New York Times*, 1 July, p. 42.

Review of film of *NI*. "Who are these dislocated wanderers? From what Freudian cell have they sprung and why are they so aggressive in punching their loneliness home to the world? These are the basic revelations that are not communicated by the film, which follows fairly closely the diologic substance of the play."

9   DAVIS, JAMES. "New 'Milk Train' Bows; A New Play Is Shelved." New York *Daily News*, 1 January, p. 35.

Brief notice of *MT*'s opening that night at Brooks Atkinson Theatre.

10 DAWSON, WILLIAM MEREDITH. "The Female Characters of August Strindberg, Eugene O'Neill, and Tennessee Williams." Ph.D. dissertation, University of Wisconsin.

Examines the authors' own childhood experiences with and attitudes toward women as basis for study of their female characters. The ego-centered domination by women of men is illustrated—as is the distrust and fear of women—in the plays. (*DA* 25:2663.)

11 DENT, ALAN. "Funny Formidable." *Illustrated London News* 245
    (26 September):480.
    Review of film of *NI*. Compares TW's work with that of
    Dickens, saying TW "has the same passion for grotesques and
    something of the same literary potency in their delineation. . . .
    The only radical difference is that Charles knew when he was
    being funny, and Tennessee doesn't." Praises only Gardner for
    performance; indifferent to the film.

12 DIDION, JOAN. "The Dream and the Nightmare." *Vogue* 144 (1
    September):106.
    Review of film of *NI*. "The entire Williams style is based upon
    the use of romantic conventions, certain shortcuts. . . . The hotel
    on the coast of Mexico is a convention; the drinking is a conven-
    tion; the beach boys are a convention. . . . [*NI*] is so good a
    movie . . . only three flaws: an inscrutably upbeat ending; a fist
    fight . . . that falls into the category of TV humor; a quite un-
    necessary establishing scene before the titles."

13 DONAHUE, FRANCIS. *The Dramatic World of Tennessee Williams.*
    New York: Frederick Ungar, 243 pp.
    Begins with assertion that the book is "a work of literary
    reporting. It seeks to capture the spirit of a Bohemian artist
    struggling with self-doubts, beset by a troubled personal life,
    who has written some of the most compelling works of the mod-
    ern theater." Goes on to try to interweave TW's life and work,
    with attention to critical reaction. Discusses his early successes
    and failures and presents an analysis of the action of the major
    plays. Quotes directly from newspaper and popular periodicals
    to show contemporary reaction to the plays. Also covers the
    fiction from early and mid periods, as well as the poetry.

14 "Drama Critics Consensus." New York *Morning Telegraph*, 3 Janu-
    ary, p. 2.
    Capsule statement of major New York dailies' reviews of *MT*.

15 EYLES, ALLEN. "Allen Eyles sees Huston Reaffirm his Skill." *Films
    and Filming* 11 (October):28.
    Praises Huston's handling of the plot, in film of *NI*, from first

moments in the church. Claims he was sensitive to TW's original script, "and certainly preserved its construction and drive."

16 FREEDLEY, GEORGE. "Of Books and Men." New York *Morning Telegraph*, 13 July, p. 2.
Brief negative mention of publication of *MT*.

17 GASSNER, JOHN. Review of *MT*. *Educational Theatre Journal* 16 (March):76.
"The fiasco . . . cannot but serve as a reminder that silk purses simply cannot be made out of sows' ears. . . . The sow's ear in this case is the appalling female on whom the author wasted his talent and his public's patience." TW "could not disentangle himself from the coils of his original conception of the characters." Reprinted: 1968.14.

18 *GM*. *New York Times*, 7 June, sec. 2, p. 3.
Photo of R. Nelson as Amanda in *GM* revival in Minneapolis.

19 HALE, WANDA. " 'Iguana'—Huston-Burton Triumph." New York *Daily News*, 1 July, p. 77.
Review of film of *NI*. "Better than the theatre presentation of the Tennessee Williams play." Attributes improvement to John Huston's direction; focuses on the acting.

20 HARTUNG, PHILIP T. "Man's Inhumanity to God." *Commonweal* 80 (21 August):580.
Review of film of *NI*. "The movie is a considerable improvement over the play [because] earlier scenes, not in the play, were added" to give more opportunity for the characters to illustrate themselves and each other. "Huston's first rate direction" emphasizes TWs capacity for overflowing "compassion." The film is "well-designed, with a fine cast and superb photography."

21 HEWES, HENRY. Review of *MT*. *Saturday Review* 47 (18 January): 22.
Review appearing after revival had closed. "Mr. Williams ought not to give up his efforts to put 'The Milktrain' on the right track."

22 HOBE. "Show on Broadway: 'The Milk Train Doesn't Stop Here Anymore.' " *Variety*, 8 January, p. 272.

"What was once a somewhat obscure talkfest about a dying harridan and her mysterious young poet-visitor has become a slightly clearer conversational jamboree, but an absurdly pretentious, over-produced, exasperating bore." Notes that play closed after four days.

23 HOUSTON, PENELOPE. "Making of a President." *New Statesman* 68 (11 September):370.
Review of film of *NI*. "The dialogue . . . is festooning itself all over the screen like some gaudy and irrepressible tropical plant. . . . [TW] always satisfies Hollywood's craving for the theatrical. . . . American baroque played rather more than up to the hilt."

24 HURLEY, PAUL J. "The Sad Fate of Tennessee Williams." *Shenandoah* 15 (Winter):61–66.
Starts with an analysis of the public's "outraged cries" against themes in early plays (*SND, SLS, SB*), and claims that now clearer critical responses are possible. Uses reference to Tischler, Nelson, and Falk and rates their critical studies of TW comparatively/relatively. Claims, however, that a truly quality study of TW has yet to be published.

25 _____. "Tennessee Williams: The Playwright as Social Critic." *Theatre Annual* 21:40–56.
Proposes "sober analyses of his concerns as a dramatist." Indicates that subject matter of his plays has "obscured attempts to analyze his thematic preoccupations," which are shown to be "typically American." Addresses issue of place of individual in modern society as it's illustrated in *CAT*, as well as the same play's evidence of TW's interest in the force of love, the desire for land, human renewal, and avarice.

26 _____. "Williams' 'Desire and the Black Masseur': An Analysis." *Studies in Short Fiction* 2 (Fall):51–55.
Argues that some find TW's fiction "often as penetrating . . . as his dramatic works." Selects "Black Masseur" as an illustration of "one of Williams' most 'shocking' and best known stories." Claims the "primary concerns of the story are both social and psychological," and traces where "the real horror" of the story

lies. Closes with an analysis of the story relative to "the perversion of values" of twentieth-century man.

27 "Imaginary People, Real Hearts." *Time* 84 (17 July):86, 88.
    Review of film of *NI*. "A picture that excites the senses, persuades the mind, and even occasionally speaks to the spirit—one of the best movies ever made from a [TW] script.... It's an absolute delight to watch the most perverse of playwrights tell a tale in which the nadir of naughtiness is attained by a man with a harmless though peculiar passion for ladies' underwear."

28 KERR, DEBORAH. "The Days and Nights of the Iguana: A Journal." *Esquire* 61 (May):128–30, 132, 134, 136, 139–42.
    Diary-like account of time during filming *NI*. Quotes numerous news headlines; newsy and gossipy.

29 KERR, WALTER. "Williams' Reworked 'Milk Train' Is Back." *New York Herald Tribune*, 2 January, p. 11.
    Review of *MT*. "The sorry, indeed the shocking fact is that in nearly all respects [*MT*] is now worse than it was before.... Mr. Williams'... predicament [is that] he has not yet heard from his muse... what needs to be said." Reprinted: 1968.26.

30 KNIGHT, ARTHUR. "Where There's a Williams...." *Saturday Review* 47 (18 July):22.
    Review of film of *NI*. Discusses his plays' gift of characterization, the transition from stage to screen ("more successfully than most") with *NI*; the film actually improves upon the play.

31 LAW, RICHARD A. "'A Streetcar Named Desire' as Melodrama." *English Record* 14 (February):2–8.
    Starts with premise that *SND* "does not happily bear critical analysis." Cites "sensational scenes," "lack of definite theme," and failure to establish a "clear dialectic" as the play's faults. Claims Blanche "is not a tragic figure," and that the play can be read successfully with Stanley as "the misunderstood good man," thus making the play successful melodrama. Finally contends that it's "the most successful melodrama in contemporary theater."

32 LAWRENSON, HELEN. "The Nightmare of the Iguana." *Show* 4 (January):49, 104–5.

Discusses Huston's filming on location; about her being there and talking with crew and cast; focus on Huston.

33 LEYBURN, ELLEN DOUGLASS. "Comedy and Tragedy Transposed." *Yale Review* 53 (Summer):553–62.

Talks of the difficulty of putting a label on TW's plays. "Arthur Miller and Tennessee Williams are perhaps the most striking examples of contemporary dramatists who consider themselves writers of tragedies and yet have produced plays in which the themes and characters resemble those of earlier critical comedy." Discusses Blanche's role in *SND* particularly.

34 McCLAIN, JOHN. "Still on Wrong Track." *New York Journal-American*, 2 January, p. 17.

Review of *MT*. "It cannot long endure. . . . There is something wrong with the play; it is not fundamentally a drama with the importance or depth of most of Mr. Williams' better achievements."

35 MILLER, JORDAN Y. "Myth and the American Dream: O'Neill to Albee." *Modern Drama* 7 (September):190–98.

Delves into the symbolic properties of setting and characterization in *CR*, with particular emphasis on Kilroy and how he fares in "Williams' Way of Life." Shows this to be one other dimension of the "Myth of the American Dream."

36 MISHKIN, LEO. "'Night of the Iguana' Fitfully Compelling." New York *Morning Telegraph*, 1 July, p. 2.

Review of film of *NI*. "Falls a good distance short of complete satisfaction." General rundown of plot and characters.

37 MUELLER, W.R. "Tennessee Williams: A New Direction?" *Christian Century* 81 (14 October):1271–72.

The difference "between the Williams of the mid-1940s and the early 1960s is that between one who describes and one who prescribes." Refers to "the quality of the poetry" in the plays and how TW occasionally relies on sentimentality.

38   NADLE, NORMAN. " 'Milk Train' Never Gets Rolling." *New York World-Telegram & Sun*, 2 January, p. 18.

Review of *MT*. The original was "infinitely superior to this new version [which] has become a grotesque hybrid of a play. . . . [It's] a spectacularly unsuccessful display of theatrical gimmicks."

39   " 'Night of the Iguana' Sets Records for Opening Day." *New York Times*, 7 August, p. 14.

News item. Release of film version of *NI* sets new records in two theaters in Manhattan.

40   OLIVER, EDITH. "Let My Iguana Go." *New Yorker* 40 (15 August): 84–85.

Review of film of *NI*. "A dreary mess—all bald and coarse on the surface, and all slick, pulpy and inexcusably uplifting underneath." Calls the original play "shoddy," and "much of the picture can be considered just an exercise in bravado."

41   OULAHAN, RICHARD. " 'Iguana' with Punch and Passion." *Life* 57 (10 July):11.

Discusses TW's concerns for the filming of his play *NI*. TW "invest[s] his characters with unsuspected qualities. . . . Studies of good in conflict with evil, of weakness struggling with strength, are the essence of any first-rate Tennessee Williams play."

42   PEDEN, WILLIAM H. "Mad Pilgrimage: The Short Stories of Tennessee Williams." *Studies in Short Fiction* 1 (Summer):243–50.

Begins with the claim that TW's stories are important in their own right and are "at their best a permanent addition to the 'sick' fiction of the forties and fifties." The stories are similar in their attachment to the grotesque, in their melancholy; his characters are found to be consistently "adrift, unloved and unwanted." Refers to the issue of "pathological or societal outcasts" as character types in the stories and ends up treating humor as a device, especially in "The Yellow Bird."

43   "Personal, Allusive Fantasy." *Times* (London), 28 January, p. 13.

CR. Comments on British TV production of *CR* by Granada Television. Generally favorable.

44 "Premiere of 'Iguana' Will Aid Heart Fund." *New York Times*, 13 May, p. 52.

  News item. World premiere of *NI* to donate proceeds to heart fund.

45 QUIGLY, ISABEL. "From the Play." *Spectator* 213 (11 September): 340.

  Review of film of *NI*. "Despite his golden (though garrulous) tongue, Tennesee Williams is filmable; *anzi*, he is cinematic. . . . He deals in symbols, treats objects metaphorically, looks at things sidelong. . . . One of Williams' least exotic plays: least far-fetched, least full of laughter at the wrong moment." Examines theme of "loneliness, lack of communication."

46 QUIRINO, LEONARD SALVATOR. "The Darkest Celebrations of Tennessee Williams: A Study of *Battle of Angels, A Streetcar Named Desire, Orpheus Descending, Camino Real, Cat on a Hot Tin Roof*, and *Suddenly, Last Summer*." Ph.D. dissertation, Brown University.

  Examines the imagery and symbolism of the plays in the title; elements of solitary experience of nightmare and the ceremonializing of the powers of darkness addressed as important motifs. (*DA* 25:4706.)

47 "'Rose Tattoo' in New TV Series." *Times* (London), 14 January, p. 12.

  RT, British TV production. Brief reference to parts of the play and cast.

48 ROTHSCHILD, ELAINE. Review of film of *NI*. *Films in Review* 15 (August–September): 439–41.

  "Pieces of pasteboard have never been juxtaposed more inanely. And people who consider themselves hep—or is it hip—take Williams' tripe seriously."

49 ROULET, WILLIAM M. "'Sweet Bird of Youth': Williams' Redemptive Ethic." *Cithara* 3:31–36.

  Focuses on the inherent morality in TW's work, particularly *SB*; cites the naturalistic aspects of the "redemptive ethic," calling attention to symbolism of the seagulls and Easter Sunday. Emphasis on Chance's submission.

50   SARRIS, ANDREW. Review of film of *NI*. *Village Voice*, 13 August, p. 12.
Generally negative comments concerning director Huston, the cast, and TW. "Here comes [TW] up from the beach with his pet iguana on a leash. The iguana looks miserable, but that's just the human condition, isn't it, Tennessee?"

51   "The Second Mrs. Goforth." *Time* 83 (10 January):52.
Review of *MT*. Comments on this second Broadway attempt within the year for this play to make a showing. Generally negative.

52   S[MITH], M[ICHAEL]. Review of *MT*. *Village Voice*, 9 January, p. 10.
MT "terminated its reincarnation after five painful performances last week." TW has "still failed to confront the subject of death as directly as he intends."

53   STEIN, ROGER B. " 'The Glass Menagerie' Revisited: Catastrophe without Violence." *Western Humanities Review* 18 (Spring): 141–53.
Discusses the division of TW's plays (the violent and nonviolent); suggests TW was "uneasy" with plays whose "sole dramatic technique" was violence. Analyzes *GM*, *NI*, and the structure and dramatic situations they depend on; goes on to relate TW's "imagery" to the point. Ends his essay with discussion of the religious motifs in his work—and the degrees of his success. Reprinted in abridged form: 1977.88.

54   SUSSEX, ELIZABETH. Review of film of *NI*. *Sight and Sound* 33 (Autumn):199.
Brief. Some plot summary. Primarily a negative review of the director's (John Huston's) interpretation of *NI*.

55   "Tallulah and Tennessee." *Newsweek* 63 (13 January):70.
Review of *MT*. A TW "play tortured into a Brechtian produc-

tion ... [making] it seem wholly alien to Williams' sensuous imagination."

56 TAYLOR, STEPHEN. Review of film of *NI*. *Film Quarterly* 18 (Winter):50–52.
    Begins with "the incontestable fact that both Huston's and Williams' reputations are on the wane." Goes on to insist that TW is an "ingrown, simpering analysand." Details of the on-location filming; claims TW "has fallen behind, has been overtaken by America." Emphasis on Huston and the cast.

57 THELDA, VICTOR, with DAVIDSON, MURIEL. "The Drama the Cameras Missed." *Saturday Evening Post* 237 (18 July):24–33.
    Victor, secretary to production executives of film of *NI*, keeps diary of the shooting. Basically gossipy; TW mentioned occasionally.

58 "Tropical Blooms." *Newsweek* 64 (13 July):85.
    Review of film of *NI*. Compares play and film. *NI* "is that fine rarity, an improvement on the play. Everything good has been retained and refined."

59 WALSH, MOIRA. Review of film of *NI*. *America* 111 (15 August):161.
    "All but the best of his plays seem detached from the reality he means to illuminate. I found this to be true of the film version of *NI*. ... In the interaction of [the main characters] there is much that is valid and deeply moving."

60 WATTS, RICHARD, JR. "The Revised Williams 'Milk Train.'" *New York Post*, 2 January, p. 42.
    Review of *MT*. "Arresting, disturbing, somewhat enigmatic. ... [TW] seems to have done some clarifying of the second act. ... Still seems too vague and too long, but it is a curiously fascinating conception."

61 WEALES, GERALD. "The Beast under the Porch." *Reporter* 31 (8 October):49–50.
    Review of film of *NI*. Relates it to other of TW works and motifs; refers to variations in the script and Huston's accepting "Williams' view of the human condition." "The film, in being

faithful [to the play], has borrowed some of the faults of the play. *Iguana* is late Williams, which means lifeless Williams."

62   WHIT. Review of film of *NI*. *Variety*, 1 July, p. 6.
"One of the best Tennessee Williams efforts to emerge on the screen." Includes details of plot and production, praise for actors and crew.

63   WINSTEN, ARCHER. " 'Night of the Iguana' at Philharmonic." *New York Post*, 1 July, p. 54.
Review of film of *NI*. "Was probably a better play than it is a movie. . . . The picture doesn't send me. . . . I wouldn't want to sit through it again."

64   ZOLOTOW, SAM. "New 'Milk Train' Stops Tomorrow." *New York Times*, 3 January, p. 13.
News item. *MT* to close after five performances.

65   _____. "Williams Plays Shift Producers." *New York Times*, 6 October, p. 34.
News item. Two *SST*s will be produced by C. Bowden instead of Actor's Studio Theater. Actor's Studio to get *BA* and *CR*.

1965

1   "An American Classic." *Time* 85 (14 May):64.
Review of *GM*. "The most Chekhovian play of the U.S.'s most Chekhovian playwright." Positive review of this revival.

2   ANNAN, GABRIELE. "Eros Denied." *Times Literary Supplement*, 1 August, p. 865.
Book review of *8M*. Short synopsis of the lives of the eight mortal ladies, with an even shorter consumer note concerning the first publication sources of the stories in the collection.

3   BEAURLINE, LESTER A. " 'The Glass Menagerie': From Story to Play." *Modern Drama* 8 (September):145–49.
Traces evolution of *GM*, with reference to an e.e. cummings quote TW used in one of its early original drafts. Discusses the

"at least four stages in the composition of" *GM*—and the years each represented. Comments on the effects of the gradual metamorphosis in tone and characterization, specifically.

4   BENEDICTUS, DAVID. "Southern Style." *Observer*, 5 December, p. 24.
Review of *GM*, London production. Brief analysis of this revival production.

5   "Brandeis Presents Awards in the Arts." *New York Times*, 29 March, p. 43.
Creative Arts Awards Medal and $1000 stipend presented to TW by Brandeis University.

6   BRIEN, ALAN. *GM*. *Sunday Telegraph* (London), 5 December, p. 12.
Review of *GM*, London production. *GM* is "sentimental, unrealistic, old-fashioned, static, anecdotal."

7   BRUSTEIN, ROBERT. Reviews of *PA*, *NI*, and *MT*. In *Seasons of Discontent: Dramatic Opinions 1959–1965*. New York: Simon & Schuster, pp. 117–18, 126–29.
Reprints of 1960.22, 1962.11, 1963.7.

8.   CASSIDY, CLAUDIA. "Cheers and Sighs over Tennessee's 'Menagerie.'" *Life* 58 (28 May):16.
Review of *GM*, twentieth anniversary revival. Discusses original production and its effect of fame on TW. "Williams' prodigal talent enriched the theatre forever."

9   CASTY, ALAN. "Tennessee Williams and the Small Hands of the Rain." *Mad River Review* 1 (Fall–Winter):27–43.
Quotes "the motto Williams affixed" to *GM* and goes on to show its pertinence as "one of the most valuable perspectives from which to examine his work and the present impasse of his career." Ties Jung's "mandala" into the analysis, taking it to the realm of "the archetypal." Among other themes, his analysis touches on struggle, sexuality, defeat, atonement, "magic vitality," self-parody. Specific reference to *GM*, *SND*, *CR*, *SLS*.

10 "Change of Cast." *New York Herald Tribune*, 18 August, p. 12.
    Cast change notice for Broadway *GM* revival.

11 DaPONTE, DURANT H. "Tennessee Williams' Gallery of Feminine
    Characters." *Tennessee Studies in Literature* 10:7–26.
        Examines first TW's work in light of so-called "school of
    Southern decadence," and the criticism of TW's tragic, "ambigu-
    ous" characters. "Not the least ambiguous of Mr. Williams' char-
    acters . . . are his women—an incredibly varied portrait gallery of
    female types which he has succeeded in investing with one
    common quality—an ability to fascinate. . . . Paradoxical as it may
    seem, these lost, abandoned and thoroughly bereft creatures
    stand out in the hierarchy of Williams' characters with such
    luminosity that they totally eclipse the normal, well-adjusted
    ladies." Reprinted: 1971.19.

12 DAVIS, JAMES. " 'Glass Menagerie' Back to B'Way Next Month."
    New York *Daily News*, 9 April, p. 72.
        Advance notice of *GM* revival coming to Broadway.

13 DILLARD, ROBERT LEE. "The Tennessee Hero: An Analytic Survey."
    Ph.D. dissertation, University of Missouri.
        Protagonists of *YTM*, *GM*, *S&S*, *CR*, *CAT*, *BA* and *OD*, *SB*,
    PA, *NI*, and *MT* examined; references also to those of *SND*
    and *RT*. Illustrates the composite Williams hero, and the theme
    of struggle against female dominance that involves them all.
    (DA 26:5592–93.)

14 DUKORE, BERNARD F. "American Abelard: A Footnote to 'Sweet
    Bird of Youth.' " *College English* 26 (May):630–34.
        Parallels are drawn between *SB* and the love story of Abelard
    and Heloise. Many devices that both stories have in common are
    detailed: the castration of Chance Wayne and Abelard, each at
    the order of their lovers' guardians, the primitive sort of justice
    involved, and the possible outcome of the characters.

15 "The Final Horror." *Observer*, 28 March, p. 23.
        Interview-commentary. TW in London at time of opening of
    NI; TW discusses the movies, Albee, Pinter.

16   FREEDLEY, GEORGE. "2 Versions of Play by Williams." New York
     Morning Telegraph, 17 February, p. 2.
        Notice of publication of two versions of same play—*EN* and
     S&S.

17   FUNKE, LEWIS. " 'Cottage' for Miss Dennis." *New York Times*, 13
     June, sec. 2, p. 1.
        News item. Because M. Stapleton does not wish to fly to
     Washington, D.C., *GM* at White House arts festival will be
     canceled.

18   GARDNER, R.H. "Streetcar to the Cemetery." In *The Splintered
     Stage: The Decline of the American Theater*. New York: Mac-
     millan, pp. 111–21.
        Questions the constancy of TW's talent and refers to *GM*
     as "his best play" and *MT* as "unquestionably his worst." Despite
     the variations in the quality of his plays, "he continues to be
     one of the most talented artists ever to write for the American
     theater." Refers to his "preoccupation with illness, disease, and
     death" and concentrates on *SND* for character and theme anal-
     ysis. Subsequent comments on *SLS*, *OD*.

19   GILLIATT, PENELOPE. "Taking Risks." *Observer*, 28 March, p. 24.
        Review of *NI*, London production. "The risks he takes [in *NI*]
     are breathtakingly dangerous."

20   GOLDSTEIN, MALCOLM. "Body and Soul on Broadway." *Modern
     Drama* 7 (February):411–21.
        Surveys the interest in psychological drama. Ties TW into
     the analysis, referring to his most popular plays. "The glowing
     solicitude of his first hit has returned only fitfully, to make a
     chiaroscuro effect against the grim anxieties he habitually puts
     on view."

21   *GM. New York Times*, 2 May, sec. 2, p. 1.
        Photo with caption to announce the opening of *GM* at Brooks
     Atkinson Theater.

22   GRUEN, JOHN. "The Inward Journey of Tennessee Williams." *New
     York Herald Tribune Magazine*, 2 May, p. 29.

Interview-commentary. In anticipation of *GM*'s twentieth anniversary revival, comments on TW in 1965 as opposed to 1945. TW discusses being "far happier" now, what he writes about and why, Southern women as characters, *SST*, being a good writer.

23 GUTHRIE, TYRONE. "Poetry Is Where You Find It." *New York Times*, 18 April, sec. 2, pp. 1, 3.
    GM mentioned in article about poetry and problems of defining poetry. Quotes a passage from *GM* and subtitles it "A Moment of Poetry."

24 HEILMAN, ROBERT B. "Tennessee Williams: Approaches to Tragedy." *Southern Review* 1 (Autumn):770–90.
    Bases investigation on premise of TW's "persistent interest in the idea of tragedy." Relegates term *tragedy* to "drama centrally concerned with a split personality"—but not pathologically so. Distinguishes between earlier and later TW plays; focuses on *GM*, *SND*, and *S&S*. Investigates possibility of TW "unconsciously seeking ground for sticking to the disaster of personality." Reprinted: 1973.29. Excerpted in 1977.88.

25 HETHMAN, ROBERT. "The Foul Rag-and-Bone Shop of the Heart." *Drama Critique* 7 (Fall):94–102.
    Investigates why *CAT* is not taken as seriously as it should be. He insists that "the play is theatrical. It grapples attention. It evokes concerted emotion." However, he admits that *CAT* "raises issues that our society can probably discuss only with difficulty." Highlights "the drama of naturalism," the play's "principal technical problems," and "the central duplicity of the play." Also calls attention to the play's mythic bases.

26 HIRSHHORN, CLIVE. "When I'm Alone I'm Just Hell." *Sunday Express* (London), 28 March.
    Interview. TW discusses his way of life, fear of death, shyness, analysis, depression, swimming, going to the movies, finding friends, failure in his work, smut.

27 HOBSON, HAROLD. "Beautifully Played." *Christian Science Monitor*, 9 December, p. 20.
    Brief reference to London production of *GM*.

28 HOFMANN, PAUL. "'A Streetcar Named Desire' Is Cheered in Havana." *New York Times*, 19 February, p. 27.

News item. *SND* successful in Havana. Troupe resists temptation to change play into a caricature of life in the U.S.

29 ISAAC, DAN. "Big Daddy's Dramatic Word Strings." *American Speech* 40 (December):272–78.

Questions the nature of the "excitement about Big Daddy," and concludes it's TW's "use of language" that makes him the successful character he is. Among other devices, he illustrates repetition, word clustering, word strings, phrase nuclei, broken rhythm—all as demonstration of his thesis.

30 JACKSON, ESTHER MERLE. *The Broken World of Tennessee Williams.* Madison: University of Wisconsin Press, 179 pp.

Starts with assertion that *GM* opened "a new epoch in the history of Western theatre," and that it made TW the successor to O'Neill "as the architect of form in the American drama." Claims his success derives from the plays covering the period of *GM* through *CAT* (1955). And suggests that TW ushers in "an aspect of a second American Renaissance." Covers his technique, his formal variety, his place within and outside the tradition. Going back to Greek sources, she places him historically; addresses his handling of "reality"; links with Kant and Coleridge and expressionism; discusses his lyric properties and leanings, his imagery, his use of myth, his interest in ritual, salvific history; concludes that "thus far, the drama of Williams has not seemed to achieve complete organic unity." Excerpted in 1967.17, 1977.88.

31 KERR, WALTER. "'Glass Menagerie'—Walter Kerr's Review." *New York Herald Tribune*, 5 May, p. 19.

TW is "ruthlessly fair," and *GM* stands "firm as a rock today. ... Mr. Williams will not cheat for an emotional effect ... and this is why the play is so moving." Praises cast generally, but singles out Pat Hingle's performance as the only one "to have found all of its nuances and to have named them."

32 KNOX, COLLIE. "Letter from Collie Knox." New York *Morning Telegraph*, 5 April, p. 2.

Brief mention of premiere of London production of *NI*; personal data on TW.

33   LAING, MARGARET. "Day after the 'Night of the Iguana.'" *Sunday Times* (London), 28 March, p. 12.

Interview (following opening of *NI* in London). TW discusses drinking, pills, children, friends.

34   ————. "Tennessee Williams—a Loner." *New York Journal-American*, 11 April, p. 38L.

Interview in London after opening of *NI* at the Savoy. TW discusses drinking, pills, psychiatrists, having children, being religious, suicide.

35   "Landscape of the Fallen." *Times* (London), 18 February, p. 16.

Review of *NI*, London production. Critical of script itself; more favorable about cast.

36   LEWIS, ALLAN. "Tennessee Williams—the Freedom of the Senses." In *American Plays and Playwrights of the Contemporary Theatre.* New York: Crown Publishers, pp. 53–65.

Begins by noting how "prolific and compulsive" a writer TW is, and how this has advanced him to "world reputation and financial security." Traces TW's loss of "purity" through *SB, NI, PA, MT,* among others. Shows how this relates to TW's dealing with "the four essential ingredients of commercial success: sex, violence, God, and communism." How TW works these themes, directly and symbolically.

37   LEWIS, THEOPHILUS. Review of *GM. America* 112 (19 June):888–89.

Discussion of the play as a play, on its twentieth anniversary. "After two decades the work remains as fresh and appealing as ever." *GM* "can endure in any spiritual climate"; praises M. Stapleton's performance.

38   LITTLE, STUART W. "Star-Studded Cast for Millburn." *New York Herald Tribune*, 17 March, p. 16.

News item. Pre-Broadway run of *GM* revival going into rehearsals in Millburn, New Jersey.

39 LOTERSZTEIN, S. *Tennessee Williams: Poeta del Nanfragio*. Buenos Aires: Instituto Amigos del Libro Argentino, 93 pp.

Refers to TW as "poet of failure," and to the spiritual and physical "landscape" in his work, how he places his characters into these landscapes, the perspectives he maintains with the landscapes. In Spanish.

40 McCARTEN, JOHN. "The Wingfields Revisited." *New Yorker* 41 (15 May):158.

Review of *GM*. Discusses the "stark simple-mindedness" of the interpretation; however, he does praise the play itself.

41 McCLAIN, JOHN. "Depth in Simplicity." *New York Journal-American*, 9 May, p. 32L.

Review of *GM*. Refers to the "most persuasive simplicity" of this revival.

42 ————. " 'Menagerie'—Great Drama." *New York Journal-American*, 5 May, p. 23.

Review of *GM*. The revival is "an excellent" work. *GM* is TW "at the top of his game. . . . A top production of a great play in our time."

43 MAXWELL, GILBERT. *Tennessee Williams and Friends*. Cleveland: World Publishing Co., 333 pp.

Biographical work relying on reminiscences dating back to the author's first meeting with TW in 1940, but going back for information. Substantial data on early professional years—in Chicago for opening of *GM*, for example. Heavy concentration on the author's own biography as basis for details on TW's.

44 " 'Menagerie' Due in Millburn." *New York Times*, 25 March, p. 44.
News item. *GM* revival to be produced in New Jersey.

45 NADEL, NORMAN. " 'Menagerie' Still a Major Play." *New York World-Telegram & Sun*, 5 May, p. 39.

Review of *GM*. *GM* is "a modern classic"; M. Stapleton's performance praised for positively changing "the tone" of the play. Recommends viewing because of this cast's interpretation.

46 "New 'Menagerie' Cast Taking over Tonight." New York *Daily News*, 18 August, p. 81.
    Change of cast notice for *GM* revival.

47 "Nine More Days." *New York Herald Tribune*, 21 April, p. 20.
    Rehearsal report for Broadway revival of *GM*.

48 "No Language Barrier." *New York Herald Tribune*, 3 December, p. 2.
    Helen Hayes appears in Japanese TV production of *GM*.

49 OLLEY, FRANCIS. "Last Block on the Camino Real." *Drama Critique* 8 (Fall):103–7.
    Focuses on the place of "sentimentality in American drama as a whole." Concludes that although "all major American dramatists are fundamentally realists . . . the trap of sentimentality is virtually unavoidable." Says the basis of the success of *GM* and *SND* is that they are "solidly within a realistic framework." *CR* is called "a symbolic play into which Williams pours all his essentially romantic concerns." Foresees TW's "venturing into terra incognita in his future work."

50 "People of Pity and Poetry." *Times* (London), 25 March, p. 16.
    Review of *NI*, London production. Brief synopsis and praise for production.

51 PHILLIPS, JOHN, and HOLLANDER, ANNE. "Lillian Hellman: An Interview." *Paris Review* 9 (Winter-Spring):65–94.
    "I think [TW] is a natural playwright. He writes by sanded fingertips. I don't always like his plays. . . . He is throwing his talent around."

52 "The Play's the Thing." *Newsweek* 65 (17 May): 92.
    Review of *GM*. Background history; mixed review of this revival. Reprinted: 1971.11.

53 POPKIN, HENRY. "Realism in the U.S.A." *World Theatre* 14 (March-April):119–26.
    After reference to new image of realism indicated by Le Roi Jones' *The Toilet*, moves on to TW, among others. TW "and

William Inge have left O'Neill far behind in their bold treatment of sex and in their arguments for individual freedom." Brief reference to TW.

54 "Record for Revival." *New York Herald Tribune*, 5 October, p. 18.
    Notice of closing of *GM* revival after 176 performances.

55 SHEED, WILFRID. "Tennessee Foxtrot." *Commonweal* 82 (4 June): 356–57.
    Review of *GM*. Claims its revival makes it seem even more solid than it had years ago. "The play is full of acute social observations." Reprinted: 1971.26.

56 SPEVACK, MARVIN. "Tennessee Williams: The Idea of the Theater." *Jahrbuch für Amerikastudien* 10:221–31.
    Survey's TW's own statements on and about the theater; says he's "struck by the intensely personal nature of the utterances." Focuses on the psychological ills that TW writes about, and discusses the ways in which he shows his "dedication to his art," the desire on his part "to lay bare the primordial condition."

57 SPURLING, HILARY. "Swannee Williams." *Spectator* 215 (10 December):778.
    Review of *GM*, London production. Details on play's background; analyzes flaws in characters themselves; says this revival production "has an air of making the best of a bad job."

58 STANG, JOANNE. "Maureen into Amanda." *New York Times*, 16 May, sec. 2, pp. 1, 3.
    Biography of M. Stapleton. Focuses on her role as Amanda in *GM*.

59 ———. "Williams: 20 Years after 'Glass Menagerie.'" *New York Times*, 28 March, sec. 2, pp. 1, 3.
    Interview-commentary. TW discusses the feelings he has when he's finished writing a play; literary prizes and critics' awards; twentieth anniversary of *GM*; flying into rages when confronted with bad reviews; *SST* production problems; *NI* production; traveling to Rome; Anna Magnani; his influences; his characters.

60 STARNES, R. LELAND. "Comedy and Tennessee Williams." Ph.D.
     dissertation, Yale University.
        Examines the use of comedy in TW's work by showing the
     antinaturalist conventions he uses in every play, and by showing
     the normal irrelevancies covered by naturalism that TW uses
     for further comic possibilities.

61 TAUBMAN, HOWARD. "Diverse, Unique, Amanda." *New York Times,*
     16 May, sec. 2, p. 1.
        Analysis of the character Amanda and the diversity of inter-
     pretations over the years by different actresses.

62 ————. "Theater: 'Glass Menagerie' Returns." *New York Times,*
     5 May, p. 53.
        Review of *GM*. Favorable about the play itself as well as this
     particular revival.

63 ————. "Theater: 'Milk Train' Revised Again." *New York Times,*
     27 July, p. 25.
        Review of *MT*. Criticism of revised version. "Revisions are
     useful ... remains disappointing."

64 "Theater Tonight." *New York Times*, 4 May, p. 50.
        News item. *GM* to open tonight.

65 ULANOV, BARRY. "The Theatre." In *The Two Worlds of American
     Art*. New York: Macmillan, pp. 325–55.
        Addresses TW's association, within his characters, of death
     and sexuality—and his obsession with it. Finds TW's characters
     to be less than whole, to be humanoids who are lacking in
     humanity. TW "lacks O'Neill's heart and soul."

66 "The Unbreakable *Glass Menagerie*." WPAT *Gaslight Review*
     (July), pp. 31–36.
        Refers to revival of *GM*; discusses its history, monetary suc-
     cess, its revivals.

67 *Variety*, 28 April, p. 62.
        Brief gossip item. Quotes Williams on youth and work.

68 WATT, DOUGLAS. "An Eloquent Revival of Williams' 'Glass Menagerie' Reaches Town." New York *Daily News*, 5 May, p. 92.

Review of *GM*. "The most genuinely appealing, and most poetic of Williams' creations." Cast is "exceptional. . . . The production . . . has been staged with full respect for the honest comedy values that make it so real."

69 WATTS, RICHARD, JR. "Good, Early Tennessee Williams." *New York Post*, 5 May, p. 78.

Review of *GM*. "A poignant and lovely play," one of TW's "finest and most sensitive creations." This revival captures its quality "skillfully."

70 WEALES, GERALD. *Tennessee Williams*. Minneapolis: University of Minnesota Press, 46 pp.

Brief study (pamphlet) covering biographical data (such as writers who influenced him, early writing experiences), goes into the "fugitive" motif in his plays, his forms of "social comment," the issue of God and his pursuit of "truth." Focuses also on such things as TW's use of light and sound, and the presence of myth as a device.

71 ———. "Tennessee Williams Borrows a Little Shaw." *Shaw Review* 8 (May):63–64.

Begins with assertion TW "makes constant use of other authors, borrowing a character here . . . , a symbol there . . . and turning them to his own use." Then goes on to claim: "*Heartbreak House* seems to have made two contributions to" *YTM*; cites the use of Capt. Shotover and of Randall and his flute.

72 ———. "Tennessee Williams' 'Lost' Play." *American Literature* 37 (November):321–23.

Discusses *At Liberty*. Cites where it first appeared and under whose auspices; plot summary and theme delineation.

73 WEISSMAN, PHILIP. "A Trio of Tennessee Williams' Heroines: The Psychology of Prostitution." In *Creativity in the Theatre: A Psychoanalytic Study*. New York: Basic Books, pp. 173–89.

Reprint of 1960.129. Reprinted: 1971.19.

74 "What Other Critics Say." *New York World-Telegram & Sun,* 5
    May, p. 39.
    Brief commentary on *GM* on its twentieth anniversary.

75 WILLETT, RALPH W. "The Ideas of Miller and Williams." *Theatre
    Annual* 22 (1965–66):31–40.
    "In general their plays are concerned with the role of the
    individual in modern society, particularized in . . . the vulgar-
    ized New South of *Cat on a Hot Tin Roof* and *Sweet Bird of
    Youth.* . . . From Williams' total dramatic work emerges a social
    order of sorts, 'sick with neon' and compounded of greed, preju-
    dice and violence." Makes reference to TW's "sympathy for the
    outsider in modern society," and his values of "sexual joy and
    poetic apprehension." Neither dramatist is likely "to be indexed
    in a history of ideas."

76 ZOLOTOW, SAM. "Prince Resigns Presidency of the Theater League."
    New York Times, 1 June, p. 45.
    News item. *GM* matinee has declining attendance.

1966

1 ADLER, RENATA. "Adapted." *New Yorker* 42 (27 August):88.
    Brief review of film of *TPC.* Surveys its background history;
    refers to the way the film abuses the play and the cast's struggle
    to overcome the script.

2 ALPERT, HOLLIS. "Instant Tennessee Williams." *Saturday Review*
    49 (25 June):40.
    Review of film of *TPC.* "Williams is not too badly served" in
    this film adaptation; but still, the product is "ersatz." Talks of how
    it departs from a Williams conceit in subtle ways.

3 "Belle Wringer." *Time* 88 (22 July):62.
    Review of film of *TPC.* "Begins and ends with excerpts from
    a fragile one-act play by" TW. "What condemns 'This Property'
    is a plot tacked on by three zealous screen writers."

4 "Boardinghouse Reach." *Newsweek* 68 (1 August):83–84.
Review of film of *TPC*. Film does not match "the little play-let from which it derives." Natalie Wood "is the main attraction," while others (Robert Redford, Kate Reid) are either "indolent" or "poor." The screen writers "have no grasp of the sort of intuition that prompted Williams to write."

5 BOLTON, WHITNEY. "Tennessee Williams' 'Slapstick Tragedy.'" New York *Morning Telegraph*, 24 February, p. 3.
"Mr. Williams is turning old ground and re-working old characters . . . offering old goods in new parcels." The effect is that we "will and do accuse him of stealing from himself."

6 BRUSTEIN, ROBERT. "A Question of Identity." *New Republic* 154 (26 March):34, 36–37.
Review of *SST*. Brief and fairly neutral; treats plot and theme. Reprinted: 1969.5.

7 CALLAGHAN, BARRY. "Tennessee Williams and Cocaloony Birds." *Tamarack Review* 39 (Spring):52–58.
TW's characters (especially in *CAT*, *LLL*, *SLS*, *SB*, *NI*) are usually mutilated or mutilators; focuses on *GF*; examines its departure from the TW method in allowing the deformed fraulein to survive.

8 CANBY, VINCENT. "I Never Depended on the Kindness of Strangers." *New York Times*, 8 May, sec. 2, pp. 1, 3.
Interview with Audrey Wood. Discusses what it's like to be agent for people like Inge and TW.

9 CARLISLE, OLGA, and STYRON, ROSE. "Arthur Miller: An Interview." *Paris Review* 10 (Summer):61–98.
Refers briefly to themes and characters in *CAT*.

10 CARROLL, KATHLEEN. "Williams' Tragic Belle Back in Stunning Film." New York *Daily News*, 4 August, p. 67.
Review of film of *TPC*. "Moves with grace and facility." Addresses theme and characterization.

11 CHAPMAN, JOHN. "'The Rose Tattoo' Is Enjoyable." New York *Daily News*, 21 October, p. 70.

Review of *RT*. This revival "carri[es] its age—15 years—lightly. . . . [TW] must have had sex on his mind when he wrote this, his most affectionate play."

12 CLURMAN, HAROLD. Review of *RT*. *Nation* 203 (7 November):493. "Tennessee Williams' most sanguine play." Contains "a deeper note, a feeling for the fierce sanctity of carnal commitment. This aspect was missed in its first production (1950) and it is still diluted at the City Center [revival]."

13 ———. Review of *SST*. *Nation* 202 (14 March):309. Defends TW against the critics; likes *GF* better than *M*; praises some in cast. Reprinted: 1977.88.

14 ———. "Tennessee Williams." In *The Naked Image: Observations on the Modern Theatre*. New York: Macmillan, pp. 123–43. Reviews of *SB*, *NI*. Reprints of 1959.33, 1962.14.

15 "Crass Menagerie." *Newsweek* 67 (7 March):90. Review of *SST*. TW "seems in the sad position of an aging soprano." Praises Zoe Caldwell in *GF*. Reprinted: 1971.11.

16 CROWTHER, BOSLEY. "Screen: 'This Property Is Condemned.'" *New York Times*, 4 August, p. 24. Review of film of *TPC*. "As soggy, sentimental a story . . . as ever oozed from the pen of [TW]."

17 "Eros and the Widow." *Time* 88 (18 November):80. Brief review of *RT*. Discusses the mythic implications seen in this revival production.

18 FEDDER, NORMAN J. *The Influence of D.H. Lawrence on Tennessee Williams*. The Hague: Mouton & Co., 131 pp. Attempts to show influence of Lawrence on TW's drama, poetry, and fiction. Uses "Background Forces" to try to couple their response to "prevailing twentieth century ideas and similar early environmental experiences." Later attempts to compare their relative "artistic achievement." Traces the connections and influences in plots, themes, characters, citing specific references from Lawrence's work and tracing general theme alliance. Covers the plays through *MT*.

19 GARDELLA, KAY. "Shirley Leery of 'Menagerie.'" New York *Sunday News*, 4 December, sec. S, p. 32.

Comments on TV production of *GM* and Shirley Booth's reaction to doing the part.

20 _____. "'Streetcar' Brushes ABC." New York *Daily News*, 16 June, p. 92.

News item. TW didn't want *SND* done on TV.

21 _____. "Williams' Symbolic Work: Is It for (Camino) Real?" New York *Daily News*, 8 October, p. 14.

Review of *CR*, TV (NET) production. "Confusing...theatrical portrait." Plot summary and cast appraisal. "What Williams is trying to say . . . has been said before—and better."

22 *GM*. New York *World-Journal Tribune Magazine*, 4 December, p. 13.

Photo and brief caption on cast in TV production.

23 GOULD, JACK. "Suddenly, a Pleasant Surprise." *New York Times*, 18 December, sec. 2, p. 21.

Discusses upcoming TV production of *GM*; refers to the management angles of getting quality material on TV.

24 _____. "TV: 'Glass Menagerie' with Taste and Perception." *New York Times*, 9 December, p. 95.

Review of *GM*, TV production. Positive regarding cast and production generally.

25 _____. "TV: A Somber Premiere." *New York Times*, 8 October, p. 63.

10B was opening night for National Educational Television Playhouse. Author considered *10B* to be an odd choice.

26 GOULD, JEAN R. "Tennessee Williams." In *Modern American Playwrights*. New York: Dodd, Mead & Co., pp. 225–46.

Biographical details—early development and influences; discusses circumstances of earliest compositions and publications, parents' reactions. Data on first successes and grants. Then covers, historically, the adventures of all the major plays up to *NI*.

27   GROSS, BEN. "T.V.'s 'Glass Menagerie': A Memorable Experience." New York *Daily News*, 9 December, p. 100.
     Review of *GM*, TV production. "An offering truly of star quality"; not positive toward Shirley Booth though.

28   HALE, WANDA. "Williams' One-Acter on Screen." New York *Sunday News*, 31 July, p. 57.
     Production notes on making *TPC* into film.

29   HARDWICK, ELIZABETH. "The Theater of Decadence." *New York Review of Books* 6 (28 April):8–9.
     Review of Broadway season just past. Says TW, Albee, and Inge "produced plays of startling antiquity." About *SST*: "sentimentality is [TW's] vice"; his "mixture of the sentimental and the strangely unwholesome . . . alienated most of the critics and all of the audience. . . . [TW] did not seem in control of the mood; he put in and took out without any artistic direction."

30   HARTUNG, PHILIP T. Review of film of *TPC*. *Commonweal* 84 (19 August):533–34.
     Brief, negative. Deals with it primarily as a script.

31   HAYS, PETER L. "Tennessee Williams' Use of Myth in 'Sweet Bird of Youth.'" *Educational Theatre Journal* 18 (October):255–58.
     Attempts to clarify Chance's role in the play; focuses on the castration theme; agrees with Popkin's characterization of him as "an Adonis figure." Calls attention to the symbolism of nomenclature, and the parallels to Shelley's "Adonais." Ends with note on Chance's "manliness."

32   HENDRICK, GEORGE. "Jesus and the Osiris-Isis Myth: Lawrence's *The Man Who Died* and Williams' *The Night of the Iguana*." *Anglia* 84 (4 March):398–406.
     Discusses the affinity TW had for Lawrence's work. Focuses first on the short story *NI*, finding Shannon to be "both the *Man Who Died* and Lawrence himself, just as Lawrence wrote himself into the part of Jesus." Emphasizes the symbols in *NI* that link it to the Lawrence story and the original Egyptian myth.

33   HEWES, HENRY. "Theater—Off the Leash." *Saturday Review* 49 (26 November):60.

Review of *RT*. This revival is "richly rewarding." Provides a survey of its background.

34　————. "Tripping on the Light Fantastic." *Saturday Review* 49 (12 March):28.
　　Review of *SST*. Likes *GF* better than *TM*; makes plea for not holding their meagerness against TW. Reprinted: 1978.23.

35　Hobe. "Shows on Broadway: 'Slapstick Tragedy.'" *Variety*, 2 March, p. 56.
　　The two plays "contain vivid writing, but they are too vague and rambling for general acceptance." Details on plot and scenery design, with praise for Leighton. "'Slapstick Tragedy' amounts to a double portion of uneven theater. Both plays are intermittenly [*sic*] interesting, but neither is quite satisfying."

36　Hurley, Paul J. "'Suddenly Last Summer' as 'Morality Play.'" *Modern Drama* 8 (February):392–402.
　　Argues that because of its subject matter, *SLS* "has been misread and misviewed." Surveys some pertinent criticism which demonstrates the content-based misunderstanding. Suggests that certain elements (i.e., homosexuality and cannibalism) function as metaphors and argues for not "ignor[ing] the symbolic function" of the more strident plot details in *SLS*. Refers to language, TW's "inversion of symbol," vision, love impulse, self-destruction, as they pertain to this theory.

37　Kauffmann, Stanley. "Theater. 'Nathan Weinstein' Arrives." *New York Times*, 26 February, p. 15.
　　News item. Correction of error in original review of *SST* by same author.

38　————. "Theater: Tennessee Williams Returns." *New York Times*, 23 February, p. 42.
　　Review of *SST*. Provides synopsis; generally negative about production. Reprinted: 1976.33.

39　————. *A World on Film: Criticism and Comment.* New York: Harper & Row, pp. 79–87.
　　Reprints of 1958.52, 1960.68-69, 1962.52.

40 KERR, WALTER. "Kerr Reviews Two by Tennessee Williams." *New York Herald Tribune*, 23 February, p. 18.
    Review of *SST*. "Mr. Williams has leaned too far, though in the first he has nearly come to rest on something solid." *M* is "a very possible play which I suspect we shall see better done one of these days. . . . Savage slapstick is not the playwright's happiest vein."

41 ————. "A 'Rose' Flowers Anew." *New York Times*, 20 November, sec. 2, p. 1.
    Review of *RT*. Generally positive review of *RT* revival and praise for M. Stapleton and TW's work.

42 KRACHT, FRITZ ANDRE. "Rise and Decline of U.S. Theater on German Stages." *American-German Review* 22 (June-July):13–15.
    Speaks of the "reeducation" of the Germans after the war, and the revitalization of theater in Germany. "Much of the tremendous success [of TW's plays] enjoyed in Germany rested on their shock value . . . and a latter-day apotheosis of dramatization."

43 LANGSAM, PAUL A. "A Study of the Major Characters in Selected Plays of Tennessee Williams." Ph.D. dissertation, State University of New York.
    Treats major characters and their development within the plays; maintains that there are definite identifiable patterns for the characters (*DAI* 27:3972A.)

44 "Lanier Flying to London." New York *World-Journal Tribune*, 16 November, p. 43.
    Sidney Lanier going to London to arrange production of *2CP*.

45 LAPOLE, NICK. "Williams Built Actors." *New York Journal-American*, 20 February, p. 35L.
    Discusses how TW "spurred, nourished and/or resuscitated the careers of Laurette Taylor, Marlon Brando, Margaret Leighton, Bette Davis, Maureen Stapleton, Elizabeth Taylor, Jessica Tandy, Geraldine Page" and others. Some of them also are quoted on TW.

46 LES. " 'The Glass Menagerie.' " *Variety*, 14 December, p. 33.
    Review of TV version of *GM*. "But for some lapses in the integrity" in this production, "it was television at its most sublime."

47 LEWIS, THEOPHILUS. "The Rose Tattoo." *America* 115 (10 December):786.
    Review of *RT*. The revival "shows no sign of aging." *RT* "will resist the attrition of time. . . . A durable and treasured showpiece of our theatre." Praises M. Stapleton.

48 LITTLE, STUART W. " 'Summer and Smoke' Will Be an Opera." *New York Herald Tribune*, 23 February, p. 19.
    Announcement concerning TW's giving permission to L. Holbly to write an opera based on *S&S*.

49 MCCARTEN, JOHN. "Quick Exits." *New Yorker* 42 (5 March):83–84.
    Brief review of *SST*. Focuses on plot and character comparisons; generally negative.

50 MCCLAIN, JOHN. "The Out and the Abstract." *New York Journal-American*, 23 February, p. 17.
    Review of *SST*. "What has happened to Tennessee Williams is the saddest thing that has happened to the current theatre in the last decade. . . . The real tragedy . . . that he should dissipate this gift in a series of irritating, vague and formless vignettes."

51 "Major Plays Listed for CBS in Color." *New York Times*, 10 June, p. 91.
    Brief announcement of TV production of *GM*.

52 MISHKIN, LEO. "One-Act Play by Williams Made a Film." New York *Morning Telegraph*, 4 August, p. 3.
    Review of film of *TPC*. "The original play was never really considered among the stronger pieces written by Mr. Williams in the first place. . . . [This] emerge[s] as more or less superior fare."

53 ———. " 'Rose Tattoo' Still Warm, Wonderful." New York *Morning Telegraph*, 22 October, p. 3.
    Review of *RT*. Advances the "theory that [*RT*] is the warmest

and most ingratiating play ever written by [TW]. . . . This present revival . . . may be played much more broadly, much more for farce, than the original was back in 1950."

54 MURF. "This Property Is Condemned." *Variety*, 15 June, p. 6.
      Review of film of *TPC*. Explanation is made that what was TW's original work has been trimmed down to the prologue and the epilogue; generally positive review.

55 MUSEL, ROBERT. "Miss Booth Comes to Tea." *TV Guide*, 3 December, pp. 38–40.
      Review of film of *GM*. Focuses on Shirley Booth and her reflections on *GM* and on her own career.

56 NADEL, NORMAN. "Bizarre, Grim 'Slapstick Tragedy.'" *New York World-Telegram & Sun*, 23 February, p. 30.
      Review of *SST*. Refers to it as "Theater of the Absurd." Calls *GF* "the more eye-popping of the two"; *M* "almost conventional in form."

57 ———."Serafina Soars Again." New York *World-Journal Tribune*, 21 October, p. 33.
      Review of *RT*. Mostly a focus on M. Stapleton in central role of Serafina; other performance analyses.

58 NOLAN, PAUL T. "Two Memory Plays: *Glass Menagerie* and *After the Fall*." *McNeese Review* 17:27–38.
      Contrasts "memory play" technique with dream play and expressionist drama and with "the traditional drama-of-action." Claims that in the memory play "as a particular form, the world of the drama is the memory of a single character." Goes on to discuss Tom and Quentin; cites "the advantage to the playwright of the memory play," and the disadvantages ("abdication of responsibility" as one).

59 "On the Air." *New York Post*, 9 December, p. 94.
      Brief mention of TV production of *GM*.

60 "Pastiche and Departure: Tennessee Williams Double Bill." *Times* (London), 7 March, p. 9.

Review of *SST*. Treats *M* and *GF* separately; compares to other TW works (*SND*, *SB*, *NI*, and *CR*); brief synopsis of each play.

61 "Penwiper Papers." *Time* 87 (4 March):88.
Review of *SST*. Extremely negative brief review of both plays in this series.

62 REED, REX. "Tennessee Williams Took His Name off It." *New York Times*, 16 January, sec. 2, p. 13.
Discusses filming of *TPC* in New Orleans. Many gossip details and logistics of filming.

63 ROGOFF, GORDON. "Tennessee Williams." *Tulane Drama Review* 10 (Summer):78–92.
Discusses TW as being "in crisis" and attempts to assess reasons (popular press plus his "twin obsessions, money and sex"). Talks of popular image and private person; elaborates on issue of crisis generally in writers and how TW's own homosexuality causes and predicts a public response to his work.

64 RUSSELL, RAY. "My Gorge Rises in Flame, Cried the Phoenix." In *The Little Lexicon of Love*. Los Angeles: Sherbourne Press, pp. 157–70.
A parody of *IR*. Its introduction claims "any resemblance to the Williams play is, of course, unintentional, coincidental, and entirely malicious."

65 SACKSTEDER, WILLIAM. "The Three Cats: A Study of Dramatic Structure." *Drama Survey* 5 (Winter 1966–67):252–66.
Claims the three versions of *CAT* offer "a special experimental opportunity, for we can inspect different fulfillments of what is presumably the same germinal conception." Surveys the history of the first two versions, importance of the Act III changes on "the lights their respective denouements cast on the drama as a whole." Eventually concludes with a preference for *CAT B*.

66 SALERNO, AL. " 'Menagerie' Properly Done." New York *World-Journal Tribune*, 9 December, p. 39.
Review of *GM*, TV production. Praise of the production, the adaptation, and the cast.

67   SHEED, WILFRID. "Two for the Hacksaw." *Commonweal* 84 (8 April):82.

Review of *SST*. Calls it "across-the-board disaster." Castigates TW for his frivolity: "what we want from Williams is the nightmare itself, one more time."

68   SMITH, HARRY WILLARD, JR. "Mielziner and Williams: A Concept of Style." Ph.D. dissertation, Tulane University.

TW's plays examined relative to the structure and texture of their sets: *GM, SND, S&S* have "memory sets"; *CAT, SB, MT* have "open sets"; *PA, RT, OD, CR, NI* have "solid sets." (*DA* 27:552A.)

69   SMITH, MICHAEL. Review of *SST*. *Village Voice*, 3 March, p. 19.

"The emotion that dominates [*SST*] is desperation, and Tennessee Williams' prescription is: persist.... Unfortunately the plays are very bad. In both of them Williams has tried tricks with form and style, and the result has been to diffuse the emotions and muddle the themes.... [But] for all its faults, [*SST*] was well worth seeing."

70   SULLIVAN, DAN. "Theater: 'Minor Artist' in a Major Key." *New York Times*, 21 October, p. 36.

Review of *RT*. "Fine revival... at the City Center.... The play contains all of Mr. Williams's strengths." Praises M. Stapleton.

71   TALLMER, JERRY. "Worth Waiting for." *New York Post*, 21 October, p. 56.

Review of *RT*. "This *is* theater... a triumphant revival.... Finally there is the craftsmanship of Tennessee Williams, the counterpoint, the specificity."

72   "Tennessee Williams' Name in Mysterioso Fade from 'Property' Film Credits." *Variety*, 11 May, p. 1.

TW's name omitted in credits of film of *TPC*.

73   "Tennessee Williams—Retrospective." WPAT *Gaslight Review* (March), pp. 20–49.

Pictures and brief notes on the plays and movies, their casts, and relative success.

74 "Tennessee Williams Today." WPAT *Gaslight Review* (March), pp. 15–18.
   Interview. TW discusses critics, Albee, *SST*, previous reviews, expenses and backing, Kazan.

75 "The Triumphs and Torments of Tennessee." WPAT *Gaslight Review* (March), p. 13.
   Brief assessment of TW's "stunning talent," citing his probing of "new depths of men's souls and new areas of man's torture and torment."

76 "Two on the Dial." *New York Times*, 4 December, sec. 2, p. 23.
   Photo with caption announcing *GM* on TV.

77 VON SZELISKI, JOHN. "Tennessee Williams and the Tragedy of Sensitivity." *Western Humanities Review* 20 (Summer):203–11.
   Questions the possibility of an American tragedy and cites "tragedy of sensitivity" as a "misconceived tragic philosophy," and relates his point to TW—using *SND* as example, in its "disorientation-through-sensitivity." Among those aspects of TW he presents for scrutiny are his pessimism, his dark world view, his use of "sexual action" in his plays. Ends with an examination of the "generic faults" in TW's work, focusing finally on "dread." Reprinted: 1971.19.

78 WATT, DOUGLAS. "Two Black Williams Comedies." New York *Daily News*, 23 February, p. 70.
   Review of *SST*; in *GF*, TW "has broken completely with the world of reality. . . . [*SST*] is a black comedy."

79 WATTS, RICHARD, JR. "Flight of the Cocaloony Bird." *New York Post*, 23 February, p. 54.
   Review of *SST*. "Opened disappointingly." *M* is better than *GF*; "Mr. Williams is having himself quite an adventurous fling with" *SST*.

80 WEALES, GERALD. "Of Human Badinage." *Reporter* 34 (24 March): 49–50.
   Review of *SST*. "A lively graveside rite for a dying art." Discusses them vis-à-vis TW's "lifelong preoccupation with the

'fugitive kind.'" References to his characters as victims; they "provide a fragile evening at the theatre."

81 WEST, ANTHONY. "*Slapstick Tragedy*, 'Drill to a Dull Soup.'" *Vogue* 147 (1 April):109.

Review of *SST*. Features *GF*; says "it relied heavily on the other standard Williams gambit of bringing a pretty young man on stage in a costume largely composed of Man Tan." Finds the "first play pivoting on mammectomy." Neither play adds "any lustre to the reputation of America's most renowned playwright."

82 WILLIAMS, RAYMOND. "Private Tragedy: Strindberg, O'Neill, Tennessee Williams." In *Modern Tragedy*. London: Chatto & Windus, pp. 106–20.

Explores several alternative modes and definitions for modern tragedy itself and then ties TW into the plan. Says TW is the logical extension of the tragic tradition of Strindberg, passing first to O'Neill, then to him. He cites "the sense of reality of the isolated human beings, the fierce *impersonal* rhythms" in *BD*, *SND*, *CAT*.

83 "Williams in Sicily Never Saw 'Condemned.'" *Variety*, 1 June, p. 15.

TW claims never to have seen film of *TPC*. Contract stipulated his name was *not* to appear in credits "because most of it is something he never wrote."

84 WINSTEN, ARCHER. "'This Property Is Condemned' Arrives." *New York Post*, 4 August, p. 18.

Review of film of *TPC*. "A one-act play by Tennessee Williams has been greatly expanded. . . . [It] has a Hollywood gloss laid on the Tennessee Williams view of Southern scene and personnel."

85 ZOLOTOW, SAM. "The Martin Beck Is Sold by Widow." *New York Times*, 17 February, p. 29.

Brief prerelease publicity for *DC* and *SST*.

86 ———. "'The Rose Tattoo' to Continue Run." *New York Times*, 26 October, p. 40.

Brief item noting move of revival of *RT* from City Center (New York City) to Broadway. Details about critical response.

1967

1 ATKINSON, BROOKS. "A Theatre of Life." *Saturday Review* 50 (25 February):53.

Book review of *KQ*. "Nothing in [it] will enhance the reputation of Tennessee Williams." Explores TW's commitment to "the unceasing discipline of writing." It's interesting to see him at work in "another medium."

2 BERKMAN, LEONARD. "The Tragic Downfall of Blanche DuBois." *Modern Drama* 10 (December):249–57.

Considers whether "victory" was ever within Blanche's grasp. Claims at outset that *SND* "is an inspired refutation of the linking of modern American drama with the common man." Cites critics on the subject of tragedy in *SND* and Blanche; also questions whether Blanche represents TW's use of a " 'Lawrencian' plea for primitive, spontaneous passion." Denies that Blanche can be read "as a weak hypocrite."

3 BOLTON, WHITNEY. "Critics Confounded by Williams Play." New York *Morning Telegraph*, 14 December, p. 3.

Commentary on London production of *TPC*. Surveys and summarizes the various reviews.

4 BRANDT, GEORGE. "Cinematic Structure in the Work of Tennessee Williams." In *American Theatre*. Stratford-upon-Avon Studies. London: Edward Arnold, pp. 162–87.

Movie-by-movie examination of TW's works translated for the screen, mentioning specific and corresponding scenes in the stage and screen versions.

5 "Burtons Taking 'Milk Train' for a 3d Run." *New York Times*, 3 October, p. 55.

Production notes. Film tentatively titled "Goforth," based on *MT*; to include Burton, Taylor, N. Coward, and M. Dunn.

6 CROCE, ARLENE. "New-Old, Old-New, and New." *National Review* 19 (24 January):99.

Review of *RT*. This revival is "worse for wear." Claims it shows how popular theater has changed.

7   DOBSON, EUGENE, JR. "The Reception of the Plays of Tennessee
    Williams in Germany." Ph.D. dissertation, University of Arkansas.
        Examines the reception of TW's plays in Germany "in terms
    of literary criticism and theatrical success or failure and to clarify
    the reason for Tennessee Williams' popularity." (*DA* 28:226A–
    27A.)

8   "Film Rights Are Sold to a New Williams Play." *New York Times*,
    8 December, p. 60.
        News item. Concerns purchase of *KE* by Warner Bros.-7 Arts,
    to be made into *LM*.

9   FREEDMAN, MORRIS. *The Moral Impulse: Modern Drama from Ib-
    sen to the Present*. Carbondale and Edwardsville: Southern Illi-
    nois University Press, pp. 115–16.
        Refers to Stanley's being "firmly and contentedly established
    in a social arrangement" in *SND*; also discusses "his dirtiness,"
    calling it "the consequence of an undirected anger, a never sub-
    dued inner violence." Compares him to Porter in *Look Back in
    Anger*.

10 GOLDEN, JOSEPH. *The Death of Tinkerbell*. Syracuse: Syracuse Uni-
    versity Press, pp. 123–31.
        Says it's time to "take [TW's] vision of the world quite seri-
    ously. It's an unhappy vision, one that reflects the infinite dis-
    tortions and inversions of human values that tend to stifle most
    of the old platitudes about love, loyalty, personal freedom, and
    sexual liberation." Among TW's dilemmas is his being "the sen-
    sualist in combat with the puritan." Cites this in *GM, MT*. Also
    makes reference to his use of metaphor, symbolism, allegory.

11 GOROWARA, KRISHNA. "The Fire Symbol in Tennessee Williams."
    Literary Half-Yearly 8 (January-July):57–73.
        Starts with assertion: "A creative wish wants to use symbols
    and metaphors. They illumine a situation. Often a dramatist is
    obsessed with one particular symbol." Goes on to trace fire sym-
    bolism in *BA, OD, BD, NI, CAT, GM, MT, SU, SLS, PA*: "Fire
    being almost always at the back of Tennessee Williams's mind,
    the word 'burn' seems to fit his expression better than any other."

12 Gottfried, Martin. *A Theater Divided: The Postwar American Stage.* Boston: Little, Brown, pp. 248–57.
     TW "has probably completed the work that will represent him to long-term American theater. . . . Williams was a true artist and a definite left-winger during the early years of his development." Surveys the plays, explaining their themes (and origins) and summarizing plots. "When a master playwright begins his descent, his artistic maturity turns toward second childhood. . . . I have implied that Williams's career is over."

13 Gresset, Michel. "Orphée sous les Tropiques où les thèmes dans le théâtre de Tennessee Williams." In *Le Théâtre Moderne II.* Edited by Jean Jacquot. Paris: Éditions du Centre National de la Recherche Scientifique, pp. 163–76.
     Surveys the plays of TW which contain elements of depravity and which he localizes in a Southern setting; attempts to place TW in the American dramatic tradition, and maintains it's too early to determine whether Albee will replace him. In French.

14 Hagopian, John V., and Dolch, Martin. "Tennessee Williams." In *Insight I: Analyses of American Literature.* Frankfurt: Hirschgraben, pp. 271–80.
     Usual biographical details in synopsis; complete textual analysis and plot summary of *GM*, plus study guide-type questions and answers.

15 Hainsworth, J.D. "Tennessee Williams: Playwright on a Hot Tin Roof?" *Études Anglaises* 20 (July-September):225–32.
     Claims need for a reassessment of TW's merit, since such works as *PA* have eclipsed his previous stature. Covers the ground of TW's themes ("troubled people," "social structures," etc.) Cites Arthur Miller on *CAT* and rehashes the problems there with Act 3; concludes that the quality in TW's writing "transcends" all the quibbling over other issues.

16 Hewes, Henry. "The Theater." *Saturday Review* 50 (25 November):71.
     Brief review of *GM*. Quite positive comments on Long Wharf Theater (New Haven, Connecticut) production.

17 JACKSON, ESTHER M. "Tennessee Williams." In *The American Theater Today*. Edited by Alan S. Downer. New York: Basic Books,
pp. 73–84.
    Excerpt from Jackson's *The Broken World of Tennessee
Williams* (1965.30).

18 " 'Knightly Quest' Has a Familiar Ring: Has Mr. Williams Said
It All Before?" *National Observer* 6 (6 March):23.
    Book review of *KQ*. "Is it that the times have changed and
there is no four-letter word, no form of human behavior left
that can shock, or even seem fresh on paper? Or is it really that
Mr. Williams has said it all before, and said it better? I suspect
the latter."

19 "London Stage: A Streetcar Named Despair." *Time* 90 (22 December):63.
    Review of *2CP*, London production. Tries to sort out plot—
treats it with respect. Little production commentary.

20 MAROWITZ, CHARLES. "Williams Premiere." *Village Voice*, 21 December, p. 35.
    Review of *2CP*, London production. Maintains London critics
would have damned it had anyone other than TW written it;
analysis of plot and theme; laments this "most pretentious play."

21 MRAZ, DOYNE JOSEPH. "The Changing Image of the Female Characters in the Works of Tennessee Williams." Ph.D. dissertation,
University of Southern California.
    Posits that Williams's early female characters all have the
same basic characteristics, and that they are reflections of the
females he knew as a young man in the South. Further argues
that his latter female characters are all more or less reflections of
the more theatrical, less vulnerable modern women of New York.
Cites *GM*, *SND*, *S&S*, *RT*, *CR*, *CAT*, *SB*, *NI*, and *MT*. (DA
28:4304A.)

22 NATHAN, DAVID. "Rather a Muddled Guide to Despair." *Sun* (London), 12 December, p. 7.
    Brief review of *2CP*, London production. Finds the play con-
fusing.

23 PETERSON, WILLIAM. "Williams, Kazan, and the Two Cats." *New Theatre Magazine* 7 (Summer):14–20.

Considers the (then) two versions of the third act of *CAT*. TW "wrote the first for himself and the second for his brilliant director, Elia Kazan. The first is known chiefly by people who read plays, for the second was used in the original Broadway production and in the film." Gives history of the dispute, and examines textual distinctions in tone, language, and emphasis; calls attention to relative levels of parallel structure; claims the first version is of greater merit "because it maintains and expands the structural devices of verbal repetition and variation."

24 "Playwrights in Print: Homo Hero." *Time* 89 (10 March):102.

Brief book review of *KQ*. Primarily a plot summary of the stories.

25 PRYCE-JONES, ALAN. "World of Books: Tennessee Williams' Nuclear Whimsey Deals with a Dolorous Dixie Quixote." New York *World-Journal Tribune*, 28 February, p. 24.

Book review of *KQ*. Detailed plot and character descriptions for the story "The Knightly Quest." Briefly mentions other stories, with special praise for "Kingdom of Earth."

26 Review of *KQ*. *Critic* 25 (June-July):90.

Brief. "The five [stories] are thoroughly entertaining and occasionally flash with the genius that has made Williams a savior of the modern American theater. But the stories add nothing to his reputation."

27 ROWLAND, JAMES L. "Tennessee's Two Amandas." *Research Studies* 35 (December):331–40.

Discusses the two versions of *GM* extant—a "'reading version' . . . copyrighted in 1945, and the so-called 'acting version' [of] . . . Dramatists Play Service." Traces the pointed evolution of both versions, and the relative distinctions, paramount in Amanda.

28 SHEFFER, ISAIAH. "Storytelling Dramatists." *New Leader* 50 (5 June):23–24.

Reviews *KQ* along with Miller's *I Don't Need You Anymore.*

"These collections are of interest for what they indicate about the current vitality in each writer's talent." TW's collection is "written with the same vivid sensory detail found in his plays, but containing few surprises. . . . Williams is at his funniest and best in describing the new age, in burlesquing the war-production mentality."

29   SHIVAS, MARK. "Was It Like This with Louis XIV?" *New York Times*, 15 October, sec. 2, p. 15.

Production notes on *Boom*; bits of on-location gossip. Some bantering between Burton and Taylor. No mention of *Boom* as title, and no mention of TW.

30   "Tennessee Williams' Fiction." *New York Times*, 25 January, p. 40.

Brief announcement of forthcoming collection of his fiction, *KQ*.

31   TYNAN, KENNETH. "American Blues: The Plays of Arthur Miller and Tennessee Williams." In *The Modern American Theatre: A Collection of Critical Essays*. Edited by A.B. Kernan. Englewood Cliffs, N.J.: Prentice-Hall, pp. 34–44.

Reprint of 1954.11, 1961.41.

32   WAKEMAN, JOHN. "Story Time." *New York Times Book Review*, 2 April, p. 4.

Book review of *KQ*. Plot summary; focuses on one story which he claims has enough "logical inconsistencies [to] invalidate it as effective satire."

33   WELLS, JOEL. "Goldilocks and the Three Bears." In *Grim Fairy Tales for Adults*. New York: Macmillan; London: Collier Macmillan, pp. 21–30.

A parody of Williams' style in a retelling of the conventional fable.

34   "Williams Drama Baffles Critics." *New York Times*, 13 December, p. 54.

Survey of media critics' reviews of London production of *2CP*.

35   ZIMMERMAN, PAUL D. "Offstage Voices." *Newsweek* 69 (27 February):92, 94.

Book review of *KQ*. Claims TW "is less concerned with ethics than with the survival of the poetic and romantic in a monstrous society." Finds that "in Williams' world, the isolated individual survives and endures."

36 ZOLOTOW, SAM. "Williams to Have Play Next Season." *New York Times*, 11 July, p. 29.
   Announcement of upcoming David Merrick production of *KE*. Discusses the metamorphosis and history of the play.

1968

1 BARNES, CLIVE. "Theater: Williams Drama." *New York Times*, 28 March, p. 54.
   Review of *7D*. Says it's more a list of characters than a play; discusses theme and gives plot details; generally negative.

2 BENTLEY, ERIC. Reviews of *CR* and *CAT*. In *What Is Theatre? Incorporating the Dramatic Event and Other Reviews 1949–1967*. New York: Atheneum, pp. 74–78, 224–31.
   Reprints of 1953.4, 1955.12.

3 BRUCE, ALAN N. "The Seven Descents of Myrtle." *Christian Science Monitor*, 9 April, p. 6.
   Review of *7D*. The "striking humor of the dialogue . . . saves much of the shaky tale. . . . [It] runs to . . . strained, unproductive lengths. . . . It glows with a sickly energy."

4 CAPASSO, RALPH. "Through a Glass Starkly: A Class Paper on 'The Glass Menagerie.' " *English Journal* 4 (February):209–12, 20.
   A high school English class group-analysis of *GM*. Starts with premise: "The characters in Tennessee Williams' *The Glass Menagerie* are trapped in their worlds, worlds which they neither understand nor accept," and proceeds in much the same vein.

5 CHAPMAN, JOHN. "Tennessee Williams, Durable Mystic." New York *Sunday News*, 7 April, sec. 5, p. 3.
   Review of *7D*. Gives details of its history in the canon; surveys

its problems; mentions its going into movie form. "I think [7D] is among the best of Williams' seventeen plays."

6   CLURMAN, HAROLD. Review of 7D. *Nation* 206 (15 April):516–17.
"I was not simply disappointed. I was sore. . . . It end[s] in a conceptual bog. . . . The dialogue is lambently vivid, graceful, streaked with pungent humor." Analysis of themes.

7   COAKLEY, JAMES. "Williams in Ann Arbor." *Drama Critique* 11 (Winter):52–56.
CR "remains an enigma. . . . Stylistic disparity promotes the play's bold efforts to break loose from the stage and spill into the house. . . . The play is non-linear in structure." Claims the play is informed by "a particularly modern notion of time which is [its] organizing principle. . . . A most ambitious play."

8   CONWAY, MARY L. "Williams in Cleveland." *Drama Critique* 11 (Winter):58–60.
"A report of an interview with a director in rehearsal." Highlights Mario Siletti's directional techniques for RT.

9   CORLISS, RICHARD. Review of film BD. *Film Comment* 4 (Summer):44–47.
Concerns the production of BD and subsequent reaction by Legion of Decency, and result of the Legion's action.

10   ————. Review of film of SND. *Film Comment* 4 (Summer):44–47.
Concerns the production of SND and the modifications necessary for the film to pass Legion of Decency censorship.

11   DRAKE, CONSTANCE. "Blanche DuBois: A Re-evaluation." *Theatre Annual* 24:58–69.
Establishes the "difficulties to the critic" that TW's heroines pose, since they don't fit the conventions of either Aristotelian or Elizabethan tragic figures. Takes on the "ambiguous" Blanche and attempts to give her clearer interpretation. Involves analysis of Stanley and Stella, the kind of sympathy Blanche receives from Williams. "Blanche is the South that no longer exists and Stanley, in destroying her, represents the forces that have destroyed the South."

12   GAGH. "Shows Out of Town: 'The Seven Descents of Myrtle.'" *Variety*, 13 March, p. 68.

      Philadelphia production. "An overly melodramatic yarn. . . . [But there's a] seeming lack of development in characterizations."

13   GASSNER, JOHN. "Anchors Aweigh: Maxwell Anderson and Tennessee Williams." In *Dramatic Soundings: Evaluations and Retractions Culled from 30 Years of Dramatic Criticism.* Edited by Glenn Loncy. New York: Crown, pp. 304–13.

      Refers to TW's only verse play ("The Purification") and goes on to discuss the poetic possibilities of his plays; ties in an analysis of TW's handling of realism and tragedy. Discusses the ways in which *GM, SND, S&S* fall short of their possibilities, and how "Williams' individuality has not yet acquired a specific character; it is as yet predominantly intuitive and wayward."

14   ———. "Time and Tennessee Williams." In *Dramatic Soundings: Evaluations and Retractions Culled from 30 Years of Dramatic Criticism.* Edited by Glenn Loncy. New York: Crown, pp. 585–90.

      Reviews of *CR, MT.* Reprints of 1960.46, 1964.17.

15   GILL, BRENDAN. "Before the Flood." *New Yorker* 44 (6 April):109–10.

      Review of *7D.* "A rueful-comical lament over human misery"; praises the script and the production.

16   HARTUNG, PHILIP T. Review of film *Boom. Commonweal* 88 (14 June):385.

      "I'm not sure what 'Boom' is trying to prove." Praise for Noel Coward, Elizabeth Taylor, and Richard Burton, but considers the film to be "jammed with symbols . . . signifying little."

17   HEILMAN, ROBERT BECHTOLD. *Tragedy and Melodrama: Versions of Experience.* Seattle: University of Washington Press, pp. 120–22.

      Refers to TW's "recurrent interest in women who withdraw from the world"; specific, brief reference to Laura and Blanche.

18   HEWES, HENRY. "Down the Down Staircase." *Saturday Review* 51 (13 April):30.

Review of *7D*. "Slow going and dramatically ambiguous. . . . Its poetic setting . . . suggests . . . the play is a great deal more profound than its plot. . . . Most of the play's magnificence is visual."

19   HOBE. "Show on Broadway: 'The Seven Descents of Myrtle.'" *Variety*, 3 April, p. 72.

The play needs editing "desperately. . . . [It] isn't a good play." Williams wanted to call it "The Kingdom of Earth." David Merrick insisted on *7D*.

20   HOFMANN, PAUL. "Williams Tells Brother He's Doing Fine." *New York Times*, 30 June, p. 54.

News item. TW surfaced long enough yesterday to phone his brother and assure him he was alive and well. Reports from his secretary that he will be leaving New York for Key West, possibly Cuba.

21   HOWARD, MAUREEN. "Other Voices." *Partisan Review* 35 (Winter):141–52.

Book review of *KQ*. Discusses *KQ* among five other authors' work. Calls *KQ* "consistently uneven. . . . He is possessed by his material. . . . The title novella is full of the shimmering old razzmatazz, as badly faulted as *Camino Real*. . . . The best piece in the collection is 'Grand,' a reminiscence of his grandmother."

22   "In the Flesh." *Times Literary Supplement*, 11 July, p. 721.

Brief book review of *KQ*. Primarily plot summary of "Desire and the Black Masseur" and "The Knightly Quest."

23   ISAAC, DAN. "'A Streetcar Named Desire'—or Death." *New York Times*, 18 February, sec. 2, pp. 1, 7.

Discusses history of *SND*; mentions reputation of TW in academe and elsewhere; whether or not TW has "written himself out." Anticipates *KE* which is about to have New York premiere.

24   KAHN, SY. "Through a Glass Menagerie Darkly: The World of Tennessee Williams." In *Modern American Drama: Essays in Criti-*

cism. Edited by William E. Taylor. DeLand, Fla.: Everett/Edwards, pp. 71–89.

"For many he is the *bete noir* of contemporary literature and a moral deformity, . . . charges against him [that] are half-truths at best, and usually based on an essentially naive and irrelevant attitude toward literature." Essay includes detailed biography, comparisons to and contrasts with Arthur Miller, an examination of TW's hero-victims through an examination of his prose and poetry—which suggests the Christian position that we are all fallen creatures struggling toward godhood, or at least salvation.

25 KAUFFMANN, STANLEY. "Booms and Busts." *New Republic* 158 (8 June):26.

Review of film *Boom*. Says the director and designer "have turned this ridiculous Tennessee Williams script into a rococo romp." Refers to its *"Harper's Bazaar* metaphysics. . . . Williams' screenplay is a hollow pomposity."

26 KERR, WALTER. "Albee, Miller, Williams: Floodwaters." In *Thirty Plays Hath November*. New York: Simon & Schuster, pp. 224–30. Reprint of 1964.29.

27 ———. "The Name of the Game is Blame." *New York Times*, 7 April, sec. 2, pp. 1, 3.

Review of *KE-7D*. Blames Quintero's direction, Jo Mielziner's staging, a badly cut opening act, Estelle Parson's voice, and Harry Guardino's uneven performance for the mishandling of the play. *7D* is not so much "ill-conceived" but "unrealized. . . . With some luck . . . it is possible that it could be finished."

28 KNIGHT, ARTHUR. "Tennessee's Waltz." *Saturday Review* 51 (1 June):19.

Review of film *Boom*. "The chances are that at last Williams has achieved a version of his play that will satisfy both him and its audience. . . . One of the film's few flaws is a brief, curiously self-conscious appearance by Noel Coward."

29 KROLL, JACK. "Old Man River." *Newsweek* 71 (8 April):131.

Brief review of *7D*. TW "tossed [*7D*] off as a souffle that is more steamy air than anything else." The play is TW's attempt "to exorcise his own devils."

30   KUNKEL, FRANCIS L. "Tennessee Williams and the Death of God." *Commonweal* 87 (23 February):614–17.

Traces numerous characters relative to supernal forces; relates this technique to general decadence in TW's work; conversion and apotheosis referred to; discusses their peculiar "theology." TW's "inability to grasp the possibility of the world being grounded in a transcendent Presence and his reliance on secular values as a source of moral action and religious belief explain, in part at least, why his literature is a literature of decadence." Reprinted: 1975.27.

31   LEE, TIMOTHY. "Writer Tennessee Williams Drops from Sight Here." *New York Post*, 29 June, p. 4.

News item. After telling brother he was afraid he'd be murdered, TW disappears; police hunt for him.

32   LEON, FERDINAND. "Time, Fantasy, and Reality in 'Night of the Iguana.'" *Modern Drama* 11 (May):87–96.

Says *NI* fits into the "memory play" conceit as TW used it in *GM*. Its plot "is one of the flimsiest in the Williams canon." Discusses TW's handling of psychological history through dialogue, "timelessness," memory, function of setting, poetry—all as elements within the play.

33   LEWIS, EMORY. "Ascent for Bullins and Foster, Descent for Williams." *Cue* 37 (6 April):9.

Review of *7D*. "It is sad." Cites TW as "member of the dreary platoon of self-caricatures.... [It's] a melodramatic, funereal parody of everything he has ever written."

34   MOODY, R. BRUCE, and COTTRELL, BECKMAN H. "Two Views of 'Summer and Smoke.'" In *Contexts of the Drama*. Edited by Richard Goldstone. New York: McGraw-Hill, pp. 664–70.

Moody begins with question: "Is John Buchanan the heat of summer, and Alma Winemiller the spiritual distillation which hangs over it?" Calls *S&S* "a period piece ... and yet it is a comedy.... Tennessee Williams is funniest when saddest." Cottrell argues that *S&S* "continues to deal with the same central concerns as did 'Glass Menagerie.'" Highlights Alma's attempt to change, compares her to others of TW's heroines.

35 NELSON, BENJAMIN. "Avant-Garde Dramatists from Ibsen to Ionesco." *Psychoanalytic Review* 55:505–12.

Creates a specific ordering of dramatists: "Ibsen and Strindberg are proto-Freudians; Williams, Miller, Albee are Freudian, whatever else they may be; Beckett, Ionesco and Genet are post-Freudians." Claims TW has "given expression to passionate intensities of members of families caught in agonizing familial and extrafamilial traps."

36 "New Movies: Boom!" *Time* 91 (31 May):56.

Review of film *Boom*. "This film makes it official: Richard Burton and Elizabeth Taylor . . . have given up acting for entertaining. . . . They display the self-indulgent fecklessness of a couple of rich amateurs hamming it up at the country-club frolic, and with approximately the same results." Calls it "worse" than *MT*.

37 "New Plays: The Seven Descents of Myrtle." *Time* 91 (5 April):72.

Review of *7D*. "The play becomes a sleepwalking tour of the dusty attic of memory." Refers to TW's "comic sense."

38 "New Williams Play Embroiled in Fight over Shifting Title." *New York Times*, 21 February, p. 61.

Brief item discussing dispute between two titles: *KE* or *7D*. Mentions David Merrick's role in dispute.

39 NIGHTINGALE, BENEDICT. "Lost Innocence." *New Statesman* 76 (29 November):765.

Review of *SB*, London production. Brief exploration of the play's theme; mixed reaction.

40 *OA*. New York *Sunday News*, 14 April, sec. S, p. 13.

Brief news item. *OA* will be made into film, TW to do the screen play.

41 PAVLOV, GRIGOR. "A Comparative Study of Tennessee Williams' *The Glass Menagerie* and 'Portrait of a Girl in Glass.'" *Annuaire de Université de Sofia, faculté des lettres*, i, 57, 111–31.

Says his "aim . . . is to analyze the short story . . . and the play . . . and to compare the manner in which he [TW] handles basically the same thematic material in two genres." Argues that "the main theme running both through play and short story is the disintegration of a petty bourgeois family." Focuses on such things as introductory speech and highlights the role of the 1930s in the play.

42   PRICE, R.G.G. Review of *KQ*. *Punch* 255 (24 July):135.
     Book review. "They have the weaknesses but not the virtues of the plays.... Mr. Williams has always been in danger of having his universe deliquesce about his ears.... His intensity slackens into shrillness."

43   QUIRINO, LEONARD. "Tennessee Williams' Persistent 'Battle of Angels.'" *Modern Drama* 11 (May):27–39.
     Discusses *BA* as "blueprint to [TW's] desperate vision and baroque theatre." Sees *BA* as attempt at "amalgamation of tragedy, melodrama, morality play and romantic mood play," an illustration of TW's "quarrel with God and existence."

44   RECK, TOM STOKES. "The First *Cat on a Hot Tin Roof*: Williams' 'Three Players.'" *University Review* 34 (Spring):187–92.
     Discusses the evolution of TW's story "Three Players of a Summer Game" into *CAT*, and claims the story has merits on its own, apart from the celebrated play that grew out of it. Treats story's setting, hero, sense of retreat; much analysis of Brick role; goes on to discuss similarities and differences in story and play, referring to Kazan's observations.

45   Review of *7D*. *Village Voice*, 4 April, p. 42.
     "Has bloated, distorted, and altogether ruined" the original short story in lengthening it to a three-act play. It "doesn't hold much interest.... [Its] direction does nothing to redeem Williams' artistic sins."

46   SCANNELL, VERNON. "Distortions." *New Statesman* 76 (12 July):56.
     Brief book review of *KQ*. The stories in this collection "are strongly earth-rooted ones that deal with the impenetrable mystery of love, with age and failure and frustration."

47   SCHICKEL, RICHARD. "Dick and Liz Dare Us to Stay Away." *Life* 64 (21 June):12.

Review of film *Boom*, TW's "latest self-satire" whose characters "no longer even titillate us, let alone stir authentic emotion, and even Mr. Williams appears bored with them." Disparages Burton and Taylor as being lazy and insulting with a "kind of arrogance" that is particular to actors who have attained some sort of "clout."

48 SCHUMACH, MURRAY. "Tennessee Williams Expresses Fear for Life in Note to Brother." *New York Times*, 29 June, p. 19.
TW's letter to Dakin expressing fear he'll be murdered; message unclear; TW can't be located.

49 SHEED, WILFRID. "Tired Scene Turned into Sad Parody." *Life* 64 (26 April):18.
Review of *7D*. "Unfortunately it seems there are no more masterpieces to be coaxed out of Mr. Williams' corner of the South. . . . [This] kind of play . . . went out of business a long time ago." Reprinted: 1971.26.

50 SIMON, JOHN. Review of *7D*. *Hudson Review* 21 (July):322–24.
Speaks of TW as "a compulsive self-parroter," *7D* as "a lumbering pastiche . . lacking even inner consistence."

51 ———. "The Self-Tormentor." *Commonweal* 88 (3 May):208–9.
Review of *7D*. Criticizes TW's rewriting old plays; traces the parodying TW does with this play: "the appalling self-parroting and self-parody. . . . Worst of all is the humor."

52 SISTER MARY JOHN, O.S.U. "Williams in Cincinnati." *Drama Critique* 11 (Winter):56–58.
Report on John Going's direction of *SND* in Cincinnati. Provides data on his interpretation and staging notions.

53 STYAN, JOHN. *The Dark Comedy*. Cambridge: Cambridge University Press, pp. 208–17.
Wiliams' "work reflects strikingly the American condition, found generally throughout serious American drama; in a world of prosperity and of unlimited opportunity for prosperity there remains the great immovable doubt that the central values are not yet discovered." Makes reference to "Williams' peculiar sen-

sationalism. . . . Williams' plays have been all of a piece, and his earlier ones mere trials for his later ones." Surveys the plays chronologically. "He does not trust his audience to accept his cronies."

54   "Tennessee Williams Safe: Missing Writer Feared Murder." *Sunday Times* (London), 30 July, p. 1.
     News item. Recounts events of his disappearance after supposed immediate danger.

55   TOMALIN, CLAIRE. "Shaking Down the Stucco." *Observer*, 7 July, p. 27.
     Book review of *KQ*. Brief favorable analysis; focuses on the aspects of the South, sex, old age.

56   WALSH, MOIRA. Review of film *Boom*. *America* 118 (8 June):760–61.
     "One could wax indignant over Williams' apparent use of Christian symbolism to express a despairing view of humanity. . . . His screen play employs floods of baroque language, almost unsupported by dramatic thrust."

57   WARDLE, IRVING. "After Nine Lost Years." *Times* (London) 20 November, p. 9.
     Review of *SB*, London production. "No piece of Williams's comes closer to self-parody."

58   ———. "Amateurs Do Well by Tennessee Williams." *Times* (London), 2 December, p. 16.
     Review of *MT*, London production by amateur company, Tower Theatre. Compares to *SB* but considers *MT* to be "stronger."

59   WATTS, RICHARD, JR. "The Drama of Three Misfits." *New York Post*, 28 March, p. 67.
     Review of *7D*. It contains "some of [TW's] most probing and compassionate reflections."

60   ———. "Word from Tennessee Williams." *New York Post*, 13 April, p. 23.

Commentary after 7D's failure. Lack of a powerful third act is its "one serious defect. . . . Everything depends on that climactic conclusion."

61 "Williams Writes Meller on a Restaurant Menu; Playwright Cancels It." *Variety*, 3 July, pp. 2, 61.
Concerning TW's letter to his brother when he thought his life was in danger.

62 ZIMMERMAN, PAUL D. "Under the Rock." *Newsweek* 71 (3 June): 104.
Review of film *Boom*. " 'Boom!' is a dud. . . . Nothing can make much sense out of Tennessee Williams' vagrant self-parody of a screen play." Praise for Burton and Taylor, but regards *Boom* as TW "at his tired worst." Despite good acting, all "wind up merely as confederates in a pointless, pompous nightmare."

63 ZOLOTOW, SAM. "Quintero Leaves Williams' Comedy." *New York Times*, 28 February, p. 39.
Production notes announcing Quintero's resignation as director of 7D because of interference from the producer.

64 ———. *New York Times*, 29 February, p. 30.
Additional production notes. Quintero resumes the direction of 7D—TW intervened on his behalf.

65 ———. "Williams Comedy 'Kingdom of Earth' to Open in March." *New York Times*, 25 January, p. 33.
Brief announcement of planned opening of *KE* in March.

1969

1 "Asides and Ad-Libs." *Variety*, 12 February, p. 56.
TW to receive National Institute of Arts and Letters Gold Medal for Drama on 21 May.

2 "Audrey Wood Deplores N.Y. Times' Acceptance of Life's Williams Ad." *Variety*, 23 July, p. 67.
Angry letter to editor from Wood, as per title.

3 BARNES, CLIVE. "Theater: 'In the Bar of a Tokyo Hotel.'" *New York Times*, 12 May, p. 54.

Review of *BAR*. "The play seems almost too personal, and as a result too painful." Generally negative.

4 BIGSBY, C.W.E. "Tennessee Williams: Streetcar to Glory." In *The Forties: Fiction, Poetry, Drama*. Edited by Warren French. Deland, Fla: Everett/Edwards, pp. 251–58.

Brief initial examination of TW's growth as a playwright, his personal development, and his early plays, followed by an examination of *SND*'s theme in a post–world war context, and the development of the Blanche and Stanley characters prior to the writing of *SND*. Reprinted: 1971.19.

5 BRUSTEIN, ROBERT. "A Question of Identity" and "America's New Culture Hero: Feelings Without Words." In *The Third Theatre*. New York: Alfred A. Knopf, pp. 98–100, 204–17.

Reprints of 1958.12, 1966.6.

6 CLURMAN, HAROLD. Review of *BAR*. *Nation* 208 (2 June):709–10.

Details on plot and themes. "I hope [it's] not Williams' last testament." Compares to *GF*.

7 CURLEY, DOROTHY NYREN, et al., eds. *A Library of Literary Criticism: Modern American Literature*. Vol. 3. New York: Frederick Ungar, pp. 531–34.

Excerpts from popular critical sources with emphasis on the plays.

8 DAVIS, RONALD L. "All the New Vibrations: Romanticism in 20th Century America." *Southern Review* 5 (Summer):256–70.

Refers to TW, along with Hemingway, Fitzgerald, O'Neill, Salinger, as a "Romantic" in a twentieth-century guise.

9 "A Demand for an Apology." *New York Times*, 22 June, sec. 2, p. 11.

Letters in "Drama Mailbag" protesting *New York Times* printing full-page *Life* ad that demeaned Williams. Ad appeared 10 June.

10 DICKINSON, HUGH. "Tennessee Williams: Orpheus as Savior." In *Myth on the Modern Stage*. Urbana: University of Illinois Press, pp. 278–309.

Cites Williams' use of the Orpheus and Eurydice myth in *BA* and *OD*. Claims both are significant to an understanding of his career. "His extremely conscious, even self-conscious, recourse to myth would seem to run counter to his natural talents." Considers also TW's "comic talent" in his use of the myth. Further, TW "frequently adds parallels from the passion, death, and resurrection of Jesus Christ to his modern treatment of an ancient story." Pointed and explicit tracing of the myth in both plays.

11 FORSYTHE, RONALD. "Why Can't 'We' Live Happily Ever After, Too?" *New York Times*, 23 February, sec. 2, p. 1.

Reference to homosexuality in *CAT* and *NI*.

12 FOSBURGH, LACEY. "Art and Literary People Urged to Look Inward." *New York Times*, 22 May, p. 52.

American Academy of Arts and Letters and National Institute of Arts and Letters award Gold Medal for Drama to TW.

13 "Gold Medal for Drama to Tennessee Williams." New York *Daily News*, 25 January, p. 24.

Brief news item. National Institute of Arts and Letters award to TW.

14 HERRIDGE, FRANCES. "Tennessee Williams Adds to 'Bar of a Tokyo Hotel.'" *New York Post*, 25 April, p. 40.

Interview-commentary. TW, in New York to make script changes on *BAR*, discusses the play and what it's about.

15 HEWES, HENRY. "Tennessee's Quest." *Saturday Review* 52 (31 May):18.

Review of *BAR*. TW "in his later period appears to be turning to more personal material." *BAR* "seems concerned with expressing Williams's agony both at the difficult process of artistic creation and at the specter of old age, waning sexual magnetism and death. . . . [Its] failure is unimportant compared with our concern for its author."

16   HILFER, ANTHONY C., and RAMSEY, R. VANCE. "*Baby Doll*: A Study
     in Comedy and Critical Awareness." *Ohio University Review*
     11:75–88.
        Surveys the "hostile" critical reaction to *BD*, gives particulars
     about the making of the film; widens analysis and relates it to
     "the usual pattern of Williams' creative process." Relates *BD* to
     earlier *27W*; then proceeds to comment on the comic elements
     in the film and explains how that element fanned the "critical out-
     rage."

17   HILL, FRANCIS A. "The Disaster of Ideals in *Camino Real* by Ten-
     nessee Williams." *Notes on Mississippi Writers* 1 (Winter):100–
     109.
        Discusses the Don Quixote conceit in *CR*. "Set in the aura of
     a dream world, the play is almost entirely symbolic. . . . The char-
     acters . . . remain dehumanized composites of the characters who
     fail in all his other plays. . . . In Williams' plays there is an over-
     burden of physical and mental cruelty."

18   HUCKER, CHARLES. "Tennessee Williams Goes Back to UMC for
     Honorary Degree." Kansas City *Times*, 4 June, sec. A, p. 8.
        News item. TW returns to alma mater (University of Missouri-
     Columbia) for honorary Doctor of Humane Letters.

19   ISAAC, DAN. "Talking with Tennessee Williams." *After Dark* 6
     (October):46–50.
        Interview-commentary. TW discusses life style, several plays,
     his writing.

20   JAUSLIN, CHRISTIAN. *Tennessee Williams*. Berlin: Friedrich Verlag
     Velber, 154 pp.
        Brief chronology of events in TW's life, his place in the
     Southern Renaissance, the autobiographical details in his work,
     the influence of D.H. Lawrence; treats all plays produced—plot
     summary and brief theme detailing. In German.

21   KALSON, ALBERT E. "Tennessee Williams' 'Kingdom of Earth': A
     Sterile Promontory." *Drama and Theatre* 8 (Winter 1969–70):90–
     93.
        Sees *KE* as "Williams' tired return to the locale and characters

of his earlier works, and surprisingly, a reaffirmation of the redemptive possibilities of the life-force." Finds Myrtle, Lot, and
Chicken to be "no longer recognizable human beings, but instead
as the last mutations of a withering humanity—in fact as carnival
freaks." Close dialogue analysis to demonstrate his theory. *KE*
"reinforces [TW's] increasingly despairing vision of existence
without hope."

22 KANFER, STEFAN. "White Dwarf's Tragic Fadeout." *Life* 66 (13
June):10.
Review of *BAR*. "Nothing about the work justifies its production, least of all its plot." Refers to it as "almost free of incident
or drama." TW "has at least retained his craftsmanship, his celebrated ability to construct scenes," but apparently has "suffered
an infantile regression from which there seems no exit."

23 KERR, WALTER. "The Facts Don't Add up to Faces." *New York
Times*, 25 May, sec. 2, p. 5.
Review of *BAR*. Analyzes its problems; discusses the play's
"theoretical people" rather than actual characters and its lack of
concreteness; the problem is anticipated only in *CR*.

24 KROLL, JACK. "Life Is a Bitch." *Newsweek* 73 (26 May):133.
Review of *BAR*. TW's "recent plays have been more imitations
of an earlier, more resilient self than his new creations." In *BAR*
"he has allowed his real concerns to appear in a stark and raw
form.... It is terror that activates the play.... 'Life is a bitch'
might be Williams' rubric.... The play itself rattles with melodrama."

25 MACEY, SAMUEL L. "Nonheroic Tragedy: A Pedigree for American
Tragic Drama." *Comparative Literature Studies* 6 (March):1–19.
Investigates the European plays that influenced "American
tragic drama... nonheroic tragedy." Emphasis on work of
O'Neill, Miller, and TW. Admits the continued interest in classi-
cal themes, but sees bourgeois tragedy as the dominant influence.
Refers to TW's own biography for sources.

26 MANNES, MARYA. "Morbid Magic of Tennessee Williams." In *The*

Reporter Reader. Edited by Max Ascoli. Freeport, N.Y.: Books for Libraries Press, pp. 145–50.
   Reprint of 1955.78.

27 NEWLOVE, DONALD. "A Dream of Tennessee Williams." *Esquire* 71 (November):172–78.
   Interview. References to TW at American Academy of Arts and Letters; sickness; going to see *Midnight Cowboy*; Catholicism; *BAR*.

28 "New Plays: Torpid Tennessee." *Time* 93 (23 May):75.
   Review of *MT*. "Tennessee Williams is lying on the sickbed of his talents." Refers to his "esthetic impotence." Surveys past works and negatively contrasts this one. Still, TW "is a thoroughbred."

29 "Played Out?" *New York Times*, 10 June, p. 96.
   Full-page advertisement for *Life* magazine. "'Tennessee Williams has suffered an infantile regression from which there seems no exit.... Almost free of incident or drama ... nothing about *In the Bar of a Tokyo Hotel* deserves its production.'"

30 PORTER, THOMAS E. "The Passing of the Old South: 'A Streetcar Named Desire.'" In *Myth and Modern American Drama*. Detroit: Wayne State University Press, pp. 153–76.
   Initially contrasts "Death of a Salesman" with *SND* (*Death* "dramatizes the death of a myth" and *SND* "deals with the same theme"), and finds Blanche to be the embodiment of a legend about the passing of the Old South. Says TW "is dealing with a more comprehensive myth" than Miller (who is really writing about "the success myth"). Discusses "the popular image of the romance," the complex of southern attitudes, southern heroes, and applies particular elements of *SND* to this motif. Surveys some contemporary criticism.

31 PRESLEY, DELMA EUGENE. "The Theological Dimensions of Tennessee Williams." Ph.D. dissertation, Emory University.
   Studies *GM*, *SND*, *S&S*, *CAT*, *CR*, *SLS*, *NI*, and *MT*. Traces the development of themes of isolation, despair, materialism vs.

religion, death. Looks forward to future TW plays producing an actual theological vision. (*DAI* 30:2038A.)

32 REED, REX. "Our Man Flint, Meet Georgy Girl." *New York Times*, 8 June, sec. 2, pp. 15, 17.
    Sunday piece on making film *BK*, based on TW's play *7D*. TW had nothing to do with it.

33 *7D*. *Newsweek* 73 (2 June):61.
    Announcement of Lynn Redgrave to be cast in *BK*, film version of *7D*.

34 STEEN, MIKE. *A Look at Tennessee Williams*. New York: Hawthorn Books, Inc., 318 pp.
    Assembles a host of "contributors" ("who have known Tennessee socially or professionally or both") and interviews them about TW—as a substitute for a biography. In the course of the work, biography does "occur"; also numerous production data and trivia, personal reminiscences.

35 TAFT, ADON. "Tennessee Williams Converts." *Christianity Today* 31 (January):39–40.
    Brief piece discussing the path to his conversion to Catholicism. Mentions the roles of those he consulted and how he considers many of his plays "Catholic plays."

36 "Tennessee Williams Ailing." *New York Times*, 22 February, p. 20.
    Brief news item. Miami: TW reported in satisfactory condition at Mercy Hospital. Nature of illness not disclosed.

37 "Tennessee Williams Ill." *New York Times*, 4 October, p. 24.
    Brief news item. TW in St. Louis hospital for treatment of drug abuse.

38 "Tennessee Williams Turns to Roman Catholic Faith." *New York Times*, 12 January, p. 86.
    Brief item on TW's conversion at time he thought he was dying of flu.

39 TISCHLER, NANCY M. *Tennessee Williams*. Southern Writers Series, no. 5. Austin, Texas: Steck-Vaughan, 42 pp.

Focuses on TW's place in the "Southern Renaissance." Establishes that TW "considers the split between the Cavaliers and the Puritans to be basic to the confusion of the Southern thought pattern." Cites enough data to support her claim that "his background helps to explain many of his ideas and his techniques," and goes on to treat the fiction and plays in customary summary, theme-analysis fashion.

40 " 'Tokyo Hotel' Closes." *New York Times*, 28 May, p. 34.
Brief note on closing of *BAR* after twenty-five performances.

41 "To Williams from Mailer." New York *Daily News*, 5 June, p. 16.
News item. Norman Mailer replies to TW's assertion that Mailer's running for mayor of New York City was "ridiculous."

42 WATTS, RICHARD, JR. "Notes on Tennessee Williams." *New York Post* (31 May), p. 17.
Review of *BAR*. Comments on its failure and TW's enduring genius.

43 WEALES, GERALD. "Williams and Miller." In *The Jumping-Off Place*. London: Collier, Macmillan, Ltd., pp. 1–23.
Examines TW's work in the '60s: *PA, NI, MT, EN, SST, KE, 7D, 2CP*. These plays have in common the story of the outsider, "one of the fugitive kind," who by virtue of his nonconformity— "his artistic inclinations, his sexual proclivities, his physical defects"—becomes the victim of "an uncongenial society." In view of the direction in which TW's latest plays are moving, it is clear that despite tentative forays into such areas as the absurd (*SST, 2CP, 7D*), "Williams . . . has no intention of abandoning familiar ground." Excerpted in 1977.88.

1970

1 BARNES, CLIVE. "Theater: 'Camino Real' after 17 Years." *New York Times*, 9 January, p. 42.
Review of *CR*. Barnes agrees with judgment that *CR* is TW's best play. It's "a play that seems to have been torn out of the

human soul." This production seems a "model of clarity." Praises Pacino and Tandy among others.

2 BARRY, JACKSON G. *Dramatic Structure: The Shaping of Experience.* Berkeley and Los Angeles: University of California Press, pp. 53–55.

Uses TW's *SND* as an example of how action "introduces a number of elements which sometimes confuse the descriptions of drama's structure." In Scene 7, consideration is given to "the place of immediate action," which "forms the basis on which the dramatic image grows." Also calls attention to "the element of character" as it participates in establishing impact.

3 BERKMAN, LEONARD. "Intimate Relationships in Tennessee Williams' Plays." D.F.A. dissertation, Yale University.

Demonstrates the struggle for and failure of intimacy in TW's characters; also considers self-definition within the characters as they attempt to form intimate relationships. Considers the issue of morality as it pertains to the same point. (*DAI* 40:5249A–50A.)

4 BLACKWELDER, JAMES RAY. "The Human Extremities of Emotion in 'Cat on a Hot Tin Roof.'" *Research Studies* 38 (March):13–21.

Discusses TW's use of "'extremes' in human nature, the animal and the spiritual, to structure and unify the play." Relates this to major characters. Discusses the play's imagery; finds the resolution of the play "highly moral, almost allegorical."

5 BLACKWELL, LOUISE. "Tennessee Williams and the Predicament of Women." *South Atlantic Bulletin* 35 (March):9–14.

Discusses the misinterpretation commonly rendered to TW's handling of women as characters. Refers to four groups, "according to their situation at the time of action," and applies characters from various plays to support the categories. Reprinted in revised form: 1977.88.

6 BLITGEN, SISTER M. CAROL, B.V.M. "Tennessee Williams: Modern Idolator." *Renascence*, 22 (Summer):192–97.

"There is no doubt that Williams wants to believe in a God; he posits His existence by questioning His role and function." Cites this phenomenon in *KE, OA, SLS, NI, MT, SB*. Says his "problem is historically older, of the order of faith and can be ascribed to the Old Testament man." Also cites TW's questioning of "the minute distinction between theism and non-theistic humanism," and concludes that TW "is a theist with an Old Testament mind-set."

7 BUCKLEY, TOM. "Tennessee Williams Survives." *Atlantic* 226 (November):98, 100–108.
   Interview-commentary. TW discusses Key West, the plays in general, his working schedule, sickness, Audrey Wood, public readings, psychiatric treatment, *BAR*.

8 CALANDRA, DENIS M. "Comic Elements in the Plays of Tennessee Williams." Ph.D. dissertation, University of Nebraska.
   Analyzes the comic aspects (comic elements of character, comic satire, and technical use of comedy) in *SND*, *RT*, *NI*, *PA*, *GM*; *MT*, *SST*, and *KE* are mentioned as inferior plays. (*DAI* 31:5390A–91A.)

9 CANBY, VINCENT. "The Screen: Last of the Mobile Hot-Shots." *New York Times*, 15 January, p. 38.
   Review of film *LM*. Film based on *7D*; TW had nothing to do with it.

10 CLURMAN, HAROLD. Review of *CR*. *Nation* 210 (26 January):93–94.
   "Its faults have become more glaring" over the years. Analyzes the deficiencies of this particular revival; negative on cast, too.

11 ————. "Tennessee Williams: Poet and Puritan." *New York Times*, 29 March, sec. 2, pp. 5, 11.
   A twenty-fifth anniversary tribute for *GM*. Traces TW's career; tries to establish the TW persona; refers to significant characters in the canon; encourages the continuance of the career "which has brought distinction and honor to our stage." Reprinted: 1974.9.

12 CROWTHER, JOHN. " 'Camino Real' Sags in London Revival." New York *Morning Telegraph*, 10 January, p. 3.
   Review of *CR*, London production. Although "not among his

better plays . . . it is here being rendered aimless, unfocused and pretentious. . . . a heavy-handed revival of one of his lesser plays."

13 DRAKE, CONSTANCE M. "Six Plays by Tennessee Williams: Myth in the Modern World." Ph.D. dissertation, Ohio State University.

Examines the myths TW employs in his work, especially in *SLS, SB, NI, MT, KE,* and *OD* (which was a prototype for all the other myth-infused plays). In his use of myth, TW presents a metaphor for man's struggle to attain completeness.

14 DRIVER, TOM F. *Romantic Quest and Modern Query: A History of the Modern Theater.* New York: Delacorte, pp. 309–10, 13.

Discusses original production of *SND;* refers to TW's writing ("prose that kept turning into a kind of poetry"), the influence of Chekhov and Strindberg. "Later it became obvious that Williams' attitude toward violence was highly ambivalent."

15 FRITSCHER, JOHN J. "Popular Culture as Cyclic Phenomenon in the Evolution of Tennessee Williams." In *Challenges in American Culture.* Edited by Ray B. Browne et al. Bowling Green, Ohio: Popular Press, pp. 258–64.

Places TW at the front of the "popculture" movement. "The artist who comes out of his culture takes that culture's disparate ends, pulls them together, and in-forms (that is, gives new form) to that culture. In this doublefeed [TW]—so long *in, of* and *with* the Popular Culture—offers himself . . . to new Popcultists."

16 ————. "Some Attitudes and a Posture: Religious Metaphor and Ritual in Tennessee Williams' Query of the American God." *Modern Drama* 13 (September):201–15.

TW's philosophy is generally "as religious as the source of classical drama." Relates religious imagery and motifs to *SND, NI, CAT, MT, SLS, GM.*

17 FROST, DAVID. "Will God Talk Back to a Playwright?" In *The Americans.* New York: Stein and Day, pp. 33–55.

Interview, from Frost's TV show. TW discusses Roman Catholicism, God, prayer, insomnia, *CR* (calls it perhaps his "most personal" play), drinking, "cover[ing] the waterfront."

18   FUNKE, LEWIS. "Williams Revival? Ask the Playwright." *New York Times*, 8 January, p. 45.
     Brief interview-commentary. TW discusses his hospitalization and recovery, his feelings about his writing.

19   GILL, BRENDAN. "The Boulevard of Broken Dreams." *New Yorker* 45 (17 January):50, 52.
     Review of *CR*. "Turns out to be one of the most entertaining shows in town." Calls it "this loosely stitched-together grab bag of gothic wonders [from] . . . the purple palace of Mr. Williams' imagination." Refers to original production; discusses themes and plot details. *CR* is "the good time a man of genius can fashion for the rest of us out of his bad dreams."

20   *GM*. *Newsweek* 75 (23 February):82.
     Brief news item. $6000 paid for corrected typescript of *GM*.

21   GOULD, JACK. "TV: Tennessee Williams Twin Bill." *New York Times*, 4 December, p. 95.
     Review of *ICI* and *TTM*. TV production of these two obscure one-acters. Calls the production "a viewer's disappointment and Mr. Williams' creative problem." Finds them to be "further evidence of the playwright's stark preoccupation with troubled souls."

22   HASHIM, JAMES. "Violence in the Drama of Tennessee Williams." *Players* 45 (February–March):125–28.
     Discusses TW's "journey of violence . . . to destroy the myth of art. . . . The dramatist's superimposed veil of sexual-spiritual sublimation." Insists that one first has to understand "the archetypal structure of the Southern milieu" in order to understand the violence in TW's plays. Discusses it in Southern fiction also. And then postulates the presence of a "Southern Gothicism" in TW's work. Refers to *SLS* and *GF*.

23   HEWES, HENRY. "Errant Knightmare." *Saturday Review* 53 (24 January):24.
     Review of *CR*. "Succeeds in saying something about modern America that goes beyond any of the dialogue. . . . The current

revival...reaffirms the play's quality, but falls short of realizing it consistently."

24 HOBE. "Shows on Broadway: 'Camino Real.'" *Variety*, 14 January, p. 84.

Calls current production better than when produced seventeen years ago, but still "an over-long, unsatisfying work." TW describes (no direct quotations) his play (in a *New York Times* interview with Lewis Funke) as "presenting the dilemma of an individual caught in a fascist state."

25 HOWELL, ELMO. "The Function of the Gentleman Caller: A Note on Tennessee Williams' *Glass Menagerie*." *Notes on Mississippi Writers* 2 (Winter):83–90.

Concludes that TW's "most striking effects are derived from the ambivalence produced by a Puritan conscience and a delight in shock," and further insists that TW "frequently uses the South in his equation as symbolic of an elusive grace." From there he goes on to show the relationship between Jim and the rest of the characters, giving special emphasis to the way in which Amanda actually comes to define Jim.

26 ISAAC, DAN. "Tennessee Williams' Dream World." *New Leader* 53 (19 January):32–33.

Review of *CR*. Provides background on the play's production history, its "sources." Praises the script; negative about this revival production.

27 KERR, WALTER. "Blanche DuBois Was Here." *New York Times*, 18 January, sec. 2, pp. 1, 3.

Review of *CR*. Focuses on the dreamlike and abstract qualities of *CR*. "The one play of Tennessee Williams that must surely have come from his college trunk and belonged to the days when a Platonic idealism...occupied a young man's mind.... [*CR*] doesn't happen. The poem doesn't rise.... No true people are there, no true event takes place."

28 KROLL, JACK. "Road to Tennessee." *Newsweek* 75 (19 January):82.

Review of *CR*. "Too much verbal and philosophical gumminess." Wishes it were simpler in intent and design.

29   LEVY, VALERIE B. "Violence as Drama: A Study of the Use of Violence on the American Stage." Ph.D. dissertation, Claremont Graduate School.

Posits that the plays of TW, with their heavy emphasis on disturbed sexuality, have their roots in Jacobean drama. Further states that the traditional manifestation of violence in American drama has been cruelty through dialogue, as illustrated by the works of O'Neill, Albee, and TW. (*DAI* 31:6618A–19A.)

30   LEWIS, THEOPHILUS. Review of *CR*. *America* 122 (7 February):140–42.

TW's "most thoughtful—and probably best—play. . . . Not to be missed."

31   LYONS, LEONARD. "The Lyons Den." *New York Post*, 14 January, p. 55.

Brief news item. Al Pacino cast for lead in *CR* revival at Lincoln Center.

32   MILLER, JORDAN Y. " 'Camino Real.' " In *The Fifties: Fiction, Poetry, Drama.* Edited by Warren French. DeLand, Fla.: Everett/Edwards, pp. 241–48.

Review of *CR*. Calls the Broadway opening "a brilliant adventure into highly stylized theatrical experimentation," even though he finds the play "flawed." Compares it to "expressionistic" dramas of the thirties and forties. "Nowhere does Williams articulate his world view as graphically as in this brash and daring drive into an extremely difficult style."

33   NARDIN, JAMES T. "What Tennessee Williams Didn't Write." In *Essays in Honor of Esmond Linworth Marilla.* Edited by Thomas A. Kirby and William J. Olive. Baton Rouge: Louisiana State University Press, pp. 331–41.

Deals with TW characters who do not appear on stage but are only mentioned, in varying degrees of detail, by on-stage characters. The characters that are examined are Mr. Wingfield of *GM*; Blanche DuBois' ex-husband; Skipper from *CAT*; Sebastian in *SLS*; Serafina's tattooed husband in *RT*; Shannon's mother and Maxine's husband in *NI*.

34 OBERBECK, S.K. "Southern Discomfort." *Newsweek* 75 (26 January):75.

Review of film *LM*. Calls it an "adaptation of Tennessee Williams' pedestrian play 'The Seven Descents of Myrtle.'" Plot details; says it's a step down for Lumet.

35 "One Heart Breaking." *Time* 95 (19 January):61.

Review of *CR*. "The play is Williams' most ambitious departure from realism." Negative on production.

36 PRESLEY, DELMA EUGENE, and SINGH, HARI. "Epigraphs to the Plays of Tennessee Williams." *Notes on Mississippi Writers* 3 (Spring): 2–12.

Calls attention to the plays' epigraphs for the supposed critical insights they provide—as well as for their "clues for interpretation." Specific attention to *GM, SND, CR, NI, MT*. As example: "The epigraphs to *GM* and *SND* effectively suggest the frustration and despair surrounding those who inhabit each play." Lists the sources (cummings, H. Crane, Dante, Dickinson, Yeats), and faults only the choice of Yeats.

37 RAYNOR, HENRY. "Intimate Conversation." *Times* (London), 16 July, p. 9.

Critical analysis of TV interview of TW by David Frost, which was shown by BBC.

38 RICHARDSON, JACK. "Innocence Restaged." *Commentary* 49 (March): 20, 22, 24.

Discusses innocence as a theatrical convention and the difficulty of maintaining it. Relates Saroyan's *Time of Your Life* and *CR* to it. Claims that TW "fares better as a celebrant of the fragility of human time and tenderness of those innocents who try to use it with love and wonder." Despite textual obstacles, *CR* does get pulled together in its last moments. Says the play "makes a hard bargain with the intellect for its acceptance."

39 SCANLAN, THOMAS M. "The American Family and Family Dilemmas in American Drama." Ph.D. dissertation, University of Minnesota.

Attempts to show a pattern of value and ideology in the way
the family is portrayed in American drama. Further states that
TW and Miller have not advanced the subject of troubled families beyond ONeill's achievement. (*DAI* 32:1529A.)

40 SILVER, LEE. "'Camino Real' Revival." New York *Daily News*, 9
    January, p. 60.
        Review of *CR*. Production is "splendid." Calls the play TW's
    "ode to losers. . . . It is a clear reflection of the moods and ten-
    sions pervading today's world." Regards *CR* to have been far
    ahead of its time when originally written.

41 SIMON, JOHN. "Camino Unreal." *New York* 3 (26 January):64.
        Review of *CR*. The play is "on the borderline between roman-
    ticism and realism, escapism and hard awareness. . . . Everything
    in this play is self-indulgent and self-defeating." Referring spe-
    cifically to this revival, he adds, "Dredging up 'Camino Real' is an
    indecent act."

42 SPERO, RICHARD HENRY. "The Jungian World of Tennessee Wil-
    liams." Ph.D. dissertation, University of Wisconsin.
        Analysis of TW's work by means of Jungian psychological
    approaches. Uses this as basis for understanding the motivations
    of TW characters. *S&S*, *SND*, *CAT*, *OD*, *SLS*, and *NI* cited as
    examples. Notes that the four plays since *NI* represent unsuccess-
    ful regression to the use of earlier character types. (*DAI* 31:-
    6205A.)

43 STARNES, LELAND. "The Grotesque Children of 'Rose Tattoo.'"
    Modern Drama 12 (February):357–69.
        Discusses the basis for realism as "the convention fundamen-
    tal to the work of" TW, and traces influences upon him (empha-
    sis first on films); gives attention to language of poetry possible
    in regional characters that TW chooses. Argues that TW has been
    able to disguise "the characteristic exaggeration and distortion
    of reality which permeates his entire canon." Uses theme of exag-
    geration as prelude to the grotesque as it operates in *RT*. Cites
    critical response to the play which underscores his theory.

44 STASIO, MARILYN. "An Updated Look at Tennessee Williams' 'Fugi-
    tives.'" *Cue* 39 (7 February): 7.

"Easy Rider" motif traced back through *CR, S&S, NI, GM,* and others. Speculates on what their quest is in general terms; notes the "self-sacrifice" of TW's fugitives.

45 WASHBURN, MARTIN. Review of *CR. Village Voice,* 22 January, p. 45.
    Calls *CR* "Williams' mawkish self-regard." Brief, generally negative.

46 WATTS, RICHARD, JR. "Tragic World of the Romantics." *New York Post,* 9 January, p. 61.
    Review of *CR.* "Beautifully written . . . yet there is something pretentious, disordered and almost self-consciously obscure. . . . In the end I think it is a failure, but a noble and distinguished one." The play itself is "at its best in the production" at Lincoln Center.

47 "Williams, Playwright, to Try Hand as Actor." *New York Times,* 19 March, p. 60.
    Brief item about TWs involvement in Key West productions.

48 "Williams Writing Play during Pacific Cruise." *Variety,* 30 September, p. 57.
    Brief news item. TW on cruise to Japan and Thailand, working on new play.

1971

1 BLADES, LARRY J. "Williams, Miller and Albee: A Comparative Study." Ph.D. dissertation, St. Louis University.
   Thematic relationships among the works of the three are explored. *BA, Death of a Salesman,* and *Zoo Story* are said to be focused on sterile, repressive, and commercialized societies which have no room for superior individuals. Family, marriage and sex, guilt and atonement are all discussed in relation to *GM, S&S, SND,* and the story "Desire and the Black Masseur." (*DAI* 32:4600A.)

2 CATE, HOLLIS L., and PRESLEY, DELMA E. "Beyond Stereotype: Ambiguity in Amanda Wingfield." *Notes on Mississippi Writers* 3 (Winter):91–100.

Starts with assertion that many critics have "misinterpreted the very complex Amanda." Calls attention to TW's description of her at play's start, and contrasts general and specific critical response to show how TW is ignored. Disputes finding her basically nagging, and emphasizes her place as Mother in the drama. Finally cites her as "a tragic heroine who functions as a prismatic character."

3 CHESLER, STANLEY A. "Tennessee Williams' Literary Reputation in the U.S." Ph.D. dissertation, Kent State University.

A survey of a selection of TW criticism in an attempt to define and evaluate his literary reputation in the United States. Considers *GM, SND, CAT, SLS, NI*. Mentions growing respect recently accorded *CAT, NI*, and *SLS*. (*DAI* 32:6418A.)

4 COHN, RUBY. "The Garrulous Grotesques of Tennessee Williams." In *Dialogue in American Drama*. Bloomington: University of Indiana Press, pp. 97–129.

Contrasts TW's "own idiom" with that of Miller and O'Neill; refers to Tynan's already established distinctions. Eventually distinguishes Miller from Williams by reliance on background (Judaism as opposed to Southernism). Calls attention to TW's "focus on dialogue of pathos." Treats this theme: in *GM* (tracing, minutely, its evolution), showing its "Chekhovian" atmosphere; in *SND* (with special emphasis given to Blanche—her fantasies, preoccupations, cultural trailings); in *S&S*; in *RT*; in *CAT* (which "thrives on the life of its lies and animality"); in *SLS*; in *CR*. Discusses his "narrow ... range," and the way he compensates by "impos[ing] symbolic meaning upon his realistic surfaces." Excerpted in 1977.88.

5 DEBUSSCHER, GILBERT. "Tennessee Williams' Unicorn Broken Again." *Revue Belge de Philologie et d'Histoire* 49, no. 3:875–85.

Compares *GM* with TW's parallel short story "Portrait of a Girl in Glass." Takes issue with another critic (Pavlov), showing his shortcomings in discussing the same two works. Insists that Pavlov "approached the play with preconceived views" and thus gave it an inadequate reading, which reading it is Debusscher's intention firmly to correct.

6 DURHAM, FRANK. "Tennessee Williams: Theatre Poet in Prose." *South Atlantic Bulletin* 36 (March):3–16.
   Surveys the relative failure of American verse drama and shows how TW's *GM* is "a prime example" of poetic drama at its best. Cites his abandoning meter as in his favor, and claims TW was "consciously ushering in a new period in drama" with *GM*. Presents distinctions between having emphasis rest "not on the action itself but on a character's reaction to that action." Finally, he treats time, and how TW arrests it.

7 ERICSON, RAYMOND. "'Summer and Smoke' Bows as an Opera." *New York Times*, 25 June, p. 16.
   Mentions that opera of *S&S*, in St. Paul, closes.

8 FREEDMAN, MORRIS. *American Drama in Social Context*. Carbondale and Edwardsville: Southern Illinois University Press, pp. 79–80.
   "The plays of Tennessee Williams are dominated by an atmosphere of un-success and anti-success, which may be part of their total perverseness, a denial of the main American impulses of ambition and fulfillment." Refers to *GM* and *SND;* compares to O'Neill.

9 FUNKE, LEWIS. "One from Tennessee, One from Tom." *New York Times*, 19 December, sec. 2, pp. 3, 43.
   Discusses TW's work on (and Maine production of) "Confessional," later to be called *SCW*. TW's comments on its prospects.

10 ———. "Tennessee's Two." *New York Times*, 2 May, sec. 2, pp. 1, 24.
   Review of *2CP*. Discusses history of *2CP*—as it came to this country and especially to New York—and its relation to *OC*.

11 GILMAN, RICHARD. *Common and Uncommon Masks*. New York: Random House, pp. 140–51.
   His reviews of *NI, MT, GM, SST*. Reprints of 1962.44, 1963.22, 1965.52, 1966.15.

12 HAUPTMAN, ROBERT. "The Pathological Vision—Three Studies: Jean Genet, Louis-Ferdinand Celine, Tennessee Williams." Ph.D. dissertation, Ohio State University.

Investigates the nature and limits of pathological behavior and the relationship between pathology and evil. Concludes that whereas Genet's character demands this evil as a personal means of salvation and Celine's character observes and condemns the world's horrors, TW's characters seek and achieve actual redemption through personal involvement. (*DAI* 32:5229A.)

13 HIRSCH, FOSTER. "Sexual Imagery in Tennessee Williams' 'Kingdom of Earth.'" *Notes on Contemporary Literature* 1 (March):10–13.

Provides plot summary and theme analysis; "'Kingdom of Earth'... continues Williams' perennial investigation of various kinds of human sexuality. And it is as well the sexual imagery with which Williams builds up character and situation."

14 HOIBY, LEE. "Making Tennessee Williams Sing." *New York Times*, 13 June, sec. 2, p. 17.

S&S, opera. Discusses writing an opera from *S&S* script—emphasis on musical aspects.

15 HOLMES, ANN. "Baby, I've Come Back to Life." Houston *Chronicle*, 17 October, p. 15.

Interview-commentary. TW discusses the sixties, *CR*, his family, *OC*.

16 "Keathley Again Has Tennessee Williams Play." *Variety*, 3 March, pp. 1, 54.

George Keathley gets rights to produce premiere of *2CP*; he formerly did *SB*; *GM*'s twentieth-anniversary revival; *RT*; *CAT*.

17 KEITH, DON LEE. "Phoenix Rising from a Stoned Age?" *After Dark* 4 (August):28–37.

Interview-commentary. TW discusses his family, his background, creativity, *GM*, *CAT*, *SND*, *SB*, *SLS*.

18 MARKS, J. "Remembered Brilliance from a Suspiciously Gracious Artist." *Los Angeles Free Press*, 18 June, pp. 3, 18.

Interview-commentary. TW discusses contemporary work, his writing in general.

19 MILLER, JORDAN Y., ed. *Twentieth Century Interpretations of A Streetcar Named Desire: A Collection of Critical Essays.* Englewood Cliffs, N.J.: Prentice-Hall, 119 pp.

Miller's own introduction contains a biographical sketch of TW, and sections entitled "The Place of *Streetcar* in the Postwar Theater," "*Streetcar* as Tragedy," and "The Critical Spectrum." The twenty essays he includes are all reprints from other publications. Reprints of 1947.2, 1947.5, 1947.9, 1947.11, 1947.21, 1947.23, 1947.26, 1947.35, 1947.44, 1949.14, 1950.34, 1953.31, 1955.98, 1960.129, 1961.26 (chap. 3), 1963.39, 1963.48, 1965.11, 1966.77, 1969.4.

20 *Newsweek* 78 (20 December):55.

Brief item and photo of TW and Norman Mailer meeting.

21 POPKIN, HENRY. "Tennessee Williams Reexamined." *Arts in Virginia* 11 (Spring):2–5.

A retrospective of his career. "It is astonishing, even now, to recall the power and the energy that he possessed." Refers to TW's works as well as to significant criticism (Donahue's *The Dramatic World of Tennessee Williams* [1964.13] for example). "Williams was the next true innovator in the American Theatre after Eugene O'Neill. He found new themes and new characters, and with them he shocked the public as thoroughly as an innovator should." Focuses on his contemporaries, on the politics of the theater, and on his, then, last works (*7D* and *BAR*).

22 PRESLEY, DELMA EUGENE. "The Search for Hope in the Plays of Tennessee Williams." *Mississippi Quarterly* 25 (Winter 1971–72): 31–44.

Begins with the statement that TW's heroes all face the same three theological or philosophical problems: "isolation, the absence of God, and the reality of death." These points are analyzed in comparison to specific characters in *S&S*, *GM*, *SND*. The suggestion is made that TW has only begun to realize logical solutions to these problems with the writing of *CR*, but that the stylistic flaws in *CR* obscure the solutions. However, TW has not

yet resolved any of the aforementioned problems for his characters; he supplies false resolutions for the purposes of drama, and
uses Christian-sounding language and themes, but has failed to
grasp the logic inherent in the theological issues.

23 RECK, TOM S. "The Short Stories of Tennessee Williams: Nucleus
for his Drama." *Tennessee Studies in Literature* 16:141–54.
To understand "what has been going wrong in the past ten
years for Mr. Williams," it's proposed that readers examine TW's
fiction that later became plays. Surveys pertinent fiction criticism
and quotes TW's own statements on it. Goes on to examine the
work that influenced *SND, GM, NI, CAT, S&S, MT.* "When
[TW] is most certain about the fiction . . . the chances are better
that the resulting play will be successful."

24 REED, REX. "Tennessee Williams Turns Sixty." *Esquire* 76 (September):105–8, 216–23.
Long interview. Reed and TW wander through New Orleans
discussing health, sex, theater, drugs, TW's future writing, Brando.
Reprinted: 1974.48.

25 ROBEY, CORA. "Chloroses—Pâles Roses and Pleurosis—Blue Roses."
Romance Notes 13 (Winter):250–51.
Cites Baudelaire's poem "L'Ideal" as source for the "Blue
Roses" confusion in *GM*. Addresses the "similarity in rhyme,
image, and thematic importance of the passages."

26 SHEED, WILFRID. Reviews of *GM* and *7D*. In *The Morning After:
Selected Essays and Reviews*. New York: Farrar, Straus & Giroux,
pp. 147–53.
Reprints of 1965.55, 1968.49.

27 *Time* 97 (11 January):30.
Brief gossip item. TW arrives in San Francisco on SS President
Wilson from three-month cruise; says he has just completed his
last long play, "a tragedy with humor about alienation."

1972

1   BARNES, CLIVE. "Rays of Spring Sunshine." *Times* (London), 13 May, p. 10.

Discusses television, music and theater in America. Considers Arthur Miller and TW to be America's current best. Comments on *CR* and synopsis of *SCW*. Recommends the latter.

2   ————. "Small Craft Warnings." *Times* (London), 6 April, p. 10.

Review of *SCW*. Synopsis and positive response to New York City production; compares TW's work with O'Neill's.

3   ————. "Stage: Williams Accepting Life as Is." *New York Times*, 3 April, p. 50.

Review of *SCW*. "The characters are not remarkable, although not uninteresting.... almost a dramatic essay rather than a play.... The acting did the play credit."

4   "BARTON, LEE." "Why Do Homosexual Playwrights Hide Their Homosexuality?" *New York Times*, 23 January, sec. 2, pp. 1, 3.

"Who really gives a damn that TW has finally admitted his sexual preferences in print?" Argues that it would be a greater contribution to theater in general, and gay theater in particular, if there were more plays dealing with homosexual relations than homosexual playwrights committed to "breast beating personal confessions." The author's name is, as noted, in quotes—in the article he admits the name is false.

5   BELL, ARTHUR. " 'I've Never Faked It.' " *Village Voice*, 24 February, pp. 58, 60, 62.

Interview-commentary prior to opening of *SCW*. TW discusses Rex Reed's *Esquire* article, homosexuality, his favorite plays, his health. Reprinted: 1978.23.

6   BUCKLEY, LEONARD. " 'Summer and Smoke.' " *Times* (London), 24 January, p. 15.

Review of *S&S*, British TV production. Positive response, brief.

7   CLURMAN, HAROLD. Review of *SCW*. *Nation* 214 (24 April):540–41.

Calls it an "old" play; says it reverts to old TW themes and devices. Compares to *GF* and *BAR*.

8 COSTELLO, DONALD P. "Tennessee Williams' 'Fugitive Kind.'" *Modern Drama* 15 (May):26–43.

   FK, "produced precisely in the middle of the career of Tennessee Williams,... provides us with a vocabulary for an interpretation" of the entire canon. Analyzes its merits as quintessential TW: its technique, its setting, its themes. Refers to "corruption" as a word, theme, and motif, as related to others of his plays; notion of a fugitive as integral to his plays; water symbolism; fire (as purification device); artistic vision; nonearthly symbols; his hero concept. Reprinted in abridged form: 1977.88.

9 Drama Mailbag: "Is 'Lee Barton' Copping Out?" *New York Times*, 13 February, sec. 2, p. 5.

   Letter to the editor: six replies to "Lee Barton," criticizing him for his pseudonymous attack on TW, on 23 January.

10 EFSTATE, ILEANA. "Tennessee Williams—a Few Considerations on *A Streetcar Named Desire.*" *Analele Universitatii Bueuresti, Limbi Germanice* 21:107–13.

   Analyzes briefly TW's contribution "to the development of American drama." Discusses his "main preoccupations," his use of romantic characters, the presence of animality and primitivism in his work, his attempts at assuring clarity in his work. Particular focus is *SND*.

11 EVANS, OLIVER. "A Pleasant Evening with Yukio Mishima." *Esquire* 77 (May):126–31, 174, 177–80.

   After Mishima's suicide, a detailing of TW and Mishima in New York City and their relationship and conversations.

12 FAYARD, JEANNE. *Tennessee Williams.* Paris: Éditions Seghers, 189 pp.

   Analysis of motifs and themes in TW's canon. Treats issue of "exorcism" in the plays, his use of New Orleans; quotes from TW's introductions; surveys and quotes from English and French language criticism. In French.

13 FLEMMING, WILLIAM P., JR. "Tragedy in American Drama: The Tragic Views of Eugene O'Neill, Tennessee Williams, Arthur

Miller, and Edward Albee." Ph.D. dissertation, University of Toledo.

Examines how the four playwrights use aspects of tragedy in their work. There are seven traits listed here that characterize American tragedy. TW's tragic figures are those who are hiding from their truth and stop hiding to confront their truth. (*DAI* 33:308A).

14 FUNKE, LEWIS. "Tennessee's 'Cry.' " *New York Times*, 3 December, sec. 2, pp. 1, 27.

Prepremiere piece discussing *OC*. Refers to its themes and TW's supposed intents. Also discusses *SND*. This article published on *SND*'s twenty-fifth anniversary.

15 GAINES, JIM. "A Talk about Life and Style with Tennessee Williams." *Saturday Review* 55 (29 April):25–29.

Interview in Key West, three weeks prior to *SCW*'s opening. TW discusses his life style; writing; character-making; big successes such as *SND* and *CAT*; writing power related to sexual power; psychoanalysis; his dreams.

16 GLOVER, WILLIAM. "Tennessee Williams: Outraged Puritan." *International Herald Tribune*, 10 May, p. 16.

Interview-commentary. TW discusses his "crack-up," *SCW*, his mother, Roman Catholicism, *OC*, *GM*.

17 GUSSOW, MEL. "Williams Looking to Play's Opening." *New York Times*, 31 March, p. 10.

Interview-commentary. TW discusses upcoming off-Broadway premiere of *SCW*; the history of the play; his reflections on the new venture.

18 HARRIS, RADIE. "Broadway Ballyhoo." *Hollywood Reporter*, 4 January, p. 4.

Brief item discussing relation of "Nightride," by Lee Barton, to TW's life; also reports on TW's comments on it.

19 ———. "Broadway Ballyhoo." *Hollywood Reporter*, 18 April, p. 4.

Brief news item. TW making CBS (and BBC) special, "Tennessee Williams' South," and writing his autobiography.

20 ————. "Broadway Ballyhoo." *Hollywood Reporter*, 13 June, p. 4.
News item. TW in *SCW*, and his talking to audience.

21 HEWES, HENRY. "The Deathday Party." *Saturday Review* 55 (22
April):22, 24.
Review of *SCW*. Refers to its original title, *Confessional*; it's
"less a play than it is a series of personal self-revelations offered
by seven of the play's nine characters." Plot details. Mentions
TW's "sublime" writing.

22 HUGHES, CATHARINE. "Retreading the Past." *America* 126 (29
April):462.
Review of *SCW*. "Has flickers of the same poetry and much of
the same compassion that made him . . . the most important
American dramatist to emerge since O'Neill. . . . At its best, the
play has considerable poignance and poetic eloquence; at its
worst, it is banal, sentimental and tedious, attenuated to a point
that tries the patience."

23 IACHETTA, MICHAEL. "Tennessee Williams: A Playwright Rejuve-
nated." New York *Sunday News*, 1 October, sec. 3, pp. 1, 28.
Interview-commentary. TW discusses coming out of alcohol,
drugs and "despair"; Key West; *SCW*; *OC*, which he considers
his most important play since *NI*; happiness and "the abyss"; his
memoirs.

24 KALEM, T.E. "Clinging to a Spar." *Time* 99 (17 April):72–73.
Review of *SCW*. Not "on a par with the durable canon of his
finest plays. . . . a five finger exercise from the man who is the
greatest living playwright in the Western world."

25 KAUFFMANN, STANLEY. Review of *SCW*. *New Republic* 166 (29
April):24.
Brief. Laments the deteriorated state of TW's work; calls *SCW*
"a vapid play." Reprinted: 1976:36.

26 KERR, WALTER. "Talkers, Drinkers and Losers." *New York Times*,
16 April, sec. 2, pp. 8, 29.
Review of *SCW*. Discusses its structure; "Mr. Williams' gift for
knowing how people think, feel, and speak reasserts itself at

least enough to keep us firmly attentive." In the play's second half, TW "let himself go on too long."

27 KITSES, JIM. "Elia Kazan: A Structural Analysis." *Cinema* (Los Angeles) 7 (Winter):25–36.
Surveys twenty-five-year history of Kazan's work. Refers to *SND* and *BD* as showing influence of their own time: in both "there is an absence of ethical perspective in the attack by thrusting young immigrants on pitiful figures who represent a bankrupt American past." Also claims that in both, "the ethical balance of Williams' dramas is undercut by Kazan's fascination with the resources of Brando and Wallach characters."

28 LITTLE, STUART W. " 'Summer and Smoke.' " In *Off-Broadway: The Prophetic Theater*. New York: Coward, McCann & Geoghegan, pp. 13–27.
Begins with observation: "Off-Broadway, for historical purposes, may be said to have begun in Sheridan Square on the evening of April 24, 1952, when [S&S] with Geraldine Page opened at Circle-in-the-Square and became the first major theatrical success below Forty-second Street in thirty years." Talks about opening night, Quintero, S&S's future on Broadway.

29 LYONS, LEONARD. "The Lyons Den." *New York Post*, 29 April, p. 27.
Brief news item. TW going to Academy Awards.

30 MCMORROW, TOM. "Author Takes Stage." New York *Daily News*, 8 June, p. 116.
Brief item. TW appearing in *SCW* and answering audience questions afterward.

31 MADD. "Off-Broadway Reviews." *Variety*, 12 April, p. 98.
Review of *SCW*. It "lacks the sweep, power and complexity of Williams' major works." But claims it's "an affecting 'small' play. . . . [It] does lean toward talkiness."

32 "Migration." *New York Times*, 2 June, p. 24.
Brief note on *SCW* moving uptown.

33   MISHOE, BILLY. "Time as Antagonist in the Dramas of Tennessee Williams." Ph.D. dissertation, Florida State University.

Attempts to show the idea of time-as-antagonist as central to TW's dramaturgy. A cycle of rebirth is identical (although completed only in *RT* and *CR*) in his works; this cycle of rebirth is made available to those who seek to conquer time through endurance, acceptance, understanding, and compassion. (*DAI* 33:2944A–45A.)

34   MURRAY, EDWARD. "Tennessee Williams—after 'The Celluloid Brassiere.'" In *The Cinematic Imagination*. New York: Ungar, pp. 46–67.

Starts with biographical data on TW's affinity for movies and quotes from Tom's speech on same topic in *GM*; goes on to show how TW "was soon to be disillusioned about the ways of Hollywood," and how *GM* itself grew out of abortive script work there. Claims that TW's interest in movies influenced his plays, and that his attitude toward movies "represents a mixture of childish fascination, smug condescension, and financial dependence." Traces influence in *GM*, *SB*, *SND*, et al. Discusses cinematography as well as composition, and calls attention to adaptation of the plays to film. Stops with *NI*.

35   "New Role, Not Career for Tennessee Williams." *New York Post*, 7 June, p. 60.

Brief note. TW appearing in *SCW*; his own quoted comments on it.

36   "New Williams Play Due." *New York Times*, 7 March, p. 45.

Brief item announcing arrival of *SCW* for off-Broadway premiere (2 April).

37   "Off Stage." *Village Voice*, 6 April, p. 60.

Brief negative reference to *SCW*.

38   O'HAIRE, PATRICIA. "An Old Williams Play Surfaces and So Does He." New York *Sunday News*, 2 April, p. 25.

On *SCW*, but not a review. Comments on TW at the rehearsals; TW didn't know why it hadn't been produced years before; it was originally titled *Confessional*.

39 OLIVER, EDITH. "How They Feel." *New Yorker* 48 (15 April):110.
Review of *SCW*. "The liveliest and most controlled play that Tennessee Williams has written in years." But it "should be considered work in progress."

40 PARKER, JERRY. "*Tennessee.*" *Newsday*, 15 October, part II, pp. 4, 5, 26, 27.
Interview-commentary. TW discusses politics, Yevtushenko, his childhood, *SCW*, *SND*, off-Broadway play "Nightride," how he wants to be remembered.

41 PERRIER, RONALD GORDON. "A Study of the Dramatic Works of Tennessee Williams from 1963 to 1971." Ph.D. dissertation, University of Minnesota.
Studies TW's work in this period with a view to the allegorical tendencies of these plays. Also examines the emergence of the toughened artist figure. Specific plays discussed: *MT, SST, KE, BAR, 2CP.* (*DAI* 33:1879A.)

42 "Playwright Series." *Village Voice*, 2 March, p. 1.
Brief news item. TW will be included in series called "Conversations with Playwrights," in New York City, presented by the 92nd Street YM-YWHA.

43 PRESLEY, DELMA EUGENE. "The Moral Function of Distortion in Southern Grotesque." *South Atlantic Bulletin* 37 (May):37–46.
Surveys the treatment of the "grotesque" in southern literature, showing the prevalence of treating it as a cultural or philosophical issue—eventually coming to Flannery O'Connor's criterion, "distortion." With TW, he claims his story, "Desire and the Black Masseur," is "the earliest and clearest example of his grotesque vision." Explores the possibilities also in *SLS, SND, NI,* and *MT.*

44 PROBST, LEONARD. "Tennessee Williams: The Shirley Temple of Modern Letters." *Village Voice*, 13 April, p. 64.
Interview-commentary. TW discusses his breakdown, "Clockwork Orange," the intolerability of a fully conscious existence, his physicians, drugs, violence in entertainment, *SCW*.

45 ROREM, NED. "Smoke without Fire." *New Republic* 166 (8 April):19.
Review of opera of *S&S*. Brief, negative.

46 SCHONBERG, HAROLD C. " 'Summer and Smoke' at City Opera." *New York Times*, 21 March, p. 34.
    Review of opera of *S&S*. "Everything was a success but the music."

47 *SCW*. New York *Daily News*, 6 June, p. 52.
    Brief item on TW appearing in *SCW*; photo.

48 *SCW*. *Village Voice*, 22 June, p. 55.
    Brief note on TW's acting debut in *SCW*.

49 SIMON, JOHN. Review of *SCW*. *New York* 5 (17 April):84.
    SCW is "the work of a man out of touch with the changing world, yet unable or unwilling to write honestly out of the depths of his true, immutable self." It is a "feeble self-parody, a dilution of his former glories." Reprinted: 1975.45.

50 SMITH, MICHAEL. Review of *SCW*. *Village Voice*, 6 April, p. 61.
    There's "no good news to report about Tennessee Williams' new play," *SCW*. It contains "shades of O'Neill, Saroyan, and old man Hemingway." *SCW* is "without drama."

51 *SND*. *On the Scene* (Hartford), (November-December).
    Entire journal devoted to twenty-fifth anniversary of *SND*. Reprints of original New York City reviews; comments from TW; excerpts from Kazan's notebook; photos.

52 STANGER, ILA. "Peter O'Toole Talks and Talks." *Harper's Bazaar* 106 (December): 92–93, 121.
    Interview with O'Toole in which he discusses TW; refers to *SCW*. "Tennessee Williams is the finest writer of English alive."

53 STEPHENS, SUZANNE SCHADDELEE. "The Dual Influence: A Dramatic Study of the Plays of Edward Albee and the Specific Dramatic Forms and Themes Which Influenced Them." Ph.D. dissertation, University of Miami.
    Within the context of an analysis of Albee's dramatic conventions, TW's plays are analyzed "in an attempt to establish those concepts and devices used by playwrights writing in the realist-expressionist tradition." (*DAI* 34:342A.)

54 "Tennessee Williams Acting in 'Warnings.'" *Variety*, 7 June, pp. 1, 60.

Brief announcement of TW substituting in role of doctor.

55 TISCHLER, NANCY M. "The Distorted Mirror: Tennessee Williams' Self-Portraits." *Mississippi Quarterly* 25 (Fall):389–403.

Discusses the continuing failure of *BA* in all its many guises, arguing that TW's "talent is apparently sufficiently unconscious that he cannot see why his story sometimes succeeds and sometimes fails." The point is taken that *BA* was the matrix from which *GM* and *SND* were created. *BA* and *CR*, as plays arising from TW's *art*, are contrasted to *GM* and *SND*, plays arising from TW's *nature*; in essence: "When he reveals his truth rather than pronouncing it . . . feeling it rather than thinking it, he is a powerful playwright." Reprinted: 1977.88.

56 TOPOR, TOM. "The New Tennessee Williams Retains the Old Mastery." *New York Post*, 22 March, p. 8.

Interview-commentary, on occasion of TW's 61st birthday. TW discusses his work, his health, *OC*, *SCW*.

57 WASSERMAN, DEBBI. Review of *SCW*. *Show Business* 11 (7 September):11.

"Not a play, but a series of vignettes. . . . [It] never really establish[es] a theme . . . a watchable play."

58 WATT, DOUGLAS. "A New Play by Williams Opens." New York *Daily News*, 3 April, p. 52.

Review of *SCW*. Calls it "a tired effort . . . a pretty sorry play, warmed-over Williams. . . . dangerously close to being a parody of himself."

59 WATTS, RICHARD, JR. "Evening in a California Bar." *New York Post*, 3 April, p. 23.

Review of *SCW*. The play contains "some of his characteristic eloquent writing and compassionate portraits. . . . [But it] suffers from lack of any central drive in its narrative." Compares *SCW* to Saroyan's *The Time of Your Life*.

60 WEALES, GERALD. Review of *SCW*. *Commonweal* 96 (5 May):214–16.

Brief, mainly negative. Primarily focusing on SCW's repeating old TW themes.

61   WEISMAN, JOHN. "Sweet Bird of Youth at 60." *Tropic*, 20 February, pp. 28–30.
Interview-commentary. TW discusses decadence, youth, his agent, Rex Reed, homosexuality, other writers.

62   ———. "Tennessee Williams 'Turns On' with Youth." *Philadelphia Inquirer*, 30 January, sec. G, pp. 1, 5.
Interview-commentary. TW discusses being decadent; youth; antiwar activities; his agent; breast cancer; psychiatry; writing in America.

63   "Williams Gets Theater Award." *New York Times*, 8 December, p. 33.
National Theater Conference honors TW for his contributions to American theater.

64   "Williams Joins His 'Small Craft.'" *New York Post*, 6 June, p. 65.
Brief news item. TW appearing in cast of SCW.

65   "Williams to Take Role." *New York Times*, 6 June, p. 48.
Brief item. TW to make acting debut in SCW.

1973

1   ADAMS, VAL. "Kate in 'Glass Menagerie.'" New York *Daily News*, 11 April, p. 48.
Advance notice of ABC production of GM, with Katharine Hepburn.

2   "Add 'Menagerie' to London Film Festival." *Variety*, 26 December, p. 21.
Brief mention of TV production being entered in London Film Festival.

3   ADLER, THOMAS P. "The Search for God in the Plays of Tennessee Williams." *Renascence* 26 (Autumn):48–56.

Traces the "God of Wrath" and "God of Love" motifs in the plays and TW's own definition of Hell. Adds attention to elements of disgust, rejection, obsession with evil, eternity, regeneration, vengeance, mercy—all as they pertain to the God-search in particular plays. Refers to *SND*, *SLS*, *S&S*, *NI*, and *LLL*. Reprinted: 1977.88.

4 ATKINSON, BROOKS, and HIRSCHFELD, ALBERT. *The Lively Years, 1920–1973*. New York: Associated Press, pp. 191–94, 227–31.
    Brief analysis of plot, theme, and worth of *SND* ("although the play represents the antiromantic attitude towards life, it is never hostile or censorious") and *CR* ("In 1953 [TW] wrote a beautiful play about a hideous subject . . . it had only sixty performances because audiences found it repellent")—plus plates of Hirschfeld's illustrations.

5 BARNES, CLIVE. "Stage: A Rare 'Streetcar.'" *New York Times*, 27 April, p. 31.
    Review of *SND*. "New and very persuasive 'Streetcar.'" The production is "fresh" but respectful of the play's history.

6 ―――. "Stage: A Static 'Out Cry.'" *New York Times*, 2 March, p. 18.
    Review of *OC*. "Deliberately static. . . . a play with a chance of ultimate survival. . . . Williams' writing is not always graceful. . . . a very brave and very difficult play."

7 ―――. "Stage: Subtle 'Streetcar.'" *New York Times*, 5 October, p. 19.
    Review of *SND*. "A very moving performance, low-keyed and almost stealthily effective." Praises Nettleton's Blanche in this Broadway revival production.

8 BEASLEY, HENRY R. "An Interpretive Study of the Religious Element in the Work of Tennessee Williams." Ph.D. dissertation, Louisiana State University.
    Beginning with *BA*, covers religious themes in TW's plays. *BA* and *OD*, *SLS*, *SB*, *NI*, *MT*, *BAR* are analyzed in an attempt to synthesize the Christian and Oriental religious thought that is said here to present itself. Taken as a whole, TW's work indi-

cates progress toward a set of philosophic conclusions that are religious in nature. (*DAI* 34:5954A–55A.)

9 BERKOWITZ, GERALD M. "The 'Other World' of *The Glass Menagerie*." *Players* 48 (April–May):150–53.
   Emphasizes the giving of "a definite *locus*" to the play and "the persistence of memory" as an element in its shaping. Also illustrates the effects of such a device ("we discover each aberration or peculiarity in [the Wingfields'] characters"); shows the influence on the work's sense of tragedy, and the creating of a timeliness dimension.

10 BOK. Review of TV production of *GM*. *Variety*, 19 December, p. 28.
    "Memorable" performance; Hepburn makes it worthwhile; praises production tactics.

11 BROCKETT, OSCAR G., and FINDLAY, ROBERT R. *Century of Innovation: A History of European and American Theatre and Drama Since 1870*. Englewood Cliffs, N.J.: Prentice-Hall, pp. 568–70.
    Brief reference to TW. Compares to Miller. Surveys the history of the canon. "In some ways, *The Glass Menagerie* sums up the major modern experiments in drama. . . . Williams relies rather heavily on antithesis to divide his characters into the sensitive and the complacent."

12 BRUSTEIN, ROBERT. "Portrait of a Warning." *New Republic* 168 (17 March):23.
    Review of *SCW*, London production. Finds play disappointing; its "moments of magic" are "to diffuse. . . . [TW] seems to have fallen too deeply in love with the idea of desperation."

13 CAMPBELL, MICHAEL L. "The Theme of Persecution in Tennessee Williams' 'Camino Real.'" *Notes on Mississippi Writers* 6 (Fall): 35–40.
    Opens with premise that TW "has divided his characters into two groups: the sensitive misfits and the tough realists," and concludes that TW believes "that the ultimate destructive force is life itself," and from that goes on to assert that TW thus manages to avoid "diatribe." Claims *CR* "is one of Williams' clearest statements of this favorite theme," and that "Williams is imply-

ing that repressive persecution by human beings is merely a
symbol for the more subtle cruelties inflicted upon us by life
itself." Examines the play's scope of hope, fate, "mutual persecution."

14 CLURMAN, HAROLD. Review of *OC*. *Nation* 216 (19 March):380.
    Discusses themes and motivation in the play. Hopes TW will
    end this confessional guise and turn his vision "outward again."
    OC "is essentially a soliloquy"—with each character becoming a
    part of TW himself.

15 ————. Review of *SND*. *Nation* 216 (14 May):635–36.
    Re-praises the play itself, lavishly; launches defense of Blanche
    over Stanley; praises the production and acting of this particular
    revival.

16 "Critics' Circle Award." Los Angeles *Herald-Examiner*, 22 March,
    sec. B, p. 1.
    Brief news item at time of Los Angeles revival of *SND*. TW
    being honored at luncheon; TW comments on *SND*, *SCW*, *OC*.

17 "Drama Mailbag." *New York Times*, 8 April, sec. 2, p. 6.
    Letter to the editor expressing outrage that *OC* closed after
    only thirteen performances.

18 FARBER, STEPHEN. "Blanche Wins the Battle." *New York Times*,
    1 April, sec. 2, pp. 1, 15.
    Review of *SND*, Los Angeles production. Calls this revival
    "respectful, cautious, traditional and straightforward ... [with]
    very little genuine artistry." Suspects the production is closer to
    TW's original intentions. TW "comes through virtually un-
    scathed."

19 FAWKES, SANDY. "Still Laughing—though Love Has Passed Him
    by." *Daily Express* (London), 15 August, p. 8.
    Interview-commentary. TW discusses drinking, his background,
    Roman Catholicism, companionship, need for good directors.

20 GARDELLA, KAY. "Hepburn Picks 'Menagerie' for T.V. Bow." New
    York *Sunday News*, 9 December, sec. 3, p. 19.

Primarily focuses on Katharine Hepburn, relative to her role as Amanda in upcoming ABC production of *GM*.

21   ————. "Katie Did It Again." New York *Daily News*, 14 December, p. 114.
      Advance praise for Katharine Hepburn in ABC's production of *GM*.

22   GILL, BRENDAN. "Happy Birthday." *New Yorker* 49 (5 May):81.
      Review of *SND*. An "able and affecting revival.... It remains remarkably unaging.... The present production of 'Streetcar' is not merely a worthy successor to the original but an illuminating companion to it."

23   ————. Review of *OC*. *New Yorker* 49 (10 March):104.
      Brief. TW is "writing about himself.... How empty I find his 'Out Cry.'... It is an exercise in dramatic composition but not a play.... I was bored to the point of indignation."

24   *GM*. *New York Post*, 18 December, p. 75.
      Brief mention of Katharine Hepburn in the upcoming ABC production of *GM*.

25   "The Great Survivor." *Sunday Times* (London), 28 January, p. 32.
      Gossip piece. Anecdotes and quotes by TW.

26   GUSSOW, MEL. "Catharsis for Tennessee Williams?" *New York Times*, 11 March, sec. 2, pp. 1, 5.
      Review of *OC*. Attempts to analyze its properties and problems. "The play is never as interesting as it sounds.... The best thing about [*OC*] is the quality of the playwright, here working in an adventurous, Pirandellian vein." Finds the play "rewritten to the point of metamorphosis."

27   ————. New Life for 'Cat on a Hot Tin Roof.'" *New York Times*, 12 November, p. 50.
      Review of *CAT*, Boston production. Discusses play's history of textual changes as well as this production's problems ("mostly in the casting"). "The play survives ... mightily."

28 HAYMAN, RONALD. "Frances de la Tour." *Times* (London), 10 March, p. 11.
   Refers briefly to *SCW* in an article about de la Tour.

29 HEILMAN, ROBERT B. *The Iceman, The Arsonist and the Troubled Agent: Tragedy and Melodrama on the Modern Stage.* Seattle: University of Washington Press, pp. 115–41.
   Reprint of 1965.24.

30 HENENBERG, ROSEMARY ELAINE. "The Psychomachian Dilemma in the Middle Ages and in the Twentieth Century in 'Camino Real' by Tennessee Williams and in Paintings by Max Beckman." Ph.D. dissertation, Ohio University.
   Attempts to "establish the pattern of the medieval mode of spiritual allegory, the psychomachia," and to place *CR* and Max Beckmann's paintings within the context of that pattern. Concludes that these works of art reveal, as their ultimate concern, the attempt to reconcile into wholeness the fragments of man as he is confronted with the loss of his beliefs. (*DAI* 34:5834A.)

31 HIGHAM, CHARLES. "Private and Proud and Hepburn." *New York Times*, 9 December, sec. 2, pp. 3, 21.
   Katharine Hepburn interview. She discusses *GM*: "Amanda is the most *accessible* woman he [TW] ever created."

32 HIRSCH, FOSTER. "The World Still Desires 'A Streetcar.'" *New York Times*, 15 April, sec. 2, pp. 1, 3.
   Commentary on *SND* in advance of its revival premiere. *SND* in TW's "fullest play, the canon's one undoubted masterpiece, and a serious contender for the best American play ever written." Analyzes its characters and staying powers, its morality; focuses on Blanche.

33 HOBE. "Shows on Broadway." *Variety*, 7 March, p. 70.
   Review of *OC*. "A beautiful, baffling play." Calls it "this poetic, anguished work." Warns that "for the literal-minded, [the play] may seem talky and pointless."

34 ———. "Shows on Broadway." *Variety*, 2 May, p. 66.
   Review of *SND*. "A superb revival." Production is "thoroughly professional and tasteful." Praises Farentino and Rabb.

35 HOBSON, HAROLD. "A Craft in Difficulties." *Sunday Times* (London), 4 February, p. 36.
Brief review of *SCW*, London production. Mixed review; calls the writing "repetitive."

36 HUGHES, CATHARINE. "The Good with the Bad." *America* 128 (17 March):242.
Review of *OC*. It "regrettably invites" negative critical response; by second act, it's "so dull as to be almost deadening." Plot details; praises cast.

37 ————. "Playing with the Past." *America* 128 (26 May):495.
Review of *SND*. "Ellis Rabb's production is a good one though not without problems." Gives details on cast and individual performances for this revival production.

38 JACOBS, JODY. " 'Streetcar': It's a Cause for Celebration." Los Angeles *Times*, 22 March, sec. IV, pp. 4, 15.
Review of *SND*, Los Angeles production. Positive review of this revival; praises cast.

39 JENNINGS, C. ROBERT. "Playboy Interview: Tennessee Williams." *Playboy* 20 (April): 69–84.
Interview-commentary. TW discusses impotence; luxury; the sixties; *SCW*; the androgynous; homosexuality; *CR*; reviews and reviewers; friends; Bill Barnes—Audrey Wood; *OC*; women in his life; Beautiful People; his "greatest gifts."

40 JOHNSTON, LAURIE. "Tennessee Williams Receives Centennial Medal of Cathedral Church of St. John the Divine." *New York Times*, 10 December, p. 13.
News article on event; first centennial medal conferred.

41 JONES, MARVENE. "The VIP's." *Hollywood Reporter*, 23 March, p. 4.
Brief item about TW and his response to Los Angeles revival of *SND*.

42 KAEL, PAULINE. "Survivor." *New Yorker* 49 (31 December):50.
Brief review of TV production of *GM*. The director "obviously had no grasp of the comedy or vitality in the Tennessee Williams material."

43 KALEM, T.E. "Beast v. Beauty." *Time* 101 (7 May):88, 90.
Review of *SND. SND* is "25 years old, and . . . ranks first among all plays written anywhere during that time. . . . Like all great works of art, it has been internalized. It is part of our sensitivity." The revival production though is "slightly but naggingly off balance."

44 ———. "The Crack-Up." *Time* 101 (12 March):89.
Review of *OC*. It "is devoid of [TW's] gifts." Finds "a Williams groping for words, parched for images, fumbling in dramatic craft—all these seem incredible, but alas, it is true."

45 KALSON, ALBERT E. "Tennessee Williams Enters 'Dragon Country.'" *Modern Drama* 16 (June):61–73.
Discusses TW's "continuing preoccupation with the relationship and interdependence of life and art." Refers to TW's early assumption that he "knew all the answers," and traces his maturing beyond that through *IR, BAR, KE*. Notes "the growing bleakness of Williams' negative vision," and the aspects most haunting and persistent in "the private Williams world."

46 "Katharine Hepburn to Make TV Debut." *New York Times*, 20 June, p. 82.
Brief announcement of Hepburn playing Amanda in *GM*, upcoming TV version.

47 KAUFFMANN, STANLEY. Review of *OC*. *New Republic* 168 (24 March):22.
"The most grievous disappointment is in the writing and in the roles as theatrical entities." Refers to watching TW's "sad descent." Play is "a bore." Reprinted: 1976.36.

48 KAZAN, ELIA. "Tennessee Williams and the South: *A Streetcar Named Desire* (1950), *Baby Doll* (1956)," In *Kazan on Kazan*. Cinema One Series. Edited by Michel Ciment. London: Secker & Warburg, pp. 35, 45, 47, 66–82.
Kazan discusses making films of *SND* and *BD*. "I feel closer to Williams personally than to any other playwright I've worked with. Possibly it's the nature of his talent—it's so vulnerable, so naked. . . . The strength of *Streetcar* is its compassion. . . . I think

the end of the stage play is better than the end of the film. . . .
In [BD] there is the dark, fertile outsider who is brought into
a dead area and will rejuvenate it. . . . I like the film [BD] better than the film [SND] and the reason is, it's more ambivalent."

49 KERR, WALTER. "Of Blanche the Victim—and other 'Women.'" *New
York Times*, 6 May, sec. D, pp. 1, 10.
    Review of *SND*. Considers it "the finest single work yet cre-
ated for the American theater." Focuses on Blanche and Rosemary Harris' interpretation.

50 KING, THOMAS L. "Irony and Distance in 'The Glass Menagerie.'"
Educational Theatre Journal 25 (May):207–14.
    Begins with premise that *GM* is often "distorted, if not mis-
understood" because of "overemphasis of scenes involving Laura
and Amanda." Cites consequent lack of attention to Tom's soliloquies. Traces the distortion back to the play's original production. Quotes from and surveys early criticism. Maintains "the
play is Tom's," and discusses the "meaning" of the play in light
of that assertion. Thorough analysis of Tom's soliloquies.

51 KROLL, JACK. "Battle of New Orleans." *Newsweek* 81 (7 May):
109–10.
    Review of *SND*. Refers to Blanche and Stanley as "archetypal
figures, as real as our dreams, nightmares and desires." In TW,
"a profound puritanism warred with a fierce sensuality." Blanche
and Stanley are "perfect objective correlatives" for his own
opposites.

52 ————. "Prisoners' Base." *Newsweek* 81 (12 March):88.
    Review of *OC*. It "is in every respect a disaster . . . a stale
Pirandellicatessen." TW "has turned a theater into a prison for
audiences."

53 "The Lady of Larkspur Lotion and Bird Food." *Show Business* 12
(25 October):8.
    Brief. A bit of plot summary and acting data.

54 LEES, DANIEL E. "'The Glass Menagerie': A Black Cinderella."
Unisa English Studies 11 (March):30–34.

Cites TW's reference to the Cinderella story as "our favorite national myth," and goes on to characterize *GM* as "an indictment of the myth." Claims TW is using the myth "eclectically." Demonstrates several examples of the "inversion of the myth," and shows the "altered treatment" given symbolically.

55 LONGO, CHRIS. "A 'Diaphanous Afternoon' with Tennessee Williams." *Los Angeles Free Press*, 30 March, p. 18.
Report on the USC luncheon in TW's honor at time of *SND's* Los Angeles revival. TW speaks in "free form panel" on critics, competition, the theater.

56 LOYND, RAY. "Faye Dunaway as Williams' Blanche DuBois." Los Angeles *Herald-Examiner*, 18 March, sec. G, p. 1.
Discusses Dunaway's interpretation in the Los Angeles revival of *SND*. Also focuses on TW's rewrites, his current productions, his work-in-progress.

57 ————. "Voight, Dunaway Star in 'A Streetcar Named Desire.'" Los Angeles *Herald-Examiner*, 21 March, sec. D, p. 2.
Review of *SND*, Los Angeles production. Generally positive; refers to change in way Stanley is portrayed.

58 MEAD, MIMI. "Katharine Hepburn's First TV Role Is in 'The Glass Menagerie.'" *Christian Science Monitor*, 14 December, p. 24.
Synopsis of the play and announcement of Hepburn's part in it; more focus on her than on the play.

59 MOOD, JOHN J. "The Structure of *A Streetcar Named Desire*." *Ball State University Forum* 14 (Summer):9–10.
Takes Blanche's entrance speech in *SND* and claims, for the first time, to examine it as "a clue to the structural development and design of the play itself." Details of analysis include Blanche's ultimate fate.

60 NIGHTINGALE, BENEDICT. "Down at Monk's Place." *New Statesman* 85 (9 February):208–9.
Review of *SCW*, London production. "Often sounds as if it was written amid stained glasses and reeking butts at or around midnight.... It is, in effect, two hours of confession.... Every-

thing and everyone in this play bears Williams' own inimitable brand." Refers to "the moral torpor at the play's boosy, tearful centre."

61 NOVICK, JULIUS. "Honest or Merely Disarming?" *Village Voice*, 8 March, p. 58.
    Review of *OC*. "An annoying, pretentious, slightly maudlin piece of work, but I found it impossible to dismiss it entirely; there is something haunting about it. . . . [It's] a repetitive, ever insistent piece of work."

62 ————. "A Token of Love for Blanche." *Village Voice*, 3 May, pp. 68, 86.
    Review of *SND*. Focuses mainly on Blanche-interpretation in this revival and praises Rosemary Harris.

63 O'CONNOR, JOHN J. "TV: Williams' Haunting 'Menagerie.'" *New York Times*, 14 December, p. 94.
    Review of *GM*, TV production. Focuses on Katharine Hepburn's performance; mentions past productions and the minor problems with this production.

64 PENNINGTON, RON. "Tennessee Williams Believes Rivalry Threat to Creativity." *Hollywood Reporter*, 21 March, p. 15.
    Brief item on TW's comments at USC luncheon in his honor at time of Los Angeles revival of *SND*. Refers to his comments about the theater, *SND*, and *OC*.

65 PHS. "The Times Diary." *Times* (London), 27 June, p. 18.
    Brief news item announcing plans for revival of *SND* after twenty-five years.

66 PIT. "Shows Abroad." *Variety*, 28 March, pp. 74, 79.
    Review of *SCW*, London production. It's significant because of Stritch's performance; praises production.

67 PRESLEY, DELMA EUGENE. "Tennessee Williams: 25 Years of Criticism." *Bulletin of Bibliography* 30 (January-March):21–29.
    Thorough check list of secondary material.

68 REED, REX. "New York Is Its Old Self Again." New York *Sunday News*, 9 December, sec. 3, p. 5.

Review of *GM*, TV production. The play, in this production, "comes close to perfection."

69 ————. "No One but Hepburn Can Fill Her Shoes." New York *Daily News*, 14 December, p. 106.

Brief praise for Katharine Hepburn in upcoming ABC production of *GM*.

70 ————. "Tennessee's 'Out Cry': A Colossal Bore." New York *Sunday News*, 11 March, sec. 3, p. 5.

Review of *OC*. "Boring . . . pretentious, static, and all but incomprehensible. . . . perhaps it should have been performed in colleges, where the kids could write papers about it. . . . Should have stayed in [TW's] trunk."

71 ————. "An Unhappy Birthday to 'Streetcar.'" New York *Sunday News*, 13 May, sec. 3, p. 5.

Review of *SND*. "The only play he ever wrote that shows no signs of aging." But in this particular revival, "Rosemary Harris was kicking the hell out of Blanche before we got a chance to know her." Blistering attack on the Lincoln Center production. Quotes TW at the opening: "Who are all these people? I never wrote all those parts, and what the hell is going on there?"

72 SIMON, JOHN. Review of *OC*. *New York* 6 (19 March):66.

OC is "lusterless concatenations of strained dialogue issuing from attitudinizing shadows in lines." Also refers to it as "this sorry farrago." TW is conducting his own "unsuccessful psychoanalysis in public and call[ing] it theater."

73 ————. Review of *SND*. *New York* 6 (14 May):97.

After 25 years, *SND* "reaffirms its position as one of the most poetic, witty, moving, shrewd and stageworthy plays in the American theater. . . . The tones of Tennessee Williams continue to be varied and ravishing."

74 SKLOOT, ROBERT. "Submitting Self to Flame: The Artist's Quest in Tennessee Williams, 1935–1954." *Educational Theatre Journal* 25 (May):199–206.

Gives attention to TW relative to "the dilemma of the artist in the modern world." Then goes on to examine "the moral and aesthetic implications" of TW's credo of "romantic escapism and sexual sensationalism." Argues that "Williams' characters . . . are physically incomplete, the physiological emblem of their psychological or spiritual truncation." Examines the "freaks" among his characters. Ample attention to how imagination, as a prime factor in TW's labor and craft creates and preserves "beauty, purity, and love" in the plays' themes.

75 *SND. Guardian* (Manchester), 27 June, p. 7.
Photo of TW and Claire Bloom plus caption announcing the upcoming London revival.

76 *SND. Newsweek* 81 (2 April):44.
Brief item mentioning cast in Los Angeles revival of *SND*.

77 SNYDER, CAMILLA. "USC's Libraries Conduct the Tennessee Wait." Los Angeles *Herald-Examiner*, 22 March, sec. A, p. 12.
Brief item. Luncheon in TW's honor at USC at time of Los Angeles revival of *SND*.

78 SORELL, WALTER. "The Case of Tennessee Williams." *Cresset* 36:26–27.
Brief. Cites faults and weaknesses in TW (his attraction toward violence, decadence; his frankness in revealing himself through his characters, and his occasional failure in this), and the plays that Sorell likes. *GM, CR, OC, 2CP, IR*, and *SND* are mentioned in brief detail with references to current productions.

79 " 'Streetcar' to End Run." *New York Times*, 19 October, p. 58.
Brief notice of *SND* closing its Broadway revival run after twenty performances.

80 SULLIVAN, DAN. " 'Streetcar' On, Off the Track." Los Angeles *Times*, 21 March, sec. IV, pp. 1, 10.
Review of *SND*, Los Angeles production. Generally positive review; praises TW, and the strength of the script itself.

81 ———. "Tennessee Williams on a Streetcar Named Restraint." Los Angeles *Times*, 11 March, calendar sec., pp. 1, 32.

Interview-commentary prior to Los Angeles opening of *SND* revival. TW discusses mental health, *OC*, *SND* revival, Roman Catholicism, marriage.

82 VILS, URSULA. "A Lunch with Tennessee Williams." Los Angeles *Times*, 25 March, sec. IV, p. 16.
Report on luncheon in TW's honor (at time of Los Angeles revival of *SND*) at USC. Primarily gossip-human interest.

83 WARDLE, IRVING. "Miss Stritch Shines as Bar Room Wit." *Times* (London), 30 January, p. 9.
Review of *SCW*, London production. Analyzes themes and provides synopsis. Goes on to compare it to O'Neill's "Iceman Cometh."

84 WATERS, HARRY F. "Deb Party." *Newsweek* 82 (17 December):61.
Advance note of the TV production of *GM* and Katharine Hepburn's role in it.

85 WATSON, ROY A. "The Archetype of the Family in the Drama of Tennessee Williams." Ph.D. dissertation, University of Tulsa.
Attempts to show that the family archetype is central to TW's best plays. Examines *BA, GM, SND, PM, S&S, SLS, CAT*, and *YTM*. Concludes that the family archetype ceased to be the primary thematic concern of TW's plays after 1958. (*DAI* 34:1299A.)

86 WATT, DOUGLAS. "Another 'Streetcar' Happily Comes Along." New York *Sunday News*, 6 May, sec. 3, p. 3.
Review of *SND*. "Unquestionably a masterpiece." Recalls original opening as "a shattering experience." Praises the revival although "the magic of the original production is missing."

87 ————. " 'Out Cry' Is Williams Puzzler." New York *Daily News*, 2 March, p. 50.
Review of *OC*. "An extremely mystifying evening of theater all by itself. . . . Solely by reason of Williams' poetic vision" does it even survive. "The play is schizophrenia given dramatic shape. . . . The play is . . . entirely elusive."

88   ————. "Rep. Ends Era with 'Streetcar.' " New York *Daily News*,
     27 April, p. 66.
        Cast and stage business. Calls the production "worth seeing."
     SND is TW's "enduring masterpiece."

89   ————. " 'Streetcar' Back With New Leads." New York *Daily
     News*, 5 October, p. 54.
        Review of *SND*. A "flawed yet arresting revival" of *SND* from
     last spring by Lincoln Center "returned last night at the St.
     James Theatre with a coarser, cheaper look, demeaning the play."
     However, the play still has "power and beauty."

90   WATTS, RICHARD, JR. "The Doom of Blanche DuBois." *New York
     Post*, 27 April, p. 27.
        Review of *SND*. The play itself is "one of the masterpieces of
     the modern drama." This revival is "a satisfactory production. . . .
     I hesitate to call any modern play great, but 'Streetcar' deserves
     it."

91   ————. "Tennessee Williams' Enigma." *New York Post*, 2 March,
     p. 30.
        Review of *OC*. "I don't think he's ever given us a more
     baffling [play] than 'Out Cry.' . . . It is one riddle wrapped in-
     tricately within another. . . . [But] for all its continuous befuddle-
     ment, it is almost steadily interesting."

92   ————. "Tennessee Williams' Puzzle." *New York Post*, 17 March,
     p. 16.
        Review of *OC*. TW "is the most distinguished American drama-
     tist since Eugene O'Neill. . . . [But *OC*] was a complete puzzle
     to me. . . . I haven't the slightest idea what it's about." Compares
     TW and Pirandello.

93   ————. "That Streetcar Is Here Again." *New York Post*, 5 October,
     p. 18.
        SND is "not only Tennessee Williams' masterpiece, but also
     one of the greatest plays ever written by an American dramatist."
     This production has "tremendous power . . . [and] a beautiful
     compassion."

94 WILLIAMS, BOB. "On the Air." *New York Post*, 11 April, p. 90.
Brief advance notice of new ABC production of *GM*.

95 ————. "On the Air." *New York Post*, 14 December, p. 81.
Advance notice of Katharine Hepburn's role in ABC's *GM*.

96 "Williams to Get Medal at St. John's." *New York Times*, 8 December, p. 42.
Brief note of TW getting first of St. John the Divine's centennial medals.

1974

1 BARNES, CLIVE. "London Theatre: Classics and Sexism." *New York Times*, 17 August, p. 16.
Review of *SND*, London production. Brief notice praising Claire Bloom as Blanche. Rest of cast is applauded for their technical expertise at handling southern U.S. dialects in this revival.

2 ————. "New and Gripping 'Cat' at the ANTA." *New York Times*, 25 September, p. 26.
Review of *CAT*. "A gripping and intensely moving play, a play that can hold its own with anything written in the post-O'Neill American theater." TW "makes you care by showing you a world."

3 BARTHEL, JOAN. "A 'Cat' in Search of Total Approval." *New York Times*, 22 September, sec. 2, pp. 1, 3.
Prepremiere commentary on the revival. Analyzes themes; interviews Ashley.

4 BATCHELOR, RUTH. " 'Streetcar' Is Still Running and Desirable." *Miss London*, 25 March, p. 8.
Review of *SND*, London production. Calls TW "the American Shakespeare of today." Quite positive in its general praise of *SND*.

5 CHESLER, S. ALAN. " 'A Streetcar Named Desire': Twenty-Five Years of Criticism." *Notes on Mississippi Writers* 7 (Fall):44–53.

Surveys scholarly criticism (which "has, for the most part, con-
centrated on its two leading characters"). Particularizes the Stanley and Blanche criticism; examines "the greatest source of controversy"; and addresses TW's use of language and the response
it received. Calls attention to the prevailing view that "Williams
failed to make clear the position he took toward his material,
specifically toward his characters." Contrasts several critics: Gassner, Tischler, Quirino, et al.

6 "Circle Begins Year with Williams Play." *New York Times*, 8 October, p. 35.
    Brief announcement of *BA* billed at Circle Repertory in New
York City.

7 CLURMAN, HAROLD. Review of *CAT*. *Nation* 219 (12 October):349–
50.
    Praises the play itself, but says it never before had satisfied
him. Analyzes its built-in problems and discusses cast of this
particular revival.

8 ————. Reviews of *S&S* and *CR*. In *The Divine Pastime: Theatre
Essays*. New York: Macmillan, 18–23.
    Reprints of 1948.15, 1953.13.

9 ————. "Tennessee Williams: Poet and Puritan." In *The Divine
Pastime: Theatre Essays*. New York: Macmillan, 227–31.
    Reprint of 1970.11.

10 COLE, CHARLES W., and FRANCO, CAROL I. "Critical Reaction to
Tennessee Williams in the Mid-1960's." *Players Magazine* 49
(Fall-Winter):18–23.
    Refers to *SST, 7D, KE*; begins with premise: "Throughout his
career Tennessee Williams has engaged in unusual theatrical experiments." Goes on from there to discuss the "creative method
that is bizarre and novel" in the three cited plays. Surveys critical
responses; concludes it was a bad set of plays.

11 DAWSON, HELEN. Review of *SND*. *Plays and Players* 21 (May):28–
31.
    London production. Praise for cast and production, set design.

Notes that English tradition forces violence to be verbal rather than physical and causes actors to hold back. "What is missing is an underlying feeling of . . . humility."

12 DEBUSSCHER, GILBERT. "Tennessee Williams as Hagiographer: An Aspect of Obliquity in Drama." *Revue des Langues Vivantes* 40:44–56.

Traces the use of Christ figures, Good Friday and Easter situations, in *BA, GM, CR, SLS, SB, NI, MT*; then shifts from Christ to the Saints, about which, he maintains, critics have been relatively silent. Discusses TW's being "aware of the possibility of prolonging the meaning of his characters and of making his particulars resonate with broader overtones." Gives attention to the St. Sebastian motif in *SLS*; St. Laurence in *NI*. Reprinted: 1977.88.

13 FEINGOLD, MICHAEL. "Cooling the Tin Roof." *Village Voice*, 3 October, pp. 77, 78.

Review of *CAT*. "The most awkwardly formed and indecisive of Williams' major works." Talks of ways the script itself could have been restructured to advantage: "the portraits do not meld into a group; instead their energy pulls people away from the play's action, and the fabric of the work is shredded." Still, it's "an exciting rough sketch of what might have been Williams's best play."

14 GILL, BRENDAN. "Family Troubles." *New Yorker* 50 (7 October):73.

Review of *CAT*. "Williams is a playwright in the nineteenth century tradition." Re-examines the plot, telling the story again.

15 *GM. New York Post*, 29 May, p. 2.

Brief news item. Notice of Emmies for ABC production of *GM*.

16 GOTTFRIED, MARTIN. "Williams' 'Cat' Revived." *New York Post*, 25 September, p. 46.

Review of *CAT*. "His plot invention running thin, Williams concocted a three-hour, three-act talkathon that could have been cut to one act with its boredom intact. . . . It would be absurd to take such a play seriously."

17   GUNN, DREWEY WAYNE. *American and British Writers in Mexico,*
     1556–1973. Austin: University of Texas Press, pp. 208–15.
        Treats TW among other American writers who would "draw
     inspiration from the Mexico of 1939–1940." Begins with premise:
     "Idolizing both Lawrence and Hart Crane, he naturally had to
     travel there, and his observations had a greater influence on the
     playwright than is generally realized." Shows scope of impres-
     sions that would influence *CR*, *NI*, and *S&S*, as well as various
     works of short fiction.

18   GUSSOW, MEL. "Stage: 'Battle of Angels.' " *New York Times*, 4 No-
     vember, p. 51.
        Review of *BA*, off-Broadway production. "An evening of re-
     newal and reclamation. . . . the play can stand on its own . . .
     [even in this] vastly altered version." Praises the production of
     this revival which is actually the New York premiere of the play.

19   ————. "Williams Revises His 'Cat' for Stratford." *New York*
     Times, 22 July, p. 40.
        Review of *CAT*, Stratford (Connecticut) production. "This is
     the script that most clearly expresses the author's intentions."
     Quotes TW and praises the production of this revival.

20   HALLOWAY, RONALD. "Stop That 'Streetcar' Named Lang; Berlin
     Failed to Tell Dramatist of Slight Switch, a Black Lead." *Variety*,
     17 July, p. 103.
        Regarding *SND*, Berlin production. Court action because of
     unauthorized cuts in text and emphasis on Blanche "enjoying her
     rape."

21   HASKELL, MOLLY. *From Reverence to Rape: The Treatment of*
     Women in the Movies. New York: Holt, Rinehart & Winston;
     Penguin Books, pp. 248–53.
        "In the case of Tennessee Williams' women, there is little
     confusion. His hothouse, hot-blooded 'earth mothers' and drag
     queens . . . are as unmistakably a product of the fifties as they
     are of his own baroquely transvestized homosexual fantasies. By
     no stretch of the imagination can they be called 'real' women."
     Maintains that TW's gallery of females are charades of his own
     sexual confusion: "the homosexual writer came halfway out of

the closet, but disguised in women's clothes that bulged in the wrong places.... Williams' women can be amusing company if we aren't asked to take them too seriously or too tragically."

22 HAWK. "Shows Abroad." *Variety*, 27 March, p. 72.
    Brief review of *SND*, London production. Calls it a "plush" production; the play "remains valid."

23 HERBERT, HUGH. "The Solid Gold Streetcar." *Guardian* (Manchester), 16 March, p. 8.
    Interview-commentary. TW discusses his youth, first productions, his views of redemption and art.

24 HOBE. "Show on Broadway." *Variety*, 2 October, p. 68.
    Review of *CAT*. The play's "flaws are more apparent [now] than when it was originally produced." Discusses TW's text changes; praises Ashley and Dullea.

25 HUGHES, CATHARINE. "New York." *Plays and Players* 21 (October): 45.
    Review of *CAT*. Synopsis and comments on changes from original productions. Generally positive. Mentions how TW continually reworks his plays, cites *OD*, *BA*, *SCW*, *2CP*, *GF*, *MT*, *KE*, *7D* as examples.

26 ———. "Plays with a Past." *America* 131 (12 October):194–95.
    Review of *CAT*. " 'Cat' is one of Williams' most highly theatrical plays.... [TW] attempts to keep too many things in the air at one time for the play to be completely successful."

27 IACHETTA, MICHAEL. "Tennessee's 'Out Cry' Is at 13th St. Theater." New York *Daily News*, 26 June, p. 38.
    Review of *OC*, off-Broadway production of TW's revision. Praises it as leaner and trimmer than a year ago.

28 "IBM Quickly Sets 'Menagerie' Repeat." *Variety*, 2 January, p. 30.
    Brief item announcing rescheduling of TV production of *GM* (from December 1973) for 20 January.

29 KALEM, T.E. "Delta Wildcat." *Time* 104 (7 October):107.
    Review of *CAT*. Praises its *endurability*; calls it a "triumph";
    generally praising of cast.

30 KAUFFMANN, STANLEY. "Two Revivals." *New Republic* 171 (19
    October):16, 33–34.
    Review of *CAT*. "This production confirms that [TW] is one
    of the two American dramatists of enduring substance and that
    this is not one of his best plays." Refers specifically to the canon
    for comparison/contrast. Discusses its themes—"loneliness, buried
    and released violence, sex and 'difference.'" Also refers to the
    role of "female fecundity" as it influences the plot here. Praises
    Ashley as "more vaginal" than Bel Geddes, and "more feline"
    than Taylor, in role of Maggie. Reprinted: 1976.35.

31 KERR, WALTER. "'Cat' Revival Superior to Original Production."
    New York Times, 6 October, sec. 2, pp. 1, 3.
    Review of *CAT*. "Clearer and more honest" than original.
    Praises Ashley; refers to the lure into the "intricate psychological
    maze that the author intended as 'a snare for the truth of human
    experience.'" Concludes the revival was "well worth having
    done."

32 ———. "A Williams Tigress." *New York Times*, 17 November,
    sec. 2, p. 5.
    Review of *BA*. "An eye-opener." The play shows us that there
    were powerful themes and savageries at work in his plays even
    before *GM*. Attempts to analyze why it may originally have
    failed.

33 KINGSTON, JEREMY. "'Streetcar' Blooms." *Punch* 266 (27 March):
    519.
    Brief review of London production. Praises it as a production
    and as a revival. "Superb."

34 KOEPSEL, JURGEN. *Der Amerikanische Suden und seine Funktionen
    im dramatischen Werk von Tennessee Williams* [The American
    South and its Function in the Dramatic Work of Tennessee
    Williams]. Frankfurt/Mein, W. Germany: Lang, 263 pp.
    Attempts to rectify the problem of insufficient research on the

function of the South in TW's work. Focuses on *BA, GM, SND, 27W, LSG, CAT, OD, SB*. Inventories southern elements, evaluates individual traits, and compares historic South and TW's record of it. Establishes that "Williams' presentation of the South" is one that has "the brutality of the white inhabitants" as the most dominant feature. In German.

35   KROLL, JACK. "Southern Discomfort." *Newsweek* 84 (7 October):73.
       Review of *CAT*. "In failing to toughen [*CAT*'s] facile texture, Michael Kahn's revival tastes flat. . . . The whole thing is a kitten on a tepid tile floor."

36   LAMBERT, J.W. Review of *SND*. *Drama* 113 (Summer):45–46.
       London production. Calls *SND* "an American family play, but one which has retained tremendous power in purely theatrical terms. . . . Blanche DuBois is inadequate because she has about her something of the fallen day which Walter Pater credited to the Mona Lisa." Speculates on the themes in the play.

37   LEVY, FRANCIS. "Eight Mortal Women Possessed." *Village Voice*, 26 September, p. 33.
       Book review of *8M*. "Part of the problem with this collection comes from taking too much for granted. Images of aging, orgasm, and death are constantly juxtaposed as culminating points of insight as if mere association precluded any further elaboration."

38   LINK, FRANZ H. *Tennessee Williams' Dramen*. Darmstadt: Thesen-Verlag Vowimckel & Co., 144 pp.
       Investigates "Loneliness and Love" and motifs in TW's work. Provides a general summary of the themes of all plays through *NI*, with a closing chapter on reality and illusion. In German.

39   MALIN, IRVING. Review of *8M*. *New Republic* 171 (14 September):27–28.
       Book review. Analyzes general themes and motifs—calls it a "marvelous collection. . . . Williams plays with the word 'possessed,' implying that his ladies are mad because they hope to own mysteries of the body."

40 MATTHEW, DAVID CHARLES CAMERON. "The Ritual of Self-Assas-
    sination in the Drama of Tennessee Williams." Ph.D. dissertation,
    Columbia University.
       Relates the myth of the self-destruction of a hero to the sym-
    bolism Williams employs in many of his plays. Williams' heroes
    commit "suicides" after becoming aware of their fading youth
    and strength. These suicides can mean actual death, usually
    provoked at the hands of others, or it can be a sexual surrender-
    ing, or a complete withdrawal from reality. (*DAI* 35:6147A.)

41 MOORE, SALLY. "Lonely Loser . . . Who Has Found the Way Back."
    Daily Mirror (London), 26 March.
       Interview-commentary. TW discusses drinking, Hemingway,
    homosexuality, his autobiography, his mother.

42 NOVICK, JULIUS. "Glints and Glimmers." *Village Voice*, 30 May,
    p. 73.
       "It is said that every great opera singer, after he has begun
    to lose his voice, has one last season in which, inexplicably, all
    his powers return to him in full force, before he resumes his
    decline or falls silent forever. I have not given up hope that this
    will happen to Mr. Williams; but it has not happened with 'The
    Latter Days of a Celebrated Soubrette.' "

43 ———. "Vivid but Not So Hot 'Cat.' " *New York Times*, 28 July,
    sec. 2, p. 3.
       Review of *CAT*, Stratford (Connecticut) production. "The
    material Mr. Williams has not quite mastered is rich material,
    full of vividness large and small—vividness undimmed after 19
    years."

44 OAKES, PHILIP. "Return Ticket." *Sunday Times* (London), 17 March,
    p. 35.
       Interview-commentary. TW discusses self-doubt; *SND* revival;
    his autobiography (wanting to call it "Flee, Flee This Sad
    Hotel"); new work; oblivion.

45 O'CONNOR, JOHN J. "TV: 'Migrants' a Drama that Portrays Poverty."
    New York Times, 1 February, p. 61.

Review of TV movie "The Migrants" which was based on "an idea by Tennessee Williams ... generally effective."

46 PEDEN, WILLIAM. "The Recent American Short Story." *Sewanee Review* 82 (October):712–29.
"Tennessee Williams's success and achievement as a playwright have tended to obscure his very real significance as a writer of short fiction. . . . *Eight Mortal Ladies Possessed*, his new collection ... will not add to his reputation. . . . Gone is the compassion that gave meaning to the twisted lives of so many of Williams's earlier misfits ...; in its place is a continuing kind of ugliness."

47 PETER, JOHN. "Brothers and Strangers." *Sunday Times* (London), 13 October, p. 31.
Review of *SU*, Dublin production. Limited to brief positive comments on production.

48 REED, REX. "Tennessee Williams." In *People Are Crazy Here*. New York: Delacorte, pp. 12–40.
Interview. TW discusses his illnesses, death, breast cancer, his mother, Frank Merlo, suicide, McCullers, Vidal, many of his plays. Reprint of: 1971.24.

49 Review of *OC*. *Virginia Quarterly* 49 (Winter):vi.
Brief positive review of publication of *OC*.

50 ROREM, NED. "Tennessee Now and Then." *Saturday Review* 1 (21 September):24–26.
Book review of *8M*. Discusses style, content, his themes. Gives attention to individual stories; positive.

51 SIMON, JOHN. "A Cat of Many Colors." *New York* 7 (12 August): 48–49.
Review of *CAT*. "After 19 years, Williams' play reveals itself as lively and attention-holding, highly theatrical: worthy commercial fare, but not art. . . . Williams is not sure which of several plays he is writing here." Referring to this revival, he questions whether TW is "losing his dramatic control, projecting the weak-

ness on the audience." Because of Ashley, he advises, "miss this performance at your soul's peril."

52   "Some Notables Name Their Bests." *New York Times*, 6 January, sec. 2, p. 9.

TW, among others, names his favorite films of 1973. "Last Tango in Paris" heads his list.

53   SNYDER, LOUIS. " 'Cat on Roof' Is Back on Broadway." *Christian Science Monitor*, 27 September, p. 16.

Review of *CAT*. An "increasingly pertinent drama.... [It] is about greed, mendacity, frustration.... [It] maintains a melo-dramatic aroma that the most spectacular performance cannot conceal."

54   THOMPSON, HOWARD. "TV: Cavett and Williams." *New York Times*, 22 August, p. 62.

Details of on-location (New Orleans) interview by Cavett. Laments its pace and its slight reference to the plays.

55   TIMNICK, LOIS. "A Visit with Tennessee Williams." *St. Louis Globe Democrat*, 9 February, sec. F, pp. 1, 3.

Interview-commentary. TW discusses his work schedule, a new play, autobiography, "speed," *SCW*, psychoanalysis, mysticism, his background.

56   WALKER, JOHN. "Splendid Revival of 'Streetcar' Stars Claire Bloom." *International Herald Tribune*, 23–24 March, p. 7.

Review of *SND*, London production. "A great play and a great production"; focuses positively on Bloom's interpretation of Blanche.

57   WATT, DOUGLAS. "Playwright Williams Comes Full Circle." New York *Sunday News*, 17 November, sec. 3, p. 3.

On *BA*. Discusses the history of the play previous to its New York City revival; talks of its closeness to and distance from its successor, *OD*.

58   ———. "Season Purrs with Revival of the Fittest." New York *Daily News*, 6 October, sec. 3, p. 3.

Review of *CAT*. Discusses the effects of time on the play; focuses on the cast of "this stirring revival."

59 ————. "Williams' 'Cat on a Hot Tin Roof' in a Roughly Satisfying Revival." New York *Daily News*, 25 September, p. 74.
Review of *CAT*. "An absorbing production ... one of Tennessee Williams' major works.... [*CAT*] has a solidity and depth all too rarely encountered in today's theatre." ANTA's production "is the most persuasive account" Watt has ever seen.

60 WATTS, RICHARD, JR. "Theater Week." *New York Post*, 28 September, p. 16.
Review of *CAT*. Praises the revival lavishly; there's "no denying that Tennessee Williams is our greatest living dramatist."

61 WEALES, GERALD C. On TW and Arthur Miller. In *Literary History of the United States: History*. Edited by Robert E. Spiller et al. 4th ed. New York: Macmillan; London: Collier Macmillan, pp. 1447–49.
"The contrast between Tennessee Williams and Arthur Miller is complete in almost every respect. Miller ... was a realist with a moral, a social, vision.... Williams ... was essentially a fantasist with a lonely, poetic vision; and his dramaturgy ... welled up from untold desires." Refers to TW's "explosive contact with the human unconscious," his plays' "lurid action ..., perversion, cannibalism or rape.... Williams modified the conventions of the theater by a deep personal intuition of the irrational."

62 WEISMAN, STEVEN R. " 'Jane Pittman' Wins Emmy for Best Program." *New York Times*, 29 May, p. 82.
Mentions awards to cast members of ABC's *GM*.

63 WHITE, EDMUND. "Eight Moral Ladies Possessed." *New York Times Book Review*, 6 October, p. 14.
Book review of *8M*. "As writer of fiction [TW] ... is never dull; and he knows how to ingratiate himself." Praises his tone: "racy and genteel.... Fortunately the book is redeemed by one perfect tale, 'Happy August the Tenth.' "

1975

1   ADLER, JACOB H. "Williams's Eight Ladies." *Southern Literary Journal* 8 (Fall):165–69.

Book review of *8M*. "These stories surprise me because they are mainly good." Surveys the canon back to beginnings, and claims the stories "recall other Williams." Goes through them each, citing problems and merits. Refers to similarities in *RT*, *SU*, *OD*, *SB*, and *RSMS*.

2   ADLER, THOMAS P. "The Dialogue of Incompletion: Language in Tennessee Williams' Later Plays." *Quarterly Journal of Speech* 61 (February):48–58.

Focuses on soliloquy and "those experiments with syntactical patterns which suggest a new direction in Williams's theatrical technique." Uses *BAR* , *OC*, *SCW* as illustrations—soliloquy study in *SCW*; syntax in *BAR*; more varied techniques in *OC*. Reprinted: 1977.88.

3   BAILEY, PAUL. "Dead Stork." *New Statesman* 90 (4 July):29.

Book review of *8M*. Surveys the character types and roles; says it's sad to see TW "indulging in this faggoty fantasising," that most of TW's ladies are "the shrill size-queens you can find in any gay bar from Greenwich Village to Bootle"; calls his writing "campy kitsch, ... *nymphomainie de tête* musings on prick power."

4   BARNES, CLIVE. " 'The Glass Menagerie.' " *New York Times*, 19 December, p. 52.

Review of *GM*. "Still a magnificent play." Its revival is not merely a play, but "a generation standing up on trial."

5   ———. "Nostalgic Reunions and a Few Home Truths." *Times* (London), 22 November, p. 10.

Book review of *MEM*. "We get a hazier picture of his life—but then it seems to be a hazy life."

6   ———. "Stage: Williams' 'Kingdom of Earth' in Princeton." *New York Times*, 12 March, p. 28.

Review of *KE*, Princeton's McCarter Theater production. "The fault of the play is simply that the characters are more fully realized than are their motives."

7 ————. " 'Sweet Bird of Youth.' " *New York Times*, 4 December, p. 53.
Review of *SB*. Sees the revival as a test of TW's staying power; this production lacks the shrillness of the original and concentrates on theme rather than action.

8 BARRAS, ˈLEONARD. "Short Stories." *Sunday Times* (London), 29 June, p. 31.
Book review of *8M*. Brief neutral comments, with plot details.

9 BERKVIST, ROBERT. "Broadway Discovers Tennessee Williams." *New York Times*, 21 December, sec. 2, pp. 1, 4–5.
Interview-commentary. TW reported to be "enjoying a widespread renewal of interest." Mentions revivals of *27W*, *GM*, *SB*. TW discusses his renewed image of worth, *MEM*, his sexuality.

10 "Briefly Noted: Fiction." *New Yorker* 51 (26 May):118–19.
Brief book review of *MWR*. "A bawdy *no* drama on a lone prairie." Praises the "strong, self-mocking humor."

11 BUCKLEY, TOM. "About New York." *New York Times*, 16 June, p. 19.
Production notes on *RED*. Leaving its rehearsal space in New York City for its Boston try-out; to return for Broadway premiere 12 August.

12 CLURMAN, HAROLD. Review of *SB*. *Nation* 221 (27 December):700.
Compares cast of this revival with original cast; analyzes impact.

13 COE, RICHARD L. "Quiet Words from a Prolific Playwright." *Washington Post*, 2 March, sec. E, pp. 1, 3.
Interview-commentary. TW discusses revival of *CAT*, *RED*, *8M*, his work habits.

14 CORRIGAN, MARY ANN ROMAN. "Expressionism in the Early Plays of Tennessee Williams." Ph.D. dissertation, University of Michigan.

GM, SND, and *CR* are analyzed with respect to their expressionistic qualities. *BA* and *YTM* are said to use the trappings of expressionism without revealing their inner life. *S&S* merely uses symbolic objects. Concludes that the best plays of this period accomplish the expressionistic aim of "objectifying internal action." (*DAI* 36:6681A.)

15 EMBREY, GLENN THOMAS. "Sexual Confusion in the Major Plays of Tennessee Williams." Ph.D. dissertation, University of California at Los Angeles.
     Claims that with the exception of *GM,* all of TW's plays are weakened by a confusion about how to handle human sexuality. Mentions *SND, S&S, CAT,* and *NI.* Concludes that when TW is not writing about sexual issues, his work is more realistic, unified, and believable. (*DAI* 36:309A.)

16 GUSSOW, MEL. "Purification." *New York Times,* 10 December, p. 56.
     Review of *P.* "Ecstasy and doom—the two ride like horsemen over the cobblestones of this one-act play." TW attends performance.

17 ———. "Tennessee Williams on Art and Sex." *New York Times,* 3 November, p. 49.
     Interview-commentary, coinciding with publication of *MEM.* Data on book's composition, publication. TW discusses the book's genesis, his [own] favorite plays.

18 ———. "Williams Still Hopes to Bring 'The Red Devil' to Broadway Despite Boston Closing." *New York Times,* 15 July, p. 39.
     Discusses Boston fiasco, TW's departure for Rome, return, the genesis of the play, his attempts to rewrite.

19 HIRSCH, FOSTER. Review of *MWR. New Republic* 172 (24 May): 24–25.
     Book review. "The novel is Williams' true confession." Focuses on the autobiographical quality. Positive.

20 HUGHES, CATHARINE. "The South on Stage." *America* 133 (15 November):340–41.
     Review of *S&S.* Production is "something less than ideal," but refers to TW's "lovely evocative writing."

21 INGLIS, WILLIAM HEARD, III. "Strindberg and Williams: A Study
    in Affinities." Ph.D. dissertation, University of Washington.
        Any similarities between TW's work and the work of Strindberg
    are not due to any influence Strindberg's work may have exerted
    on TW, but rather, that major playwrights constantly re-examine
    similar aspects of life. Concludes that the affinities they share
    "indicate more about the Industrial Revolution . . . than they do
    any causal relationship between them." (*DAI* 37:698A–99A.)

22 KALEM, T.E. "Of Sin and Grace." *Time* 106 (1 December):83–84.
        Book review of *MEM*. Praises his dramatic writing, but finds
    this prose attempt weak. Finds the work important. Much sum-
    mary.

23 KAUFFMANN, STANLEY. "Inside the Menagerie." *Saturday Review*
    3 (1 November):29–31.
        Book review of *MEM*. Discusses TW and sexuality, *SCW*,
    SND, *SB*, *YTM*; emphasizes family, early career; calls it impor-
    tant because it's the autobiography of "the second most impor-
    tant dramatist this country has produced." Also, it creates a
    "perspective" for all the plays.

24 KELLY, KEVIN. "New Williams Play Opens." *Boston Globe*, 19 June,
    p. 25.
        Review of *RED*, Boston production. It "is dreadful, a further
    indication . . . of the steady decline of the American theater's
    once foremost playwright. . . . [TW] is writing now as a flickering
    shadow of his former self." Refers to the "lurking pomposity in
    his ever-darkening vision." Finally concludes: "It is all utterly
    vacuous. The real clue to this vacuity may be found in the
    desperation of the play's plotting."

25 KERR, WALTER. "A Small 'Hamlet' and a 'Menagerie' without
    Claws." *New York Times*, 28 December, sec. 2, p. 5.
        Review of *GM*. The revival production suffers from the lack of
    abrasiveness on the part of M. Stapleton as Amanda.

26 ————. "Where There's Smoke, There's Fire and Ice." *New York
    Times*, 19 October, sec. 2, pp. 1, 5.

Review of *S&S*, off-Broadway production. The play itself is
strong; discusses characters; focuses on Alma.

27 KUNKEL, FRANCIS L. "Tennessee Williams: God, Sex, and Death."
In *Passion and the Passions: Sex and Religion in Modern Litera-
ture*. Philadelphia: Westminster Press, pp. 99–107.
Reprint of 1968.30.

28 LEHMANN-HAUPT, CHRISTOPHER. "A Deeper Tennessee Williams."
New York Times, 15 May, p. 41.
Book review of *MWR*. Says because TW has dealt "overtly . . .
and graphically" with homosexuality that this "alone makes a
difference, whatever the book is finally worth as art." Plot
summary.

29 ————. "Love Songs of a Crocodile." *New York Times*, 7 November, p. 35.
Book review of *MEM*. TW "is simply *sui generis*." *MEM*
should be read "with amusement and dismay, curiosity and disgust, laughter and pity."

30 McREA, RUSSELL WILLIAMS. "Tennessee Williams: An Artifice of
Mirrors." Ph.D. dissertation, York University (Canada).
A study of frequently misleading forms of rhetoric used by
some of TW's critics; emphasis placed on the effects TW's homosexuality has on his critics. (*DAI* 36:311A–12A.)

31 MALLET, GINA. "Petit Guignol." *Time* 106 (15 December):71.
Review of *SB*. "Today it [*SB*] seems fatally misconceived, a
sentimental melodrama." Sees the revival as a showcase production.

32 MILLER, ROBERT ROYCE. "Tragedy in Modern American Drama: The
Psychological, Social and Absurdist Conditions in Historical
Perspective." Ph.D. dissertation, Middle Tennessee State Uni-
versity.
Discusses plays by O'Neill, Miller, Albee, and TW (*The Em-
peror Jones*, *Death of a Salesman*, *The American Dream*, and
The Glass Menagerie). Finds that for the most part the plays

ask questions without providing answers, and that the resultant frustrations characterize these forms of tragedy.

33 "Miss Woodward, Newman Feted." *New York Times,* 6 May, p. 48.
   Brief society piece. TW at celebration for Woodward and Newman at Lincoln Center.

34 NAVONE, JOHN. "The Myth and the Dream of Paradise." *Studies in Religion* 5:152–61.
   Applies premise of the "religious implications in the relation between dream and myth and the archetype of paradise" to *GM* and *SND.* Contends that "paradise is among the archetypal symbols repeatedly found in myths, religion, dreams, fantasies, and literature. It is a primordial image of a fundamental aspect of human experience." And finds it possible for *GM* and *SND* to "be interpreted as enacted myths of the human pilgrimage condition." Talks of place, and clash between "idealized past" and unfortunate present in both plays.

35 NORTON, ELLIOT. "Tennessee Williams' New 'Red Devil' Here." *Boston Herald American,* 19 June, p. 14.
   Review of *RED,* Boston production. It "is a presently unfocused play that teeters and totters eerily between tragedy and mawkish melodrama.... Now needs to be rewritten by Tennessee Williams if it is to match in dramatic force and conviction the best of his plays." Ample plot detailing.

36 O'FAOLAIN, JULIA. "Cats on a Hot Tin Roof." *Observer,* 3 August, p. 21.
   Book review of *8M.* Offers a defense for this collection: "One reviewer has dismissed this collection as 'kitsch.' If it is, it is purposeful kitsch." Brief plot summaries.

37 O'HAIRE, PATRICK. "Tennessee's Dream." New York *Daily News,* 3 June, p. 42.
   Interview-commentary. TW discusses *RED, MWR.* "I consider myself scattered."

38 PETERSEN, CAROL. *Tennessee Williams.* Berlin, W. Germany: Colloquium Verlag Otto H. Hess, 94 pp.

A brief psychological biography highlighting how TW's life's experiences influenced the creation of the plays and their characters. Looks upon him as something of a romantic poet. Focuses on heroes, success, and new modes. In German.

39   PHILLIPS, ROBERT. Review of *8M*. *Commonweal* 102 (11 April): 55, 57.
       Compares this collection of short stories to Joyce Carol Oates' work; mentions consistency of female characters; refers to TW's "misogynistic imagination."

40   Review of *MWR*. *Virginia Quarterly* 51 (Autumn):cxliv.
       Brief, one paragraph. Calls it "superficial" and "gratuitously insouciant."

41   RICHARDSON, JACK. "Unaffected Recollections." *New York Times Book Review*, 2 November, pp. 45, 46.
       Book review of *MEM*. "Mixture of incongruous incidents and associations." Finds TW "trying to maintain an honorable, if somewhat romantic, attitude toward his art."

42   ROOSEVELT, KARYL. *MWR*. *New York Times Book Review*, 13 July, pp. 26, 28.
       Book review of *MWR*. "Not much" comes of the struggle to move through this novel. Considerable plot summary. "Williams's dribbly prose does nothing but enhance the tedium." Calls it "this scrappy book."

43   SHARMA, P.P. "The Predicament of the 'Outsiders' in Tennessee Williams' Plays." *Indian Journal of American Studies* 5 (January– July):69–75.
       Discusses worldly pressures on the "fugitive kind" in TW's plays.

44   SHARP, CHRISTOPHER. "Tennessee Williams: 'Scandal Exists with Me Always, My Dear.'" *Women's Wear Daily*, 16 May, p. 8.
       Interview-commentary. TW discusses revivals of his plays, Frank Merlo, his sister Rose, *MWR*.

45 SIMON, JOHN. *Uneasy Stages: A Chronicle of the New York Theater 1963–1973*. New York: Random House, pp. 6–8, 392–93.
Reviews of *MT* and *SCW*. Reprints of 1963.50; 1972.49.

46 STEINBECK, JOHN. *John Steinbeck: A Life in Letters*. Edited by Elaine Steinbeck and Ralph Wallsten. New York: Viking Press, p. 471.
A letter to Richard Watts, Jr. Reprint of 1953.51.

47 ————. *John Steinbeck: A Life in Letters*. Edited by Elaine Steinbeck and Ralph Wallsten. New York: Viking Press, pp. 630–31.
A letter to Kazan discussing impact of *SB* and TW's values.

48 TYLER, RALPH. "Playwright and Prizefighter on a Streetcar Named Success." *Village Voice*, 10 November, p. 55.
Book review of *MEM*. "[Williams] says his 'Memoirs' is the first book he ever wrote to make money, although once he got into it it became more to him than that. If it makes money, he deserves it.... He merits an honorable old age not so much for his inadequate plays as for such successes as 'The Glass Menagerie,' 'A Streetcar Named Desire,' and 'Cat on a Hot Tin Roof.' His failed plays cost him sweat and grief, and they might not have faltered so dismally if the zeitgeist of revved-up America hadn't sped past and left him eating dust. For in the 1960s, gallant defeat was no longer enough; the sensitive and feeling people wanted to win. They no longer blushed before the barbarians."

49 VAN GELDER, LAWRENCE. *2CP*. *New York Times*, 22 August, p. 16.
Review of *2CP*. Extremely brief notice of off-off-Broadway production; plot details; notes its connection to *OC*.

50 WEALES, GERALD. Review of *MEM*. *New Republic* 173 (23 December):31–32.
Book review. "A melange of anecdote, rumination, opinion, grievance and celebration." Tries to make sense of the "chaotic presentation of material," the shifting sense of time; laments the lack of comment on his work, and the focus on too much "trivia."

51 "Williams's 'Red Devil' Is Closing in Boston." *New York Times*, 26 June, p. 35.

Brief announcement. *RED* to close on 28 June; Broadway premiere canceled.

52 "Williams to Get Literature Medal." *New York Times*, 15 February, p. 35.
    National Arts Club awards its gold medal to Tennessee Williams.

1976

1 BAILEY, PAUL. "Confessing Loudly." *Times Literary Supplement*, 17 December, p. 1576.
    Book review of *LDW* and *MEM*. Denounces TW's *Memoirs* as badly written and confessional; remarks that TW looks "more attractive and wittier" as he is described in the letters to Windham.

2 BARNES, CLIVE. "'The Eccentricities of a Nightingale.'" *New York Times*, 24 November, p. 23.
    Review of *EN*. "This is a warm, rich play full of that compassion and understanding and that simple poetry of the heart that is Mr. Williams at his shining and simple best."

3 ———. "Steaming in the Tropics." *New York Times*, 17 December, p. C2.
    Review of *NI*. The revival offers "fine entertainment" and a reminder of TW's talent as an "ironic comic writer musing on the lonely tragedy of separateness."

4 ———. "'Twenty-Seven Wagons Full of Cotton.'" *New York Times*, 27 January, p. 26.
    Review of *27W*. Compares *27W* and Miller's "A Memory of Two Mondays." "The Williams play is a surprise, even a discovery."

5 BARNES, JULIAN. "Ductile." *New Statesman* 91 (12 March):334.
    Brief book review of *MWR*. Book is called excessive and unorganized.

6 BLUMBERG, MYRNA. "Fiction." *Times* (London), 18 March, p. 13.
   Book review of *MWR*. Generally positive. Finds "Mr. Williams
   to be a profoundly graceful prose writer."

7 BODEEN, DEWITT. Review of *MEM*. *Films in Review* 27 (April):
   238–39.
   Refers to the quality of his various films; notes the slight discussion of his work in *MEM*, and highlights his discussion of his
   homosexuality.

8 BRIEN, ALAN. "Tennessee in Pyjamas." *Spectator* 237 (20 November):19.
   Book review of *MEM*. "This is a genuine attempt at autobiography, in which our hero more often plays a role anything
   but heroic, a kind of self-abuse almost, which (as his, and Gore
   Vidal's, third partner in the weird sisterhood, Truman Capote,
   once remarked about masturbation) has the great advantage
   that you do not have to dress up for it."

9 BUKOWSKI, ANTHONY. "The Lady and Her Business of Love in
   Selected Southern Fiction." *Studies in the Humanities* 5 (January):14–18.
   Calls attention to the problem of distortion through use of
   "idealization of women" in southern literature. Finds the women
   in TW's work "as fascinating as any, since they represent the
   horrid outgrowth of close to two centuries." References to *SND*,
   27W, *CAT*, *OD*. Talks of the "Love-Broker" role he constructs.

10 CLARITY, JAMES F. "Williams Finds Cannes Festival a Crass Menag-
   erie." *New York Times*, 24 May, p. 36.
   News item. TW having difficulty as president of jury at Cannes
   Film Festival.

11 CLAYTON, SYLVIA. "The Bird Has Flown." *Times Literary Supplement*, 12 March, p. 283.
   Book review of *MWR*. Short synopsis of novel's ending with
   this quote and comment: " 'What is the future of a being with a
   chronically inflamed libido when the bird of youth has flown
   out of body and soul?' asks the narrator; and as any of Mr. Wil-

liams' heroines could tell him, he cannot expect an encouraging answer."

12 CLURMAN, HAROLD. Review of *GM. Nation* 222 (10 January):28.
    Brief. Says it's bogged down in too much literalness.

13 ————. Review of *27W. Nation* 222 (14 February):189–90.
    Brief. Praises this short play and its interpretation.

14 COHN, RUBY. Review of *TIE. Educational Theatre Journal* 28 (October):406–7.
    Brief. "He is such a grand old man that I suppose no one will tell him when a play simply stinks."

15 COOKE, MICHAEL G. "The Hero in Autobiography." *Yale Review* 65 (Summer):587–93.
    Book review of *MEM*. Starts with Rousseau's "terrible challenge of survival, let alone self-assertion. . . . *Memoirs* is a book of mere recollection, a sequence without consequence. . . . [TW] manages to make sex dreary, the theatre silly, and politics irrelevant. . . . In the long run, he fails to look himself in the eye, the *sine qua non* of autobiography."

16 CORRIGAN, MARY ANN. "Memory, Dream and Myth in the Plays of Tennessee Williams." *Renascence* 28 (Spring):155–67.
    Contends that TW's "writing reveals a striking preoccupation with the problem of time," quoting from his "The Timeless World of the Play." Divides his work into three periods and explores them relative to the time theme; brings other elements such as setting and lighting into the discussion, and advances to concepts of illusion and escape. Asserts that "thematic considerations are but one aspect of aesthetic evaluation," and closes the study with broader comments on TW's philosophy generally.

17 ————. "Realism and Theatricalism in 'A Streetcar Named Desire.'" *Modern Drama* 19 (December):385–96.
    Begins with the Krutch observation, in 1947, that *SND* "may be the great American play." Says that its greatness "lies in Tennessee Williams' matching of form and content." Adds that in *SND*, TW "synthesizes depth characterizations," concentrates

on setting ("emotionally charged"), costuming, props, lighting, color, music, and other sounds—on subjective and objective levels. Asserts that TW "achieves his most successful revelation of human nature in its totality in this play in which he distorts the realistic surface as little as possible and only when necessary."

18 CROSSETTE, BARBARA. "Ex-Dr. Kildare Dissects 'Iguana.'" *New York Times*, 26 November, p. C3.
    Discusses Richard Chamberlain's revival of *NI*; discusses the play's and Chamberlain's histories.

19 DAVIES, RUSSELL. "Anyone for Tennessee?" *New Statesman* 92 (12 November):683.
    Book review of *MEM*. "These are uncommonly rotten old memoirs, full of junk, and shamelessly ill-organized, slapdash, maudlin and arch." Says they're not dull, but are "boring." TW is "an impossible person, a sort of male Judy Garland, always slightly out of control." Claims the work becomes progressively "less and less coherent." Finds him a "fool."

20 FALLOWELL, DUNCAN. "Oh Boy." *Spectator* 236 (20 March):23.
    Brief book review of *MWR*. "I do not know exactly what it is that causes gay American writers to flip their onions in middle age, . . . but Tennessee Williams has now taken up the melodramatic confessional posture too, screwing tears from his urbane past."

21 GILL, BRENDAN. "The Triumph of Avarice." *New Yorker* 52 (27 December):52.
    Review of *NI*. A "respectful revival. . . . The production is satisfactory . . . a garrulous and often touching play."

22 ———. "Two Fly into the Phoenix's Nest." *New Yorker* 51 (9 February):78.
    Review of *27W*. "A youthful Williams in an impish . . . mood"; praises Streep's acting.

23 ———. "Woebegone Beginners." *New Yorker* 52 (6 December): 134–35.
    Review of *EN*. "Williams' ideal hero is the incestuous homo-

sexual." Calls it an "ingenious reworking" of the original; compares it to other plays. "An excellent production."

24 GOTTFRIED, MARTIN. "An Old Pair Get New Shine." *New York Post*, 27 January, p. 16.
    Review of 27W. 27W "is a curious little item, short and yet overlong, written with that power and eloquence of Williams in his prime, but without story enough even for its brevity." Doesn't think there is "much to this playlet."

25 HUGHES, CATHARINE. "Broadway Revival Meeting." *America* 134 (31 January):75.
    Brief review of GM. Says production is too "literal and heavy-handed."

26 ———. "Broadway Revival Meeting." *America* 134 (31 January): 75.
    Brief review of SB. Praises Worth's performance; negative about production generally.

27 ———. "Playing with the Past." *America* 134 (26 May):495.
    Review of SND. "Production is a good one, though not without problems." Praises cast of this revival production.

28 ———. "Tennessee Williams at 65." *America* 134 (1 May):382–83.
    A tribute. TW "is by far the most significant American playwright to emerge during the period that began roughly at the end of World War II." Refers to many of the plays in tracing his career, citing evidence to support her praise.

29 ———. "Tennessee Williams: 'What's Left?' " *America* 134 (10 January):10–11.
    Book review of MEM. Traces his personal and professional history vis-à-vis the plays; calls the book: "unquestionably poignant memoirs."

30 KALEM, T.E. "Bad Case of the Fantods." *Time* 108 (6 December):98.
    Brief review of EN. Surveys history of other TW remakes; praises Palmer as Alma.

31   ————. "Flee as a Bird." *Time* 107 (12 January):61.
Review of GM. "This revival finds our greatest living playwright in the best possible hands."

32   ————. "God Is—Or Is He Not?" *Time* 108 (27 December):39.
Brief review of NI. This revival "lacks the luminosity of the 1962 original." Mostly plot summary.

33   KAUFFMANN, STANLEY. "About Williams: Gloom and Hope." In *Persons of the Drama.* New York: Harper & Row, pp. 165–68.
Reprint of 1966.38.

34   ————. "Acting in Williams." *New Republic* 174 (17 January):28.
Review of GM. Praises Payton-Wrights' acting—says it's better than any he's seen doing Laura. The play "was clearly defective" when it opened, and it isn't improved in this revival. "Character, not plot is Williams' strength."

35   ————. " 'Cat on a Hot Tin Roof.' " In *Persons of the Drama.* New York: Harper & Row, pp. 152–55.
Reprint of 1974.30.

36   ————. *Persons of the Drama: Theater Criticism and Comment.* New York: Harper & Row, pp. 168–71.
Reprints of 1972.25, 1973.47.

37   KERR, WALTER. "Melodrama Isn't Always a Dirty Word." *New York Times,* 8 February, sec. 2, p. 5.
Review of 27W. Defends the play and praises TW's talent in creating melodramatic plot devices.

38   ————. "Never Mind the Echoes, Listen to Williams." *New York Times,* 19 December, sec. 2, p. 3.
Review of NI. It's difficult to watch this present revival without thinking of all the past performances and performers of the play.

39   LASSELL, MICHAEL. "Williams on Williams." *Yale Theatre* 8 (Fall): 78–82.
Book review of MEM. Discusses the problem with this sort

of memoir writing; depends on Vidal's review. "We do not come to see what it is like to be Tennessee Williams, but what it is like to see Tennessee Williams more or less as he is willing to be seen." Refers to *Memoirs'* "highly touted openness about his homosexuality." Williams has "a complete, almost naive faith in the power of language to communicate . . . his intention. . . . In *Memoirs* Williams has written not so much an autobiography, but a novel about a writer named Tennessee Williams."

40 LEONARD, JOHN. "T.V.: Drama by Tennessee Williams." *New York Times*, 16 June, p. 79.
    Review of *EN*, TV production. "Although there are problems, they are nothing fine acting can't take care of." Praises Danner's interpretation of Alma.

41 MANO, D. KEITH. "A Round on the House." *National Review* 28 (16 April):405–6.
    Brief book review of *MEM*. Praises it lavishly: "Gentle and proud and fey and fearful and elegiac; so honest that honesty itself seems a put-on."

42 NEVILLE, JILL. "South Americans in Paris." *Sunday Times* (London), 7 March, p. 41.
    Book review of *MWR*. Contains plot summary and brief excerpts from the text.

43 "New Williams Drama Scheduled for April." *New York Times*, 27 December, sec. C, p. 21.
    Brief announcement of *VC* coming to Broadway.

44 "Notes on People." *New York Times*, 27 April, p. 31.
    Gossip piece concerning TW's displeasure at not having once seen a production of *SLS* that was not "revolting"—and finally seeing a "vigorous, semiprofessional production" in Key West.

45 "Notes on People." *New York Times*, 4 December, p. 30.
    Brief mention of TW as new member of American Academy of Arts and Letters.

46 O'CONNOR, JOHN J. "Depending on the Kindness of Public TV." *New York Times*, 8 December, p. C24.

Review of "Tennessee Williams' South." The PBS piece has "invaluable footage of the playwright recalling his childhood, commenting on his plays." Praises the scenes it presents of *LSG*.

47 ————. "This Tribute Smacks of Exploitation." *New York Times*, 5 December, sec. 2, pp. 29, 30.
Review of *CAT*, TV production. "Unsalvageable . . . riddled with unresolved dramatic and structural problems."

48. Review of *MEM*. *Virginia Quarterly* 52 (Spring):42.
Brief, one paragraph. "An immensely entertaining book . . . both hilarious and pathetic. . . . A delicious feast of anecdote."

49 ROSENTHAL, RAYMOND. "Inhibited Introspection." *New Leader* 59 (29 March):18.
Book review of *MEM*. Highlights aspects of TW's family background, his homosexuality, and the events that led to his having a materially disadvantaged adolescence—when TW began to write.

50 SAGE, LORNA. "Round the Cafe Table." *Observer*, 7 March, p. 27.
Book review of *MWR*. Calls book a "natural curiosity. . . . a weary study in all the ways art doesn't compensate for an empty bed."

51 SATTERFIELD, JOHN. "Williams' 'Suddenly Last Summer': The Eye of the Needle." *Markham Review* 6 (Fall):27–33.
Lengthy essay analyzing possibilities for an understanding of *SLS*; tries out etymology and genealogy to understand characters' names, some myth for theme and motif clarification, some philosophy for meaning understanding; considerable hypothesizing. Finally concludes SLS "is special. Insight, that perceptive flash that lights relationships, always is special. Special thanks are due to Tennessee Williams."

52 TRAUBITZ, NANCY BAKER. "Myth as a Basis of Dramatic Structure in 'Orpheus Descending.'" *Modern Drama* 19 (March):57–66.
Claims as its thesis that by analyzing the mythic structure, it can be shown that *OD* has generally been underrated and that it "represents a significant attempt to re-create myths in the con-

text of our time." Shows TW emphasizing "the responsibility which love places upon the poet/singer Orpheus." Draws in Christ/Veronica motif, as well as Adam and Eve, Orpheus and Adonis. Asserts that the myths used are "integral to the dramatic structure, never imposed on the naturalistic action or introduced self-consciously."

53   TRUE, WARREN ROBERTS. "Chekhovian Dramaturgy in the Plays of Tennessee Williams, Harold Pinter, and Ed Bullins." Ph.D. dissertation, University of Tennessee.

Demonstrates Chekhovian influences on twentieth-century playwrights, particularly Bullins, Albee, and TW. TW is shown to share an immobility of plot with Chekhov. (*DAI* 37:5131A.)

54   VAHLAND, BARBARA. *Der Held als Opfer: Aspekte des Melodramatischen bei Tennessee Williams* [The Hero as Victim: Aspects of Melodrama in Tennessee Williams]. Bern, W. Germany: Herbert Lang, 188 pp.

Discusses problem of tragedy; the individual and art; crisis of self-identity; guilt as societal corruption; problem of melodrama ("menace of time," "reality of power," "the hope of love,"); the problem of theater (the function of the stage and the interpretation of symbols). In German.

55   VIDAL, GORE. "Selected Memories of the Glorious Bird and the Golden Age." *New York Review of Books* 23 (5 February):13–18.

Book review of *MEM*. Discusses his own memories of TW; says his first impression of TW was that he was "every bit as ancient as Gide and Santayana." Talks of TW's days in Rome. "I picked up Tennessee's *Memoirs* with a certain apprehension . . . was startled by the technique he had chosen." Responds to mentionings of himself in *Memoirs*. Adds, "Today, at sixty-four, Tennessee has the same voracious appetite for work and applause that he had at twenty-four." References to TW's affairs and the "Monster Women" of his plays. "Tennessee is the sort of writer who does not develop; he simply continues." Reprinted: 1977.97.

56   VON BARGEN, CATHLEEN. Review of *MEM*. Cresset 39 (September):26.

"His embarrassingly frank autobiography reveals a man ravaged by his carnal appetites, suspicious and temperamental in dealing with his friends as well as the public. . . . Williams divulges his neuroses with unabashed candor. . . . He is . . . implacably defiant and self-pitying."

57 WAHLS, ROBERT. "Of Time and Money." New York *Sunday News,* 18 January, leisure sec., p. 4.
   Interview-commentary. TW turns 65 and discusses his grandfather, *NI,* Irene Worth, *MEM.*

58 WATSON, GEORGE S. "The Revision of *The Glass Menagerie*: The Passing of Good Manners." *Southern Literary Journal* 8 (Spring): 74–78.
   Refers to changes noticed in the two published texts of *GM.* "The most noticeable changes are the omission of the screen device and the increase of scenes from seven to eight." Claims need for attention to the changes since earlier edition is more often printed than later one.

59 WATT, DOUGLAS. "Miller-Williams Twin Bill." New York *Daily News,* 27 January, p. 44.
   Review of *27W.* Regards *27W* as "the ugly little Williams [play], an almost exultantly painful character sketch" that proved powerful only "because of Meryl Streep's brilliant, chillingly convincing portrait." Thinks TW's conception "is a savage one."

60 YOUNG, B.A. "The Two-Character Play." *Financial Times* (London), 11 December, p. 26.
   Review of *2CP,* London production. Plot and theme summary; refers to its element of panic. It "has very little . . . intrinsic entertainment value."

1977

1 ADLER, JACOB H. "Tennessee Williams' South: The Culture and the Power." In Tharpe (1977.93), pp. 30–52.
   Excerpted from 1961.3.

2 ARMATO, PHILIP M. "Tennessee Williams' Meditations on Life and Death in *Suddenly Last Summer, Night of the Iguana* and *The*

Milk Train Doesn't Stop Here Anymore." In Tharpe (1977.93),
pp. 558–70.

Focuses on the predominance of death images and presences
in TW's life and work. "Williams is the only American playwright who has regularly grappled with the problem of death."
Considers the three plays of the title, written during TW's
"inferno" period. *SLS* presents TW's "Christian and existential"
ways of examining death. Notions of the mock-heroic enter, particularly with use of St. Sebastian imagery. *NI* contains "the
'special' brilliance" of Hannah who is an "example of courage and
understanding in the face of tribulation." *MT* is cited for "the
severe asceticism of its statement." Concludes that TW "practices
the art of a decidedly Christian playwright."

3   BARNES, CLIVE. "Stage: 'Vieux Carre' by Williams Is Haunting."
New York Times, 12 May, p. C22.

Review of *VC*. Notes that TW's "compassion [is] always on
the boil.... Is [*VC*] a good play? Probably not.... a play of
blatant melodrama and crepuscular atmosphere." It shows "the
murmurings of genius."

4   BENNETT, BEATE HEIN. "Williams and European Drama: Infernal-
ists and Forgers of Modern Myths." In Tharpe (1977.93), pp.
429–59.

"Tennessee Williams' preoccupation with his inner world, as it
absorbs, rejects, and rebukes the outer world, belongs to [the
Romantic] tradition." Additionally cites his "fascination with
forms and forces" in defense of this categorizing. The two staples
of the Romantic tradition are limited to "infernalism" and myth
making. Cites *MWR, OC, BAR, 2CP* as examples of TW's embrace of ambiguity—especially as it shows itself in "the Absurd
artist's relationship to his environment." Also focuses on problem
of time, an "inferno vision" (*RED* and *CR*, particularly), the
two archetypes of "the fugitive exile and death by cannibalism,"
"the poet as myth maker," and the sense of "alienation" that *MEM*
attests to.

5   BERKOWITZ, GERALD M. "Williams' 'Other Places'—a Theatrical
Metaphor in the Plays." In Tharpe (1977.93), pp. 712–19.

Contrasts Williams with Miller, and says "Williams' aim, his primary obligation, is to inspire sympathy and identification with his characters." Details TW's attempts "to reverse our attitudes toward his characters" by means of "a simple but subtle geographical metaphor . . . settings for" *GM, SND, CAT, NI,* et al., "being *someplace else,* a spot cut off from the rest of the universe." Traces this convention in the works mentioned above—sees the alien place as an adjunct of alienation, reinforcing it.

6   BERLIN, NORMAND. "Complementarity in *A Streetcar Named Desire.*" In Tharpe (1977.93), pp. 97–103.

Advances the thesis that TW "wishes to keep the sides balanced" with the villain-hero argument about Blanche and Stanley. Cites some appropriate criticism, and then textually analyzes elements pertaining to his theory: desire (and Desire), past-present, light-dark, heights-depths. Finds ambiguity to be an acceptable dialectic.

7   BROOKS, CHARLES B. "Williams' Comedy." In Tharpe (1977.93), pp. 720–35.

"Although [TW's] vision of the world is not primarily comic, comedy contributes to his success." Details comic moments and motifs in his plays—use of gags, slapstick, caricatures, verbal witticisms. Maintains these devices generally "relate to character or theme rather than being gratuitous." Calls *CR* and *GF* "the most fanciful of the plays." Furthers the issue beyond language to include characterization. References drawn from nearly the full canon. Reprinted: 1980.56.

8   BRUSTEIN, ROBERT. "The Perfect Friend." *New York Times Book Review,* 20 November, p. 9.

Review of *LDW.* Discusses how "the letters grow more guarded, more defensive." Refers to Windham's tendency "to sacrifice people to his personal and professional needs." Calls it "a very damaging book."

9   CARDULLO, BERT. "Drama of Intimacy and Tragedy of Incomprehension: *A Streetcar Named Desire* Reconsidered." In Tharpe (1977.93), pp. 137–53.

Takes issue with the critical school that damns Stanley "unqualifiedly." Surveys the criticism of Clurman, Gassner, Tischler,

Jordan, Miller, and Falk. Defends Stanley since "he has not consciously plotted to destroy [Blanche] throughout the play." Cites Stanley's "blindness" to Blanche's plight (his "tragedy of incomprehension"). Claims TW structures Act 3, Scene 4 "so as to make the rape seem incidental." Goes on to argue for Blanche's tragic stature; considers what the play's basic questions or propositions might be.

10 CARRAGHER, BERNARD. "Born-Again Playwright: Tennessee." New York *Daily News*, 8 May, leisure sec., pp. 3, 14.
   Interview-commentary, prior to opening of *VC*. TW discusses *VC*, writing habits, his reading, his friends, Bankhead, his fears.

11 CASPER, LEONARD. "Triangles of Transaction in Tennessee Williams." In Tharpe (1977.93), pp. 736–52.
   Sees Williams as open "to respectful reconsideration as a precursor of the New Uncertainty." Finds Williams going beyond Romanticism and Naturalism. Cites the *"special geometry constructed of triangles"* which he sees as "organic to the shape of the plays' complications. . . . Sometimes they function as triangles of opposition" (*SLS, SND, BD*); sometimes as "triangles of compassionate apposition" (*GM, CAT, SB, MT, NI*). Elaborate philosophical and psychological examination of the plays cited. Reprinted: 1980.56.

12 CHERRY, GRADY. "Life and Art: A Classification of the Artist-Figures in Selected Fiction of Tennessee Williams." Ph.D. dissertation, Texas A&M University.
   TW's artist-figures are classified in three categories: contemplative, hedonistic, and histrionic. Classifications are further defined and compared to characters from *GM, BA, OD, CR, SLS, KE,* and *NI*. The artist-figures all seek to achieve an interdependence between life and art, a theme TW does not resolve, but illustrates with depth and insight. (*DAI* 38:2121A.)

13 CHESLER, S. ALAN. " 'Orpheus Descending.' " *Players* 52 (October): 10–13.
   Starts with premise that "the conflict in much of Tennessee Williams' work is between the ideal and the real," and goes on to attempt to show TW in *OD* affirming "the beauty of man's

reach for the ideal." Discusses the three levels of its conflict (on stage, symbolic, mythic) and cites the first as the most important. Then goes on to show the development of these three levels within the plot. Ends with argument that in *OD* "the emphasis is on the love and mutual struggles of the hero and the heroine."

14 ————. "Tennessee Williams: Reassessment and Assessment." In Tharpe (1977.93), pp. 848–80.

Survey of the criticism of the plays from *BA*. Considers original productions as well as revivals, the effect of different directors upon works, scholarly as opposed to popular work; emphasizes the place of *GM* and *SND* in forming and sustaining TW's reputation; anticipates the modification of critical estimate since the playwright's last word hasn't yet come.

15 CLARK, JUDITH HERSH. "The Countess: Center of *This Is* (*An Entertainment*)." In *Tennessee Williams: A Collection of Critical Essays*. Edited by Stephen S. Stanton. Englewood Cliffs, N.J.: Prentice Hall, pp. 179–91.

TIE "shows Williams' concern with characterization, particularly as an outgrowth of characters he explored in two earlier plays": *BAR* and *2CP*. Discusses the centrality of the Countess in the play.

16 CLARKE, GERALD. "The 89% Solution." *Time* 109 (7 February):94.

Book review of *LDW*. "One of the inestimable merits of this book is that through this newly discovered treasure of prose, the reader too sees and cares how it is and how it has been with America's greatest living playwright."

17 CLURMAN, HAROLD. Review of *NI*. *Nation* 224 (1 and 8 January): 28–29.

Refers back to original 1962 production. Says he now considers it one of TW's "better . . . later plays." Discusses the autobiographical details in the plot, linking TW to Shannon. "The glamour and soiled lyricism that the play seemed initially to possess have faded." Generally negative about Chamberlain and Miles.

18   ————. Review of *VC*. *Nation* 224 (28 May):669.
      It seems like "still another revival." Plot details, says all the
      characters "ride on the streetcar named desire. . . . The dialogue
      has some of the usual felicities of Williams' writing, though there
      are signs of a weakening in precision."

19   COAKLEY, JAMES. "Time and Tide on the Camino Real." In Tharpe
      (1977.93), pp. 232–36.
      CR "remains an enigma. . . . Stylistic disparity promotes the
      play's bold efforts to break loose from the stage and spill into
      the house, enhancing the dramatic action's reliance upon theat-
      ricalist conventions." Asserts that "In no play of Williams before
      or since does his sense of form . . . serve him more faithfully."
      Cites, among others of its characteristics: its "nonlinear" struc-
      ture, "fragmentation of experience," "refusal to accept time either
      as sequential or as the fundamental common denominator of hu-
      man affairs," and its "calculated disorder."

20   CORRIGAN, MARY ANN. "Beyond Verisimilitude: Echoes of Expres-
      sionism in Williams' Plays." In Tharpe (1977.93), pp. 375–412.
      First part of essay concerns Expressionism directly, and its
      influence on and place in TW's work. Defines the convention
      exactly, traces its pre-Williams theatrical history, mentions
      Williams' university background which brought him into con-
      tact with it, and begins to show its particular use in the canon.
      Mentions its place in, among others, *S&S*, *CAT*, *GM*, *BA*, *YTM*,
      SND—in which such elements as "the focus on internal reality
      rather than external appearance, . . . nameless figures and abstract
      characters" are referred to. Second part of essay focuses specif-
      ically on *CR*, seeing it as Williams' most specifically Expression-
      ist play. Emphasizes its dream quality, its "symbolic settings and
      props," its archetypal images.

21   DAVIS, JOSEPH K. "Landscapes of the Dislocated Mind in Williams'
      The Glass Menagerie." In Tharpe (1977.93), pp. 192–206.
      Cites TW's "dramatization of men and women by a display of
      their fragmented, tortured psychologies and the depiction of
      these characters against a haunting environment" as the bases
      of the *"landscape of the dislocated,"* and calls this a pattern that

TW repeatedly uses, even into the later plays. Focuses on "Tom's mode of dramatic presentation," and examines Laura's place as "both the lyrical and the symbolical center of the play." Cites the play as "introduc[ing] Williams' Orphic dilemma," and also traces the way the play alerts us to Williams' concern with the South.

22 DeMott, Benjamin. "Culture Watch: 10's Tones." *Atlantic* 240 (September):90.
   Book review of *LDW*. "Not since Hunter Thompson's report on Las Vegas have I read anything funnier than these letters. . . . Everywhere in Williams' pages you feel a human presence, and hear the sound of a human voice, aware of itself, listening to itself, entertaining itself at language games, remembering its past, rejoicing in its own unfathomable, immeasurably perverse complexity. In a generation of ape and computer worshippers, I call this a necessary sound."

23 Dickson, Vivienne. "*A Streetcar Named Desire*: Its Development through the Manuscripts." In Tharpe (1977.93), pp. 154–71.
   Examines the resources of the Tennessee Williams collection in the Humanities Research Center at the University of Texas (Austin), considering the five complete play and screen scripts of *SND*, and shows its "evolution . . . from a romance to a tragedy." Moves from inspection of Williams' original outline to the later versions; provides graphs; distinguishes between images for the main characters as the play evolved. Considers Blanche's confrontation with the doctor as the most important evolving detail influencing "the tone of the whole play."

24 Draya, Ren. "The Fiction of Tennessee Williams." In Tharpe (1977.93), pp. 647–62.
   Traces the consistent lines of development obvious in his fiction, from *OA* through *MWR*. Calls *OA* "an early catalogue of Williams' concerns. . . . Williams' fiction often serves as a drawing board for themes and characters later amplified in drama." Shows connections with *CAT, GM, MT, KE, NI*. Calls the plays and stories "subtle variations of the same voice." Ending with *MWR*, he calls it "Williams' dark night of the soul," and claims

351

that it "is not representative of Williams' talent as a fiction writer."

25 ————. "The Frightened Heart: A Study of Character and Theme in the Fiction, Poetry, Short Plays, and Recent Drama of Tennessee Williams." Ph.D. dissertation, University of Colorado.

TW shows all of his characters as being possessed of a frightened heart—the quality that allows them the awareness of themselves as individuals who must confront and accept their mortality. Further attention given to what frightens these characters and what traits they have in common. (*DAI* 38:2773A.)

26 EHRLICH, ALAN. "A Streetcar Named Desire under the Elms: A Study of Dramatic Space in *A Streetcar Named Desire* and *Desire Under the Elms*." In Tharpe (1977.93), pp. 126–36.

Compares the plays on basis of their "identical subjects," similar themes and sense of conflict, same "unity of place." "Both playwrights take great pains to establish their respective environments prior to the arrival of the destructive agent. . . . Confinement pervades both plays."

27 EMBREY, GLENN. "The Subterranean World of *The Night of the Iguana*." In Tharpe (1977.93), pp. 325–40.

Explores the recurrent "idea that sex is fatal" in TW's plays, and the means of escape possible. Especially concerned with the unusually "optimistic ending" which he maintains is deceptive—in fact, the standard Williams theme is seen to persist: "that sex kills, that it is disgusting and dangerous." Provides explication of play to illustrate premise; considers "Shannon's concept of God," Maxine's influence, the function of "masochistic pantomime," and the level of final despair. Continued reference to and exposure of the "subterranean" levels in the play. Reprinted: 1980.56.

28 FEDDER, NORMAN J. "Tennessee Williams' Dramatic Technique." In Tharpe (1977.93), pp. 795–812.

Recalls TW's early successes and joins the speculation about what happened after 1961 and *NI*, "the last Williams' work to date to 'sustain itelf.'" Considers the change in TW's work since 1961: "What has happened, I think, is not a change in style, but in emphasis"; defining technique as "the way a play-wright employs *plot, theatricality* and *language* to establish tone, create character and express theme," he examines the canon in light of technique, distinguishing between pre- and post-*NI* works. Reprinted: 1980.56.

29 FEINGOLD, MICHAEL. "The Gang's All Here." *Village Voice*, 30 May, p. 87.

Review of *VC*. Claims Arthur Seidleman's "clumsy directing" is responsible for most of its faults; calls attention to the "decidedly narrow and strictly circumscribed field" from which TW draws in making his drama. Laments the injury TW does himself in this play.

30 FREE, WILLIAM J. "Williams in the Seventies: Directions and Discontents." In Tharpe (1977.93), pp. 815–28.

Considers the "general themes in Williams criticism" of the seventies (that TW repeats himself and that the works are excessively autobiographical). Contends that the problem with such critical estimates is that they fail "to take [the plays] on their own terms." Goes on to examine the works of the seventies, showing their capacities beyond the range of what the prevailing criticism has acknowledged. Considers *SCW* and *OC-2CP*. Reprinted: 1980.56.

31 GILL, BRENDAN. "Consolations of Memory." *New Yorker* 53 (23 May):83.

Review of *VC*. Discusses the sense of *place* in *VC*; negative on its script: "Mr. Williams has chosen to write the play in the languidly discursive style of his recent experiments in autobiography."

32 GOLDFARB, ALVIN. "*Period of Adjustment* and the New Tennessee Williams." In Tharpe (1977.93), pp. 310–17.

General analysis of this "serious comedy," including data on its premieres, its critical and popular reception, its plot and themes, its use of slapstick, its satire. Questions how typical of Williams this work is.

33   GOTTFRIED, MARTIN. "Williams' 'Carre' a Glimmer." *New York Post*, 12 May, p. 27.

Review of *VC*. Hails it as a return to "the compassion, and poetry that once enriched Williams' plays, that gave master-pieces to the world," but faults the play as "undramatic and uninteresting." Production was "workshop level." Attacks the script as "virtually unplayable."

34   GRAUERHOLZ, JAMES. "Orpheus Holds His Own: William Burroughs Talks with Tennessee Williams." *Village Voice*, 16 May, pp. 44, 45.

Conversation between TW and Burroughs prior to premiere of *VC on Broadway*. They discuss autobiographical details in their work, New Orleans, nostalgia, actors, *VC*, drugs, death.

35   GRAY, RICHARD. *The Literature of Memory: Modern Writers of the American South*. Baltimore: Johns Hopkins University Press, pp. 258–60.

Refers to TW's use of the South in a "reductive process [which is] slightly more complicated than it is with Capote, because [TW] . . . remains less than fully aware of it." TW "depends on the romantic commonplace." Refers to the gothic quality of his plays.

36   HAFLEY, JAMES. "Abstraction and Order in the Language of Ten-nessee Williams." In Tharpe (1977.93), pp. 753–62.

Laments the failure to investigate TW's language in any but a "superficial" way; cites his language as "perhaps the chief single technical glory of our theater to date"; proposes going beyond a consideration of the often cited "poetic" quality of TW's language and investigating even "the mere vocabulary of abstraction." Focuses on TW's ambivalence about "absolutes," on what TW's "favorite abstracts" seem to be; compares him to ONeill and Albee.

37   HARWOOD, BRITTON J. "Tragedy as Habit: *A Streetcar Named Desire*." In Tharpe (1977.93), pp. 104–115.

"I mean to develop here the [assertion] that *Streetcar* is in-tended, and ought, to be understood as a sort of *double* of tragedy, the 'lurid reflection' of it . . . rather than the thing itself."

Discusses the ironic rendering of tragedy in the play. High-lights elements that are redolent of *Oedipus*, that focus on the hero, that depict the good-bad antagonism, that draw in "the Apollonian illusion of individuality."

38 HAYS, PETER L. "Arthur Miller and Tennessee Williams." *Essays in Literature* 4 (Fall):239–49.
Claims the customary critical separation of Miller and TW "obscures their similarities, and even influence by Williams on Miller, particularly that of *The Glass Menagerie* on *Death of a Salesman*." Cites "the freedom of form that *Salesman* evinces" as primary influence upon Miller by Williams, but makes no claim of conscious borrowing by Miller. Close textual comparison of both plays.

39 HUGHES, CATHARINE. Review of *NI*. *America* 136 (8 January):20.
Review of *NI*. Although she finds it funnier than she remembered, she's troubled by the "long patches of dullness and over-writing."

40 JACKSON, ESTHER M. "Tennessee Williams: Poetic Consciousness in Crisis." In Tharpe (1977.93), pp. 53–72.
Begins with premise that TW's "idea of form [has] been a primary factor in determining the course of the American drama in the last half of the twentieth century; it has had a significant effect on the interpretation of reality in our time." Compares/contrasts TW with O'Neill; discusses his work on "an American theatrical language," his attempts to "objectify poetic vision," his interest in symbols, the modifying of his "Romantic intent," and the character problems in his attempts at tragedy. Calls attention to his "concept of moral freedom." And closes with argument that "for Williams, form is the concretion of stages in the progression of the poetic consciousness."

41 JONES, ROBERT EMMET. "Sexual Roles in the Works of Tennessee Williams." In Tharpe (1977.93), pp. 545–57.
Within the period 1943–63, "Williams was a precursor . . . in the depiction of what today is known as the unisexual character, a person in whom only the organs of generation define the differences between the sexes." Refers to his Romantic tradition

roots, his use of sexually ambivalent characters, his pouring his own autobiography into his female and male characters. Says that in S&S we see the greatest range "of the varied forms taken by sexual desire," and adds that "desire and death, be the latter moral, spiritual, or physical, dominate Williams' universe. . . . The leading male characters remain essentially similar in Williams' plays and fall into several convenient categories." The categories include: "outwardly . . . masculine," possessing "animal vitality" having "the torsos of a sculpture." Other types include the "multilated" and "passive victims." Also considers the role of the poet ("poet-savior, poet-victim") and the more "savage depiction[s] of homosexuality" that TW devises. Ends with consideration of SCW wherein the first "avowedly homosexual character actually appeared on Williams' stage."

42   KAHN, SY. "*Baby Doll*: A Comic Fable." In Tharpe (1977.93), pp. 292–309.

Explores *BD*'s origins, its uniqueness in the canon, and proposes "to examine the script as one might any other of Williams' discrete works." Calls attention to Kazan's role and influence, the cast, and the location work; pointed detailing of plot and theme evolution; indication of its "prototypes," its "generating line and full significance." Following the exegesis, focuses on its critical and popular reception.

43   ———. "*The Red Devil Battery Sign*: Williams' Gotterdammerung in Vienna." In Tharpe (1977.93), pp. 362–71.

Concerns itself with play's premiere in Vienna after its Boston failure and subsequent rewriting. Provides data on its evolution, its critical reception, Williams' own reflections (principally in *MEM*). Gives plot and theme summary/analysis. "Though the play may have structural faults, the production itself suffered problems not necessarily inherent in the script nor in the limitations of a modest stage." Reprinted in abridged form: 1977.88.

44   KALEM, T.E. "Down and Out in N.O." *Time* 109 (23 May):108.

Brief review of *VC*. "As he has had less to say, Williams has adopted an assertive confessional way of saying it."

45   KALSON, ALBERT E. "Tennessee Williams at the Delta Brilliant." In Tharpe (1977.93), pp. 774–94.

Advances the theory that "for many Williams characters, Hollywood is what life never is—but ought to be." Traces the use of movies in the canon; turns to consider the influence of movies on TW personally and his "borrowings" from films, and also his "studied use throughout his career of film techniques adapted to the stage." Reprinted: 1980.56.

46 KERR, WALTER. "A Touch of the Poet Isn't Enough to Sustain Williams' Latest Play." *New York Times*, 22 May, sec. 2, pp. 5, 30.

Review of *VC*. The play is described as a victim of irresponsible production (inadequate direction, acting, sets); a major fault of the play is its lack of conflicting urgencies; it has no "hard-driven wills determined on satisfaction."

47 KLEMESRUD, JUDY. "Tennessee Williams Is a Reluctant Performer for an Audience of High School Students." *New York Times*, 13 March, p. 51.

Describes an afternoon at the Winter Garden Theater, where TW sat on stage (occasionally drinking from a small bottle of vermouth) and answered questions asked by teen-aged drama students.

48 KOLIN, PHILIP C. " 'Sentiment and Humor in Equal Measure': Comic Forms in *The Rose Tattoo*." In Tharpe (1977.93), pp. 214–31.

Surveys the early popular criticism of TW's attempt in *RT* to construct humor—shows the categorizing of it as cheap farce, absurdity, and "grotesque comedy." Traces what he considers to be the authentic comic elements of the play: its "one-liners," "Serafina's verbal assaults," Williams' comic portrait of Alvaro, the chases, the "lingo of these southern Europeans," and its adherence to conventions of "romantic comedy." Admits though that "the playwright's inability to write pure comedy throughout the play may explain why *RT* is a tragicomedy."

49 KRAMER, VICTOR A. "Memoirs of Self-Indictment: The Solitude of Tennessee Williams." In Tharpe (1977.93), pp. 663–75.

Claims that the theme of loneliness running through *MEM* sheds light on numerous of the plays and is as valuable in understanding the plays as *Moveable Feast* was to understanding

Hemingway. "*Memoirs* provides information about personal loneliness and the distillation of that loneliness into art." Cites
the disarming quality of *Memoirs* and calls the book an "odyssey
... through madness." Discusses the data from the book, useful
as analogue to the plays, the method, the journal quality, the
form which emerges from the chaotic life.

50   LARSEN, JUNE BENNETT. "Tennessee Williams: Optimistic Symbolist." In Tharpe (1977.93), pp. 413–28.
Argues the premise: "Tennessee Williams is a direct descendant
of the Symbolists, whose concern with man's struggle against
the void led them to seek refuge in dreams. . . . At the core of
the Symbolists' retreat from reality was the decadent spirit."
Makes reference to TW interview in which he "discusses his
fascination with androgyny, especially androgynous males." Other
Symbolist characteristics she notes include: "mystery of life";
"the immediacy of death" (Poe's influence cited); "a new syntax
of poetic conventions"; TW's "Symbolist titles"—*GM*, *SND*; Williams' concept of plastic theater. Gives considerable attention to
CR and *SLS*.

51   LASKO, JOANNE ZUNZER. " 'The Fiddle in the Wings': An Approach
to Music in Drama." Ph.D. dissertation, American University.
Isolates various characteristics of music in drama. Examples
are limited to the works of TW since he employs music in a
variety of ways. (*DAI* 38:1391A.)

52   LESTER, ELENORE. "Tennessee Williams: Gay in the '40s." *Soho
Weekly News*, 20 October, p. 57.
Book review of *LDW*. Claims the letters give a "much livelier
and closer glimpse of the man than we get from his *Memoirs*."
Contrasts cited between rendering of same events and issues
in *MEM* and *LDW*.

53   LEVIN, BERNARD. "Deep in the Heart of Tennessee." *Sunday Times*
(London), 12 June, p. 37.
Review of *RED*, London production. "[I] found it a dark,
haunting and coherent play, as   strong as anything he has
written except his very best." Includes lengthy plot summary.

54 "Lowell Gets Medal." *New York Times*, 19 May, p. C14.
Mentions TW being inducted into American Academy and Institute of Arts and Letters.

55 McBride, Mary. "Prisoners of Illusion: Surrealistic Escape in *The Milk Train Doesn't Stop Here Anymore*." In Tharpe (1977.93), pp. 341–48.
Examines the theme of "self-induced imprisonment—ironically the result of an effort to escape" in TW's work, particularly *MT*. "Mrs. Goforth's attempted escape is chiefly *from* three elements of reality—society, illness, and death—and *into* two areas of surrealistic illusion—the past and pretense." Addresses the kinds of reality she attempts to escape from, and the conflict caused by the "irresistible force of fate."

56 McGlinn, Jeanne M. "Tennessee Williams' Women: Illusion and Reality, Sexuality and Love." In Tharpe (1977.93), pp. 510–24.
Considers the critical history of how TW's women characters are classified; also notes the similarity of TW's treatment of women: "A woman is presented at a moment when frustration has led to a crisis. She has only two possible ways of acting: to face reality or to retreat into illusion." Considers the period 1940–60, and delineates the movement more and more toward women who are "at least ready for unselfish love." Focuses on *GM* and *SND* in tandem; proceeds to *S&S* (where "Williams' characterization of women begins to change"), and on to *RT* and *CAT* and *NI*; eventually reaches conclusion that "examination of Williams' women characters show that oversimplified classifications are inadequate."

57 MacNicholas, John. "Williams' Power of the Keys." In Tharpe (1977.93), pp. 581–605.
"The question informing the substrata of all Williams' major work is: does personal disintegration press merely toward insignificant inanition or can the soul in painful despair regenerate itself?" Central image for the question is the Fall—shown in "two aspects of primal loss"—"the obstruction of passion and the erosion of sincerity." The essay proposes "to trace the etiology of damnation in [TW's] plays" and "to discuss how redemption ... may arise out of acute despair." TW "like Lawrence

and Blake, can conceive of no greater wasteland than that which traps and neuters individual passion." Focuses on elements that characterize this decay: disease, destruction, cannibalism, sadomasochism, damnation, death, and ultimately the access to redemption. Explores this thesis in the canon generally, grouping the plays where appropriate. Reprinted: 1980.56.

58. MADD. "Vieux Carre." *Variety*, 18 May, 124.
     Review of *VC*. "Abysmally deficient in almost every respect . . . seems more non-directed than misdirected by Arthur Seidleman."

59 MAROWITZ, CHARLES. "Tennessee Revisited." *Plays and Players* 24 (September):26–27.
     Reviews of *RED* and *GM*, London productions. Generally positive review of *RED*; praise for consistency of production and "vigorous and intelligent performances." Negative review of *GM*; calls performance "undercast."

60 MATTHEW, DAVID C.C. " 'Towards Bethlehem': *Battle of Angels* and *Orpheus Descending*." In Tharpe (1977.93), pp. 172–91.
     Considers setting, use of hero, mythic base in each version of the play; cites critical commentaries. Gives attention to Williams' concern with the "divinity of the hero" as well as the presence of ritual sacrifice; shows the opposition Williams structures between "messianic revolt" and "animal nature."

61 MAY, CHARLES E. "Brick Pollitt as Homo Ludens: 'Three Players of a Summer Game' and *Cat on a Hot Tin Roof*." In Tharpe (1977.93), pp. 277–91.
     Brick is one of TW's "most metaphysically mysterious" characters. Reviews the pressing question: "What . . . does Brick's detachment mean?" Examines what TW has written about him, how Kazan views him, and what certain critics have said; also considers the third act issue. Suggests T.S. Eliot's analysis of Hamlet as a method; also cites means implicitly suggested by McCullers, Mann, Melville. Eventually concludes that the dominant clue is in the short story "Three Players of a Summer Game," where the emphasis is on "images and abstractions." Finally, though, he insists the answer is not "knowable.'" Reprinted: 1980.56.

62 MOORMAN, CHARLES. *"The Night of the Iguana*: A Long Introduc-
     tion, a General Essay, and no Explication at All." In Tharpe
     (1977.93), pp. 318–24.
     Cites Eliot's "objective correlative" theory and surveys con-
     siderable literary lore in application. Eventually ties in *NI*, call-
     ing attention to its origins and its later dramatic form. Cites the
     probable "objective correlatives" within the script ("a world of
     symbols and minor characters"). Refuses to explicate the play
     since "this is an essay, a trial-run, a fungo."

63 NAPIERALSKI, EDMUND A. "Tennessee Williams' *Glass Menagerie*:
     The Dramatic Metaphor." *Southern Quarterly* 16 (October):
     1–12.
     Discusses *action* in *GM*. Action defines "Amanda as the center
     of a metaphor that is the drama itself."

64 NIESEN, GEORGE. "The Artist against the Reality in the Plays of
     Tennessee Williams." In Tharpe (1977.93), pp. 463–93.
     Focuses on the ways TW "has indulged his penchant for cre-
     ating in his plays characters who are artists of one sort or an-
     other." All such characters are found to be "sensitive, creative,
     and paradoxically, destructive.... *In the early plays his sensitiv-
     ity usually leads to his death. In the later plays he is an 'angel
     of death.'*" This pattern "is most strikingly stated in *SLS*, also
     illustrated in *2CP, GM, CAT, BA, LLL, DC, CR, P, S&S. SLS*
     "is Williams' strongest statement concerning the artist's condi-
     tion . . . his last positive statement on the subject." Shows the
     darkening vision of *NI, SB, MT, BAR*, and in the several versions
     of *2CP*; throughout the essay, *SLS* is seen as pivotal. Reprinted:
     1980.56.

65 OAKES, PHILIP. " 'Goings On': Strictly in Character." *Sunday Times*
     (London), 24 July, p. 35.
     Brief interview with TW and Maria Britmera. Both trade
     banter and old anecdotes.

66 OWER, JOHN. "Erotic Mythology in the Poetry of Tennessee Wil-
     liams." In Tharpe (1977.93), pp. 609–23.
     "Williams is not a poet small enough to be tidily classified
     under a single heading." Rather he shows clear signs of connec-

tion with the romantic, the modern, and the "Classical." Treats various poems in *IWC* relative to this theory. As far as his Romantic side goes, "Williams uses myth and symbol, intuition and imagination, to chart the recesses of man's soul and of the universe." Cites "the influence of Freud" and treats his poem "Lady, Anemone" specifically. "Proceeds to include his inclination toward Platonist metaphysics, and the images of death, crucifixion, as well as images of softness and melting." Added to those are drug images, gestation images, and images of sexual ambivalence.

67 PEASE, DONALD. "Reflections on Moon Lake: The Presences of the Playwright." In Tharpe (1977.93), pp. 829–47.
Examines the forewords of TW's plays, emphasizing the problem of the life vs. the work theories. Shows the pressure of TW's autobiography upon the reader of the plays when the forewords are considered. Devotes considerable attention to *BA, GM, SND, CAT*. Reprinted: 1980.56.

68 PHILLIPS, GENE D. "Tennessee Williams and the Jesuits." *America* 136 (25 June):564–65.
Discusses TW's relation to Jesuits (and Roman Catholicism); claims that TW descends from the (St. Francis) Xavier family; traces religious themes through several works.

69 PHILLIPS, JERROLD A. *"Kingdom of Earth*: Some Approaches." In Tharpe (1977.93), pp. 349–53.
Attempts to go beyond the popular estimate of the work as a melodrama and find a method for revealing its worth as "a work of great imaginative power and compelling intensity." Gives its background history, explication of plot and theme; calls attention to the levels of its symbols—especially for their Biblical possibilities.

70 PHS. "The Times Diary." *Times* (London), 2 September, p. 10.
Brief gossip item. "A claim is made by someone in the know that Tennessee Williams, the American playwright, holds the record of there and back transatlantic Concorde flights. Any advance on 14?"

71 PRENSHAW, PEGGY W. "The Paradoxical Southern World of Tennessee Williams." In Tharpe (1977.93), pp. 5–29.

Quotes Hugh Holman's axiom on paradox as basic ingredient of the "Southern riddle," and goes on to associate TW with the other major southern figures. Biographical details, aspects of his "world view" (primarily "his ambivalence of belief"), his attachment to "meaninglessness." Traces this element in his plays, citing appropriate criticism; considerable attention to *GM*, *SND*, *NI*, *SB*—highlighting sexuality, suffering, "man's body-soul dilemma," and like paradoxical elements in TW's canon. Ends with reference to *MEM*. Reprinted: 1980.56.

72 PRESLEY, DELMA EUGENE. "Little Acts of Grace." In Tharpe (1977.93), pp. 571–80.

"Williams has preferred to create characters who have the kinds of problems that call for theological solutions, for little acts of grace." Involved are the problems of isolation and alienation and the issue of community—in *GM* and *SND* for example. As he developed, TW incorporated "threads of hopefulness" in the later plays—*NI* involves a patent Christ-figure. TW's turning point is *CR* where he is "developing themes of hope . . . [and] also is experimenting with a theatrical structure foreign to his genius."

73 QUIRINO, LEONARD. "The Cards Indicate a Voyage on *A Streetcar Named Desire*." In Tharpe (1977.93), pp. 77–96.

Cites gradual obfuscation of TW's original thematic intent in *SND* by so much written criticism. Selects the angle of analyzing it as "a tragic parable of dramatizing existence, the fact of incarnation, itself." Limits discussion to two symbols ("the cards of destiny and the voyage of experience") and relates dialogue, action, and situations of the play to these symbols. Tries to show the play fulfilling TW's ambition to create "timeless" worlds. Reprinted: 1980.56.

74 RADIN, VICTORIA. "Fighting off the Furies." *Observer Review* (London), 22 May, p. 32.

Interview-commentary, at time of premiere of London production of *RED*. TW discusses his brother, the New York production of *VC*, New York productions of his plays, a new, unnamed novel.

75   ————. "Wolf-Howls at the Door." *Observer Review* (London),
       12 June, p. 26.
       Review of *RED*, London production. Calls the play "three
       hours of confusion." Claims the cause is "Williams's apocalyptic
       vision of the wolf outside the door." Plot summary, and con-
       cludes: "I cannot believe that Williams is now shifting the
       responsibility for human unhappiness from the individual to
       society."

76   RICH, ALAN. "Morpheus Descending." *Village Voice*, 30 May, p. 92.
       Review of *VC*. Cites "the ineptitude, the inexactitude" of
       TW's, "imitation" of himself in the play. Claims TW leaves his
       hero "empty and unformed." Plot details.

77   RICHARDSON, THOMAS J. "The City of Day and the City of Night:
       New Orleans and the Exotic Unreality of Tennessee Williams."
       In Tharpe (1977.93), pp. 631–46.
       Cites New Orleans's image as an "overwhelmingly exotic" city,
       one whose influence TW has felt—along with a host of others:
       Cable, Whitman, Twain, Faulkner, S. Anderson, Dos Passos,
       Percy. Laments that although it's been inspiring, New Orleans
       "has failed to sustain their artistic interest." Calls attention to
       the particular influence of the city's "exotic unreality" on TW,
       tracing its effect in *SND*, *RT*, *S&S*, *OA*; gives history of TW's
       actual involvement with New Orleans, starting in 1938–39.

78   RODERICK, JOHN M. "From 'Tarantula Arms' to 'Della Robbia Blue':
       The Tennessee Williams Tragicomic Transit Authority." In
       Tharpe (1977.93), pp. 116–25.
       Denies that *SND* is a "flawed tragedy" but insists instead that
       it's "brilliant tragicomedy." Admits to the "tragic implications"
       but sees them as factors in TW's "tragicomic stance." Shows the
       characters defying "stereotyped classification" needed to call
       the play pure tragedy, and cites the "humorous incidents coun-
       terpointing the dramatic action." Finally concludes that TW "is
       not a didactic writer."

79 SCHEICK, WILLIAM J. "An Intercourse Not Well Designed: Talk and Touch in the Plays of Tennessee Williams." In Tharpe (1977.93), pp. 763–73.

Argues against the critical theory that suggests influence on TW by D.H. Lawrence and Strindberg, especially pertaining to the "dichotomy of flesh and spirit.... Williams actually perceives no *real* conflict between the spirit and the flesh." Investigates this theory in *S&S, YTM, CAT, OD, BD, NI, SND, SB, P, 27W, MT*.

80 SCHEYE, THOMAS E. *"The Glass Menagerie*: 'It's No Tragedy, Freckles.'" In Tharpe (1977.93), pp. 207–13.

Focuses on forgetting and remembering in this memory play. Attention is upon Tom, his place, and his relative attachment to the action in the play: "From the first moment he enters Tom is trying to escape." Elements of his affection for Laura are shown to be pivotal.

81 SEIDLEMAN, ARTHUR ALLAN. "Tennessee Williams: Author and Director Discuss 'Vieux Carre.'" *Interview* 7 (April):14–15.

Interview-conversation. TW discusses *MEM, FK, SLS*, President Carter, films made of his plays.

82 SHAUGHNESSY, MARY ELLEN. "Incomplete Sentences: A Study of Tennessee Williams since 1960." Ph.D. dissertation, State University of New York at Buffalo.

Examines plays from 1960 to 1975 with a view to Williams' emotional, intellectual, and artistic transition(s) in this period. Treats *SND, NI, DC, OC, SCW*, as well as *MEM. OC* is said here to complete the cycle of experimentation Williams began with *NI. (DAI* 38:5485A.)

83 SIMON, JOHN. "Warmed-Over Vice and Innocence." *New Leader* 60 (20 June):21–22.

Review of *VC*, London production. Negative about cast and production; calls *VC* "his [TW's] disaster." Refers for comparison to *SCW, BAR, OC, RED*.

84 SKLEPOWICH, EDWARD A. "In Pursuit of the Lyric Quarry: The Image of the Homosexual in Tennessee Williams' Prose Fiction." In Tharpe (1977.93), pp. 525–44.

Begins by invoking Alfred Kazin: " 'The love that dare not speak its name' (in the nineteenth century) cannot, in the twentieth century, shut up." Goes on to consider TW's relation to the dilemma as shown in *MWR* and *MEM*; in the latter, "Williams only *seems* to warn the potential critic away from his homosexuality as an approach to his work." Essay insists though, "In fact, Williams' homosexuality does provide the critic with an important way of understanding" TW's vision. Considers "a homosexual sensibility" and the changes TW's own homosexuality has undergone; separates the "characteristic homosexuals of Williams' early fiction" from those of later work.

85 SMITH, LIZ. "Truman and Tennessee Try on Some Suits." New York *Daily News*, 2 February, p. 10.
   Gossip item. TW being sued by Truman Capote for $5 million; TW suing Donald Windham.

86 "Sorry I Wrote." *Sunday Times* (London), 31 July, p. 35.
   Brief commentary by TW. Expresses his regrets over having *MEM* published, and also agrees to let Windham publish *LDW*.

87 STAMPER, REXFORD. *"The Two-Character Play*: Psychic Individuation." In Tharpe (1977.93), pp. 354–61.
   2CP "is an important play. It is not a good play; it is too long, too opaque, and too obviously therapeutic to be good." But praises it for the new territory it allows TW. Traces its evolution, and shows the attention TW gives it in *MEM*. Insists on the turn to a new theater this represents for TW; in it "Williams tentatively estatblishes himself in the new creative world he first explored in the 1960s." Highlights its "Jungian view of the subconscious," the three conclusions Williams has drafted, its chief symbols, its contact with reality.

88 STANTON, STEPHEN S., ed. *Tennessee Williams: A Collection of Critical Essays*. Englewood Cliffs, N.J.: Prentice Hall, 194 pp.
   The editor's introduction plus sixteen essays. Excerpts from 1965.24, 1965.30, 1969.43, 1971.4. Abridged text of 1964.53, 1972.8, 1977.43. Reprint of 1966.13, 1972.55, 1973.3, 1974.12, 1975.2, 1976.29. Revision of 1962.37, 1970.5.

89   SULLIVAN, JACK. Review of *LDW*. *Saturday Review* 5 (15 October):35.
     "These letters have an extraordinary immediacy of emotion and detail.... The early letters alternate between a 'serene' down-and-out romanticism and the 'blue-devils' of depression.... The letters are filled with high-spirited, if sometimes scabrous, portraits."

90   TAYLOR, WILLIAM E. "Tennessee Williams: The Playwright as Poet." In Tharpe (1977.93), pp. 624–30.
     Asserts that TW's poetry shows a mastery of two techniques, "the open, sprawling, prophetic form and the tight, delicate lyric." And also claims that his poetry has an autonomy from his plays. Analyzes structural modes, compares him to other poets, shows how "volatile" his imagination is, illustrates the "fugitive poet" motif in his work; concludes that his poetry "was ahead of its time."

91   "Tennessee Williams." *Times* (London), 9 May, p. 9.
     Small announcement of the first commercial production of *RED*.

92   "Tennessee Williams Stalks the Sweet Bird of His Youth in New Orleans." *People* 12 (14 February):50–51.
     Brief. TW and Arthur Seidleman go to New Orleans "for a sentimental scene-setting visit" before *VC* premiere on Broadway.

93   THARPE, JAC, ed. *Tennessee Williams: A Tribute.* Jackson: University of Mississippi, 896 pp.
     Collection of fifty-three essays on TW, only one of which was previously published. Sections on *SND*, other plays as a group, "European Contexts," themes, prose and poetry, techniques, assessment. All essays are cited alphabetically within this year. Abridged: 1980.56.

94   THOMPSON, JUDITH J. "Symbol, Myth, and Ritual in *The Glass Menagerie, The Rose Tattoo*, and *Orpheus Descending*." In Tharpe (1977.93), pp. 679–711.
     "Williams' dramatic use of universally evocative symbols derives from his concept of and concern with the interrelationship

of the playwright, the audience, and the play." Goes on to
cite Williams' claim that "loneliness" is his dominant recurrent
theme. Essay attempts to show means by which TW takes
stock of his personal concerns and translates them "into recog-
nizably universal feelings." The specific means is symbols, and
their "major function . . . [is] to form an emotional bridge with
the audience, to create a drama so emotionally charged with
the concrete universals of archetypal images that their realization breaks down the psychological walls of our separate selves."
Cites two kinds of symbols: "concrete and transcendent," and
goes on to show the place, structure, and use in the plays. Her
field of reference is the major works of the canon, with details
of scene, character, theme. Reference also to some poems and
stories. Finally observes: "Williams offers no solutions for metaphysical loneliness, except for that rare and transient embrace
with our fellow man." Reprinted: 1980.56.

95   TISCHLER, NANCY M. "A Gallery of Watches." In Tharpe (1977.93),
     pp. 494–509.
        Asserts as premise: "The most memorable characters created
     by [TW] are women." Lists three categories into which they
     can be grouped—cites Falk's list—"Southern gentlewomen, South-
     ern wenches, and Southern mothers." But claims the categories
     require "reconsideration, correction, and expansion," especially
     since TW's developed "interest in myth." Mentions TW's aban-
     doning of the "standard American notions of male-female rela-
     tionships, and the Southern mystique of the woman." Focuses
     on his substitutions: "the Terrible Mother," "the sexually ag-
     gressive female" (which "fascinates Williams"), both examples
     of "the more vicious archetype" he favors. Finally, claims that
     through these women, TW "has domesticated his monsters."

96   TURNER, DIANE E. "The Mystic Vision in Tennessee Williams'
     Camino Real." In Tharpe (1977.93), pp. 237–51.
        Cites the "comic myth, the myth of rebirth, renewal, and re-
     dedication" at the center of all TW's plays. In *CR* the "cultic
     themes . . . have degenerated into a grotesque parody of their
     classic versions. . . . The structure of [*CR*] is that of the dream-
     vision. . . . The major symbolic device in the play is the Camino

Real itself." Goes on to discuss the "series of rebirths" within the play: "separation phase; transition; incorporation."

97 VIDAL, GORE. "Some Memories of the Glorious Bird and an Earlier Self." In *Matters of Fact and Fiction*, pp. 129–47.
Reprint of 1976.55.

98 WARDLE, IRVING. "Public Nightmare in Dallas." *Times* (London), 9 June, p. 13.
Review of *RED*, London production. Includes plot summary. "It seems that his [TW's] personal obsessions are now expanding into the public domain."

99 WATT, DOUGLAS. "Haunting 'Vieux Carre.'" New York *Daily News*, 12 May, p. 83.
Review of *VC*. It "ranks with his finest and surely his most candid works.... The play, however lurid, rings with honesty." Sees the play as "a new flowering of the author's genius."

100 ———. "'Vieux Carre' Is Vintage Tennessee." New York *Daily News*, 22 May, leisure sec., p. 15.
Commentary on *VC* after closing. Calls its failure unfortunate; compares to *MEM*; *VC* "is the first of Williams' 19 full-length plays ... to confront us so directly with the author." It is "resonant with his very special poetic insight and compassion."

101 WEALES, GERALD. Review of *AMA*. *New Republic* 176 (4 June): 32–34.
Book review. Traces the history of these poems vis-à-vis the TW canon of plays; discusses TW's "remarkable ear.... The poems have a heavy burden of infelicity ... a penchant for cliche."

102 "Williams's 'Vieux Carre' Goes into Rehearsal." *New York Times*, 9 March, sec. C, p. 24.
Brief item announcing the who, what, where of *VC*'s Broadway engagement.

103 WINDHAM, DONALD, ed. *Tennessee Williams' Letters to Donald Windham 1940–1965*. New York: Holt, Rinehart & Winston, 333 pp. (First printed privately: Verona, Italy, 1976.)

Reprints of letters which discuss their early relationship, TW's writing, personal details of TW's own life. TW has, since the publication of this collection, denounced Windham's annotations.

104 WOLF, MORRIS PHILIP. "Casanova's Portmanteau: *Camino Real* and Recurring Communication Patterns of Tennessee Williams." In Tharpe (1977.93), pp. 252–76.

Discusses TW's fertile 1945–55 period. Questions the origin and cause of the "communication gap" of *CR*. Asks also, "Despite his sincerity of purpose, does Tennessee Williams risk plunging *Camino* from fantasy into farce by portraying diverse characters, apparently legendary, within the carnival atmosphere of a time-less, placeless arrest-point?" Discusses three separate sorts of "romantic dreamers" in the work (and in other plays, by extended reference,) adding considerations on TW's reliance on "physical settings," and "Lights, Colors, and Music."

105 YACOWAR, MAURICE. *Tennessee Williams and Film.* New York: Frederick Ungar Publishing Co., 168 pp.

Discusses, in detail, the plays that were made into films (plus those that started out as filmscripts), analyzing the characterization, theme development, filming details, general criticism, and adaptation techniques. Adds section on "filmography" in which all specifics of production and cast are provided.

1978

1 AIRE, SALLY. Review of *VC*. *Plays and Players* 25 (July):20–21.

London production. Positive criticism; plot summary; praise for production and cast.

2 ANDERSON, MICHAEL. Review of *KE*. *Plays and Players* 25 (April): 39.

Brief. Plot summary with very little analysis.

3 ARRO. " 'Vieux Carre.' " *Variety*, 23 August, 90.

Review of *VC*, London production. "The work is not so much

a play as a collection of sketches thrown together in a sleazy New Orleans setting." Praises Sylvia Miles' performance.

4 ASIBONG, EMMANUEL B. *Tennessee Williams: The Tragic Tension.* Devon: Arthur H. Stockwell Ltd., 65 pp.
A published master's thesis, revised. Studies the plays through *MT*, relative to motifs of tragedy, disaster, and melodrama.

5 BARNES, CLIVE. "Williams' Women Find a Place for Loneliness." *New York Post*, 12 June, p. 23.
Review of *CC*, Charleston production. "Williams is here probing into the simple consciousness of people. The play is an essay, a very funny essay, about human generosity. Williams has rarely been funnier." He hopes it will go on to Broadway.

6 BROWN, CECIL. "An Interview with Tennessee Williams." *Partisan Review* 45:276–305.
In Key West, question-answer format. TW discusses *RED*, Polanski, Manson gang, L.H. Oswald, Wilde, his family, his sex life, Windham, exaggeration in his work, Hemingway, Hart Crane, V. Woolf, Joyce, Liz Taylor and Elizabeth Ashley.

7 BRUSTEIN, ROBERT. "Letters." *New York Times Book Review*, 5 February, pp. 14, 15.
Brustein defends his original review of *LDW* (20 November 1977).

8 CURTIS, ANTHONY. Review of *VC*. *Drama* 130 (Autumn):52–53.
London production. Considerable plot summary; relates it in theme and structure to previous works; says the evening is a "triumph."

9 CUSHMAN, ROBERT. "Back to New Orleans." *Observer*, 20 August, p. 21.
Review of *VC*, London production. Compares it favorably to *SND*; also says it "inherits its technique" from *GM*; calls it "a tribute . . . to the theatre of Elia Kazan."

10 FERILLO, TRAYNOR. "Play Provides Satisfying Experience." Charleston (S.C.) *Evening Post*, 2 June, p. 4B.

Review of *CC*, Charleston production. The premiere provided a "satisfying emotional experience [which is] the true purpose of the theater." Discusses this play's relative mildness: "Have no fears [if you're] squeamish about taboo subjects which are often a part of the works of Tennessee Williams."

11 FLEIT, MURIEL. "The Application of Interaction Process Analysis to Selected Plays of Tennessee Williams." Ph.D. dissertation, New York University.

Attempts to demonstrate "the applicability of small group interaction analysis techniques to the study of drama." The reported results indicate that Robert F. Bales' Interaction Process Analysis system is "efficient and reliable in the study of drama, [TW's] drama specifically." (*DAI* 39:1931A.)

12 FURTWANGLER, WILLIAM. "'Creve Coeur' Poignant, Sensitive." Charleston (S.C.) *News and Courier* 2 June, pp. 1, 4.

Review of *CC*, Charleston production. "Taken as a charming unpretentious entertainment, 'Creve Coeur' works.... One thing that added immeasurably to my enjoyment of the performance was Tennessee Williams himself, who was sitting directly behind me, guffawing."

13 GUNN, DREWEY WAYNE. "The Various Texts of Tennessee Williams' Plays." *Educational Theatre Journal* 30 (October):368–75.

A bibliography of primary works. Prelude to his *Tennessee Williams: A Bibliography* (1980). Some annotations.

14 GUSSOW, MEL. "Tale of Heartbreak." *New York Times*, 7 June, sec. C., p. 19.

Review of *CC*, Charleston production. Calls it "in evolution," needing a few surface refinements. The play shows a world that is "tender, poignant and measurably human." Praise for Shirley Knight as Dorothea, "an early echo of Blanche."

15 HAMILTON, IAN. "Peek-a-Boo." *New Statesman* 96 (25 August): 251–52.

Review of *VC*, London production. "90 minutes worth of wretched self-parody (all the old Williams cliches, but with the gay stuff now permitted to be spiced up and explicit), a laughable,

ponderous production . . . and acting of a screeching falsity that
only a writer as revered and talentless as this one could so fulsomely induce. It seems to me that no sane spectator could fail
to prefer traffic noise to yet more of *that*."

16 HOBSON, HAROLD. Review of *VC*. *Drama* 130 (Autumn):45.
London production. "The Good Lord, when he was thinking
of something else, endowed Mr. Williams with a mess of pottage
as his birthright. . . . [*VC*] is a feeble echo of old glories." Sees
the play as TW's "desecrating the grave in which his once fine
talent·is buried."

17 HUMMLER, RICHARD. "Bard Still Rules Non-N.Y. Legit Roost; Williams 2d for Resident Groups." *Variety*, 26 September, pp. 83, 90.
A count of the most popular playwrights produced by non-
profit regional theaters. Shakespeare is the most popular, followed by TW, followed by Noel Coward, Ibsen, Brecht, Chekhov, Shaw, and O'Neill.

18 Interview-commentary. *Sunday Times* (London), 13 August, p. 35.
Refers to current London production of *VC* with Hack directing and Miles playing lead. Gossip details: Miles dumps plate of
spaghetti on John Simon's head; TW carries with him two un-
finished plays and *CC*; TW begins to write new book of memoirs.
("I hated what the publishers did with the last book. It was
butchered in the editing. But this time I'm trying to take a harder
view of my life and the people in it. I'm calling it 'Mes Cahiers
Noirs.'")

19 JENKINS, PETER. "Summer Treats." *Spectator* 241 (26 August):
20–21.
Review of *VC*, London production. "In *Vieux Carre* Tennessee
Williams engages in every known form of excess and yet gets
away with it—or nearly enough—in the way that only an old
magician could. The Williams play is gross autobiographical self-
indulgence." Calls the total work a "sentimental extravaganza
and bad-taste farrago."

20 JOHNSON, HARRIETT. "Tennessee Does His Own Thing in S.C."
New York Post, 10 June, p. 31.

Focuses on TW's carrying-on in Charleston at premiere of
CC. Quotes TW, at press conference, on critics, TV, taboos.

21 KALEM, T.E. "Women Alone." *Time*, 111 (12 June):84.
Review of *CC* Charleston production. Praises the humor in the
play.

22 KINNUCAN, WILLIAM A.H. " 'Tennessee Williams' Letters to Donald
Windham: 1940–1965.' " *New Republic* 178 (4 February):38.
Book review of *LDW*. "The reader can, of course, transcend
Windham's editorial presence in the *Letters*. . . . The letters themselves provide us with only the sketchiest biographical outline,
but they profit from having been written during those interesting
years when the playwright's star was definitely on the rise.
Furthermore, it matters very little how self-conscious a letter-
writer Williams was: in contrast to the *Memoirs*, Williams'
epistolary poses are breaths of spring air."

23 LEAVITT, RICHARD F., ed. *The World of Tennessee Williams*. New
York: G.P. Putnam's Sons, 168 pp.
A picture biography of TW's life and career, with facsimiles
of programs, stills of plays and films. Reprints of 1940.10; 1945.59;
1953.1; 1966.34; 1972.5.

24 "Letters: Tennessee Williams—Donald Windham." *New York Times
Book Review*, 15 January, pp. 14, 18.
Two letters to editor, one by Windham and one by TW, responding to Brustein's review of the publication of *LDW*. Williams objects mainly to way copyright was secured.

25 McCANN, JOHN. "Tennessee without Taboos." *Washington Post*,
11 June, sec. K, pp. 1, 10, 11.
Interview-commentary. TW discusses his health, Gore Vidal,
the Concorde, *CC*, his critical reputation, *LDW* and *MEM*.

26 NIGHTINGALE, BENEDICT. "Tuition Fees." *New Statesman* 95 (19
May):686.
Review of *VC*, Nottingham production. "It's hard to know how
much of his 'Vieux Carre' is directly autobiographical. Maybe he
was seduced by a wide-eyed consumptive named Nightingale. . . .

These characters don't make things happen. Things happen to them, mostly as a result of itches, aches and glandular longings. . . . His compassion for his walking wounded has tended to become a bit woozy and maudlin of late."

27 RADER, DOTSON. "The Private Letters of Tennessee Williams." *London Magazine* 18 (July):18–28.

Attempts to set record straight on circumstances surrounding publication of *LDW*. (Legal case resulted when Windham claimed this piece was libelous; adjudicated in Windham's favor on 28 November 1980.)

28 RODMAN, SELDEN. "Three Neurotics." *National Review* 30 (1 September):1094.

Book review of *LDW*. "If Williams' plays themselves are never tragedies, that is because there are no heroes with whose betrayal or fall from grace one can identify; but in the *Letters* there *is* such an undoing, and Donald Windham has had the insight to trace it with compassion all the way."

29 SAROTTE, GEORGES-MICHEL. "Tennessee Williams: Theater as Psychotherapy." In *Like a Brother, Like a Lover: Male Homosexuality in the American Novel and Theatre from Herman Melville to James Baldwin.* Translated by Richard Miller. Garden City, N.Y.: Anchor Press, pp. 107–20.

Begins with assertion that "the childhood and adolescence of Tennessee Williams can be regarded as a classic psychoanalytic homosexual case history." Treats the biographical details pertaining to his thesis and examines evidence in the plays—*SND, SB, CR, CAT, OD, SLS, SCW*; also draws attention to *MEM*.

30 SHORTER, ERIC. Review of *VC*. *Drama* 129 (Summer):68–69.

Nottingham production. "A new play that seemed to crystallise many of his old studies of emotional, sexual and economic desperation." For TW "the shape of the writing transcends any stage."

31 SHRIMPTON, NICK. "Spring in Liverpool." *Plays and Players* 25 (May):39.

In a survey of the London theatrical season, mentions productions of *CR* and *GM*. Regarding *CR*: "It is very hard to make dramatic plot out of the eternal verities and Williams doesn't seem to me to manage it."

32   SIMON, JOHN. "The Sports of Spoleto." *New York* 11 (26 June):60–61.
Review of *CC*. Assaults the play and TW: "I doubt whether a playwright with a smaller number of themes has ever existed." *CC* "consist[s] almost entirely of rechewed bits of 'Menagerie' and 'Streetcar.' . . . There is no real drama here."

33   SULLIVAN, JACK. "Books in Brief." *Saturday Review* 5 (5 December):54.
Brief book review of *WIL*. Praises the essays that are "simple and anecdotal."

34   "Tennessee Plays for New Agent." *New York* 11 (4 December):9.
Gossip item. TW drops Bill Barnes and selects Milton Goldman as his agent.

35   THOMAS, BARBARA. " 'Tiger Tail' Superb at Alliance." *Atlanta Journal*, 20 January, sec. B, p. 8.
Review of *TT*, Atlanta production. "Superbly crafted, expertly performed stage work." Traces its evolution from *BD*. Hopes the premiere will presage long run and general acclaim.

36   WHITMORE, GEORGE. "Men and Men." *Washington Post Book World*, 8 January, p. 4.
Book review of *LDW*. Placed with short descriptions of books that might be of interest to homosexuals: "Dispatches from the temperate zone. What Williams colored prettily in his *Memoirs* is more vividly rendered here in this complex chronicle of a friendship that describes his career from 'self-dramatization to self-justification.' "

37   WILSON, EARL. "Tennessee's Coming Back." *New York Post*, 27 January, p. 52.
Brief mention of *TT* premiere in Atlanta. Refers to popular and press response.

1979

1   ADLER, JACOB H. "New Books on Southern Playwrights." *Southern Literary Journal* 12 (Fall):96–99.

Book review of *WIL*. Brief survey of the essays, recapping their highlights; cites the "autobiographical fragments." "Probably the major interest in going through this volume is in comparing Williams' remarks with actual plays."

2   ADLER, THOMAS P. "Two Plays for Puritans." *Tennessee Williams Newsletter*, subscription issue (Spring):5–7.

Contends that TW "had Eugene O'Neill's *Desire under the Elms* at least unconsciously in mind when he wrote *Kingdom of Earth*." Traces similarity of imagery of a gray house, a parlor "associated with the dead mother," the role of the birde and of the men in both plays. Claims that *Desire under the Elms* succeeds and *KE* fails.

3   BAIN, CARL E. Review of *TT*. *Tennessee Williams Newsletter*, subscription issue (Spring):21–23.

Atlanta production. Business and theater details of the mounting of this world premiere; plot details. Discusses its growth from the original *BD* text.

4   BARNES, CLIVE. "Williams' 'Creve Coeur' Is an Exceptional Excursion." *New York Post*, 22 January, p. 35.

Review of *LSCC*. "Will provide an insight into the nature of Williams as a playwright." Discusses its themes and its textual changes since Charleston premiere. Calls it "totally enjoyable."

5   BIER, CHARLES RICHARD. "The One-Act Plays of Tennessee Williams." Ph.D. dissertation, University of Southwestern Louisiana.

A study of twenty-six one-acters, focusing on the works found in the collections *AB*, *27W*, *DC*. The plays are analyzed with respect to theme, characterization, style, visual and auditory adornments, concluding with the assessment that the one-acters are long overdue in terms of recognition and proper status as works of art. (*DAI* 41:2101A.)

6   CHESLER, S. ALAN. Book review of *WIL*. *Tennessee Williams Newsletter* 1 (Fall): 17–18.

Despite the varied purposes for their composition and the diverse topics, "the book coheres. The collection is unified by a pervasive spirit." Praises TW's "voice" over his intellectual capacity.

7 CHOUKRI, MOHAMED. *Tennessee Williams in Tangier.* Santa Barbara, Calif.: Cadmus Editions, 85 pp.
   Biographical account of TW's 1973 trip to Tangier during time of his work on *RED.* (Contains a note by TW.)

8 CLARK, JUDITH HERSH. "The Victims in 'A Recluse and His Guest' and 'Mother Yaws.'" *Tennessee Williams Newsletter,* subscription issue (Spring):8–10.
   Analysis of "protagonist-as-victim" in the two short stories in the title. Such characters, from all TW's genres, "share the ambiguity inherent in such a dual characterization" as their character type suggests.

9 CLUCK, NANCY ANNE. "Showing or Telling: Narrators in the Drama of Tennessee Williams." *American Literature* 51 (March):84–93.
   The unactable observations of the "narrators" make TW's dramas approach prose fiction.

10 CLURMAN, HAROLD. Review of *[LS]CC. Nation* 228 (10 February):156–57.
   Brief. "What pleases me most in *[CC]* is its light touch, its teasing humor and its freedom from bathos."

11 DEAN, JOAN F. Review of *VC. Tennessee Williams Newsletter,* subscription issue (Spring):26–27.
   London production. TW "returns to his most familiar themes—loneliness, displacement, kindness, and the struggle between brutality and humanity." Laments his "unstinted reliance upon character types."

12 DEMARET, KENT. "In His Beloved Key West, Tennessee Williams Is Center Stage in a Furor over Gays." *People* 11 (7 May):32–35.
   Discusses repercussions of "tension and violence centering on gay community" in Key West as it affects TW; recounts assault

upon TW. Includes comments from TW on the issue and his reaction to it.

13   DERVIN, DANIEL A. "The Spook in the Rainforest: The Incestuous Structure of Tennessee Williams's Plays." *Psychocultural Review* 3 (Summer-Fall):153–83.
     Refers to the dilemma of fantasy and reality as a basis for a character's life, as it is involved in the make-up of Shannon, Blanche, Val Xavier, and Sebastian; treats specifically the means by which TW structures an integration of the two polar opposites in certain of his characters' lives. Involves the issue of sublimated and suggested incest as it pertains to the battle.

14   DeVITIS, A.A. Review of *CC. Tennessee Williams Newsletter*, subscription issue (Spring):24–25.
     Charleston production. Sees it as "a welcome return to a more recognizable world, . . . [his] revisiting of several of the cherished moments of his earlier plays." Cast details.

15   EDER, RICHARD. "'Creve Coeur,' New Drama by Tennessee Williams." *New York Times*, 22 January, sec. C, p. 15.
     Review of *CC*, off-Broadway production. Plot details; "a highly polished production." TW retains his "virtuoso command of theatrical complexity."

16   FOX, TERRY CURTIS. "Faint Desire." *Village Voice*, 5 February, p. 76, 77.
     Review of *LSCC*. Contrasts *LSCC* with *SND*, claiming *LSCC* "lacks the ornate language which was the true substance of the early masterpiece." Regrets "how little language Williams has allowed to slip through his characters' mouths." *LSCC* "is a quartet for four mannequins."

17   GAMAREKIAN, BARBARA. "Kennedy Center Honors Five for Life Achievements in Arts." *New York Times*, 3 December, p. C14.
     Society item on Kennedy Center gala. TW among recipients.

18   GANZ, ARTHUR. "A Life in Fragments: Tennessee Williams' Memoirs." *Tennessee Williams Newsletter*, subscription issue (Spring):16–17.

Book review of *MEM*. Disdains the book's disorganization, poor style, and self-indulgence. Speculates on the cause of such slim references to TW's writing.

19 GILL, BRENDAN. "The Theatre: Two Classics." *New Yorker* 55 (24 December):70–73.
    Brief review of *The Invitational* which consists of four one-act plays, one of which is *Life Boat Drill* by TW—"a gruesome glimpse of senile connubiality, described with a certain relish by a bachelor playwright."

20 GRUNWALD, BEVERLY. "A Haunted Williams Is Writing about Ghosts." *Women's Wear Daily*, 9 April, p. 17.
    Interview-commentary. TW discusses the murder of his care-taker-thief, evil, loneliness, his attitude toward women, his work habits, his painting, laughter.

21 HAIRI, SALAHUDDIN. "The Conflict between the Physical and the Ideal in the Plays of Tennessee Williams." Ph.D. dissertation, Southern Illinois University at Carbondale.
    Explores the conflict between the real and the ideal in *CAT*, *SND*, *OD*, *GM*, *CR*, *RT*, *SLS*, *S&S*, and *NI*. Reports on TW's failure to create believable idealistic characters and a balance between the physical and spiritual sides in human nature. (*DAI* 40:4595A.)

22 HICKS, JOHN. "Bard of Duncan Street." *Florida*, 29 July, pp. 6–7, 14–16, 18–19.
    Interview-commentary (in form of a mock-drama). TW discusses *CSH*, current work, his "compound" at Key West, his health, regional theater.

23 HIRSCH, FOSTER. *A Portrait of the Artist: The Plays of Tennessee Williams*. Port Washington, N.Y.: Kennikat Press, 121 pp.
    Critical analysis of the plays of "our national poet of the perverse." Goes on to illustrate TW as "a popular entertainer who is at the same time a serious artist." Examines the plays for their moralism, mythology, autobiography, sexuality. Calls TW "a reluctant pagan spirit, Dionysian, a guilt-ridden reveler" and shows the place and effect of sexuality in his plays. One section

on his failures and another on film adaptations attempt to provide a contemporary critical view.

24 HOIDITCH, W. KENNETH. "Surviving with Grace: Tennessee Williams Today." *Southern Review* 15 (July):753–62.
   Book review of *LDW* and *WIL*. Begins with premise that TW
   "has been for the most part neglected by the academic community" and then goes on to review four new books on TW:
   Tennessee Williams: A Tribute (1977.93), edited by Jac Tharpe;
   Tennessee Williams' Letters to Donald Windham: 1940–1965
   (1977.103), edited by Donald Windham; *Where I Live*, by Tennessee Williams; *The World of Tennessee Williams* (1978.23),
   edited by Richard F. Leavitt. Proposes to assess the "current
   state of Williams criticism," and where TW fits among the American dramatic greats. Brief survey of TW's work. Disappointed
   with TW's selected essays (*WIL*) but claims that of the four,
   it "provides the richest reading experience."

25 HUGHES, CATHARINE. "Capsule Comments." *America* 140 (24 February):135.
   Review of *[LS]CC*. Another of "the current string of inef-
   fective and largely unaffecting dramas" by TW; "production over-
   all . . . is only so-so."

26 HUMMLER, RICHARD. "Bard Still Rules Non-N.Y. Legit Roost."
Variety, 26 September, pp. 83, 90.
   Reports that TW places second among the most often produced
   playwrights, first among the living; *GM* "is the clear fave among
   Williams' plays, with five productions on tap."

27 JAN-ORN, CHARLERMSRIE. "The Characterization of Women in Tennessee Williams' Work." Ph.D. dissertation, The University of
Nebraska-Lincoln.
   Shows the similarities in a range of TW's female characters;
   then goes on to demonstrate the evolution of psychological
   strength and morality, examining the characters chronologically.
   Plays through *SCW* considered. (*DAI* 40:4037A.)

28 KERR, WALTER. " 'Creve Coeur.' " *New York Times*, 4 February,
sec. D, p. 26.

Review of *LSCC*. TW "is still writing good parts for women." Takes TW to task for the absence of plot in the play. "The performances are sound enough to keep you gainfully employed" if one goes with prior understanding of the play's limited intent.

29 " 'Kirche, Kutchen und Kinder.' " *New York Times*, 16 September, sec. D, p. 7.
Very brief mention of *KKK* production.

30 KLEIN, ALVIN. Review of *LSCC*. *New York Theatre Review* 3 (March):19.
"A throwback to the good old days for Tennessee Williams, who seems to have discarded the metaphysical nonsense which afflicted his work for too long." Calls it "rather more an extended scene than a wholly realized play." Praises its dialogue and "clear cut" performances.

31 KROLL, JACK. "Secondhand Rose." *Newsweek* 93 (5 February):68.
Review of *(LS)CC*. Williams hasn't gotten enough past his old themes and constructs. The play is "classic Williams chemistry," but not good enough.

32 LARDNER, JAMES. "Williams on Williams." *Washington Post*, 3 December, sec. B, pp. 1, 8.
Interview-commentary. TW discusses Kennedy Center honors, his brother Dakin's politics, artists, the seventies, sex.

33 LONDRE, FELICIA HARDISON. *Tennessee Williams*. New York: Frederick Ungar Publishing Co., 213 pp.
Talks of the personality contrasts within TW and the many voices he speaks in; also refers to the widely varying critical responses. Goes through the plays chronologically, analyzing their plots and themes, and, where appropriate, relating them to each other. (Covers forty-one plays, through *2CP*.)

34 OLIVER, EDITH. Review of *[LS]CC*. *New Yorker* 54 (5 February): 99–100.
Merely plot summary and the slightest reference to the production.

35 ORTHWEIN, WALTER E. "Dakin Williams Meets Carter, Stars at
White House Reception." *St. Louis Globe Democrat* (8–9 December), p. 2A.
    TW's brother attends White House reception for TW and
other recipients of Kennedy Center honors; Dakin Williams'
political views discussed.

36 PATTERSON, JOHN S. "Tennessee Williams' Latest A First for off-
B'way Group." *Villager*, 20 September, p. 13.
    Discusses production of *KKK*; gives background on Cocteau
Repertory's affiliation with TW; the play is "committed to catching
a mood rather than charting a line of events." Gives details on
TW's involvement with the evolving script and with the production.

37 QUINBY, LEE. "Tennessee Williams' Hermaphroditic Symbolism in
The Rose Tattoo, Orpheus Descending, The Night of the Iguana,
and *Kingdom of Earth.*" *Tennessee Williams Newsletter* 1 (Fall):
12–14.
    TW's "original dramatic vision resembles an ancient version
of the hermaphroditic ideal." Finds TW's most pointed use in
RT; it "continues shifting throughout his later dramas," however.
TW denigrates the ideal in *KE*.

38 RAIDY, WILLIAM A. "Nights on the Town." *Plays and Players* 26
(April):37.
    Review of *(LS)CC*, London production. *(LS)CC* "urgently
wants to touch the heart, but it is a difficult feat to accomplish
through distorted comedy." Discusses the theme of loneliness the
play develops.

39 REPPERT, CAROL F. "*Suddenly Last Summer*: A Re-Evaluation of
Catharine Holly in Light of Melville's *Chola Widow.*" *Tennessee
Williams Newsletter* 1 (Fall):8–11.
    Surveys the ways Catharine has been consistently misinterpreted;
determines to "demonstrate that [her] character is as
ambivalent as those of her dramatic counterparts." Considers her
re-evaluation to result "in an epistemological crisis for the audience."

40 Review of *WIL*. *Antioch Review* 37 (Summer):379.
    Brief, one-paragraph review. "We gain a personal revelation
    of the man as a writer, as a singular artist. His honesty and direct-
    ness . . . comes forth."

41 SMITH, LIZ. "Tough Talk from Tennessee." New York *Daily News*,
    18 May, p. 8.
    Gossip item. Verbal skirmish between TW and Mickey Mantle
    over Mantle's antigay remarks.

42 STANTON, STEPHEN S., ed. "News, Notes and Queries." *Tennessee
    Williams Newsletter* 1 (Fall):40–46.
    TW news. MLA convention to have a special TW session; Rose
    Williams moves to Key West; TW reads poems at New York
    University; TW Fine Arts Center to open in Key West; TW
    appears on "Dick Cavett Show"; TW's participation in Visconti's
    Senso explained.

43 STEIN, HARRY. "A Day in the Life of Tennessee Williams." *Esquire*
    91 (5 June):79.
    Interview. TW discusses his "supposed 'mugging' a few months
    ago"; Key West; his sister "Miss Rose"; "the process of writing";
    about being made to compete with himself; about *CSH*, then
    being typed.

44 STUART, ROXANA. "The Southernmost *Desire*." *Tennessee Williams
    Newsletter* 1 (Fall):3–7.
    First of two parts (succeeding part in Spring 1980). Author
    discusses her admiration for TW and her pleasure in playing
    three of his "great roles." Quotes TW on Blanche, original pro-
    duction of *SND*.

45 TALLMER, JERRY. "Knight Speaks about 'Coeur'—Frankly." *New
    York Post*, 19 January, pp. 38, 47.
    Interview with Shirley Knight prior to off-Broadway opening
    of *LSCC*; says she's doing the play because of her "care about
    [TW's] sanity."

46 TAYLOR, LYLE. "*Two-Character Play*: A Producer's View." *Ten-
    nessee Williams Newsletter* 1 (Fall):20–23.

Discusses TW's concern for the quality of the San Francisco production of *TCP* after its numerous failed attempts. Praises TW's care and guidance and goes on to contend that *TCP* is one of TW's "most exciting and deeply interesting plays."

47 "Tennessee Williams (Playwright), Craig Anderson (Producer/ Director) Talk with T.E. Kalem (Theatre Critic) About 'Creve Coeur.' " *New York Theatre Review* 3 (March):14–18.
Round-table discussion about genesis, meaning, and impact of *CC*. TW discusses editing, male-female characters, Charleston premiere, exposition, members of the cast.

48 "Tennessee Williams Reflects on Fragility of Friendship." *New York Times*, 15 March, sec. C, p. 16.
Brief item. Observations on the recent murder at TW's home in Key West.

49 WATT, DOUGLAS. " 'Lovely Sunday' Is Trivial and Uneven." New York *Daily News*, 22 January, p. 27.
Review of *[LS]CC*. It "plays like a pilot for a sitcom that is destined never to reach the home screen." Dismisses the comic attempts; says audience is "left with a blurred cartoon."

50 WEALES, GERALD. Book review of *LDW*. *Tennessee Williams Newsletter*, subscription issue (Spring):11–13.
"The collection has minimal appeal as a work in its own right. The letters are too dependent on shared references to create the worlds—gay, artistic, theatrical—out of which they grew." Finds interest in anecdotes about premiere of *GM* and the "struggles with" *YTM*. Focuses on what they tell of the influences upon TW's literary output; contends that the letters are superior to *MEM*.

51 ————. "Tennessee's Waltz." *Commonweal* 106 (16 March):55– 56.
Review of *[LS]CC*. Considerable plot summary; characters "lack the urgency of the early Tennessee Williams heroines."

52 "Work in Progress." New York *Daily News*, 25 December, p. 13.
Brief mention of *KKK* at Cocteau Repertory.

1980

1 ADLER, THOMAS P., CLARK, JUDITH HERSH, and TAYLOR, LYLE. "Tennessee Williams in the Seventies: A Checklist." *Tennessee Williams Newsletter* 2 (Spring):24–29.

A checklist divided into productions of full-length and one-act works, revivals, fiction, poetry, nonfiction; brief section on secondary material.

2 ARNOLD, CHRISTINE. "Center-by-the-Sea: Key West Exalts Tennessee Williams." *Miami Herald*, (20 January), sec. L, pp. 1, 3.

Discusses impending opening of Tennessee Williams Fine Arts Center at Florida Keys Community College, near Key West; mention of *WMM*.

3 BARNES, CLIVE. " 'Clothes' Needs Some Tailoring." *New York Post*, 27 March, pp. 50, 51.

Review of *CSH*. "The biographical play is a curious and usually unsatisfactory form of theater." Prefers to call it a "memory" play, a "fantasy of reason." TW "has failed to shape it into the special surrealistic [form] that even a dramatic fantasy must have. . . . much of the writing is almost defiantly flat and banal."

4 ———. "*Going to Bat for the Stage's Big 3.*" *New York Post*, 10 April, pp. 41, 46.

Commentary on *CSH* subsequent to initial review. Cites the general critical response; discusses the ways the play might have been tailored; refers to *OC*, *SCW*, and *CC* as indications of TW's "genius."

5 "A Birthday for Williams." *New York Times*, 25 March, sec. B, p. 18.

TW to attend birthday party after opening of *CSH* in New York.

6 BLUM, DAVID J. "The Art and Anger of Tennessee Williams." *Wall Street Journal*, 21 November, p. 29.

Interview-commentary in Chicago at time of *SML* premiere. TW discusses dislike of New York and its critics, his dismay over failure of *CSH*, his thorough dislike of *New York Times*.

7 BRUSTEIN, ROBERT. "Robert Brustein on Theater: Advice for Broadway." *New Republic* 182 (3 May):27.

Review of *CSH*. "For those who are still interested in my impressions of Tennessee Williams's recent misfortune, I can say, briefly, that 'Clothes for a Summer Hotel' is another version of 'A Streetcar Named Desire,' with mad Zelda substituting for neurotic Blanche DuBois."

8 BUCKLEY, PETER. "Tennessee Williams' New Lady." *Horizon* 23 (April):66–71.

Review of *CSH*. Discusses historic, biographical basis for Zelda in *CSH* and goes on to examine the women characters in other plays, starting with *GM*; gives attention to various successful and unsuccessful periods in his work, and then reviews *CSH*—says "it is a work of moods," and therefore similar to *GM*, *S&S*, *CR*; compares Zelda and Blanche. Focuses more on heroine than on the play.

9 CARPENTER, CHARLES A. "Studies of Tennessee Williams' Drama: A Selective International Bibliography: 1966–1978." *Tennessee Williams Newsletter* 2 (Spring):11–23.

Excerpts from his international bibliography of modern drama studies published since 1966; two hundred (plus) references to TW criticism in Roman alphabet languages.

10 "Carter Gives Medal of Freedom to His Mentor, Rickover and 13." *New York Times*, 10 June, sec. D, p. 9.

TW among those receiving Medal of Freedom.

11 CLAY, J.H. "The Broken Unicorn." *Tennessee Williams Newsletter* 2 (Fall):47–52.

Mentions finding a production of *GM* unmemorable and questions why "so many 'good' productions—most it seems—[are] like this." Discusses experiments with college students in issues of creativity and is surprised by results.

12 CLURMAN, HAROLD. "'Did Shaw Quit? Or O'Neill?'" *New York Times*, 13 July, sec. D, pp. 4, 11.

Letter to drama editor, chiding TW's and Quintero's "cries

of bitterness" concerning the Broadway run of *CSH*. TW responds in *Times*, 3 August, sec. 2, pp. 4, 14.

13 ————. Review of *CSH*. *Nation* 230 (19 April):477.
   "A quick failure." Tries to point out what was wrong with the
   structure of the play.

14 COPELAND, ROGER. "The British Always Have a Word for It." *New
   York Times*, 3 August, sec. 2, pp. 1, 3.
   Lengthy article concerning modern British drama. Williams
   is mentioned briefly; his *SND* is compared to John Osborne's
   Look Back in Anger. "The male protagonists of these two plays
   ... both radiate a primal socially 'uncouth' energy. But Williams
   felt compelled to make Stanley uneducated and inarticulate in
   order to preserve his animal vitality, as if eloquence would sap
   his bodily juices and domesticate him."

15 CUMMINGS, JUDITH, and JOHNSTON, LAURIE. "14 Win Medal of
   Freedom." *New York Times*, 22 April, sec. B, p. 8.
   News item. Announcement from the White House that four-
   teen prominent Americans, including TW, are to be awarded the
   Medal of Freedom.

16 DOWLING, ELLEN, and PRIDE, NANCY. "Three Approaches to Directing *A Streetcar Named Desire*." *Tennessee Williams Newsletter* 2 (Fall):16–20.
   Comments on a particular (Texas A&M) production of *SND*
   and the audience's enthusiasm for Stanley. Presents three directing approaches "to maximize the varying levels of actor com-
   petencies while still producing a good performance." Three traditional possibilities explored.

17 "Edwina Dakin Williams Dies; Mother of Author, Playwright." *St.
   Louis Post-Dispatch*, 2 June, p. 11B.
   Obituary. Died "of infirmities" at 95. Mentions her being
   reputed source for Amanda; refers to her assistance to TW in
   his early writing years.

18 "Edwina Williams Is Dead at 95; Mother of Tennessee Williams."
   New York Times, 4 June, p. 26.

Obituary. Mrs. Williams died in a nursing home in St. Louis, Sunday, 1 June. She is survived by sons Dakin, Tennessee, daughter Rose, and two grandchildren.

19 "Edwina Williams Rites Thursday; Playwright's Mother." *St. Louis Globe Democrat*, 3 June, p. 12A.
    Obituary. Establishes place of death and illness of "Miss Edwina." Claims she "was immortalized as 'Amanda.'" Mentions her book on TW.

20 GILL, BRENDAN. "Body Snatching." *New Yorker* 56 (7 April):116, 118.
    Review of *CSH*. It contains "scarcely a shred of his talent." TW's tactics are those of a "second-rate scandal-mongering journalist." Calls it serious "mischief."

21 "Going South for Tennessee Williams." New York *Daily News*, 22 January, p. 8.
    Brief mention of opening of Tennessee Williams Fine Arts Center at Florida Keys Community College, and the premiere of *WMM*; also lists some celebrities slated to attend.

22 GUNN, DREWEY WAYNE. *Tennessee Williams: A Bibliography.* Metuchen, N.J., and London: Scarecrow Press, 255 pp.
    Thorough primary bibliography which organizes TW's publications (in English and other languages), locates extant manuscripts, lists "important productions" of the plays; also provides a checklist of secondary materials. The volume represents the only significant published attempt to organize the canon—the plays as well as the poetry and prose.

23 GUSSOW, MEL. "Stage: Julie Haydon Plays Mother in 'Glass Menagerie.'" *New York Times*, 6 November, sec.C, p. 16.
    Review of *GM*. "A memory play that shifts between the lights of remembered laughter and affection, and the melancholy of doubt and self-defeat." Concerns off-Broadway production featuring Julie Haydon (who played Laura in the original 1945 production) playing the role of Amanda. "This petite actress ... is ... the dominant figure on stage. Unhappily, her performance does not capture the essential values of the stage."

24 HEALY, PAUL. "Geraldine Page: Psyched up for Whatever the Crit-
    ics Say." New York *Daily News*, 12 March, p. 43.
    Page interviewed prior to Broadway premiere of *CSH*. She
    discusses cast attitudes and fears; lengthy comment on Washing-
    ton, D.C., tryout and negative press there.

25 HERRIDGE, FRANCES. "Quintero Finds 'Clothes' Suitable." *New York
    Post*, 21 March, p. 42.
    Pre-Broadway premiere (of *CSH*) interview with Quintero. He
    discusses the play's pre-New York record.

26 HORNAK, RICHARD WRAY. Review of *KKK*. *Tennessee Williams
    Newsletter* 2 (Spring):33–35.
    Off-Broadway production. Quotes TW's description of it as
    "an outrage for the stage." Considers TW's motives here to be
    "more Promethean than scandalous." Plot details on the three
    separate stories.

27 HOUSTON, NEAL B. "Meaning by Analogy in 'Suddenly Last Sum-
    mer.'" *Notes on Modern American Literature* 4 (Fall): Item 24.
    Discusses the "three key analogies" that demonstrate TW's
    "religious apostasy" in *SLS*: Melville's description of the Galap-
    agos Islands; Sebastian's behavior after the experience in the
    Encantadas; Sebastian's severing of the "Oedipal ties."

28 JACKSON, ESTHER M. "Tennessee Williams' *Out Cry*: Studies in
    Dramatic Form at the University of Wisconsin, Madison." *Ten-
    nessee Williams Newsletter* 2 (Fall):6–12.
    Report on research seminar, its emphases, activities, and
    participants.

29 JOHNS, SARAH BOYD. "Williams' Journey to *Streetcar*: An Analysis
    of Pre-Production Manuscripts of *A Streetcar Named Desire*."
    Ph.D. dissertation, University of South Carolina.
    Contains transcripts of fifty pages of early drafts of *SND*.
    Discusses *SND*'s evolution from a brief film scenario set in the
    Italian-American section of Chicago to its final 1947 production
    form. (*DAI* 41:3107A.)

30 KAHN, SY M. Book review of *AMA*. *Tennessee Williams News-letter* (Spring):30–32.
    "The volume articulates an outcry ... expressing the poet's distress in facing old age and loneliness. ... They are poems of honest fear and night-sweats, apprehension and wonder." Treats several poems individually.

31 KAKUTANI, MICHIKO. "'Ghosts' of the Fitzgeralds Rehearsing under the Watchful Eye of Williams." *New York Times*, 18 January, sec. C, p. 9.
    Details on prepremiere goings-on with cast and TW. Consider-able quoting of Jose Quintero, director.

32 ————. "Williams and Quintero Build a 'Summer Hotel.'" *New York Times*, 23 March, sec. 2, pp. 1, 26.
    Discusses *CSH*'s preparation for Broadway premiere. Refer-ences to recently failed TW's works, and TW's attempts to re-write this while on road.

33 KALEM, T.E. "Apparitions and Cakewalkers." *Time* 115 (4 Febru-ary):61.
    Review of *WMM*, world premiere in Key West. Gives back-ground ("written when [TW] was mourning the death of his friend Frank Merlo"). "The play most nearly resembles *CR*. But it is more pensive and muted." It "embraces the four major concerns that have spurred Williams' dramatic imagination: lone-liness, love, the violated heart and the valiancy of survival."

34 KALSON, ALBERT E. "A Source for *Cat on a Hot Tin Roof*." *Tennessee Williams Newsletter* 2 (Fall):21–22.
    Considers the possibility of J. B. Priestley's *Dangerous Corner* having "insisted itself upon Williams' consciousness" and becom-ing a source for *CAT*.

35 KERR, WALTER. "The Stage: 'Clothes for a Summer Hotel.'" *New York Times*, 27 March, p. C15.
    Review of *CSH*. "Mr. Williams's personal voice is nowhere to be heard in it. ... No one has let down the production physically or visually. ... But no one is able to do a single thing to bring the performance to plausible, troubled, passionate life." Chides

TW for not having "arrived at a definite attitude toward either of his unhappy artists.... We are simply being told what we already know.... The play is structurally wasteful." Finally concludes that *CSH* "is Tennessee Williams holding his tongue."

36   KRIEBEL, CHARLES. "An Afternoon in Gray with Tennessee Williams." *After Dark* 11 (April):39, 76–77.
     Interview in D.C., preopening of *CHS*. TW discusses his paintings, *CSH*, the Fitzgeralds, anti-Christs.

37   KROLL, JACK. "Slender Is the Night." *Newsweek* 95 (7 April):95.
     Review of *CSH*. Questions why TW wrote the play at all. Says he "adds no deep insights" to what we already know about the Fitzgeralds. Extremely negative.

38   McKENNA, JOHN J. "Interviews with Williams." *Tennessee Williams Newsletter* 2 (Fall):26–28.
     Attempts "to evaluate several [interviews] that have appeared in the last few years"—1976–79; references to *RED, CSH, CC*.

39   "Martin to Capitalize Williams' 'Summer Hotel' for 400G; No Overcall." *Variety*, 23 January, p. 93.
     Business data related to Elliot Martin's production of *CSH*.

40   NOVICK, JULIUS. "Ungreat Scott." *Village Voice*, 7 April, pp. 74, 75.
     Review of *CSH*. Relates play's themes to TW's own life during last seven years. Claims that TW "wallow[s]" in the Fitzgeralds.

41   PHILLIPS, GENE D. *The Films of Tennessee Williams*. Philadelphia: Art Alliance Press, 336 pp.
     Focuses on the films and their directors. The long second chapter on Elia Kazan and *SND* and *BD* offers a history of the *BD* dispute, especially as it was reflected in the American Catholic press. A selected bibliography as well as a filmography complete the illustrated volume. Bases his esteem on the assertion that TW's "plays, even when brought to the screen without his collaboration, remain unmistakably stamped with his personal style and vision."

42 PHILLIPS, JERROLD A., ed. "Tennessee Williams: A Re-Evaluation." *Tennessee Williams Newsletter* 2 (Fall):53–60.

Report on panel discussion on work of TW during sixties and seventies, at American Theatre Association. Summaries of participants' statements.

43 PROSSER, WILLIAM. "Loneliness, Apparitions, and the Saving Grace of the Imagination." *Tennessee Williams Newsletter* 2 (Fall): 13–15.

Analysis of *WMM* subsequent to its Key West premiere. Compares it to *CR* and discusses the history of its composition; comments on its dominant themes and questions.

44 RAIDY, WILLIAM A. "Instant in the Wind." *Plays and Players* 27 (June):33–34.

Review of *CSH*, London production. "Filled with echoes of past plays, more eloquent and more feeling, as well as personal parallels which truly touch the heart. I wish it were all in better focus.... Whatever its faults [*CSH*] has a certain rhetorical lyricism which recalls the poetic Williams of old."

45 REED, REX. " 'Summer Hotel' an Out-of-Season Eyesore." New York *Daily News*, 28 March, Friday sec., p. 3.

Review of *CSH*. "There isn't a sign of life in it." Wishes play had taken viewers' understanding of the Fitzgeralds further. Ample plot details.

46 SANDOMIR, RICHARD. "Tennessee Williams: On Age and Arrogance." New York *Sunday News*, 23 March, leisure sec., pp. 5, 12.

Interview-commentary, prior to Broadway premiere of *CSH*. TW discusses illness and pain; criticism out-of-town for *CSH*; the British response to his plays—and their love of language; the death of Frank Merlo; his paintings. "I just want to live to complete my life's work."

47 SILVERMAN, STEPHEN M. "Tennessee Takes Aim at Zelda's Life." *New York Post*, 12 January, p. 18.

Interview-commentary, prior to premiere of *CSH* on Broadway. TW discusses his rewriting, Geraldine Page, his future.

48   SIMON, JOHN. "Damsels Inducing Distress." *New York* 12 (7 April):
     82–84.
        Review of *CSH*. Examines *CSH* as an "unfocused, meandering,
     unnecessary play. . . . [TW's] Zelda is yet another lost soul, driven
     by her frustrations into lyrically foulmouthed dementia—just like
     all those other Tennessean Ophelias." Regarding the language:
     "The clever old hand reasserts itself, but the ear is failing."

49   SMITH, HELEN. "Tennesse Williams: 'I'm Hanging in There Baby.'"
     Arts Journal 5 (March):2–3.
        Interview-commentary. TW discusses theology, *NI*, O'Neill,
     Stoppard, *CSH*, *SC*.

50   SMITH, LIZ. "Making It up as We Go along." New York *Daily
     News*, 16 July, p. 8.
        Gossip item. TW said to be "now writing the whole story of his
     life." Maureen Stapleton will play his sister Rose.

51   STANTON, STEPHEN S., ed. "Abstracts of Reviews, Articles and Meet-
     ings." *Tennessee Williams Newsletter* 2 (Spring):40–57.
        Summaries of *CSH* reviews. Critical reaction to *WMM*; special
     session on TW at MLA; Gunn bibliography published.

52   ————. "News, Notes and Queries." *Tennessee Williams News-
     letter* 2 (Spring):58–66.
        TW news. TW receives Medal of Freedom at White House;
     TW's mother dies; TW's new agent, Mitch Douglas, signs con-
     tract; Kennedy Center bestows award on TW.

53   ————. "News, Notes and Queries." *Tennessee Williams News-
     letter* 2 (Fall):61–66.
        TW news. New edition of *RSMS* published; *LTD* filmscript
     finished; upcoming publications on TW.

54   STUART, ROXANA. "The Southernmost *Desire*." *Tennessee Wil-
     liams Newsletter* 2 (Spring):5–10.
        Continuation of observations begun in fall 1979 issue. Dis-
     cusses TW's reaction to a production of *SND*.

55 "Tennessee's Flying High." New York *Daily News*, 4 January, p. 28.
Brief gossip-news item. TW fails to attend rehearsals of *CSH*.

56 THARPE, JAC, ed. *Tennessee Williams: 13 Essays*. Jackson: University Press of Mississippi, 287 pp.
Thirteen of the original essays reprinted from his 1977 *Tennessee Williams: A Tribute*. Reprint of 1977.71, 1977.73, 1977.59, 1977.27, 1977.64, 1977.55, 1977.94, 1977.7, 1977.45, 1977.28, 1977.30, 1977.67, 1977.11.

57 WATT, DOUGLAS. "Williams' Ghost Play Shrouds New Insights into Fitzgeralds." New York *Daily News*, 27 March, p. 107.
Review of *CSH*. "He calls it a 'ghost play.' It is more of a blur." Ample plot problems analysis. "Scenery, costumes and lighting all conspire imaginatively to help express Williams' wispy and rather frosty enterprise. . . . But nothing can save this evening."

58 WEATHERBY, W.J. "Scott and Zelda Relive the Jazz Age." *Sunday Times* (London), 30 March, p. 38.
On *CSH*. Quotes TW admitting he fashioned Scott Fitzgerald from his own self-image: "At one point I went through a deep depression and heavy drinking. And I, too, have gone through a period of eclipse in public favour. Yes, I found Scott and I had a lot in common." Includes detailed plot and character descriptions.

59 "Williams Play Opens Florida Arts Center." *New York Times*, 26 January, p. 12.
Brief item on opening of Tennessee Williams Performing Arts Center in Key West, with premiere of *WMM*. Mentions celebrities in attendance.

60 YOUNG, MICHAEL C. "The Play of Memory: Reflections from *The Glass Menagerie*—An Interview." *Tennessee Williams Newsletter* 2 (Fall):32–35.
Recollections on events surrounding premiere of *GM* in Chicago, critical response to it, TW's activities during its rehearsal.

1981

1   ADLER, THOMAS P. "Images of Entrapment in Tennessee Williams's Later Plays." *Notes on Modern American Literature* 5 (Spring): item 11.

Begins with thesis that "Images of entrapment or confinement abound in Williams's later plays." Highlights the symbolic, allegorical levels on which we see this condition. Refers to *SCW*, *OC*, *LSCC*, *RED*, *VC*, and *GM*.

2   ————. "The (Un)reliability of the Narrator in *The Glass Menagerie* and *Vieux Carre*." *Tennessee Williams Review* 3 (Spring): 6–9.

Focuses on the narrators in *GM* and *VC* and raises question ("aesthetic issue"): "Why do we not demand the same consistency . . . of the dramatic narrator that we do of the first person narrator in a limited point of view novel. . . ?" Sees *VC*, contrary to *GM*, as "a play about the nature of art and the creative artist."

3   BARNES, CLIVE. "More Cloudy than Clear." *New York Post*, 14 September, p. 25.

Review of *SC*. "Not a particularly good work, too diffuse in its structure." Draws attention to TW's tendency to write plays "that are memory tapestries of characters, incidents, and vignettes." His tone "works better in a book such as *Memoirs* than on stage."

4   ————. "Tennessee Williams: A Toast at Turning 70." *New York Post*, 26 March, p. 39.

Tribute to TW on seventieth birthday. Brief synopsis of career and achievements. "His beachcomber genius, his defiantly tattered glory still fitfully blazes."

5   CHRISTIANSEN, RICHARD. "At 70, Even Tennessee Williams Is Impressed." New York *Daily News*, 23 April, p. 65.

Interview-commentary. TW in Chicago for *HNM*; TW discusses his past, his recent productions, works-in-progress.

6   ————. " 'House Not Meant to Stand' Needs Madness, Clarity." *Chicago Tribune*, 3 April, sec. 2, p. 3.

Review of *HNM*, Chicago production. Faults play for its lack of both "a connecting spine" and a "properly surreal tone for its hallucinatory madness." The play is not "integral" yet.

7 CLARKE, GERALD. "Summer of 1940." *Time* 118 (21 September):65.
Review of *SC*. Claims that TW's memories of his own past "would not shock a novitiate nun." Sees TW continuing like Sophocles, moving into old age, writing all the while.

8 FEINGOLD, MICHAEL. "The Playwright as Stinker." *Village Voice*, 16 September, p. 89.
Review of *SC*. Debunks script's thinly veiled autobiographical content; relates plot to *MEM*; sees TW picturing himself as "the unscrupulous horny bastard on the make . . . the playwright as stinker."

9 GOLD, AARON. "Tower Ticker." *Chicago Tribune*, 26 March, sec. 2, p. 9.
Brief news item. Crowd boos mention of President Reagan's name at TW's seventieth birthday gala.

10 GRUMLEY, MICHAEL. Review of *SC*. *New York Native*, 5 October, p. 33.
Some of the play's characters "come out looking merely like cliches; others have the familiar detailed skin of life's distress." Questions whether it "will wash on stage or screen as dramatic art."

11 HUGHES, CATHARINE. "Specters." *America* 145 (10 October):202.
Review of *SC*. "Certainly closer to success than such recent previous works as" *VC, OC, CSH*. Considerable plot summary and theme analysis. Finds TW becoming "a prisoner of a form of myopia."

12 ISAAC, DAN. "Tennessee Revisited." *Other Stages* 4 (17 December): 6, 8.
Begins with premise that "the failure . . . of Tennessee Williams' most recent plays, represents a significant chapter in the creative odyssey of America's greatest living playwright." Looks forward to reopening of *SC* in 1982; calls *SC* more autobiographical than

anything since *GM*; goes on to analyze the play as it already appeared in the unsuccessful off-Broadway run. Mentions TW's participation in the rehearsals. Calls *SC* "a work that deserves to live."

13 KAKUTANI, MICHIKO. "Tennessee Williams: 'I Keep Writing.' Sometimes I Am Pleased." *New York Times*, 13 August sec. C, p. 17.
Interview-commentary, prior to *SC* premiere off-Broadway. TW discusses his tenacity, his personal attachment to the plays, giving himself "more license," his decline in popularity.

14 KALSON, ALBERT E. "Tennessee Laughs: Three One-Act Plays." *Tennessee Williams Review* 3 (Spring):25–27.
Review of *PAG*, *FGC*, *SML*, Chicago production. Three one-acts which "all mask their anguish with peals of forced laughter, but the hollow sound evokes no echoing response from the audience." Considers all three "too shrill in tone." *MK*, premiering here, "veer[s] from parody to sentimentality."

15 "Keep Your Eye on: Tennessee Williams." *Harper's Bazaar* 114 (November):262–63.
Focuses on TW at time of New York premiere of *SC*; quotes Joseph Papp and Elizabeth Ashley on his quality and fame; refers to the then anticipated tribute for his seventieth birthday at Lincoln Center.

16 KERR, WALTER. Review of *SC*. *New York Times*, 27 September, sec. 2, p. 3.
Relates plot to TW's autobiography and to *BA*. TW "has not had the objectivity, the detachment, to make himself vivid to us. In the play at the Bouwerie Lane, he is simply a shadowy fellow trying to finish a script." Calls its language "impersonally rhetorical."

17 MOR. "A House Not Meant to Stand." *Variety*, 13 May, p. 410.
Review of Chicago production. Considers the rewrite of *MK* to amplify "the merits and defects of the original work." TW can "still burst out with a line that cuts to the bone of truth and he can delineate a character with a couple of verbal brush strokes."

18   "Playwrights Spotlighted." *New York Times*, 20 November, sec. B, p. 4.

TW and Harold Pinter accept Common Wealth Awards "for distinguished service in the dramatic arts." TW dedicates his award to his sister Rose.

19   "The 'Private' Letters of Tennessee Williams: Donald Windham Replies to Dotson Rader." *London Magazine* 20 (February–March):80–88.

Results of court hearing in which Windham successfully sues Rader and *London Magazine*, written in form of statements made in open court. A statement later from Windham (setting the record straight), and an apology for the original article upon which the suit was based (July 1978).

20   RADER, DOTSON. "Tennessee Williams." *Parade: Sunday Newspaper Magazine* (17 May), pp. 12–14.

Interview-commentary: on occasion of TW's visit to Chicago for premiere of *HNM* and his 70th birthday celebration; TW discusses Hemingway; artists; Castro; McCullers; Fitzgerald; Inge; fascism; his views on morality.

21   SCHEIDLER, KATHERINE P. "'Romeo and Juliet' and 'The Glass Menagerie' as Reading Programs." *English Journal* 70 (January):34–36.

Discusses classroom tactics to encourage remedial reading students, using *GM* along with *Romeo and Juliet*; mentions use of *GM* TV production.

22   "Sked New Williams Play Based on His One-Acter." *Variety*, 18 March, 311.

Announces opening of *HNM* in Chicago.

23   STANTON, STEPHEN S., ed. "News, Notes and Queries." *Tennessee Williams Review* 3 (Spring):34–43.

TW news. Gala in Chicago for TW's seventieth birthday; new film of *SND*; TW commissioned to write new play; upcoming publications and productions.

24   SYSE, GLENNA. "Tennessee Williams' House of Tremors and Quiet Terrors." Chicago *Sun-Times*, 2 April, p. 80.

Review of *HNM*, Chicago production. Emphasizes need to judge this play as "work in progress." Suggests remedies for tempo and characterization; the work needs to "soften some of the edges."

25 "Tennessee Williams Gala to Aid Fellowship." *New York Times*, 15 November, p. 76.
Announcement of 2 December salute to TW, slated for Avery Fisher Hall at Lincoln Center. Gives details on tickets and celebrities who will attend.

26 "True Love." *New York Times*, 25 August, sec. C, p. 8.
Announcement of opening of *SC*. Brief plot summary.

27 "Up Front." *People* 16 (23 February):24–25.
TW mentioned as being among other celebrities who have sought serenity in Key West.

28 WORTHINGTON, CHRISTA. "Eye: Brotherly Love." *Women's Wear Daily*, 16 July, p. 3.
Society notice. Dakin Williams attends organizational party to plan for gala for TW at Lincoln Center.

Index

401

Pollack, Robert, 1944.4
Pollett, Elizabeth, 1955.44
Pollock, Ellen, 1958.94
Ponder Heart, The, 1961.25
Poore, Charles, 1948.54; 1953.44
Popkin, Henry, 1950.40; 1960.98, 99; 1962.78; 1965.53; 1966.31; 1971.21
Porter, Thomas E., 1969.30
Portrait of a Madonna, 1947.4, 30; 1948-.32, 67; 1957.2, 79; 1959.7, 10-11, 14, 28, 35, 49, 60, 71, 80-81, 107-8, 113-114; 1961.41; 1973.85
Portrait of the Artist: The Plays of Tennessee Williams, A, 1979.23
Powell, Dilys, 1958.73; 1960.100
Powers, Harvey M., Jr., 1957.75
Pratley, Gerald, 1956.84
Prenshaw, Peggy W., 1977.71
Prescott, Orville, 1950.41
Presley, Delma Eugene, 1969.31; 1970.36; 1971.2, 22; 1972.43; 1973.67; 1977.73
Price, R.G.G., 1968.42
Price, Robert, 1958.74
Pride, Nancy, 1980.16
Prideaux, Tom, 1963.46
Priestly, J.B., 1980.34
Probst, Leonard, 1972.44
Prosser, William, 1980.43
Prouse, Derek, 1956.86; 1960.101
Providence, Rhode Island, 1957.7, 9
Provincetown Playhouse, N.Y.C., 1953.17
Pryce-Jones, Alan, 1961.65; 1967.25
Pryor, Thomas, 1952.14; 1954.10; 1956-.87; 1957.76; 1958.76-78
Pulitzer Prize, drama, 1945.14, 22; 1948.1, 55-56, 61; 1955.31, 36, 47-48, 87-88; 1956.60
Purification, The
—Dallas production, 1954.1-2
—New York productions, 1959.50, 101; 1975.16; 1977.64, 79
Pyro, 1960.102

Quigly, Isabel, 1957.77; 1958.79; 1960-.103-4; 1962.72; 1964.45
Quinby, Lee, 1979.37
Quinn, Anthony, 1950.10

Quint, Bert, 1956.88
Quintero, Jose, 1960.46, 48; 1961.66, 97; 1968.14, 27, 63-64; 1972.28; 1980.12, 25, 31-32
Quirino, Leonard Salvator, 1964.46; 1968.43; 1974.5; 1977.73

Rabb, Ellis, 1973.34, 37
Rader, Dotson, 1978.27; 1981.19-20
Radin, Victoria, 1977.74
Raidy, William A., 1979.38; 1980.44
Raisin in the Sun, A, 1959.69
Ramsey, R. Vance, 1969.16
Raynor, Henry, 1970.37
Reagan, Ronald, 1981.9
Reck, Tom Stokes, 1968.44; 1971.23
Red Devil Battery Sign, The
—Boston production, 1975.18, 24, 35, 50; 1977.43
—London production, 1977.53, 59, 74-75, 91, 98
—New York productions, 1975.11, 13, 37; 1977.4, 83; 1978.6; 1981.1; 1979.7; 1980.38
—Vienna production, 1977.43
Redford, Robert, 1966.4
Redgrave, Lynn, 1969.33
Reed, Rex, 1966.62; 1969.32; **1971.24;** 1972.5, 61; 1973.68-71; 1974.48; 1978-.23; 1980.45
Reid, Desmond, 1957.79; 1961.41
Reid, Kate, 1966.4
Reiley, Franklin C., 1948.57
Reisz, Karel, 1952.15
Remember Me to Tom, 1963.68
Reppert, Carol F., 1979.39
Rhode, Eric, 1962.73
Rice, Elmer, 1961.55; 1963.37
Rice, Vernon, 1949.22; 1953.47
Rich, Alan, 1977.76
Richards, Stanley, 1958.84; 1961.67; 1962.74
Richardson, Jack, 1970.38; 1975.41
Richardson, Thomas J., 1977.77
Richardson, Tony, 1959.19
Riddel, Joseph N., 1963.48; 1971.19
Rilke, Rainer Maria, 1958.74

32, 42-43, 47; 1980.6, 36, 38, 46-47, 49; 1981.13, 20
—loneliness 1977.49, 94; 1979.20
—parodied, 1961.52; 1966.64; 1967.33
—plays
—American South in, 1957.56; 1958.66, 74, 98; 1959.87; 1960.36, 39, 51; 1961-3; 26, 41; 1963.1; 1965.11, 75; 1967-.13; 1968.11; 1969.30, 39; 1970.22, 25, 43; 1971.4, 19; 1974.34; 1977.1, 21, 35, 95
—characters in, 1944.1, 4; 1945.25, 42, 62; 1948.8, 36, 39, 67, 72; 1949.14; 1950.40; 1951.62; 1952.5; 1953.18, 31, 35, 39; 1955.49, 66, 97, 102; 1956.91, 101, 107; 1957.63-64, 79, 86; 1958.12, 31, 91, 104; 1959.8, 23, 33, 46, 66, 108, 116-17; 1960.20, 29, 35, 47, 98, 108, 129, 133; 1961.26, 32, 41, 92; 1962.27-28, 39, 51, 58, 78-79, 93, 100; 1963.18, 24, 34, 37, 39; 1964.3, 10, 33, 35; 1965.11, 13, 18, 22, 29, 39, 59, 65, 73; 1966.5, 7, 14, 18, 31, 43, 57; 1967.2, 9, 20; 1968.11, 17, 24, 30, 44; 1969.4; 1970.3, 5, 11, 33, 43; 1971.2, 12, 19, 21-22; 1973.9, 13, 32, 50-51, 56, 74, 78; 1974.5, 9, 12, 21, 30; 1975.27, 38-39; 1976.8, 51; 1977.5, 12, 20, 23-25, 40-41, 45, 56, 60-61, 64, 72, 94-95; 1979.13, 21, 27, 39, 47, 51; 1980.8, 14-15, 58
—comedy in, 1959.21; 1960.12, 14, 19, 31, 71-72; 1961.26; 1964.33; 1965.60; 1969.16; 1970.8; 1971.19; 1977.7, 32, 48
—his comments on, 1945.55; 1946.11; 1947.8, 42; 1948.6, 13, 46; 1950.13; 1951.29; 1952.17; 1953.27, 47; 1955-.25; 1956.35; 1957.63, 67, 86, 89, 99; 1958.40, 74, 100, 107, 113; 1959.62-64, 87, 98, 104; 1960.15, 90, 105, 107, 124; 1961.18, 63; 1962.36; 1963-.17, 23; 1965.22, 59; 1966.74; 1969.14, 27; 1970.7, 17, 24; 1971.9, 15, 17; 1972.15-17, 23, 40, 44, 51, 56; 1973-.16, 39, 41, 55, 64, 71, 81; 1974.44,

48, 55; 1975.9, 17, 37, 44; 1976.46; 1977.10, 34, 74, 81; 1978.6, 18, 25; 1979.22, 43, 47; 1980.6, 26, 46-47, 49, 54
—conflict with censors, 1941.1, 5, 6; 1950.7-8, 13; 1951.55; 1955.98; 1956-.11, 16, 19, 63, 85, 87, 90, 92, 100; 1957.5-7, 9, 12, 20, 24, 33, 35, 69-70, 73, 84-85, 88, 91, 94, 97; 1958.20, 28, 63, 75, 89, 100; 1960.24; 1968.9-10; 1969.16; 1980.41
—dramaturgy, 1944.5, 8, 17; 1945.44, 62; 1947.35; 1949.4, 7, 15, 19; 1950.38; 1951.4, 15, 64; 1953.25, 34; 1954.6, 11; 1955.53; 1957.40, 47, 51-52, 75, 92-93; 1958.105; 1959.8, 29, 47, 50, 109; 1960.17, 20, 47, 49, 64, 85, 132; 1961.3, 20-21, 32, 41, 51, 60, 82; 1962.11, 16, 45; 1963.4, 8, 15, 18, 21-22; 1964.6, 31, 46, 53; 1965.25, 30, 60, 70; 1966.58, 68, 77; 1967.17, 23, 31; 1968.7, 30, 32, 41; 1969.10; 1970.2, 4, 36, 44; 1971.6, 19; 1972.8, 33, 41, 53; 1973.9, 11, 14, 30, 50, 59, 74; 1974.7, 61; 1976.16-17, 51-52; 1977.5, 11, 13, 19, 24-26, 28, 38, 40, 51, 60, 63, 80, 93-94, 96, 104; 1979.2, 23, 27, 36-37; 1980.44; 1981.2
—evil in, 1960.127; 1961.26, 42; 1963.8; 1971.12, 19
—evolution of films from, 1960.3, 35, 101, 106; 1961.26, 37, 69, 98; 1962.25, 39, 107; 1963.17, 64, 70; 1964.15, 30, 61; 1966.1-4, 54, 83; 1967.4; 1969.16; 1971.19; 1972.34; 1973.48; 1977.81, 105
—imagery in, 1947.35; 1957.71, 101; 1958.43; 1959.56; 1963.39; 1964.46, 53; 1965.30; 1970.4, 16; 1971.13, 19, 25; 1974.37; 1977.2, 20; 1981.1
—language in, 1956.51; 1957.95; 1959.17; 1960.83; 1961.26; 1964.6; 1965.29; 1968.41; 1970.43; 1971.4, 6, 19, 22; 1974.5; 1975.2; 1977.28, 36
—plots, 1944.1, 3-4; 1945.26-27; 1947.11, 23; 1948.7, 16, 31, 41, 44; 1949.11; 1950.38; 1951.25, 28; 1955.99; 1956-